Takeshi Obata

Regarding the debate about my use of the expression "yosogoto" on page 94 of *Hikaru no Go* vol. 13: I really do use the phrase a lot.

—Takeshi Obata

It all began when Yumi Hotta played a pick-up game of go with her father-in-law. As she was learning how to play, Ms. Hotta thought it might be fun to create a story around the traditional board game. More confident in her storytelling abilities than her drawing skills, she submitted the beginnings of **Hikaru no Go** to **Weekly Shonen Jump**'s Story King Award. The Story King Award is an award that picks the best story, manga, character design and youth (under 15) manga submissions every year in Japan. As fate would have it, Ms. Hotta's story (originally named, "***Kokonotsu no Hoshi***"), was a runner-up in the "Story" category of the Story King Award. Many years earlier, Takeshi Obata was a runner-up for the Tezuka Award, another Japanese manga contest sponsored by **Weekly Shonen Jump** and **Monthly Shonen Jump**. An editor assigned to Mr. Obata's artwork came upon Ms. Hotta's story and paired the two for a full-fledged manga about go. The rest is modern go history.

HIKARU NO GO VOL. 14
The SHONEN JUMP Manga Edition

STORY BY YUMI HOTTA
ART BY TAKESHI OBATA
Supervised by YUKARI UMEZAWA (5 Dan)

Translation & English Adaptation/Naoko Amemiya
English Script Consultant/Janice Kim (3 Dan)
Touch-up Art & Lettering/Inori Fukuda Trant
Design/Julie Behn
Additional Touch-up/Rachel Lightfoot
Editor/Annette Roman

Editor in Chief, Books/Alvin Lu
Editor in Chief, Magazines/Marc Weidenbaum
VP, Publishing Licensing/Rika Inouye
VP, Sales & Product Marketing/Gonzalo Ferreyra
VP, Creative/Linda Espinosa
Publisher/Hyoe Narita

Printed in the U.S.A.

Published by VIZ Media, LLC
P.O. Box 77010
San Francisco, CA 94107

SHONEN JUMP Manga Edition
10 9 8 7 6 5 4 3 2 1
First printing, February 2009

www.viz.com

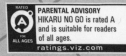

PARENTAL ADVISORY
HIKARU NO GO is rated A
and is suitable for readers
of all ages.
ratings.viz.com

THE WORLD'S
MOST POPULAR MANGA

www.shonenjump.com

Hikaru no Go

14 sai vs. toya koyo

STORY BY
YUMI HOTTA

ART BY
TAKESHI OBATA

Supervised by
YUKARI UMEZAWA
(5 Dan)

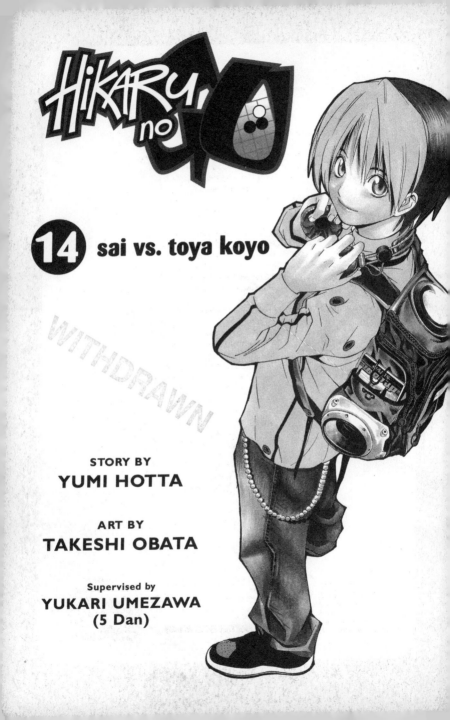

Character Introductions

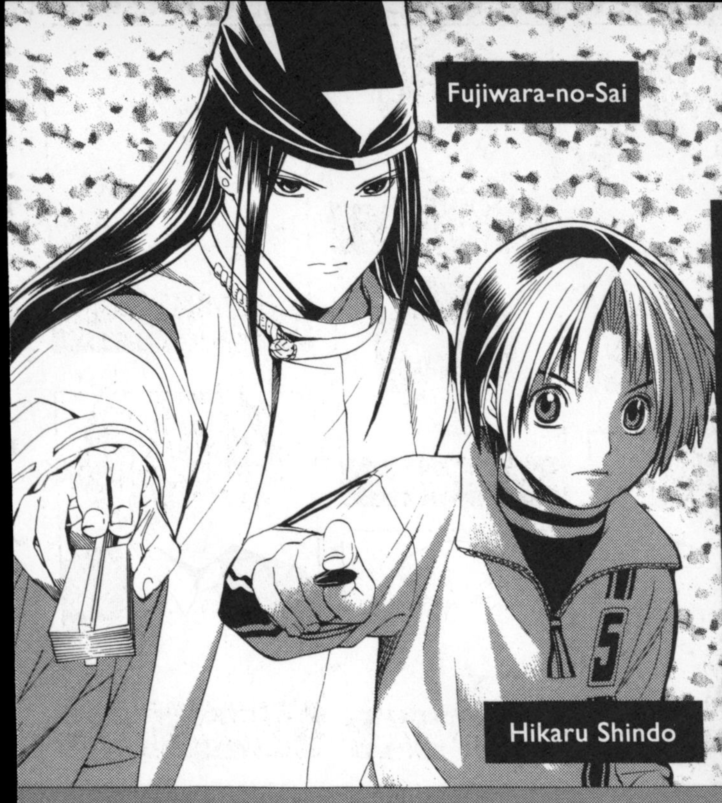
Fujiwara-no-Sai
Hikaru Shindo

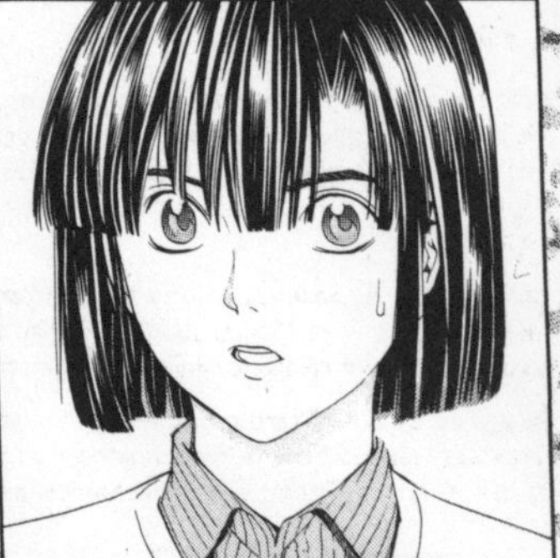
Akira Toya

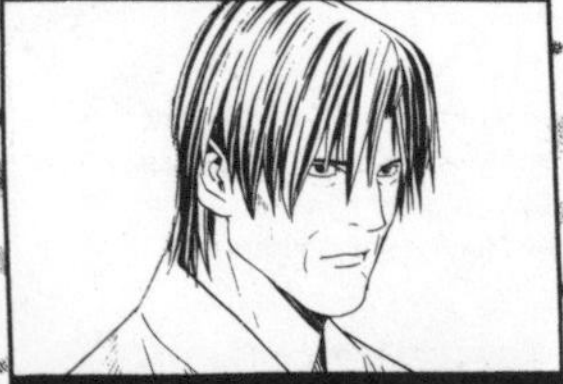
Toya Meijin

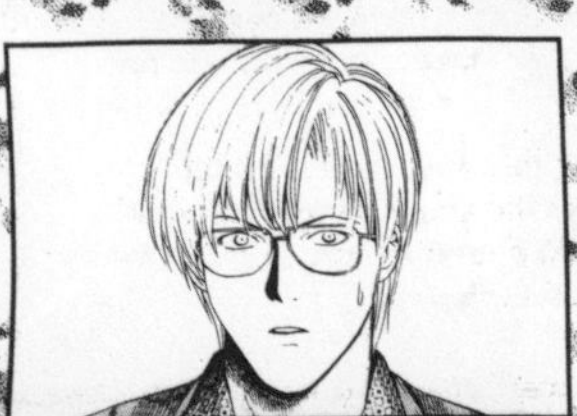
Ogata 9 dan

Koji Saeki
Ichiryu Kisei
Kurata 6 dan
Akira's mother
Yoshitaka Waya
Kuwabara Hon'inbo
Morishita 9 dan

Story Thus Far

Hikaru Shindo discovers an old go board one day up in his grandfather's attic. The moment Hikaru touches the board, the spirit of Fujiwara-no-Sai, a genius go player from Japan's Heian Era, enters his consciousness. Sai's love of the game inspires Hikaru, as does a meeting with the child prodigy Akira Toya—son of go master Toya Meijin. Now Hikaru has become a professional go player…

Hikaru's first pro tournament opponent is Akira Toya. Hikaru heads to the game with great anticipation, but Akira's father, Toya Meijin, suddenly collapses from heart trouble and Akira doesn't show up to play. The two rivals' long-awaited rematch at the go board will have to wait.

A few days later, badgered by Sai, Hikaru pays the meijin a visit in the hospital. There he learns that the master player has learned how to play online go to pass the time. Hikaru begs the meijin to play sai on the internet. The meijin finally agrees, and even stakes his retirement on the outcome.

Finally, the day of the big game arrives. Toya Meijin refuses all visitors and devotes his full attention to his battle with sai. The online match rapidly captures the attention of go players around the world, including Akira, who watches the game on a computer at a study group for young pro players. Can his father hang onto his lead as the game develops…?!

CONTENTS

14

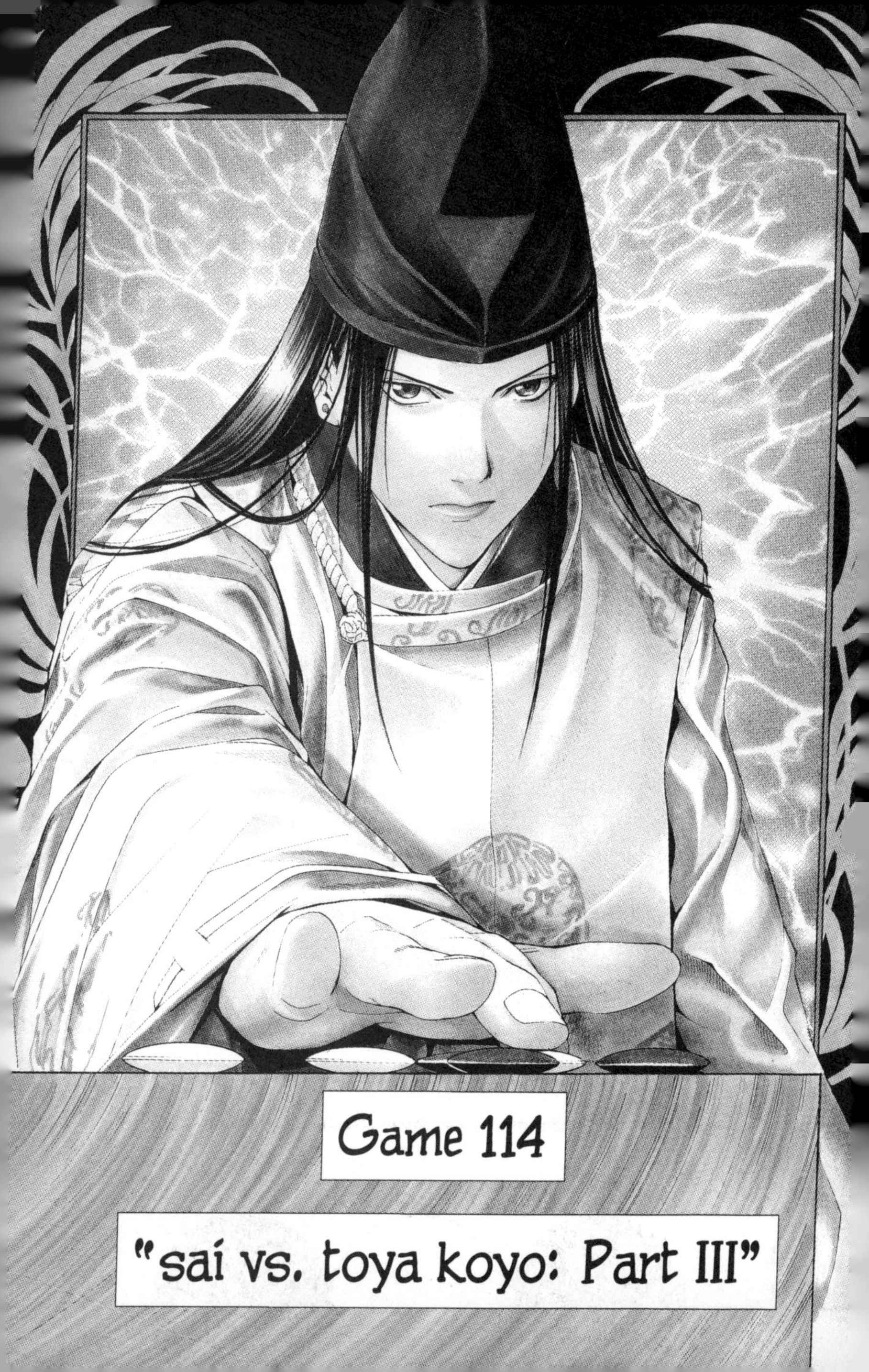
Game 114
"sai vs. toya koyo: Part III"

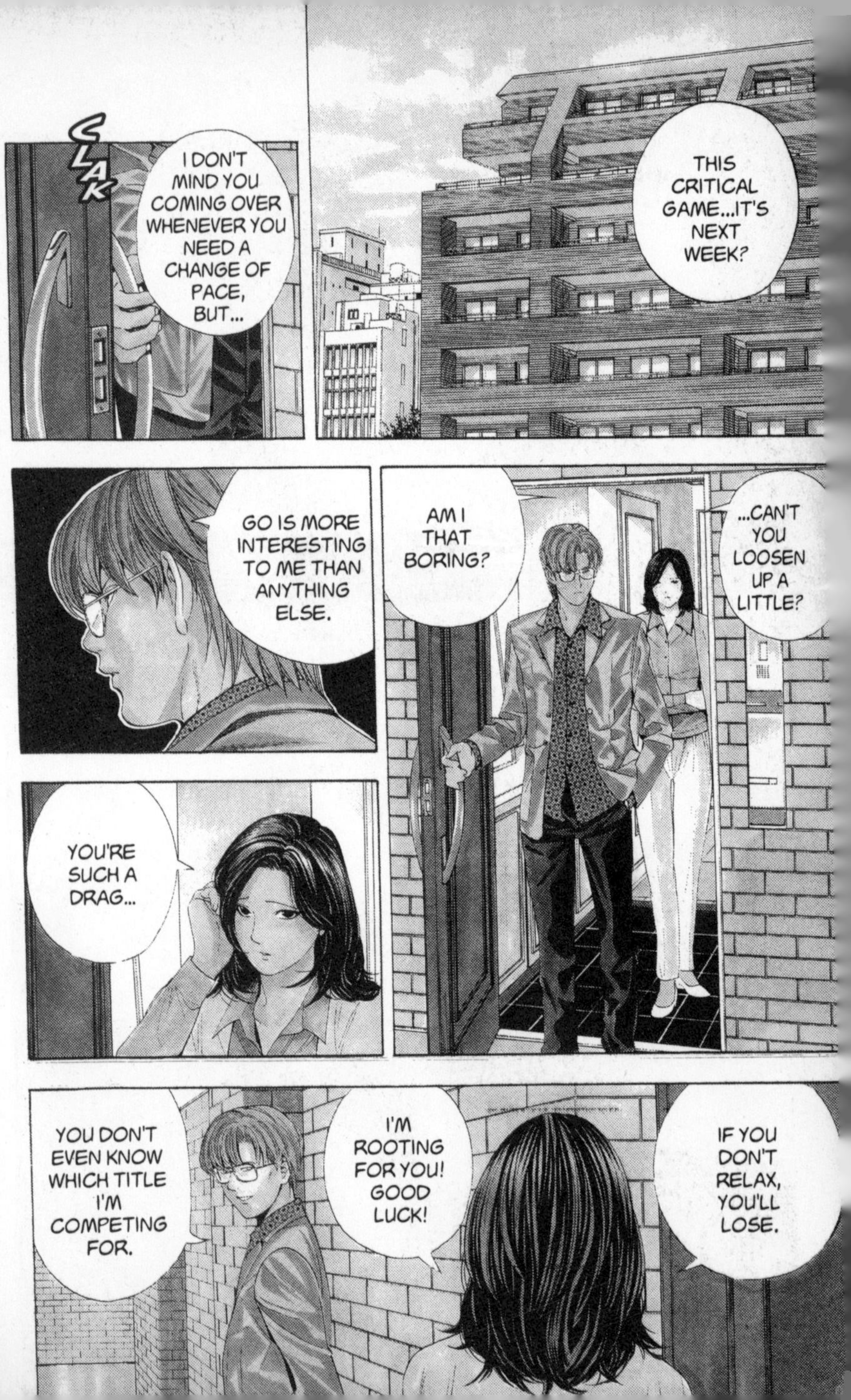
THIS CRITICAL GAME...IT'S NEXT WEEK?
CLAK
I DON'T MIND YOU COMING OVER WHENEVER YOU NEED A CHANGE OF PACE, BUT...
...CAN'T YOU LOOSEN UP A LITTLE?
AM I THAT BORING?
GO IS MORE INTERESTING TO ME THAN ANYTHING ELSE.
YOU'RE SUCH A DRAG...
IF YOU DON'T RELAX, YOU'LL LOSE.
I'M ROOTING FOR YOU! GOOD LUCK!
YOU DON'T EVEN KNOW WHICH TITLE I'M COMPETING FOR.

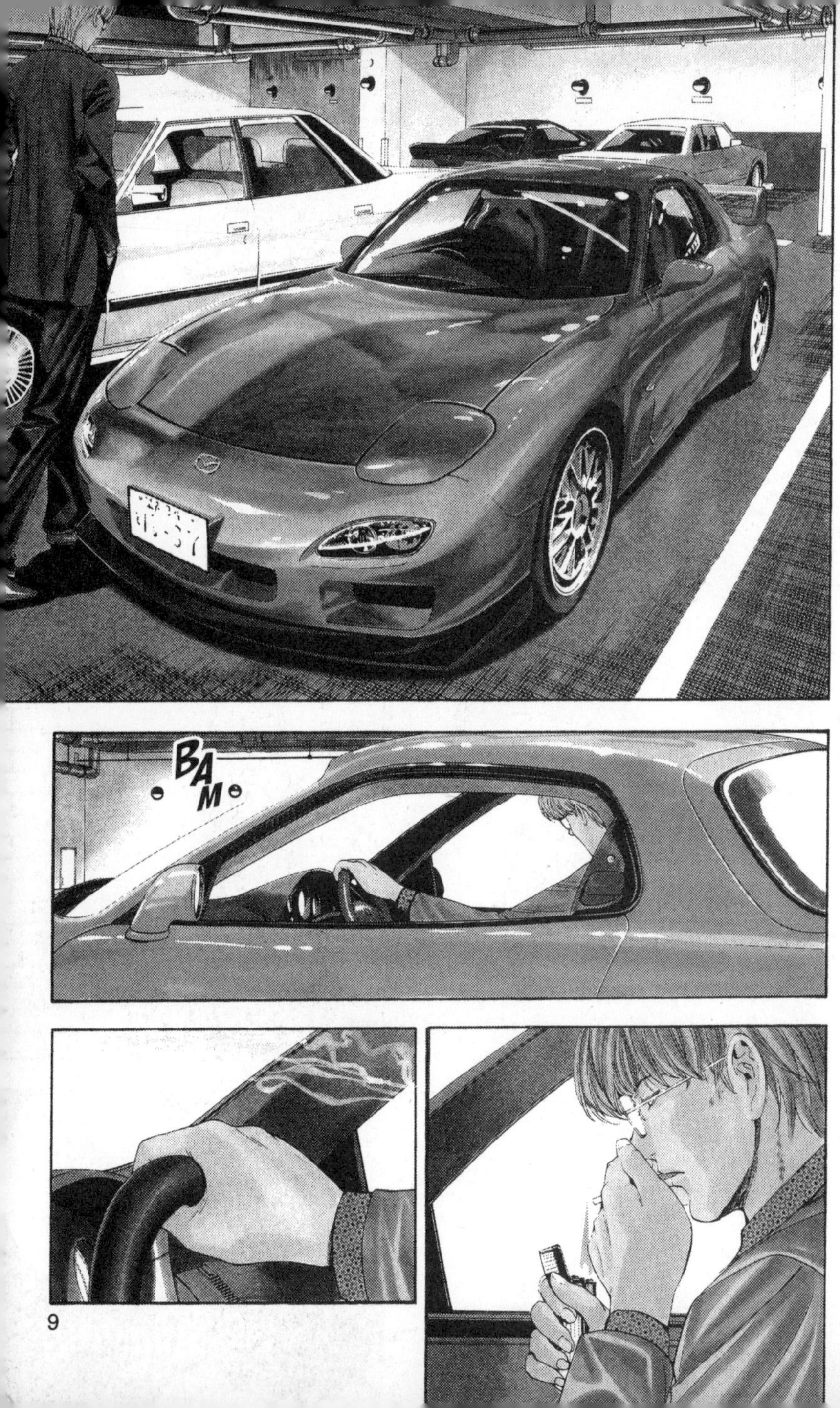
BAM

Sai: Spacesuit Version

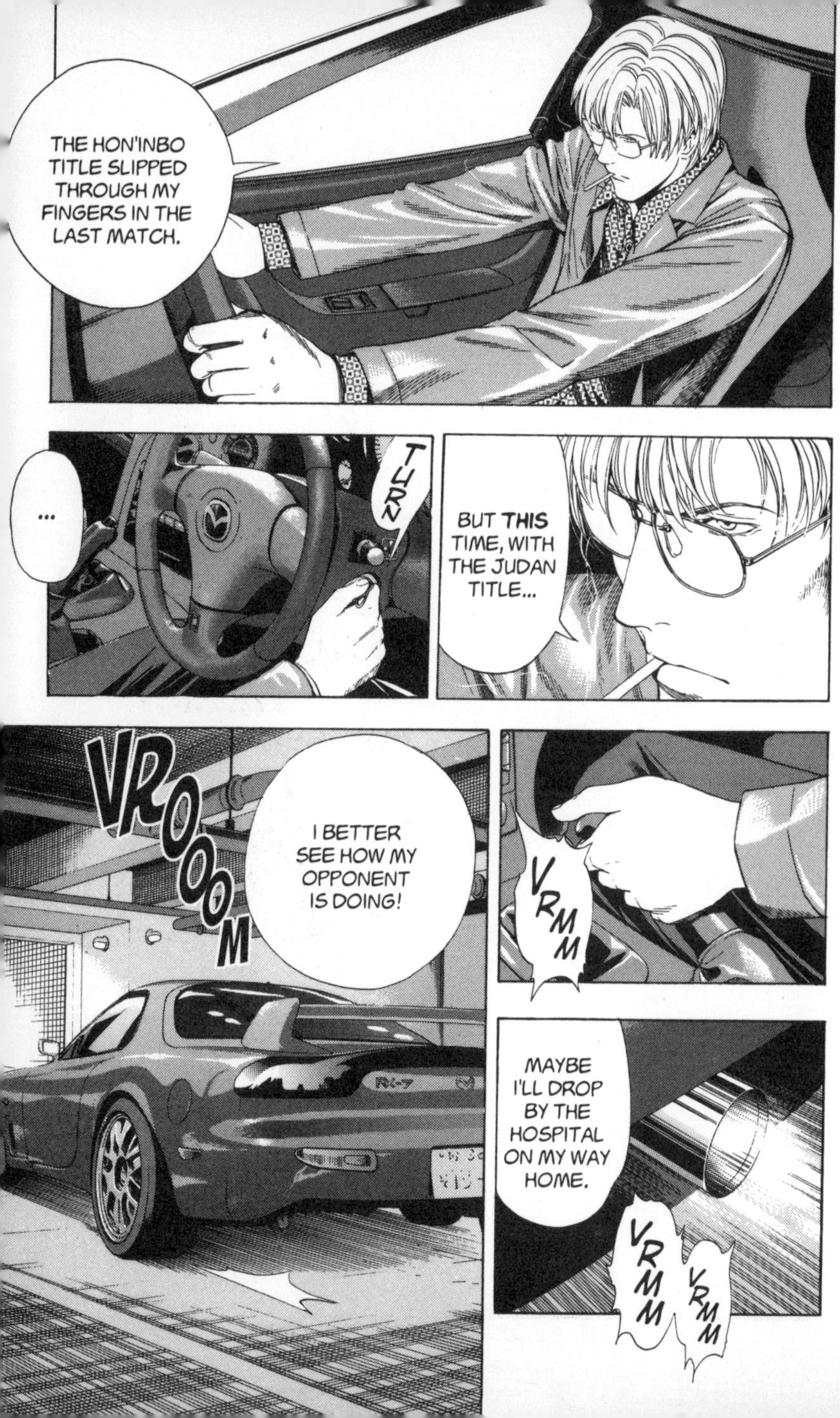
THE HON'INBO TITLE SLIPPED THROUGH MY FINGERS IN THE LAST MATCH.
BUT **THIS** TIME, WITH THE JUDAN TITLE...
TURN
...
VRMM
MAYBE I'LL DROP BY THE HOSPITAL ON MY WAY HOME.
VRMM
VRMM
VROOOOM
I BETTER SEE HOW MY OPPONENT IS DOING!

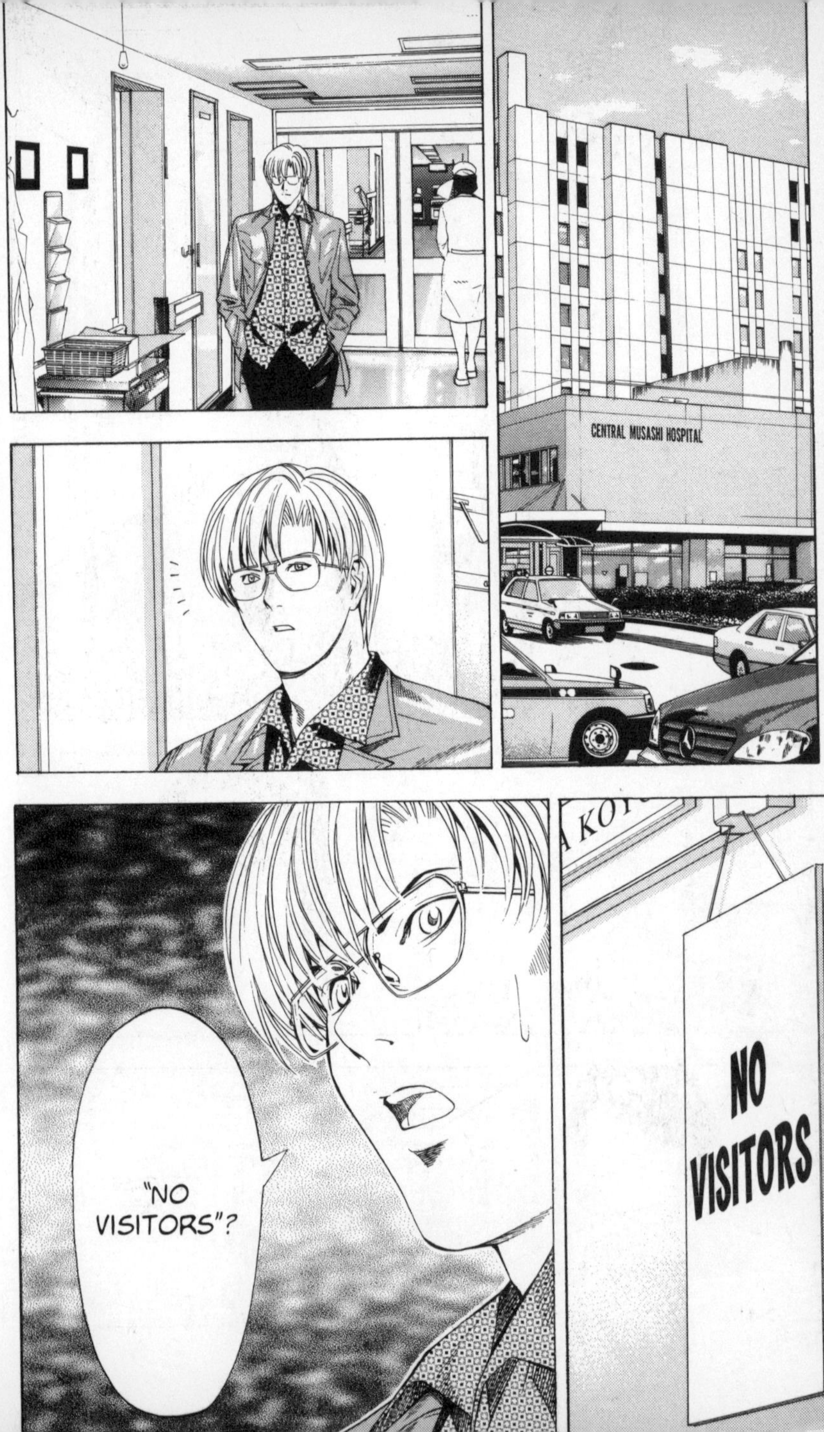
CENTRAL MUSASHI HOSPITAL
NO VISITORS
"NO VISITORS"?

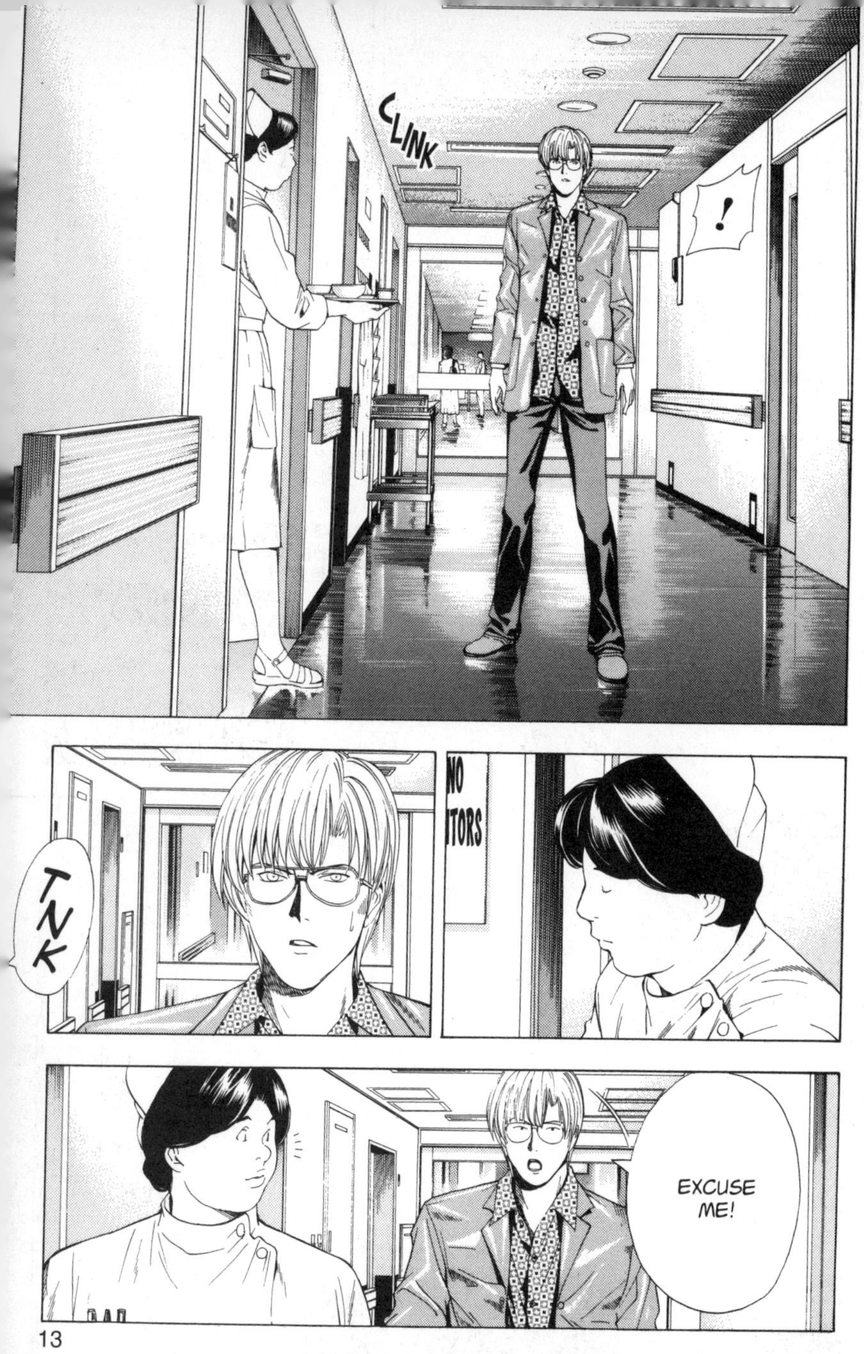
CLINK
!
TNK
EXCUSE ME!

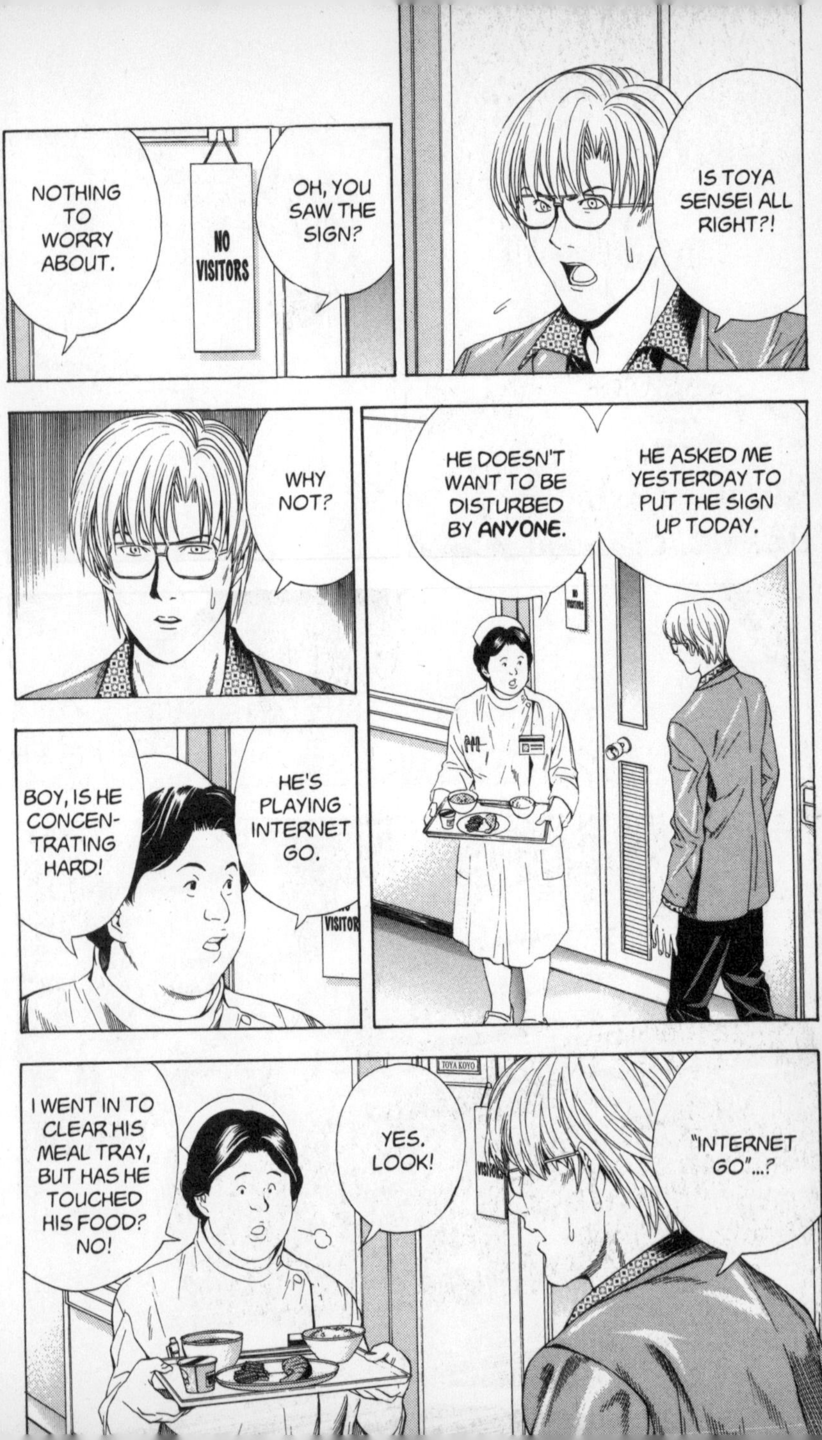
IS TOYA SENSEI ALL RIGHT?!
OH, YOU SAW THE SIGN?
NOTHING TO WORRY ABOUT.
NO VISITORS
HE ASKED ME YESTERDAY TO PUT THE SIGN UP TODAY.
HE DOESN'T WANT TO BE DISTURBED BY **ANYONE.**
WHY NOT?
HE'S PLAYING INTERNET GO.
BOY, IS HE CONCENTRATING HARD!
TOYA KOYO
"INTERNET GO"...?
YES. LOOK!
I WENT IN TO CLEAR HIS MEAL TRAY, BUT HAS HE TOUCHED HIS FOOD? NO!

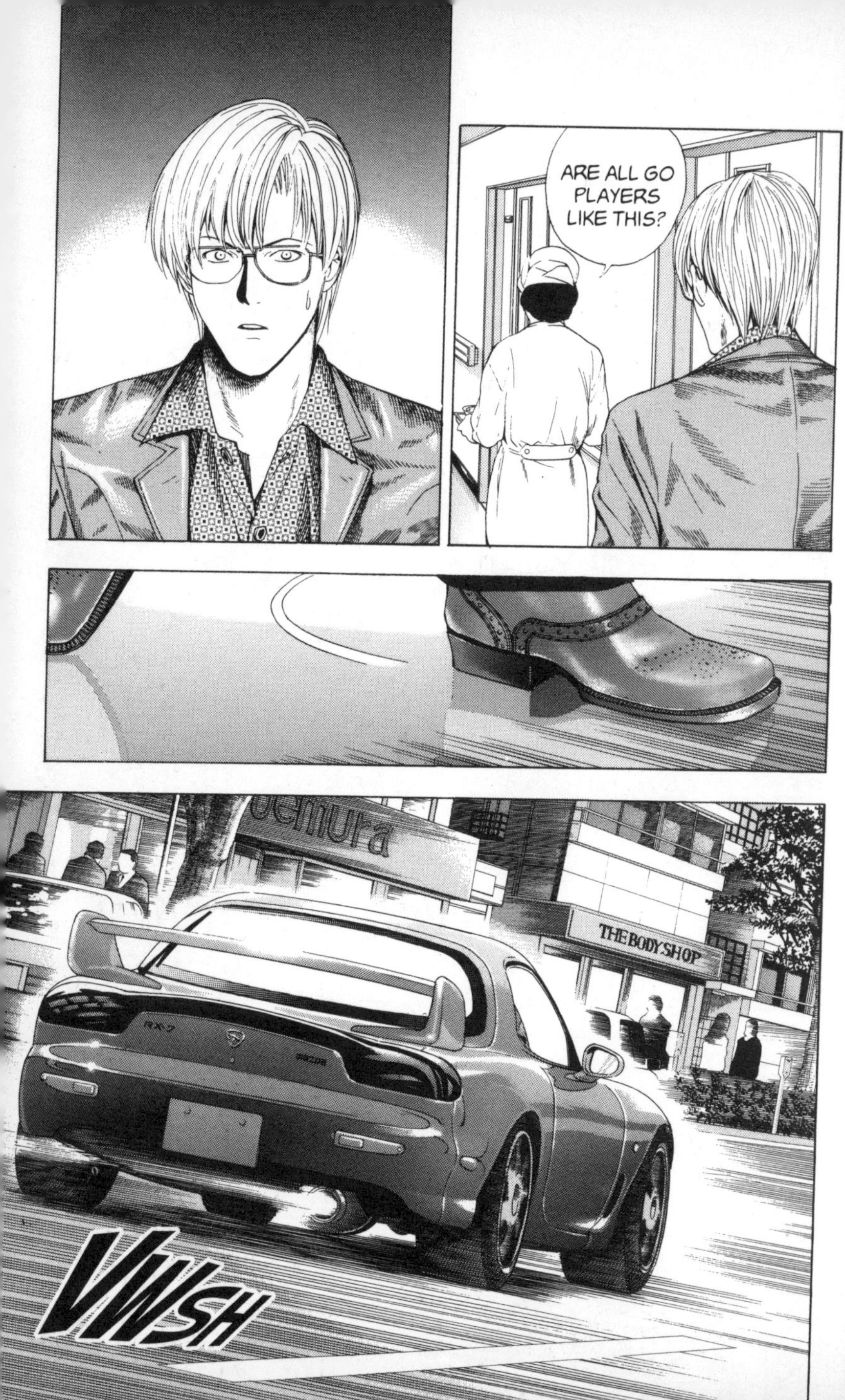
ARE ALL GO PLAYERS LIKE THIS?
THE BODY SHOP
RX-7
VWISH

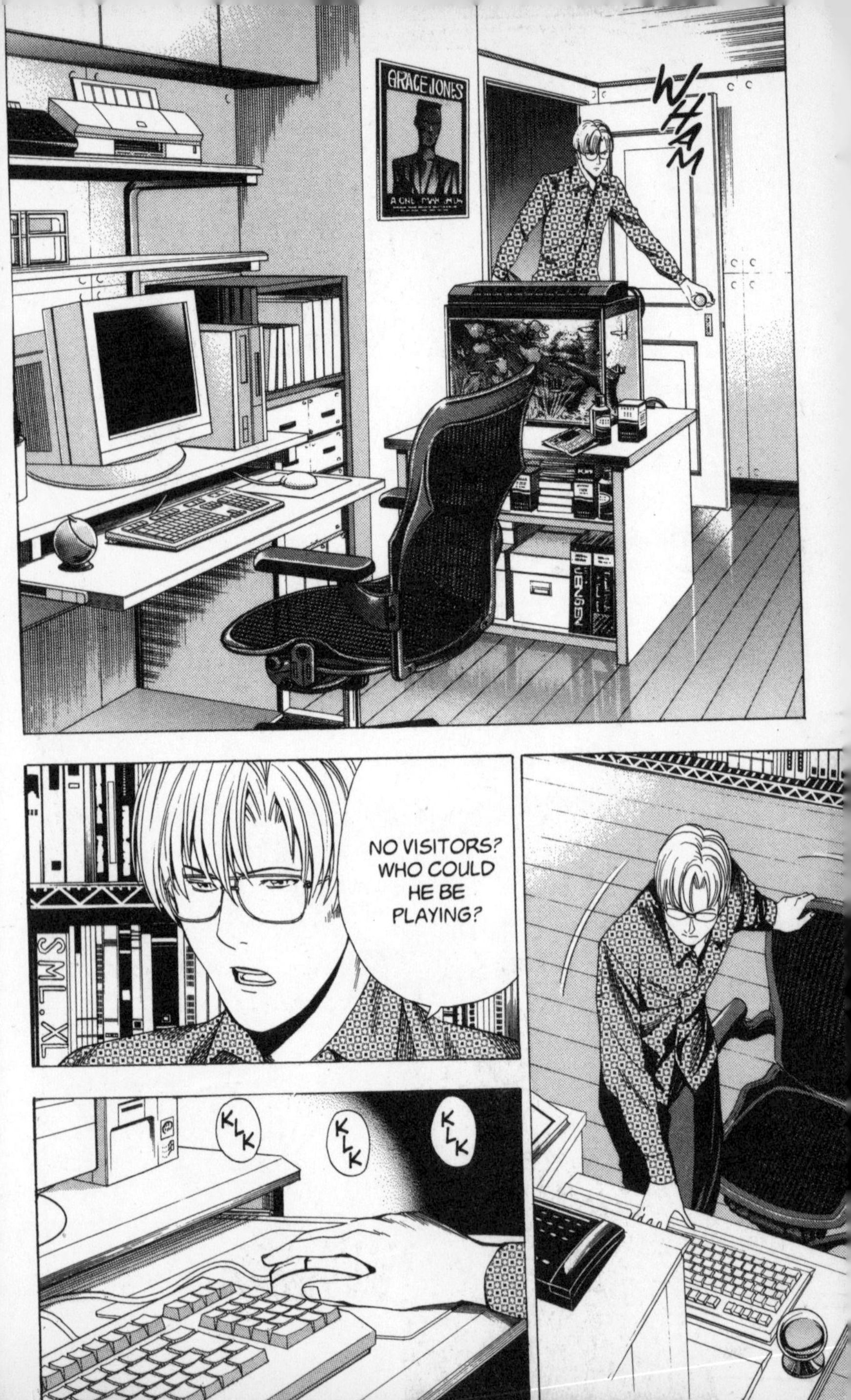
GRACE JONES
WHAM
NO VISITORS? WHO COULD HE BE PLAYING?
SML.XL
KLK
KLK
KLK

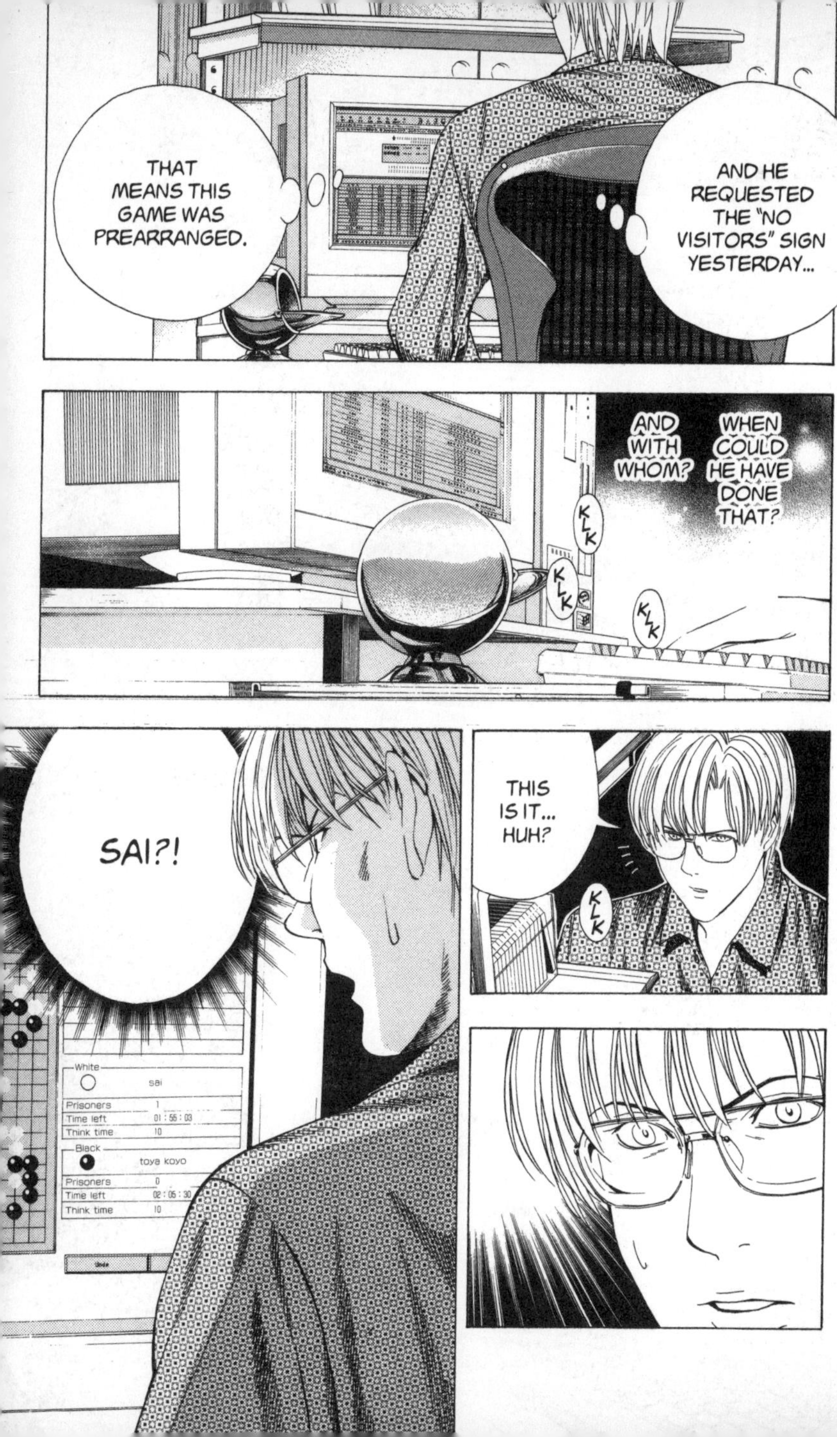
AND HE REQUESTED THE "NO VISITORS" SIGN YESTERDAY...
THAT MEANS THIS GAME WAS PREARRANGED.
WHEN COULD HE HAVE DONE THAT?
AND WITH WHOM?
KLK
KLK
KLK
THIS IS IT... HUH?
KLK
SAI?!
White
sai
Prisoners 1
Time left 01:55:03
Think time 10
Black
toya koyo
Prisoners 0
Time left 02:05:30
Think time 10

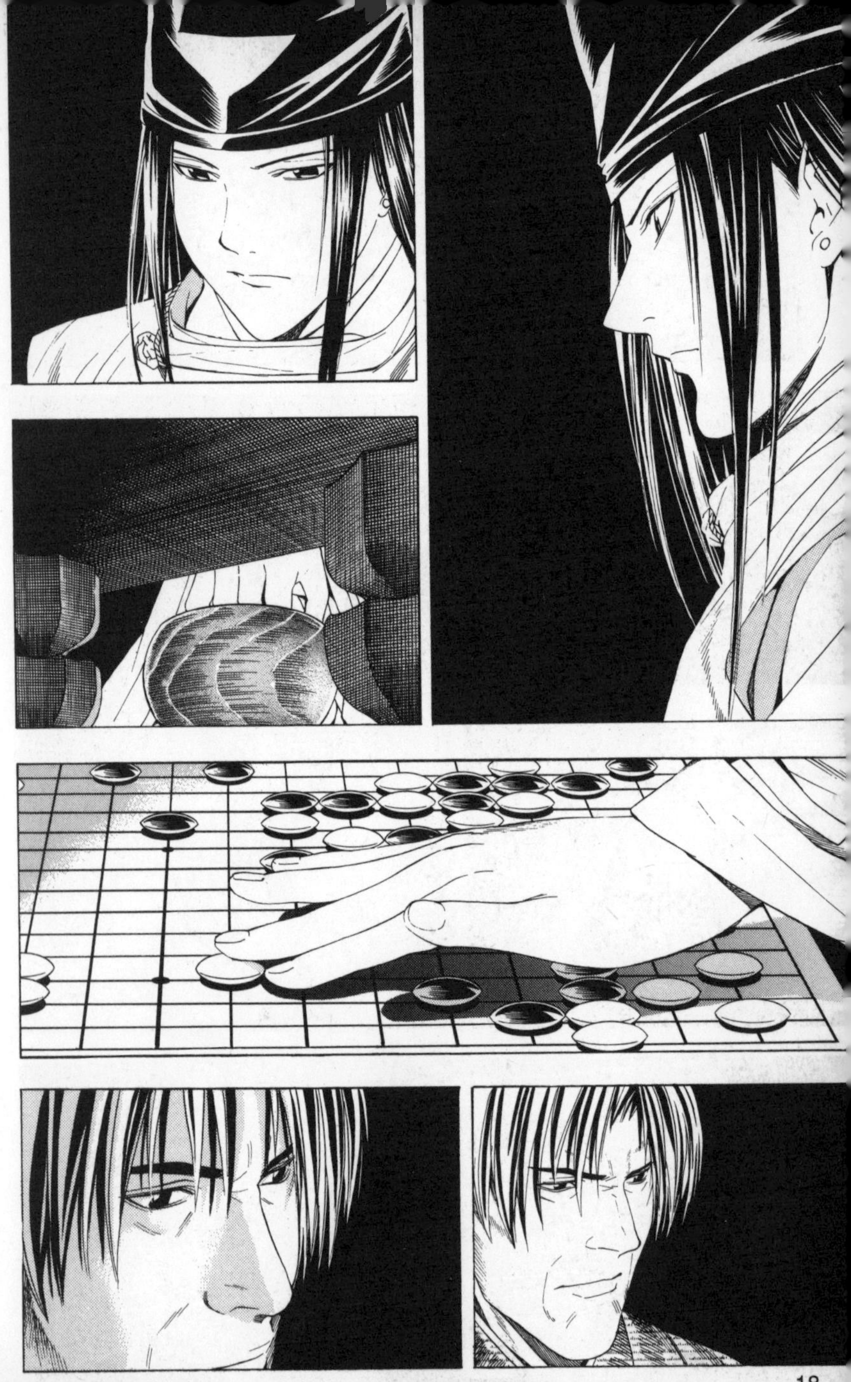

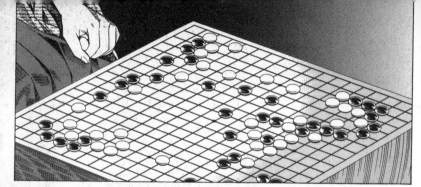

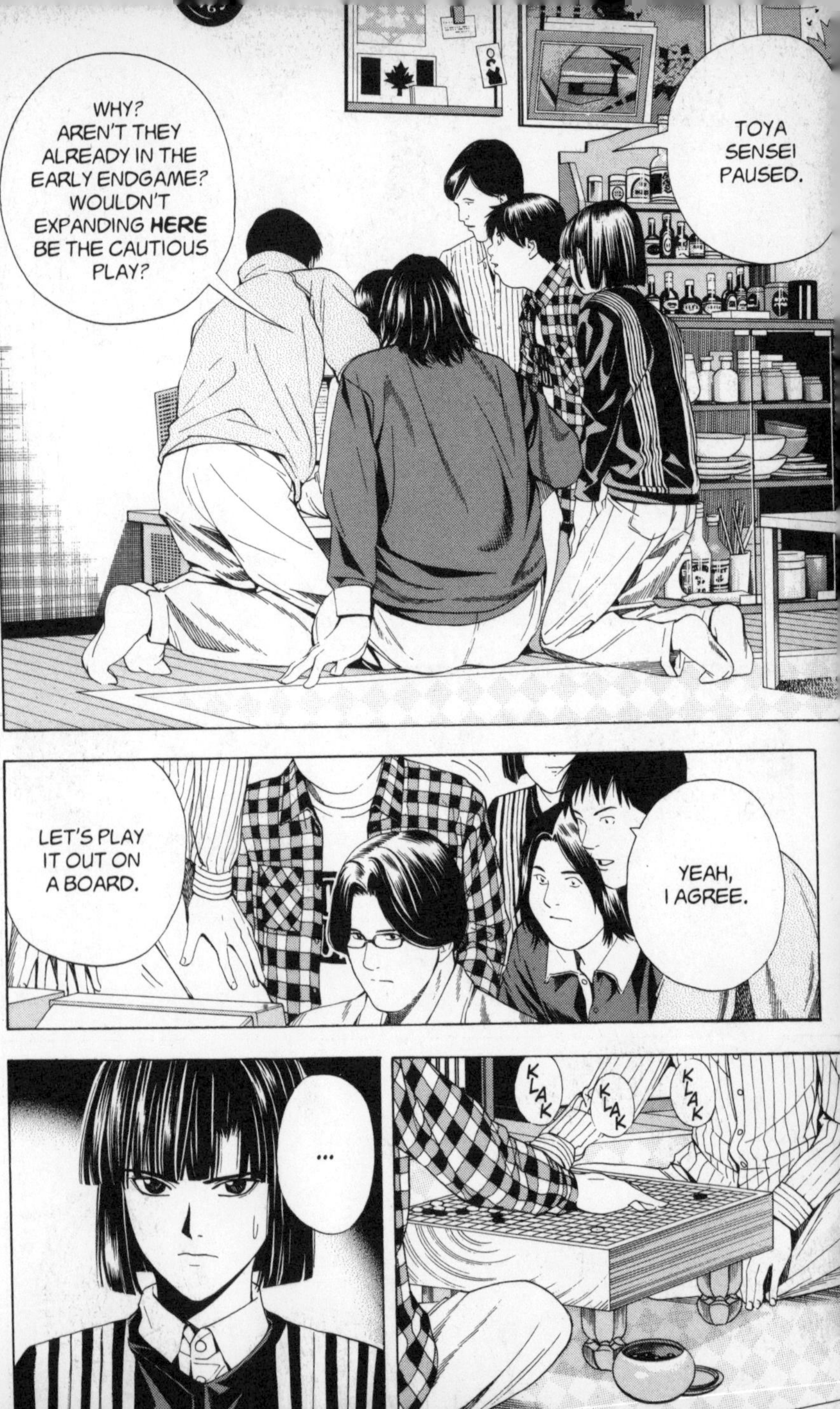
TOYA SENSEI PAUSED.
WHY? AREN'T THEY ALREADY IN THE EARLY ENDGAME? WOULDN'T EXPANDING **HERE** BE THE CAUTIOUS PLAY?
YEAH, I AGREE.
LET'S PLAY IT OUT ON A BOARD.
KLAK
KLAK
KLAK
...

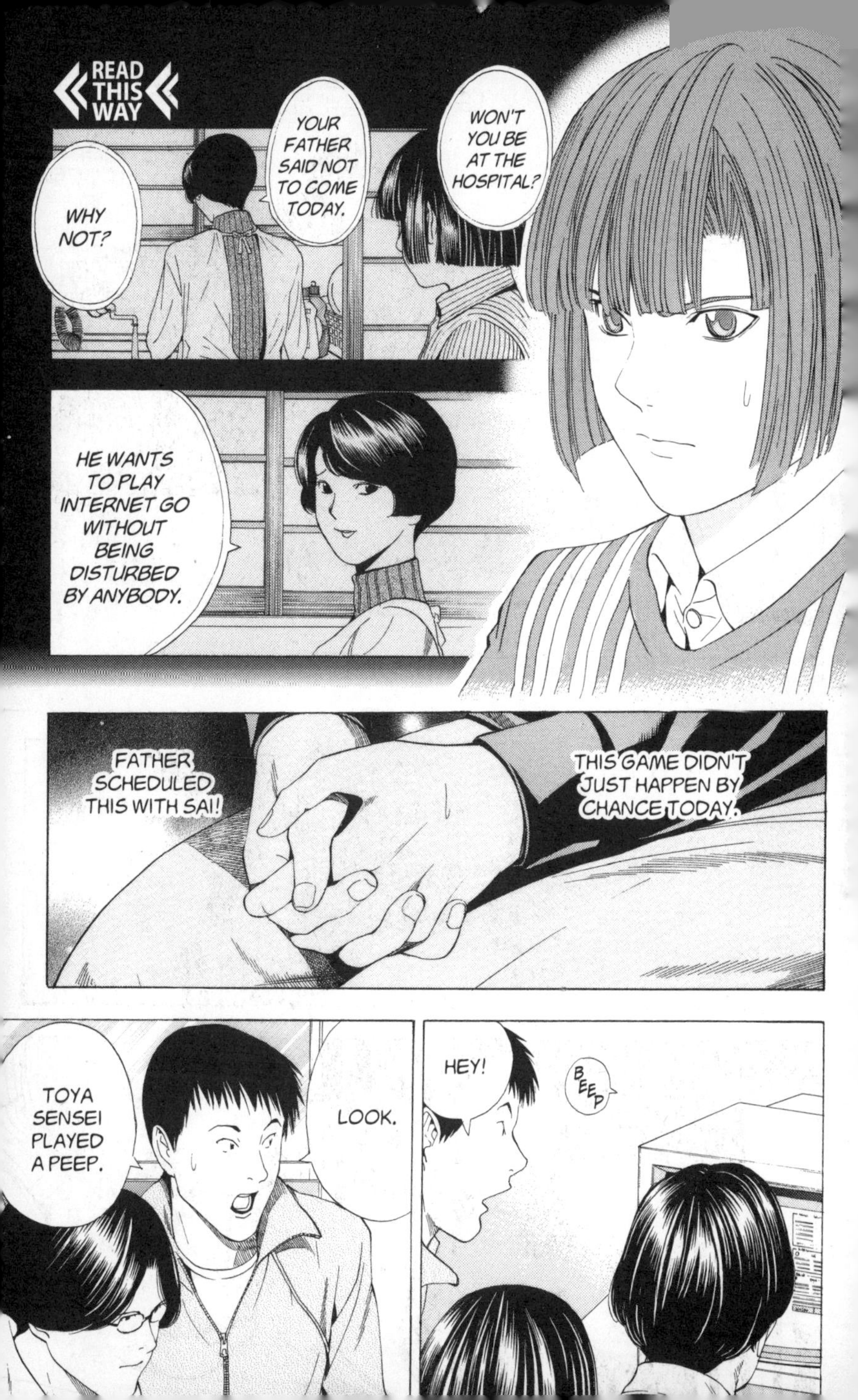
READ THIS WAY
WON'T YOU BE AT THE HOSPITAL?
YOUR FATHER SAID NOT TO COME TODAY.
WHY NOT?
HE WANTS TO PLAY INTERNET GO WITHOUT BEING DISTURBED BY ANYBODY.
THIS GAME DIDN'T JUST HAPPEN BY CHANCE TODAY.
FATHER SCHEDULED THIS WITH SAI!
BEEP
HEY!
LOOK.
TOYA SENSEI PLAYED A PEEP.

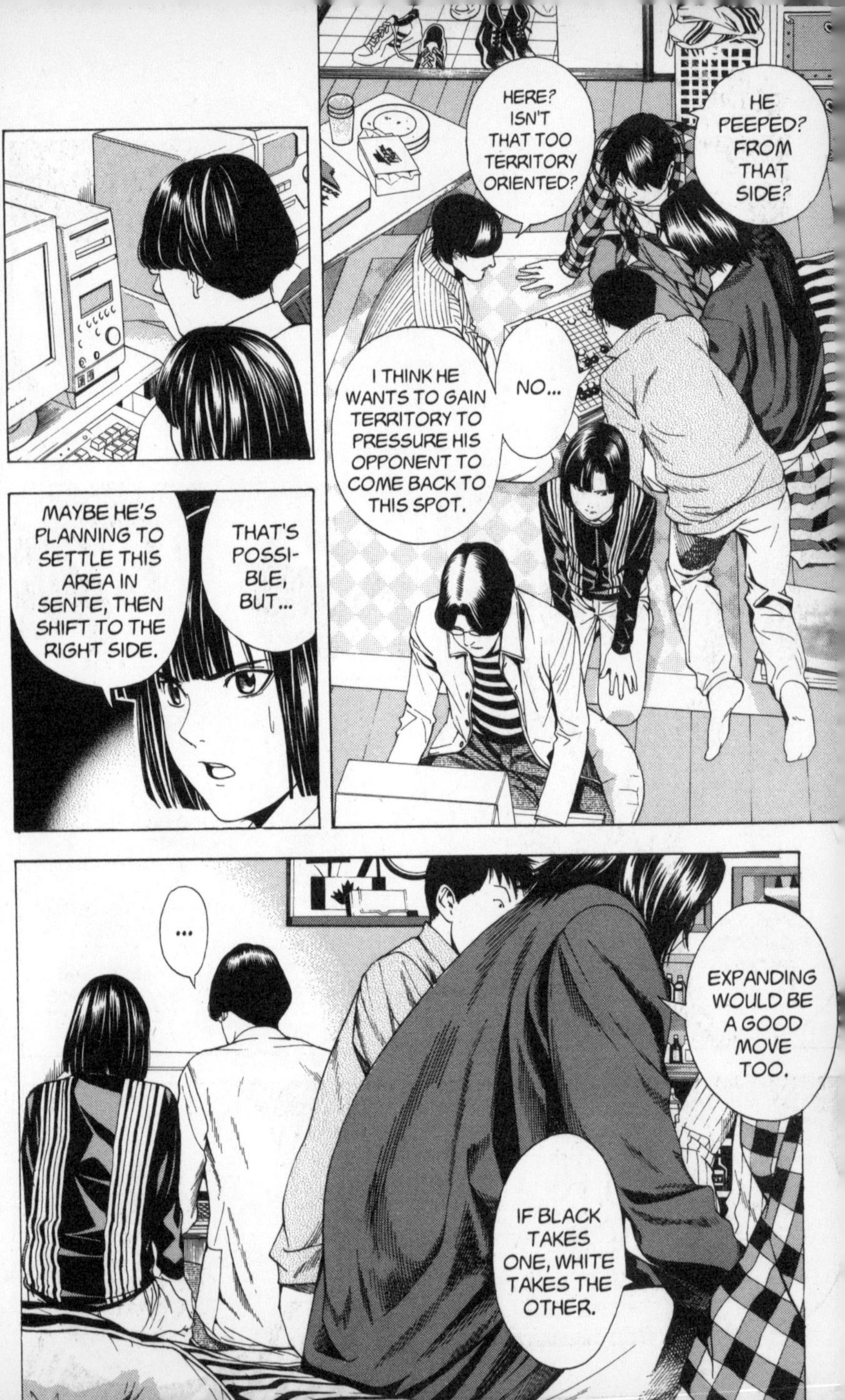
HE PEEPED? FROM THAT SIDE?
HERE? ISN'T THAT TOO TERRITORY ORIENTED?
NO...
I THINK HE WANTS TO GAIN TERRITORY TO PRESSURE HIS OPPONENT TO COME BACK TO THIS SPOT.
THAT'S POSSIBLE, BUT...
MAYBE HE'S PLANNING TO SETTLE THIS AREA IN SENTE, THEN SHIFT TO THE RIGHT SIDE.
EXPANDING WOULD BE A GOOD MOVE TOO.
IF BLACK TAKES ONE, WHITE TAKES THE OTHER.
...

READ THIS WAY

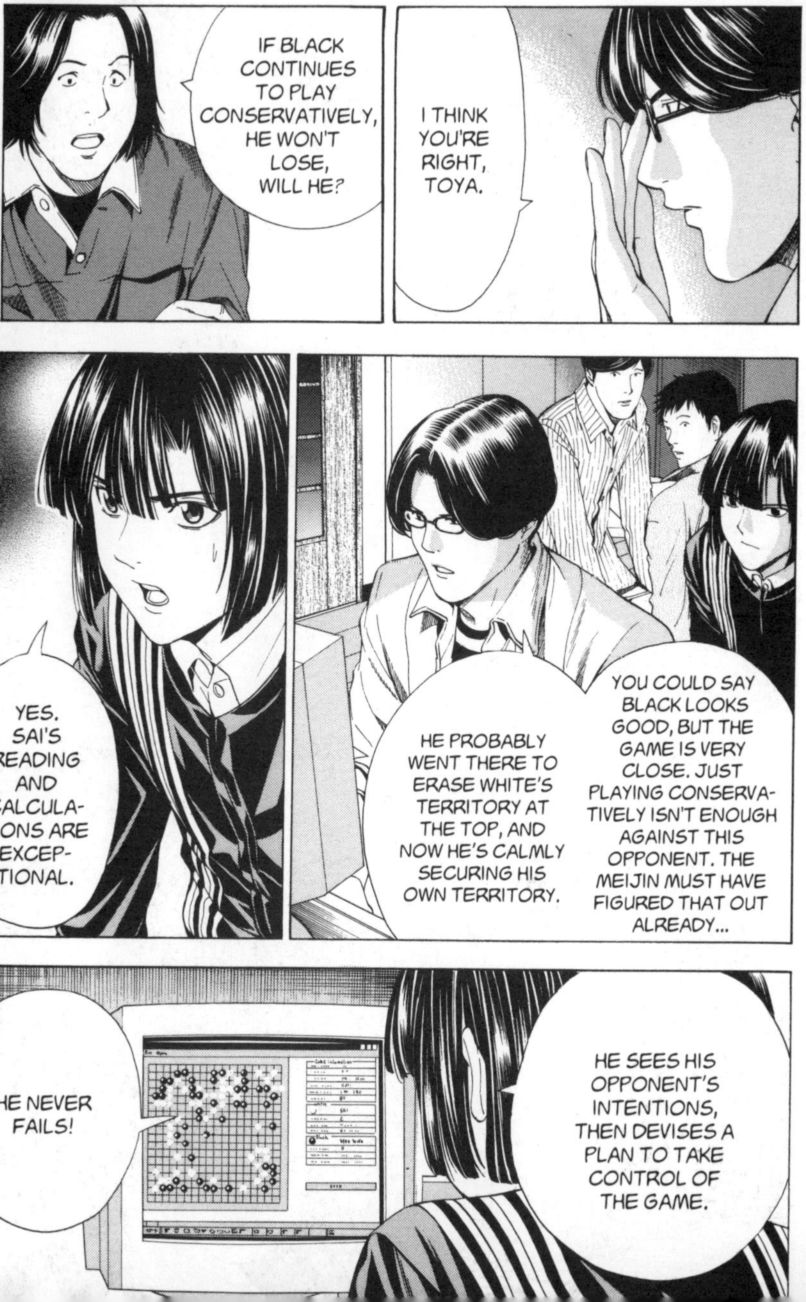
I THINK YOU'RE RIGHT, TOYA.
IF BLACK CONTINUES TO PLAY CONSERVATIVELY, HE WON'T LOSE, WILL HE?
YOU COULD SAY BLACK LOOKS GOOD, BUT THE GAME IS VERY CLOSE. JUST PLAYING CONSERVATIVELY ISN'T ENOUGH AGAINST THIS OPPONENT. THE MEIJIN MUST HAVE FIGURED THAT OUT ALREADY...
HE PROBABLY WENT THERE TO ERASE WHITE'S TERRITORY AT THE TOP, AND NOW HE'S CALMLY SECURING HIS OWN TERRITORY.
YES. SAI'S READING AND CALCULATIONS ARE EXCEPTIONAL.
HE SEES HIS OPPONENT'S INTENTIONS, THEN DEVISES A PLAN TO TAKE CONTROL OF THE GAME.
HE NEVER FAILS!

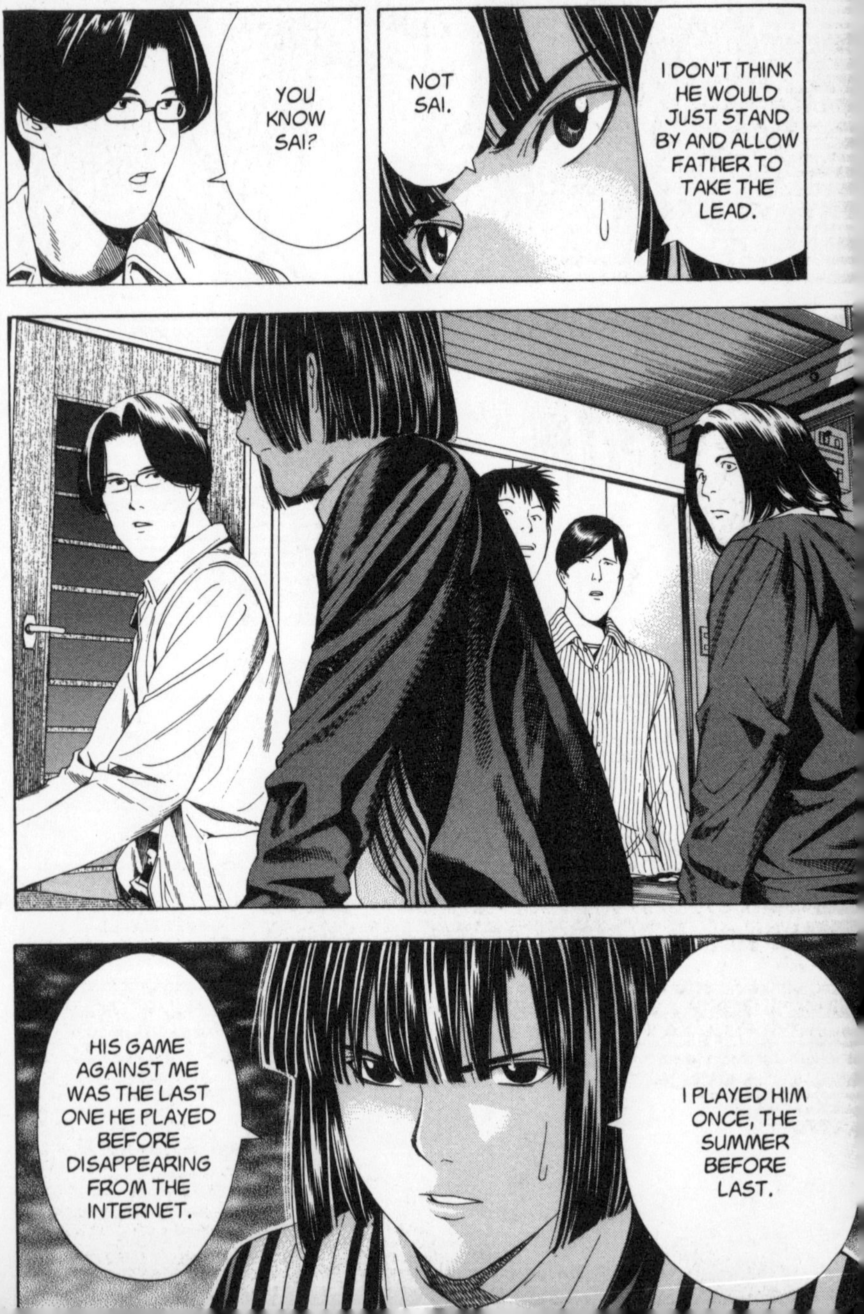
I DON'T THINK HE WOULD JUST STAND BY AND ALLOW FATHER TO TAKE THE LEAD.
NOT SAI.
YOU KNOW SAI?
I PLAYED HIM ONCE, THE SUMMER BEFORE LAST.
HIS GAME AGAINST ME WAS THE LAST ONE HE PLAYED BEFORE DISAPPEARING FROM THE INTERNET.

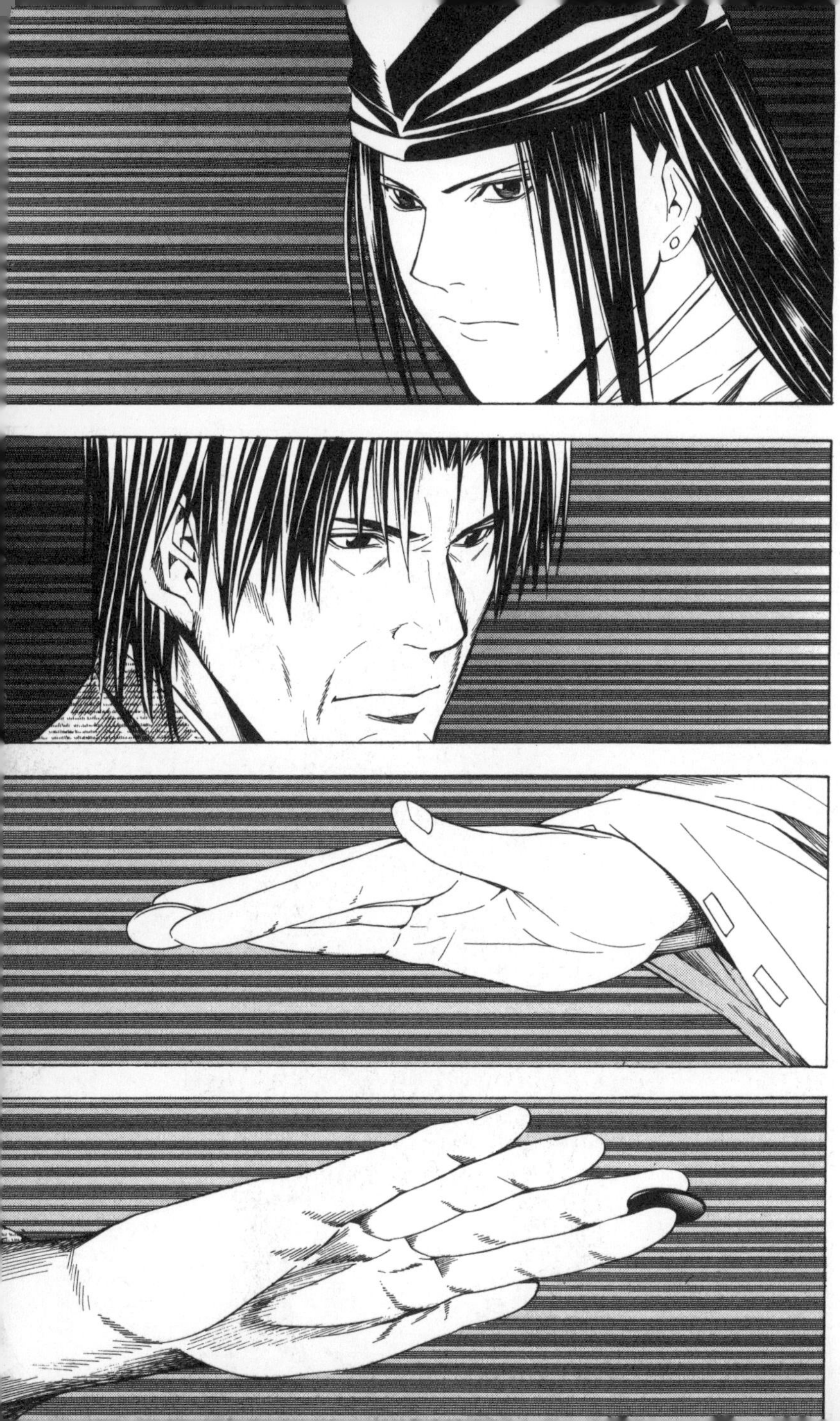

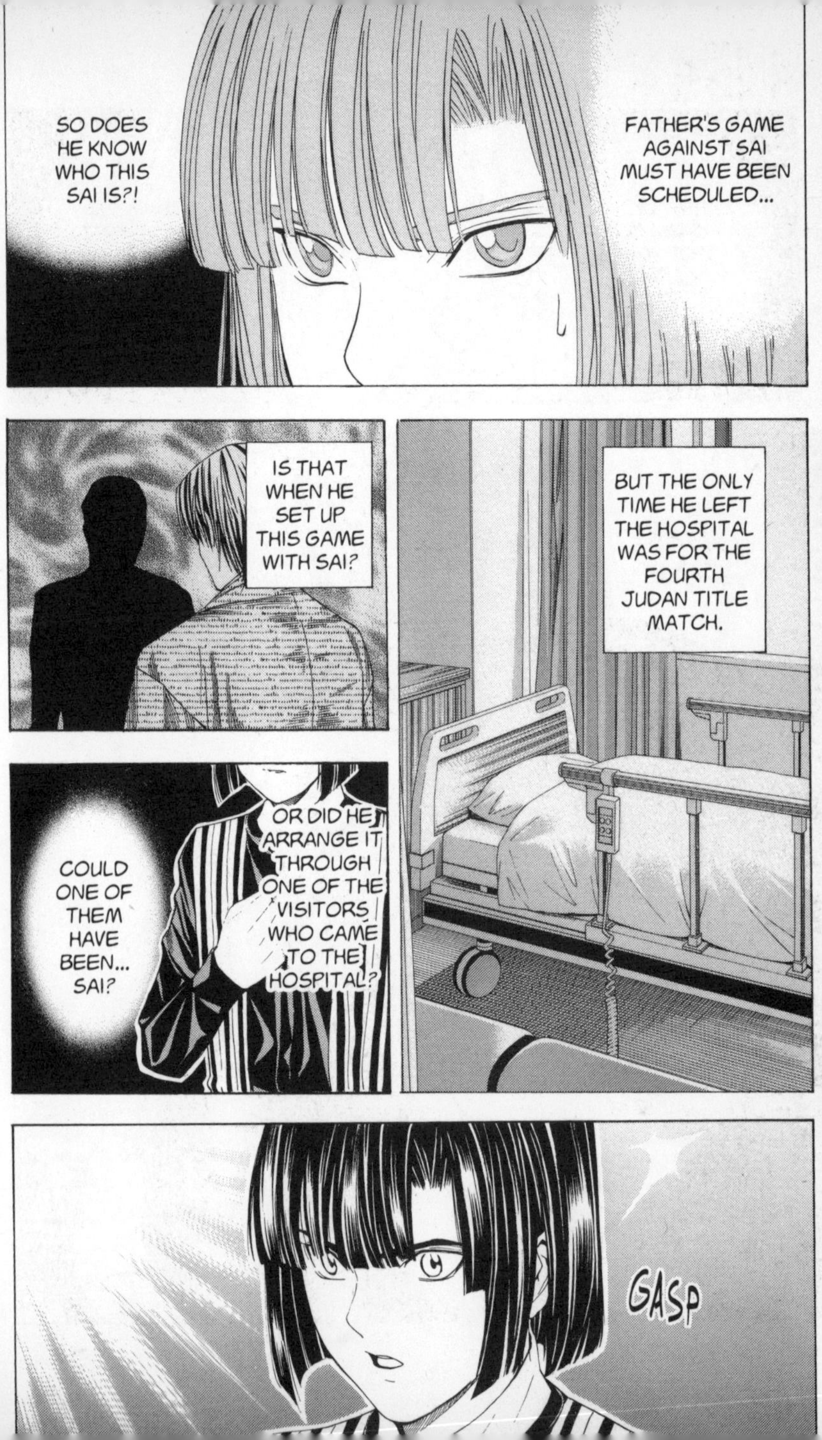
FATHER'S GAME AGAINST SAI MUST HAVE BEEN SCHEDULED...
SO DOES HE KNOW WHO THIS SAI IS?!
BUT THE ONLY TIME HE LEFT THE HOSPITAL WAS FOR THE FOURTH JUDAN TITLE MATCH.
IS THAT WHEN HE SET UP THIS GAME WITH SAI?
OR DID HE ARRANGE IT THROUGH ONE OF THE VISITORS WHO CAME TO THE HOSPITAL?
COULD ONE OF THEM HAVE BEEN... SAI?
GASP

READ THIS WAY

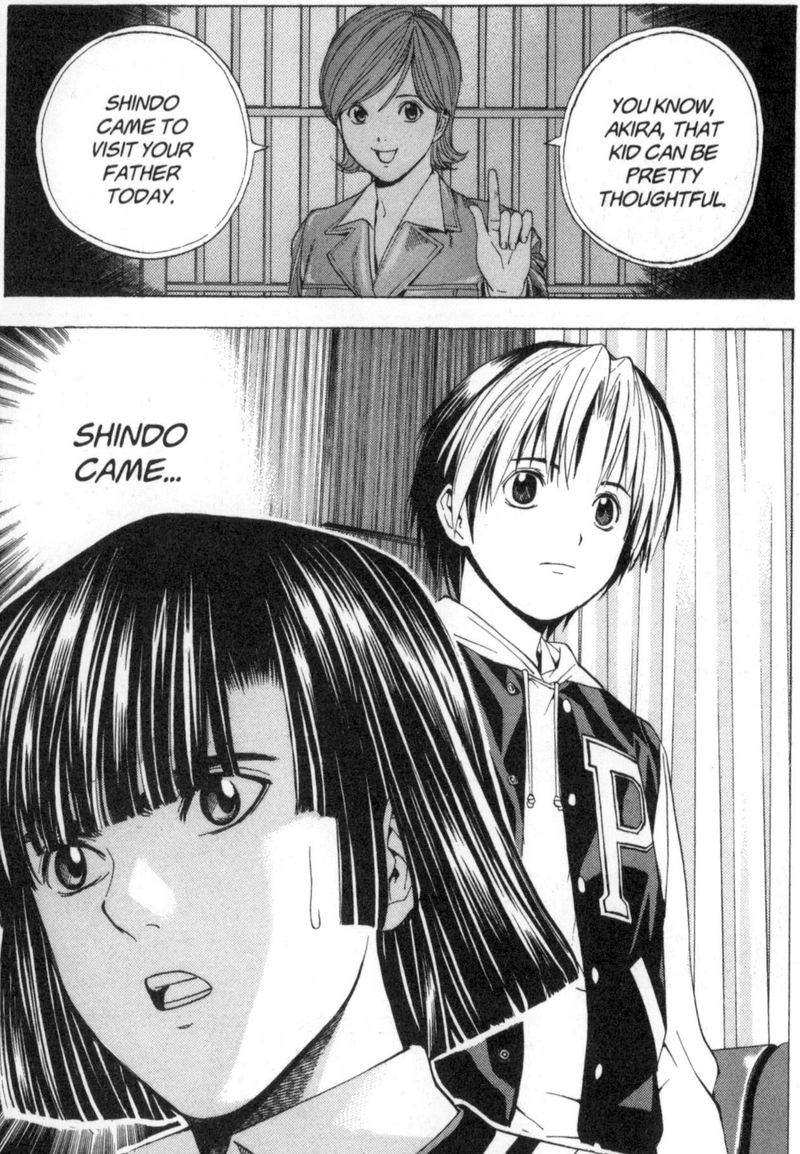

YOU KNOW, AKIRA, THAT KID CAN BE PRETTY THOUGHTFUL.
SHINDO CAME TO VISIT YOUR FATHER TODAY.
SHINDO CAME...

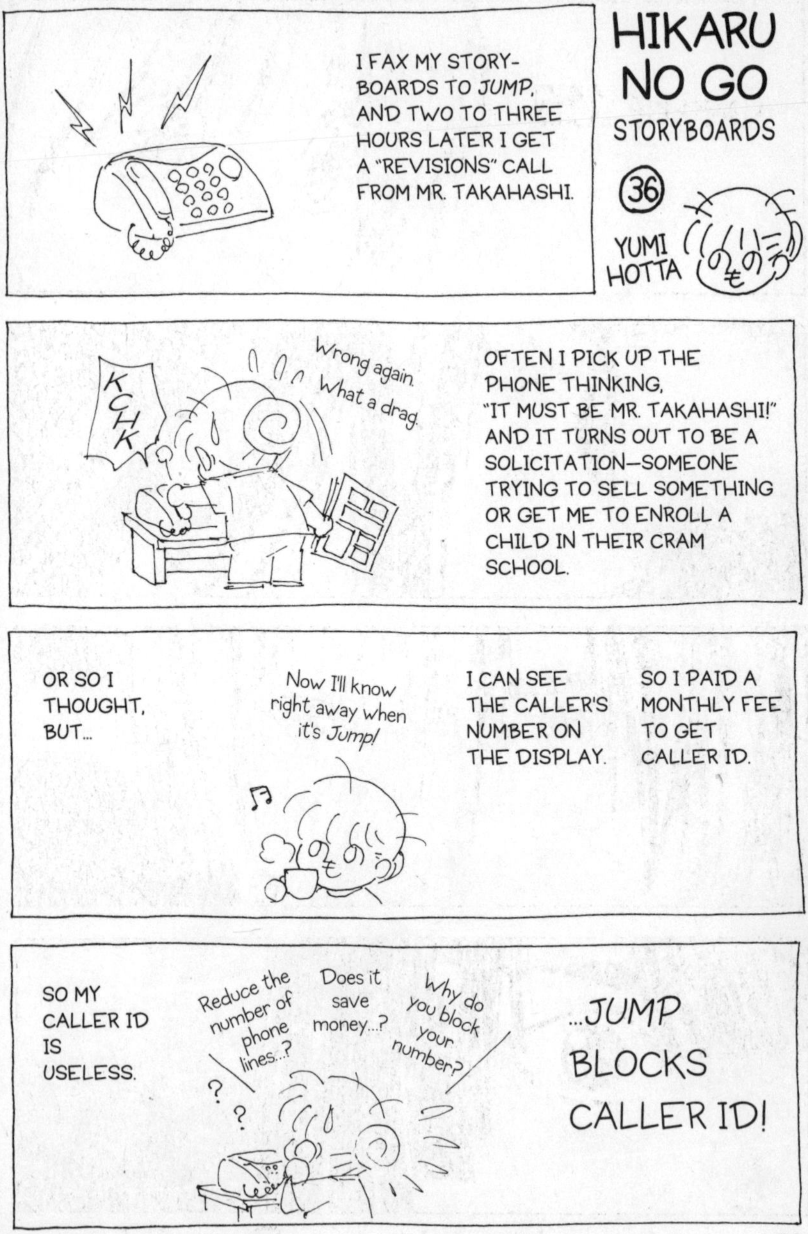
HIKARU NO GO
STORYBOARDS
36
YUMI HOTTA
I FAX MY STORYBOARDS TO JUMP, AND TWO TO THREE HOURS LATER I GET A "REVISIONS" CALL FROM MR. TAKAHASHI.
OFTEN I PICK UP THE PHONE THINKING, "IT MUST BE MR. TAKAHASHI!" AND IT TURNS OUT TO BE A SOLICITATION—SOMEONE TRYING TO SELL SOMETHING OR GET ME TO ENROLL A CHILD IN THEIR CRAM SCHOOL.
Wrong again. What a drag.
KCHK
SO I PAID A MONTHLY FEE TO GET CALLER ID.
I CAN SEE THE CALLER'S NUMBER ON THE DISPLAY.
Now I'll know right away when it's Jump!
OR SO I THOUGHT, BUT...
...JUMP BLOCKS CALLER ID!
Why do you block your number?
Does it save money...?
Reduce the number of phone lines...?
SO MY CALLER ID IS USELESS.

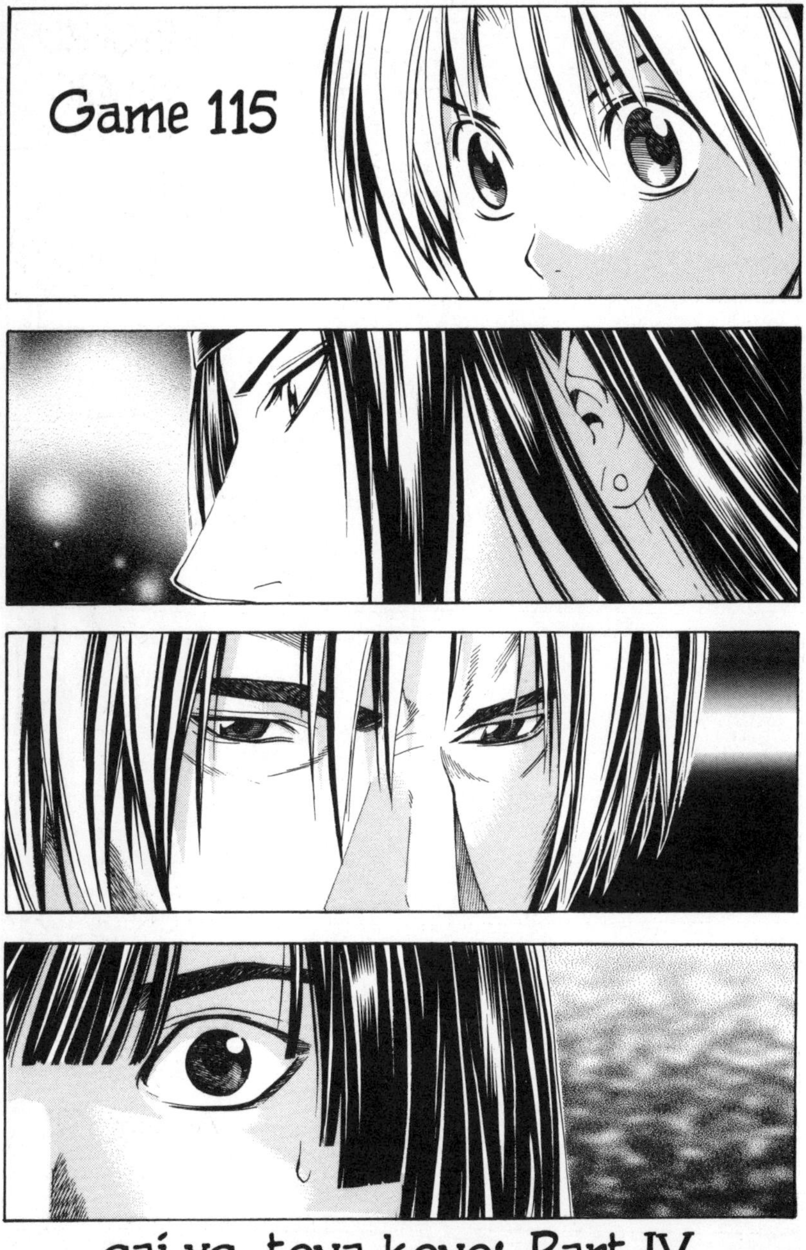
Game 115

sai vs. toya koyo: Part IV

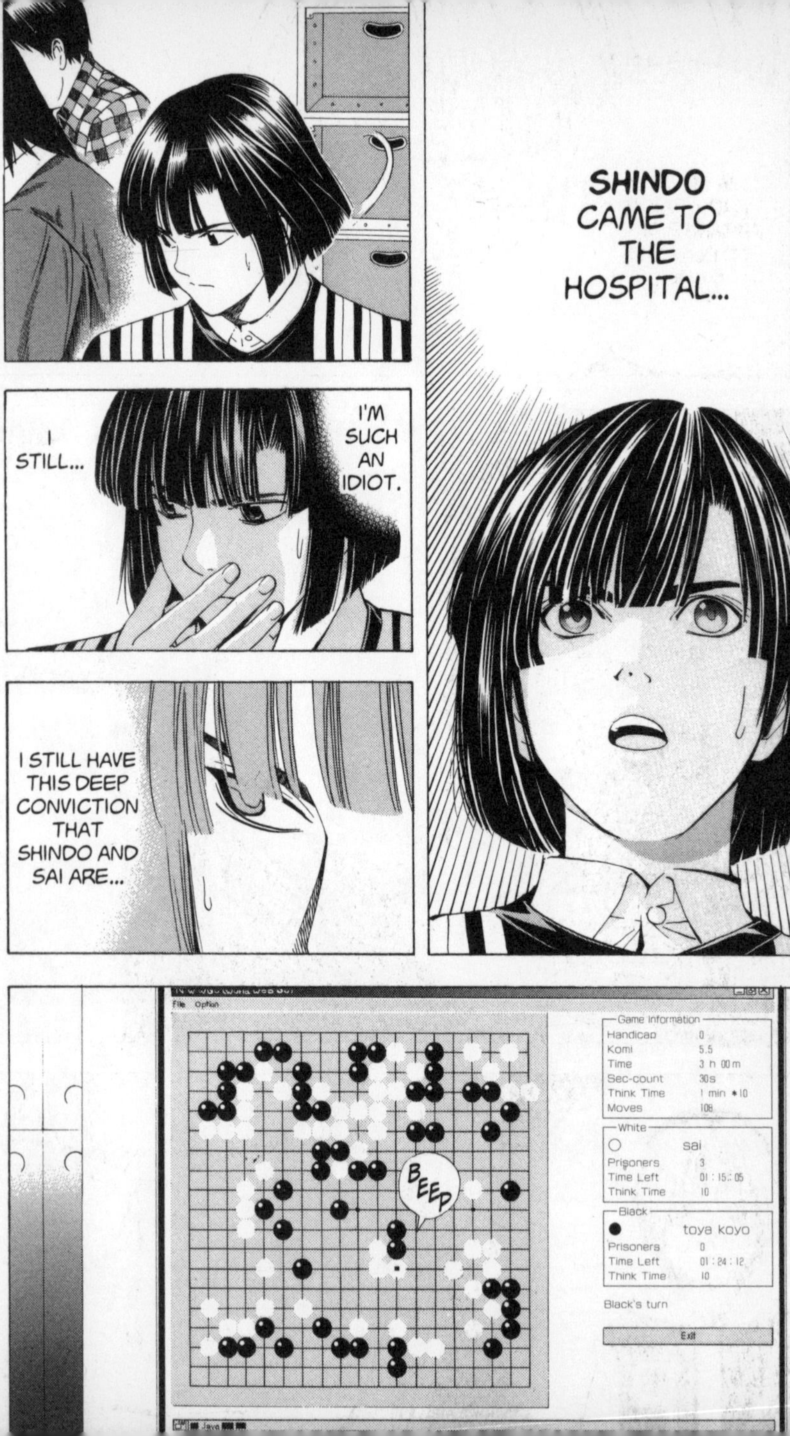
SHINDO CAME TO THE HOSPITAL...
I'M SUCH AN IDIOT.
I STILL...
I STILL HAVE THIS DEEP CONVICTION THAT SHINDO AND SAI ARE...
File Option
Game Information
Handicap 0
Komi 5.5
Time 3 h 00 m
Sec-count 30s
Think Time 1 min *10
Moves 108
White
sai
Prisoners 3
Time Left 01 : 15 : 05
Think Time 10
Black
toya koyo
Prisoners 0
Time Left 01 : 24 : 12
Think Time 10
Black's turn
Exit
BEEP

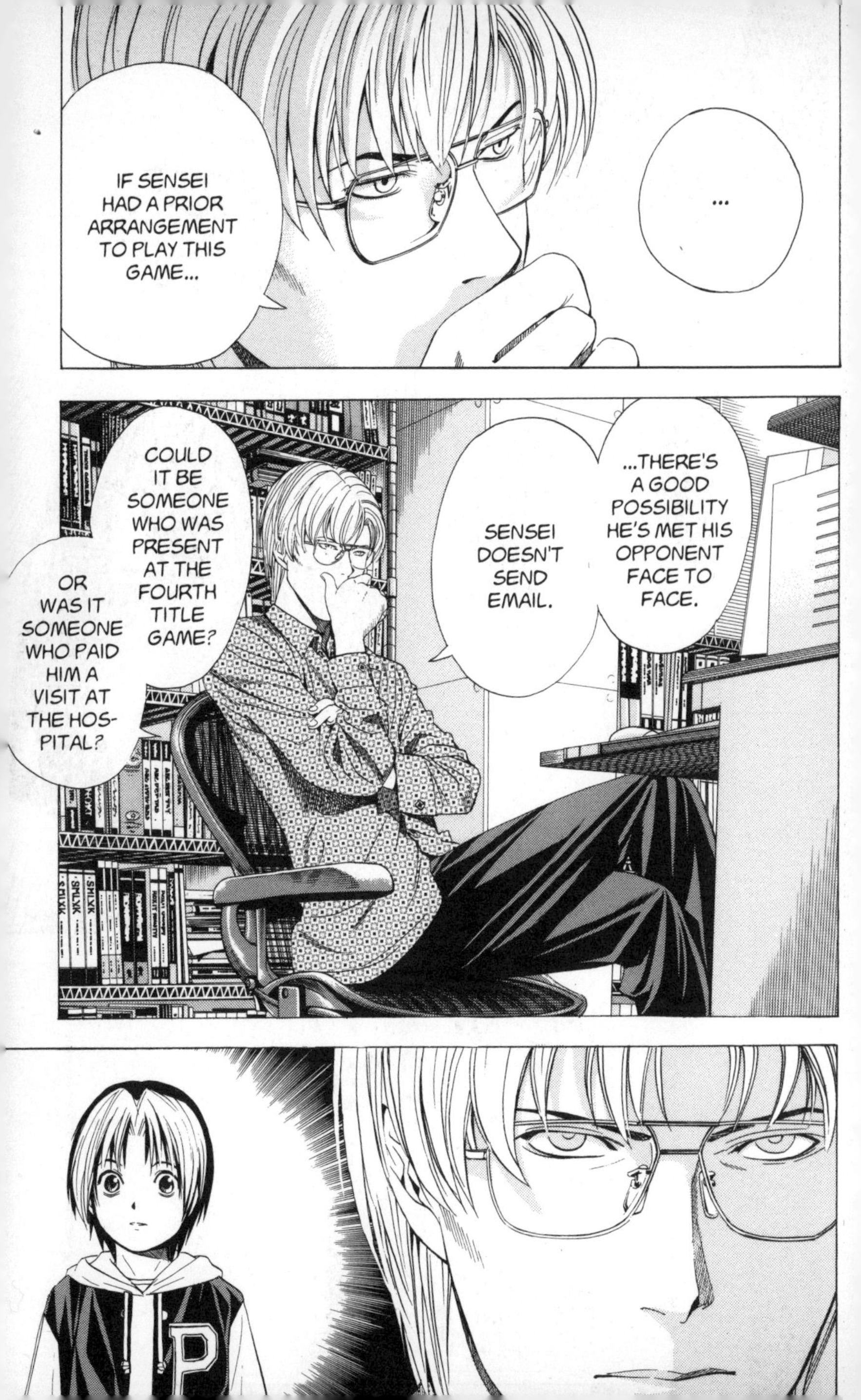
...
IF SENSEI HAD A PRIOR ARRANGEMENT TO PLAY THIS GAME...
...THERE'S A GOOD POSSIBILITY HE'S MET HIS OPPONENT FACE TO FACE.
SENSEI DOESN'T SEND EMAIL.
COULD IT BE SOMEONE WHO WAS PRESENT AT THE FOURTH TITLE GAME?
OR WAS IT SOMEONE WHO PAID HIM A VISIT AT THE HOS-PITAL?

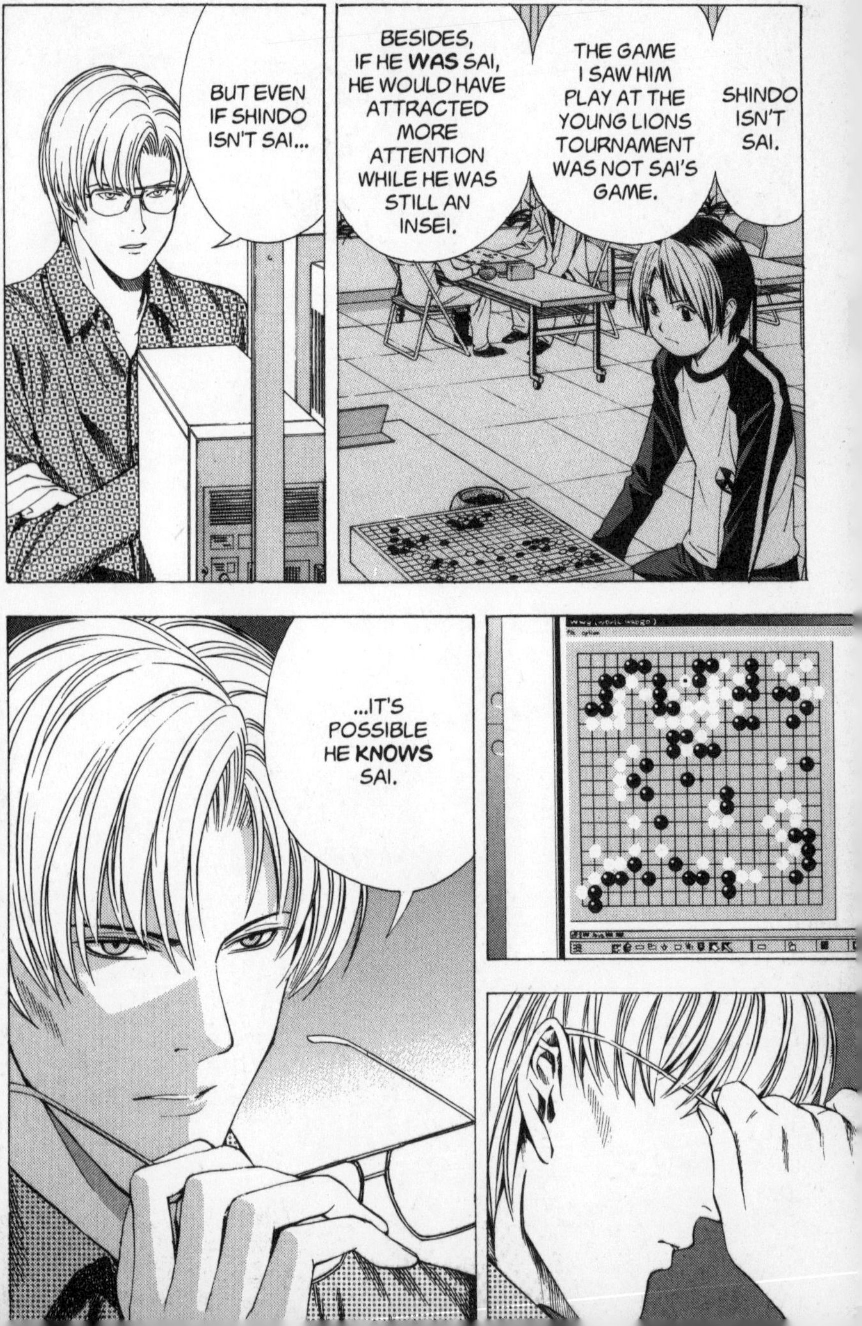
SHINDO ISN'T SAI.
THE GAME I SAW HIM PLAY AT THE YOUNG LIONS TOURNAMENT WAS NOT SAI'S GAME.
BESIDES, IF HE **WAS** SAI, HE WOULD HAVE ATTRACTED MORE ATTENTION WHILE HE WAS STILL AN INSEI.
BUT EVEN IF SHINDO ISN'T SAI...
...IT'S POSSIBLE HE **KNOWS** SAI.

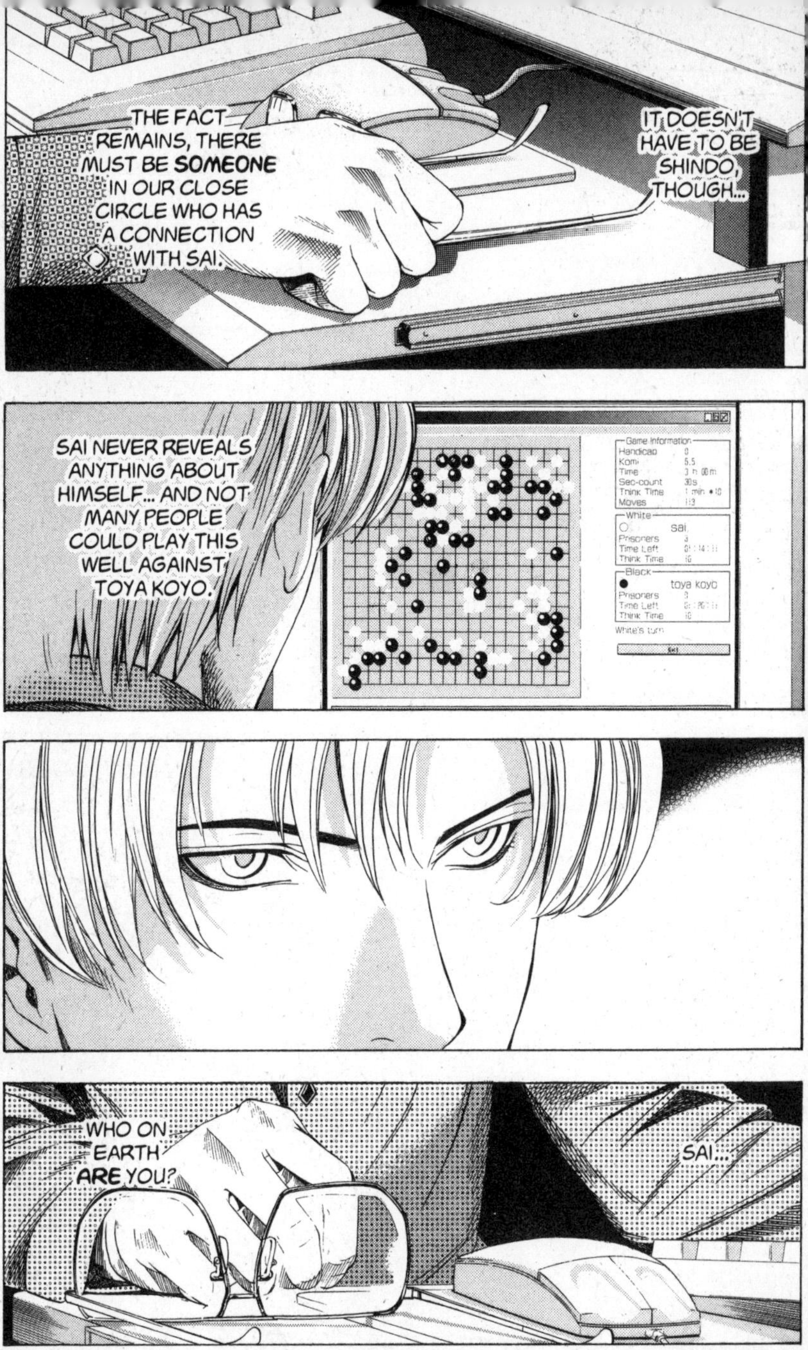
IT DOESN'T HAVE TO BE SHINDO, THOUGH...
THE FACT REMAINS, THERE MUST BE **SOMEONE** IN OUR CLOSE CIRCLE WHO HAS A CONNECTION WITH SAI.
Game Information
Handicap
Komi
Time
Sec-count
Think Time
Moves
White
sai
Prisoners
Time Left
Think Time
Black
toya koyo
Prisoners
Time Left
Think Time
White's turn
SAI NEVER REVEALS ANYTHING ABOUT HIMSELF... AND NOT MANY PEOPLE COULD PLAY THIS WELL AGAINST TOYA KOYO.
SAI...
WHO ON EARTH **ARE** YOU?

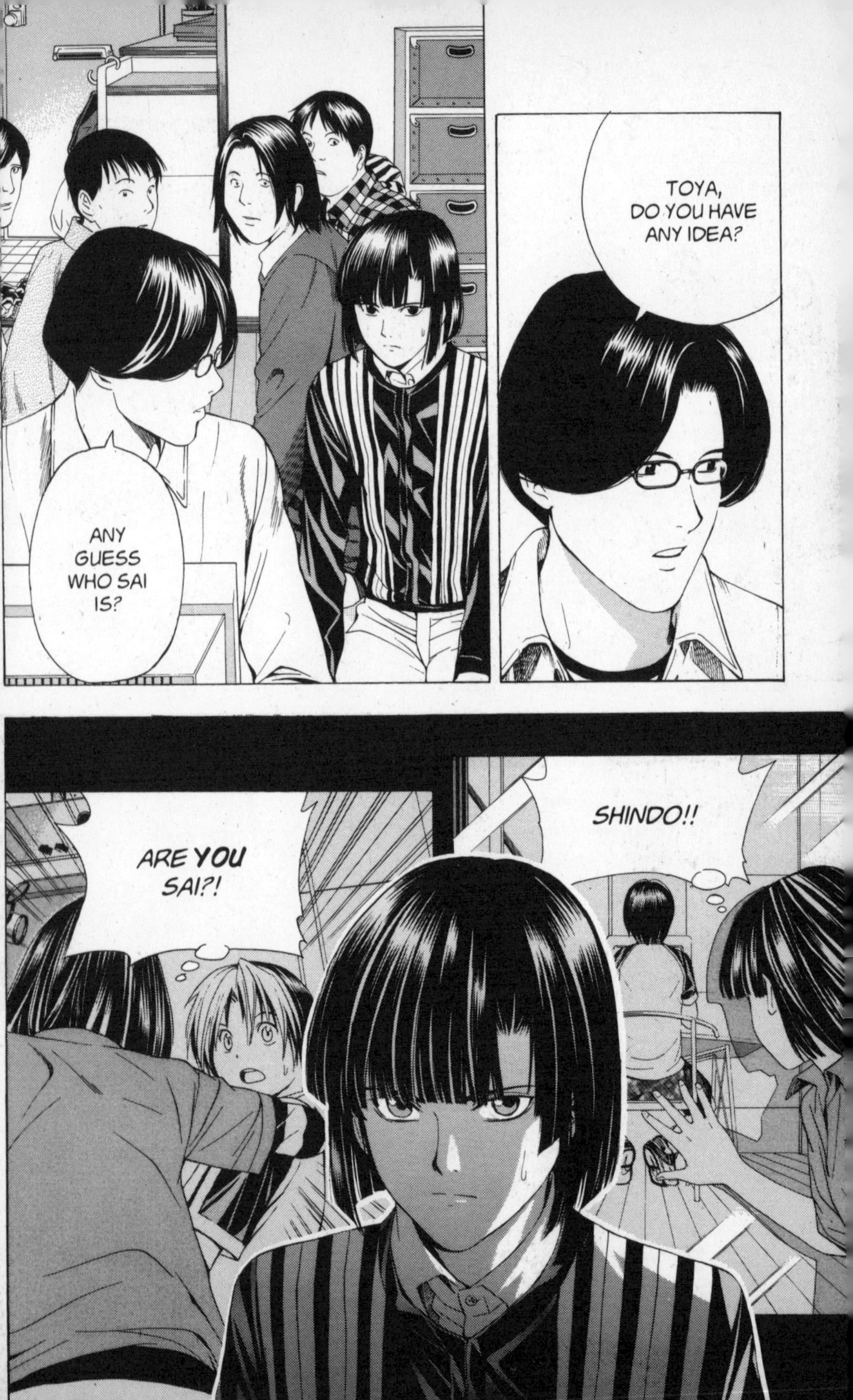
TOYA, DO YOU HAVE ANY IDEA?
ANY GUESS WHO SAI IS?
SHINDO!!
ARE YOU SAI?!

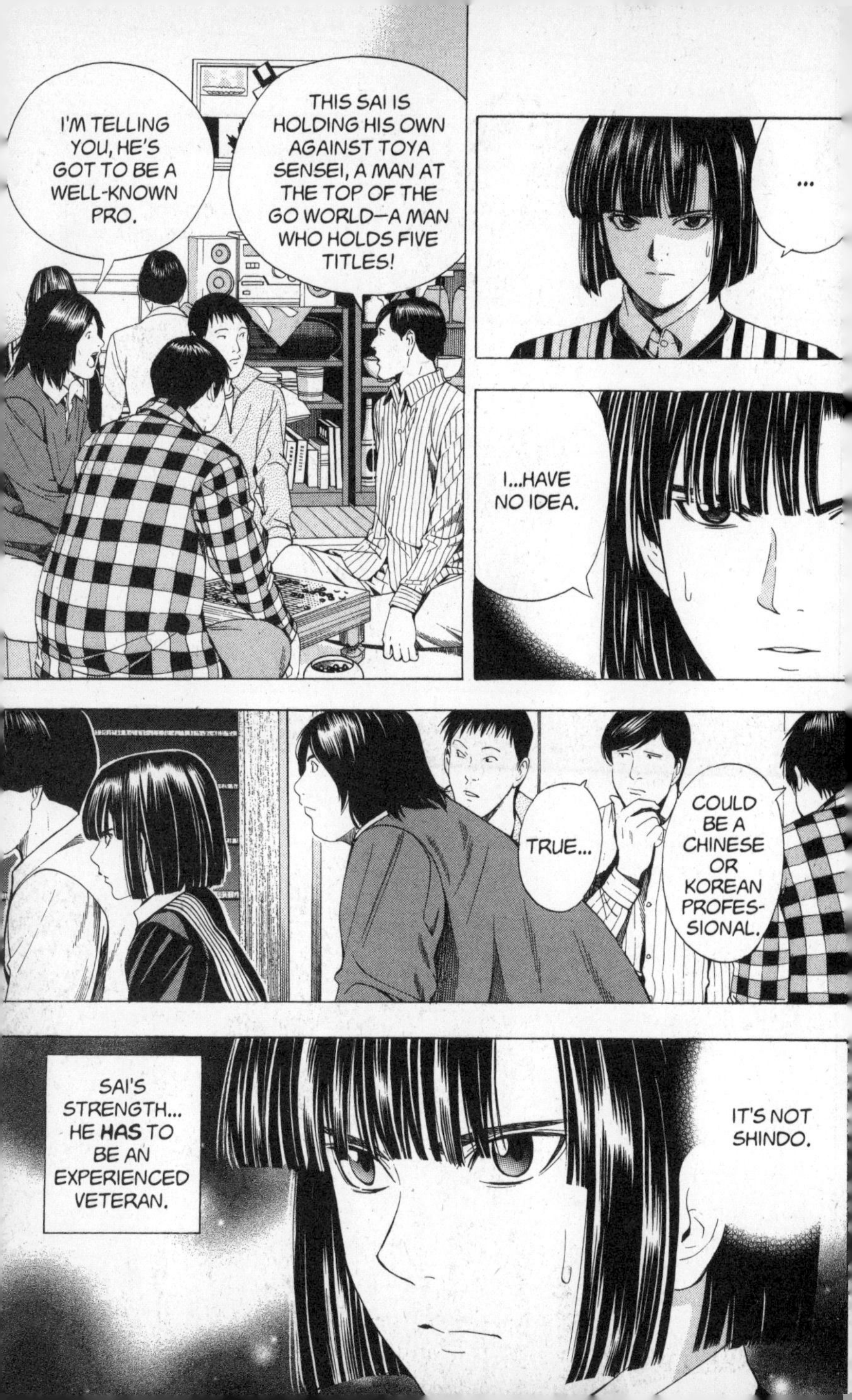
...
I...HAVE NO IDEA.
THIS SAI IS HOLDING HIS OWN AGAINST TOYA SENSEI, A MAN AT THE TOP OF THE GO WORLD—A MAN WHO HOLDS FIVE TITLES!
I'M TELLING YOU, HE'S GOT TO BE A WELL-KNOWN PRO.
COULD BE A CHINESE OR KOREAN PROFESSIONAL.
TRUE...
IT'S NOT SHINDO.
SAI'S STRENGTH... HE **HAS** TO BE AN EXPERIENCED VETERAN.

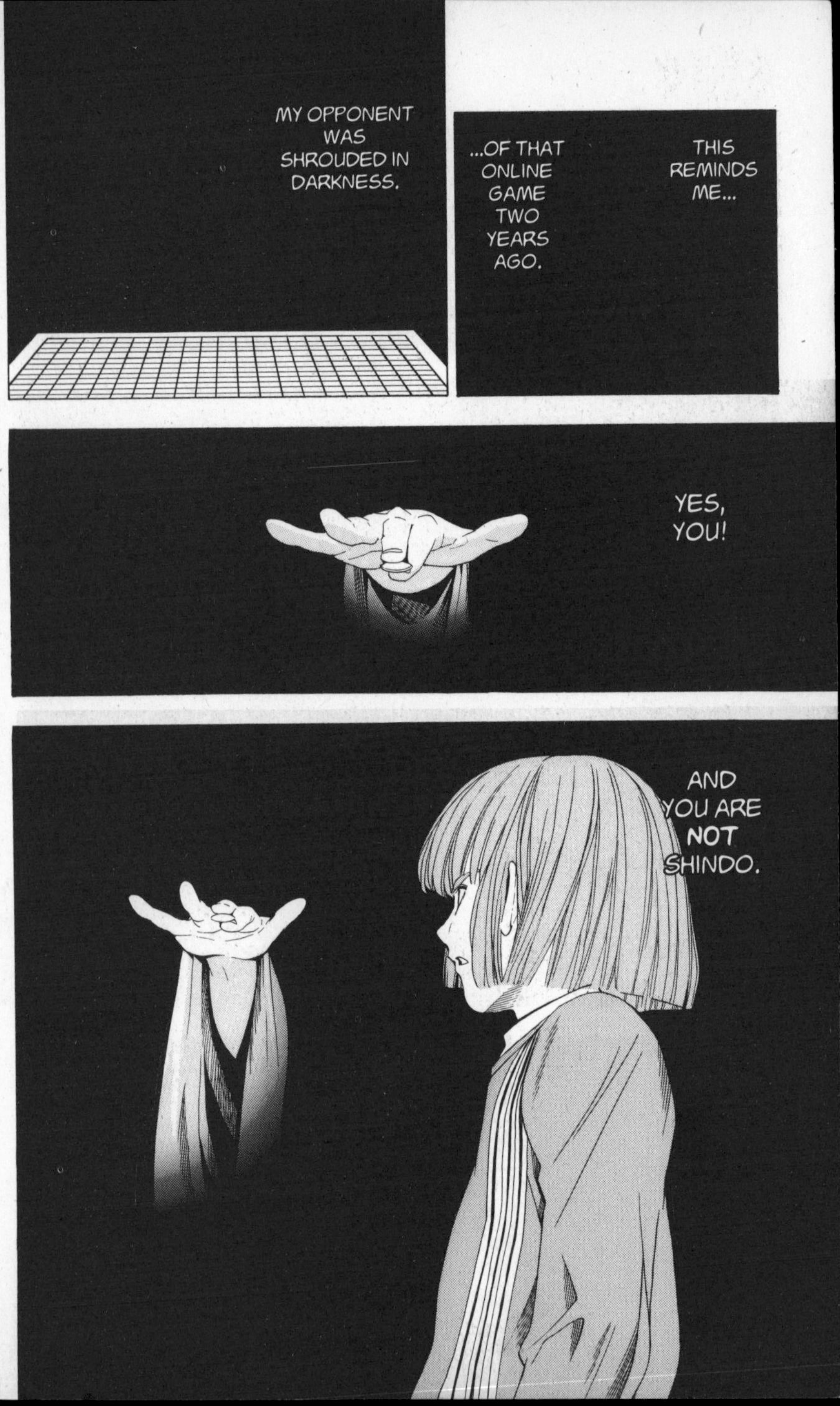
THIS REMINDS ME...
...OF THAT ONLINE GAME TWO YEARS AGO.
MY OPPONENT WAS SHROUDED IN DARKNESS.
YES, YOU!
AND YOU ARE **NOT** SHINDO.

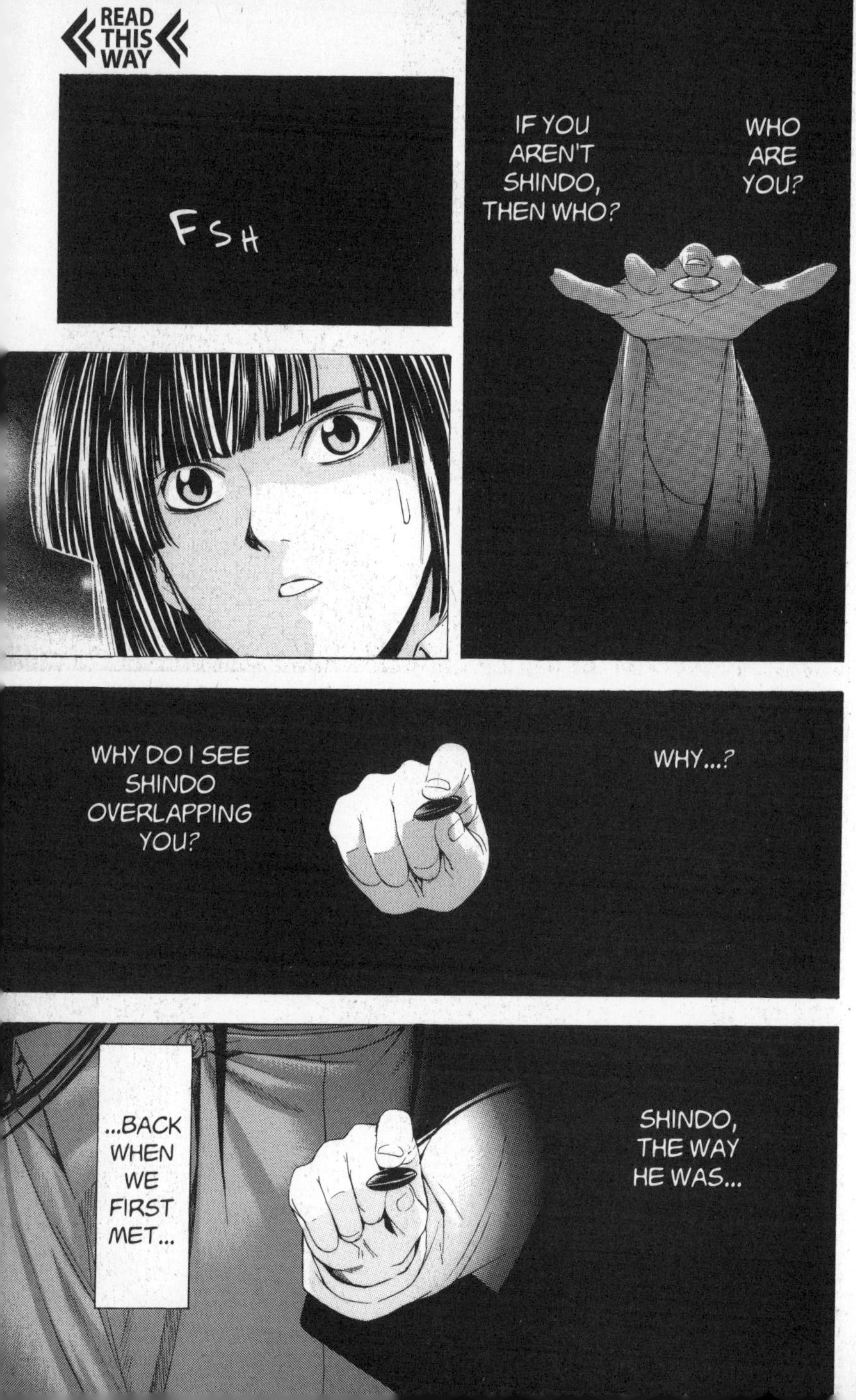
READ THIS WAY
WHO ARE YOU?
IF YOU AREN'T SHINDO, THEN WHO?
FSH
WHY...?
WHY DO I SEE SHINDO OVERLAPPING YOU?
SHINDO, THE WAY HE WAS...
...BACK WHEN WE FIRST MET...

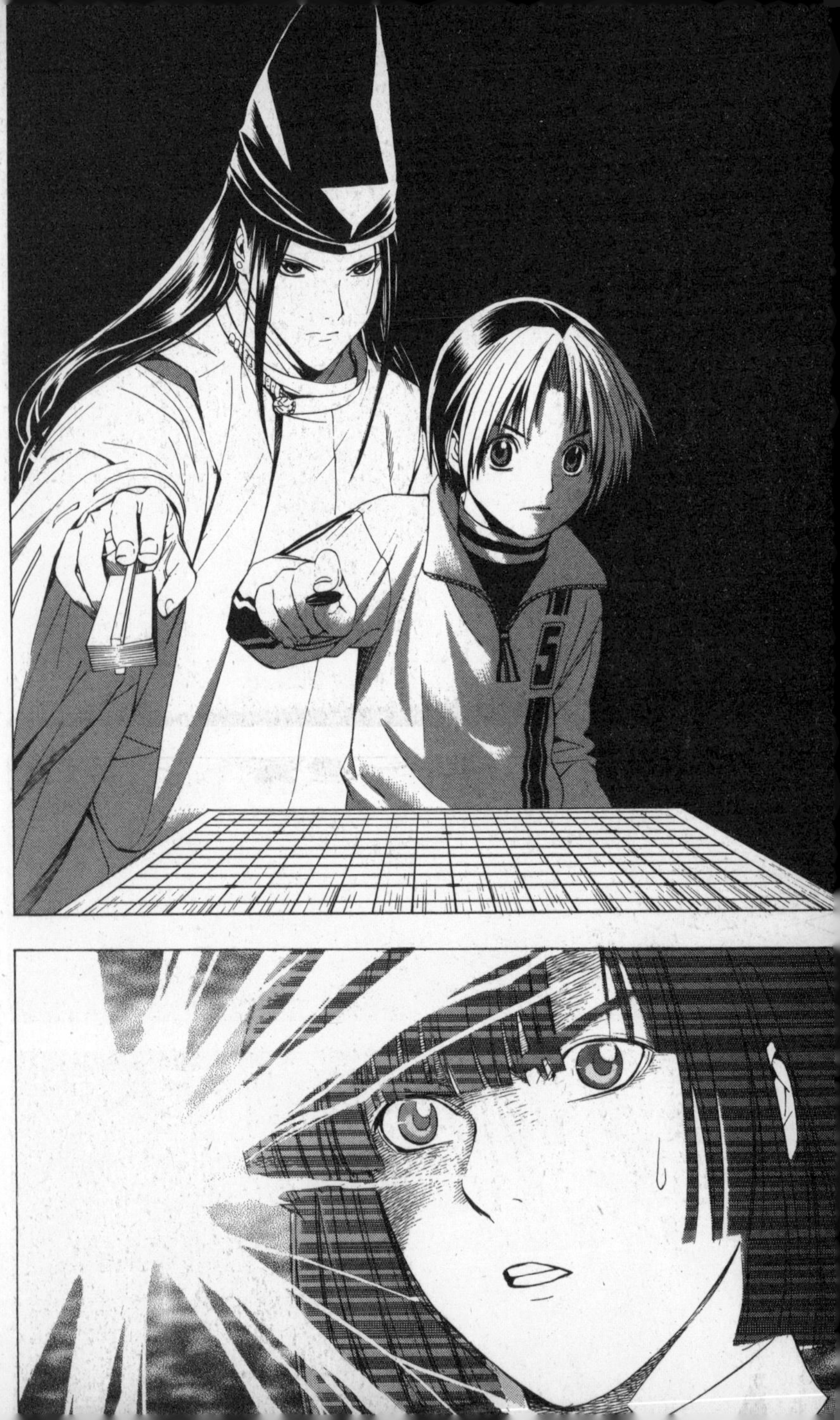

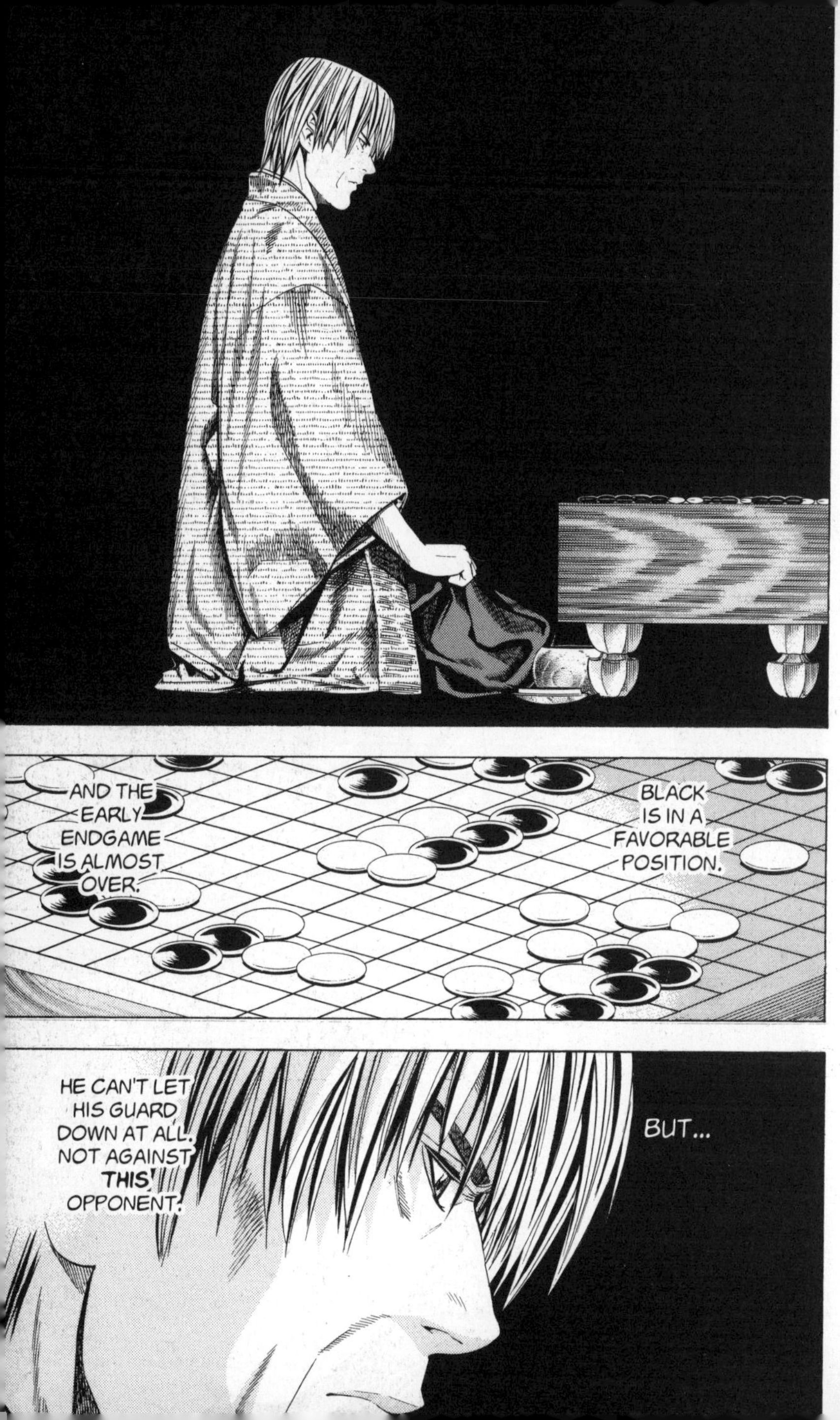
BLACK IS IN A FAVORABLE POSITION.
AND THE EARLY ENDGAME IS ALMOST OVER.
BUT...
HE CAN'T LET HIS GUARD DOWN AT ALL. NOT AGAINST **THIS** OPPONENT.

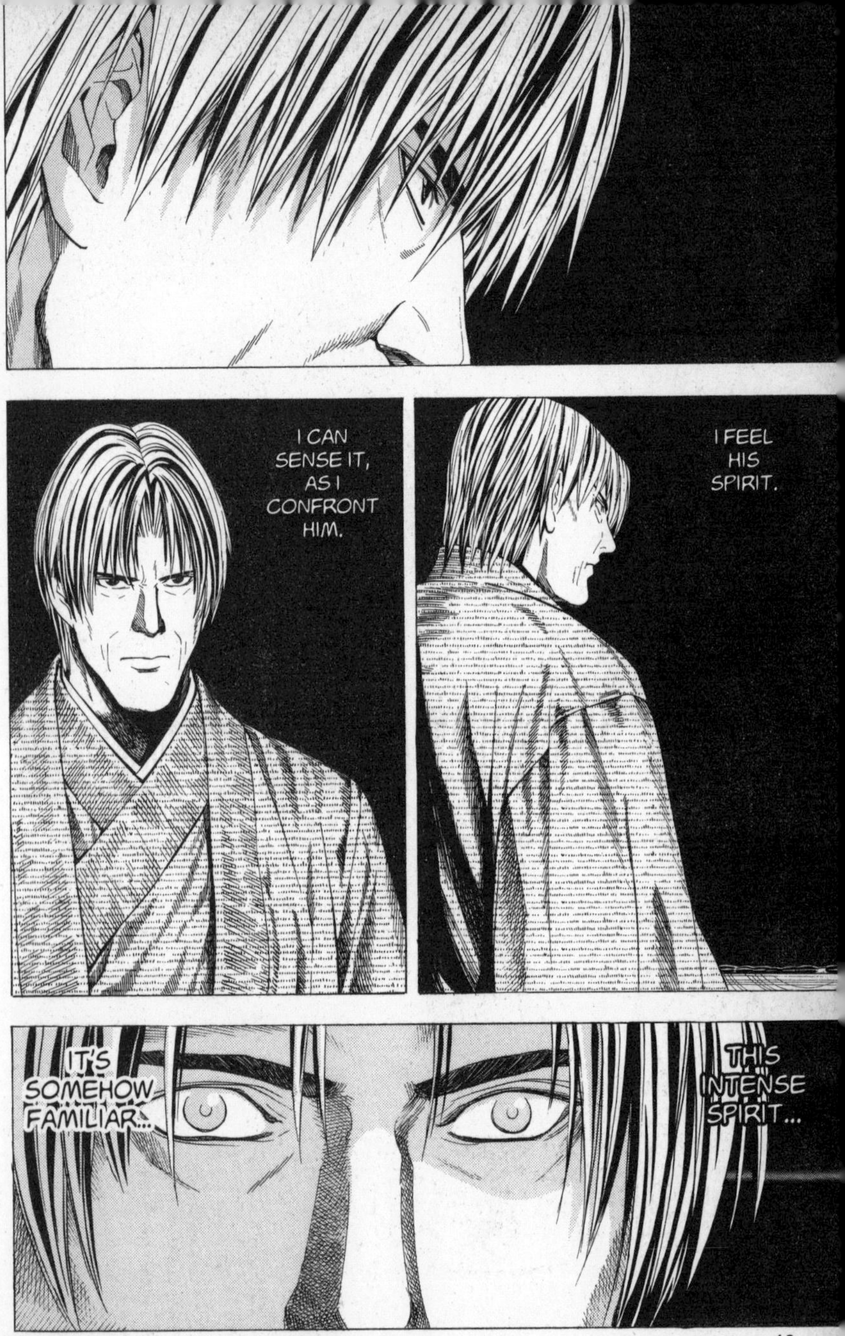
I FEEL HIS SPIRIT.
I CAN SENSE IT, AS I CONFRONT HIM.
THIS INTENSE SPIRIT...
IT'S SOMEHOW FAMILIAR...

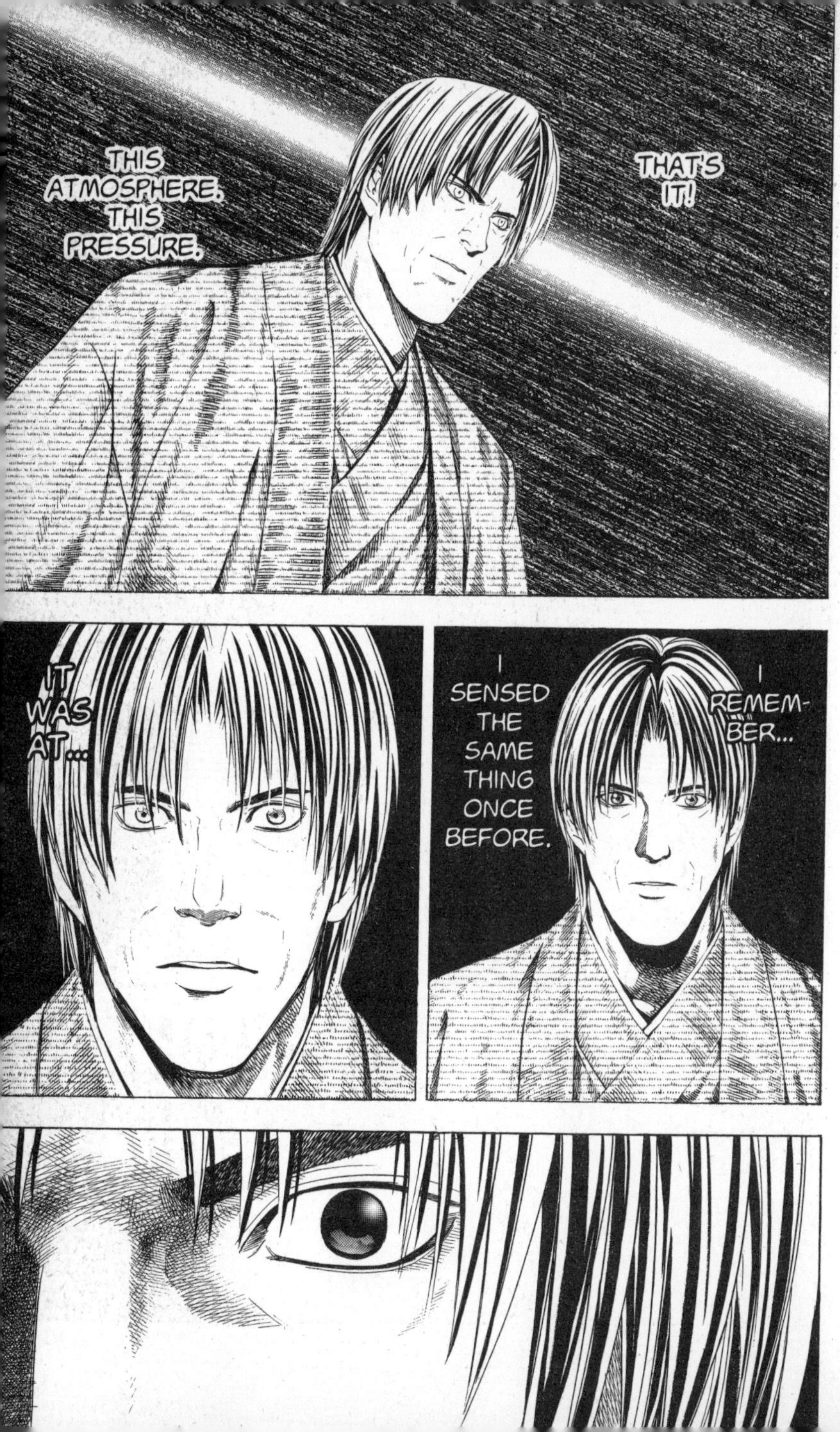
THAT'S IT!
THIS ATMOSPHERE. THIS PRESSURE.
I REMEMBER...
I SENSED THE SAME THING ONCE BEFORE.
IT WAS AT...

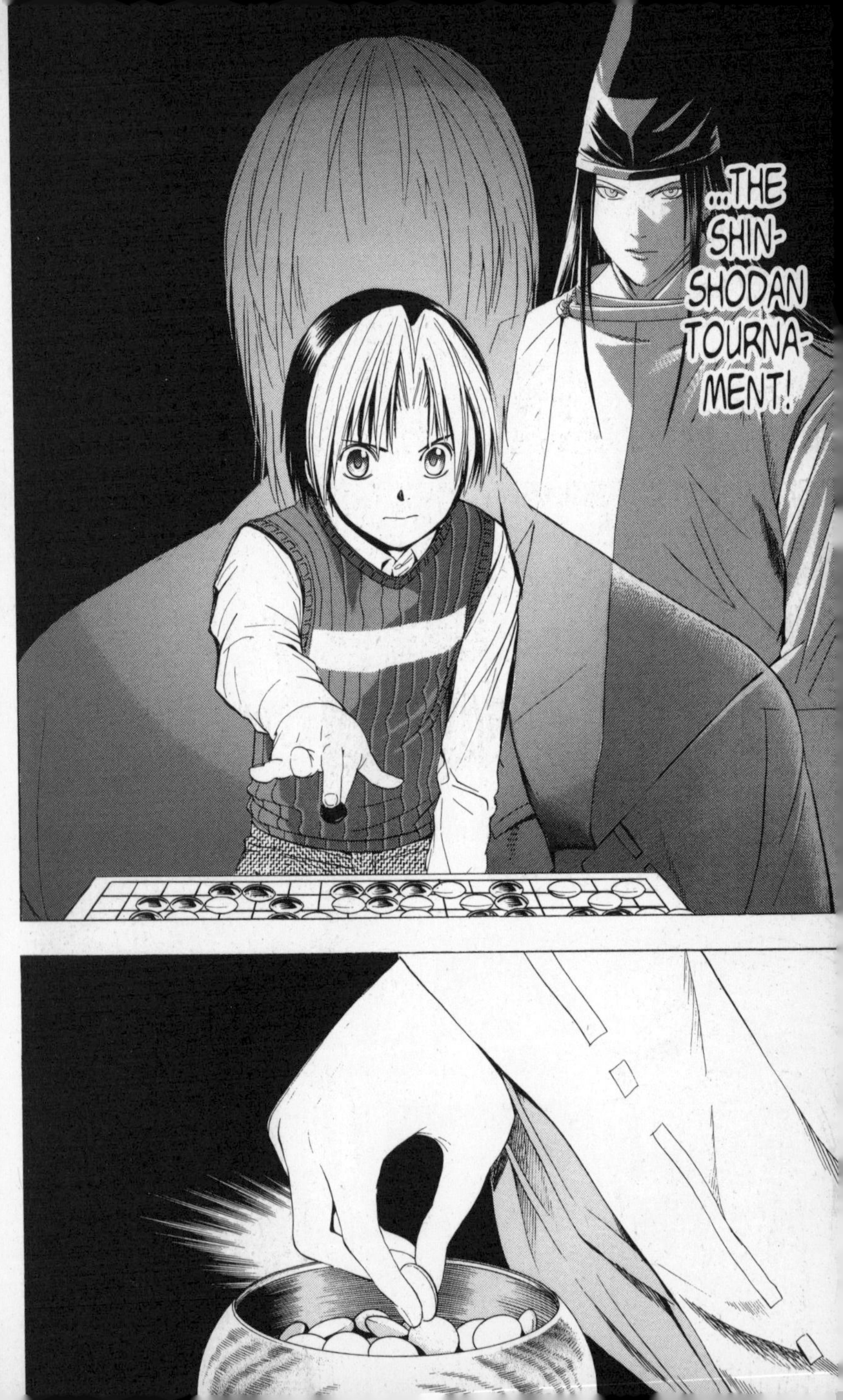
...THE SHIN-SHODAN TOURNA-MENT!

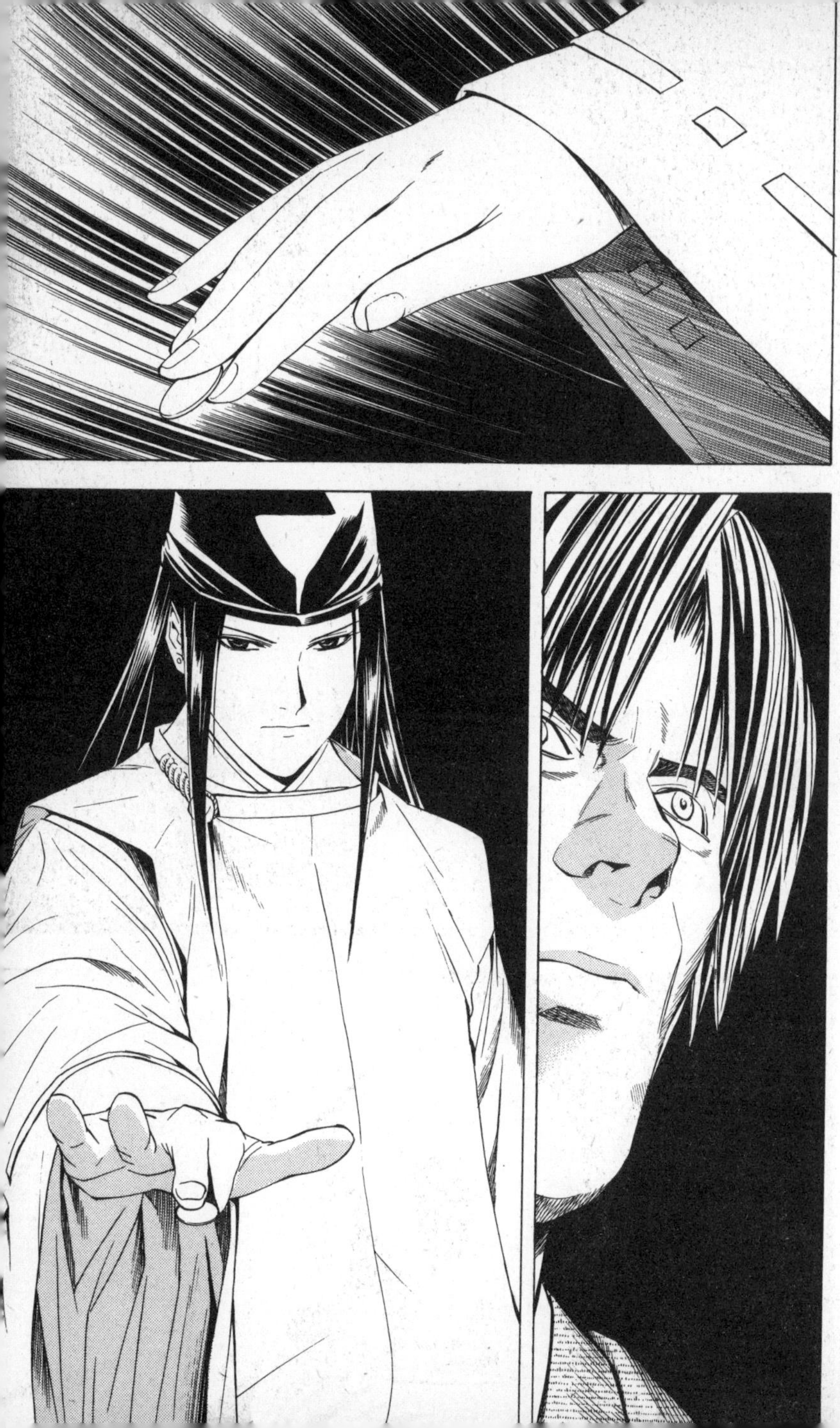

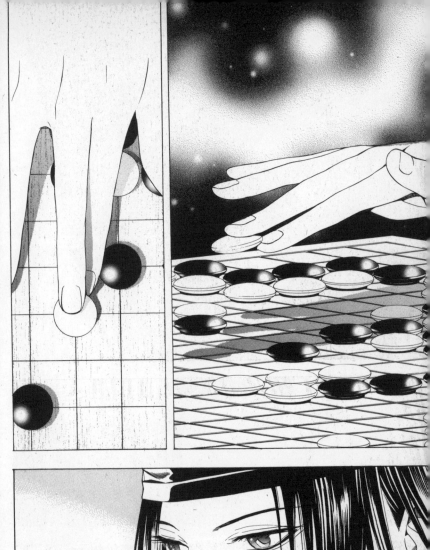

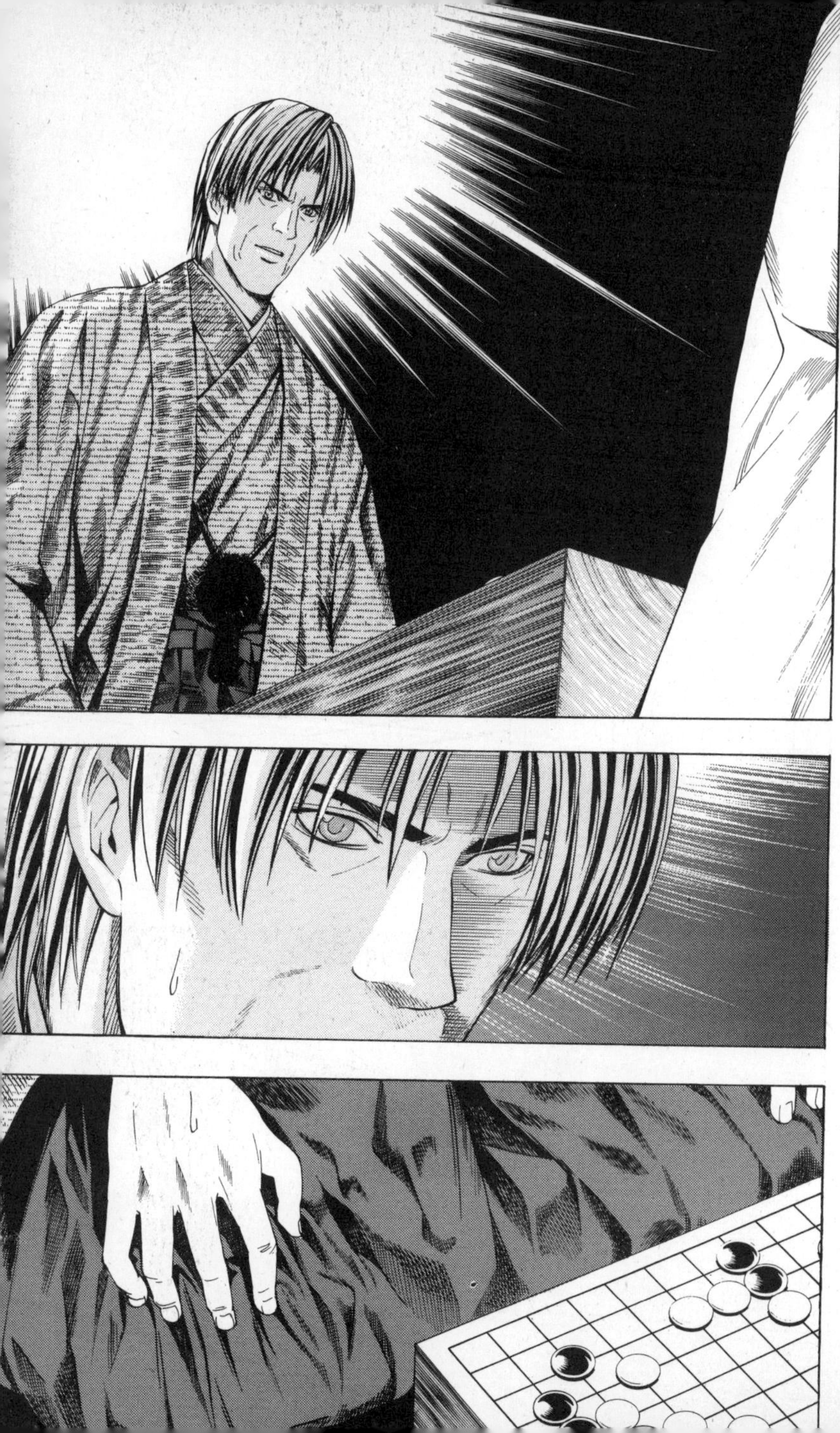

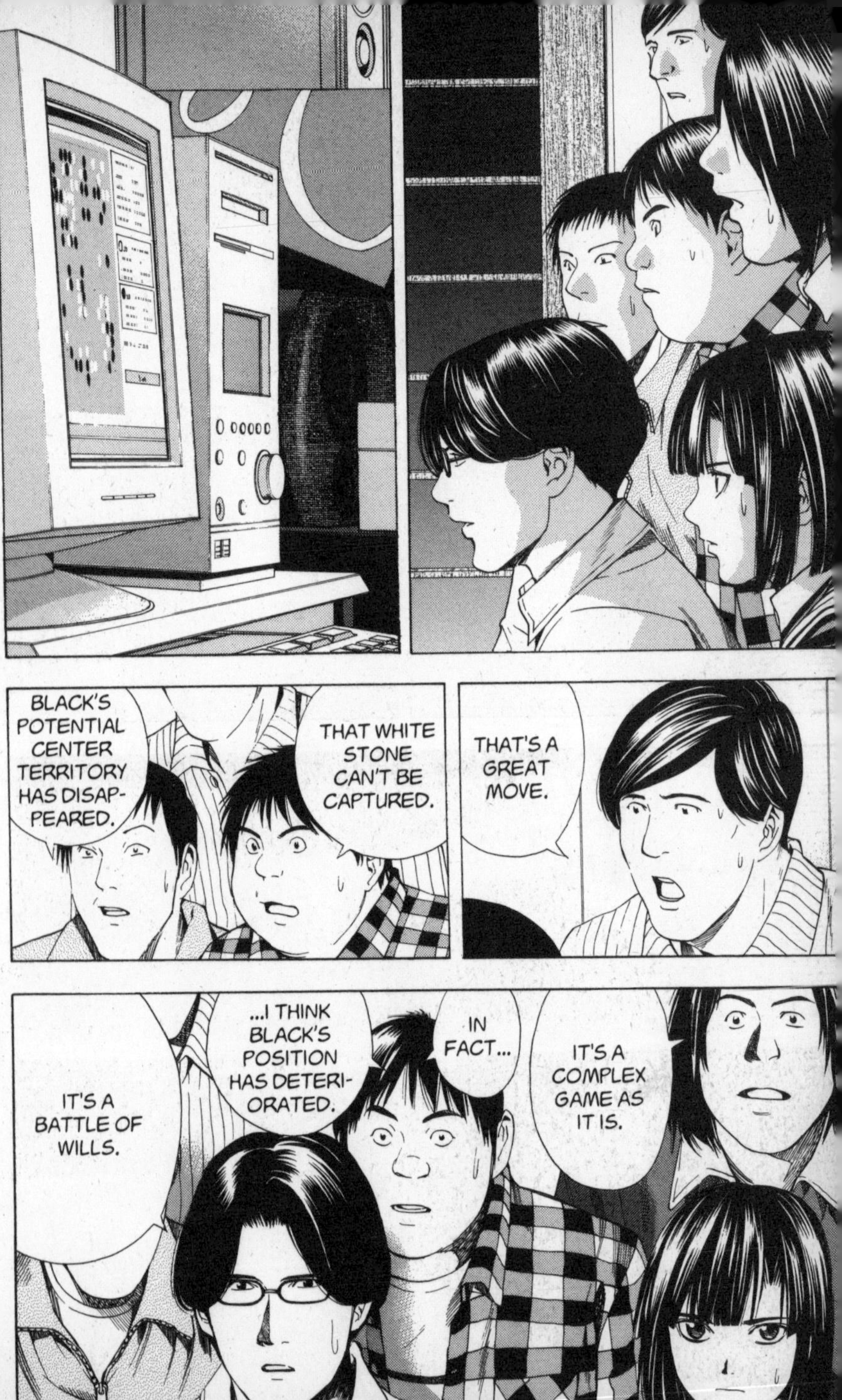
THAT'S A GREAT MOVE.
THAT WHITE STONE CAN'T BE CAPTURED.
BLACK'S POTENTIAL CENTER TERRITORY HAS DISAP-PEARED.
IT'S A COMPLEX GAME AS IT IS.
IN FACT...
...I THINK BLACK'S POSITION HAS DETERI-ORATED.
IT'S A BATTLE OF WILLS.

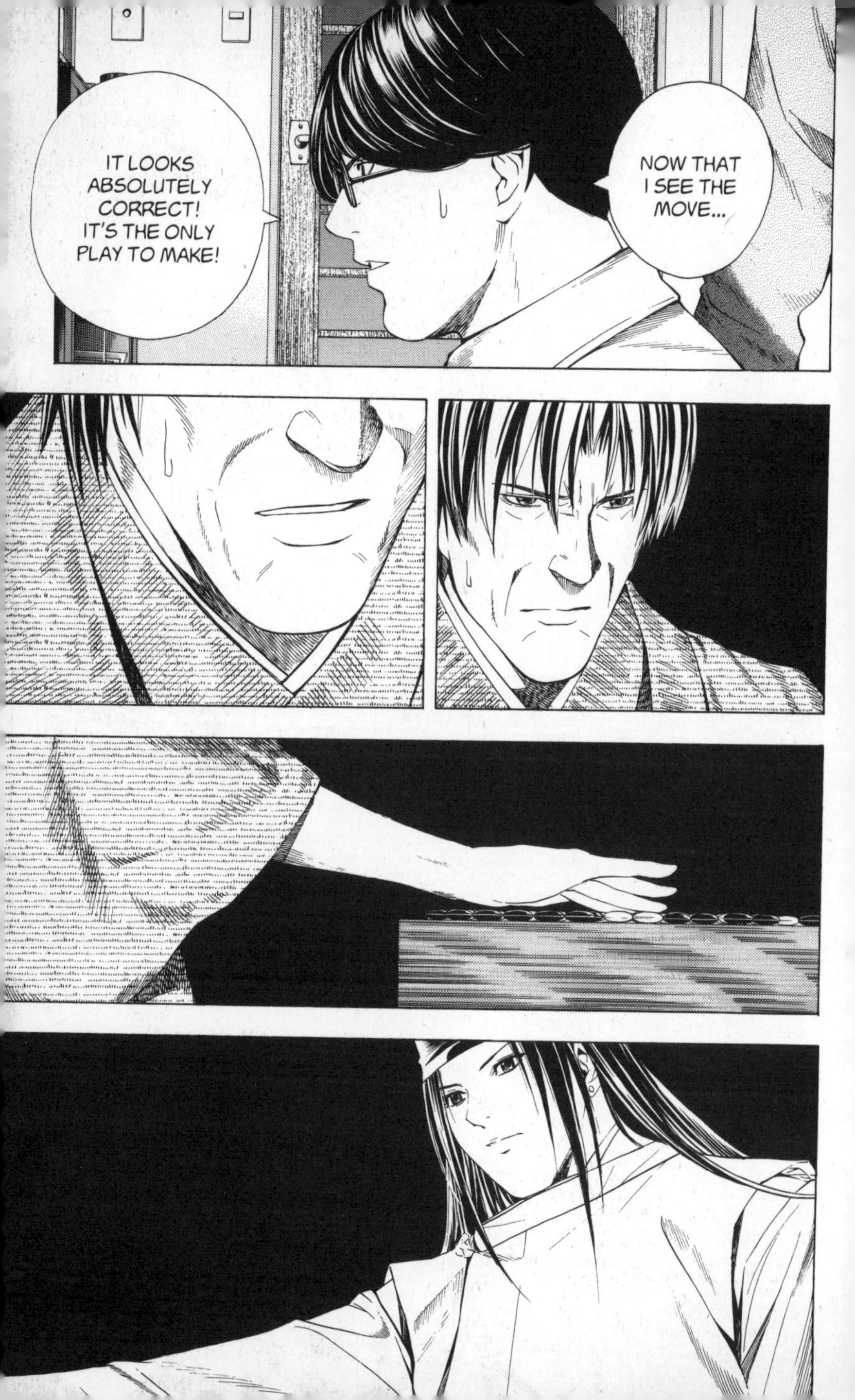
NOW THAT I SEE THE MOVE...
IT LOOKS ABSOLUTELY CORRECT! IT'S THE ONLY PLAY TO MAKE!

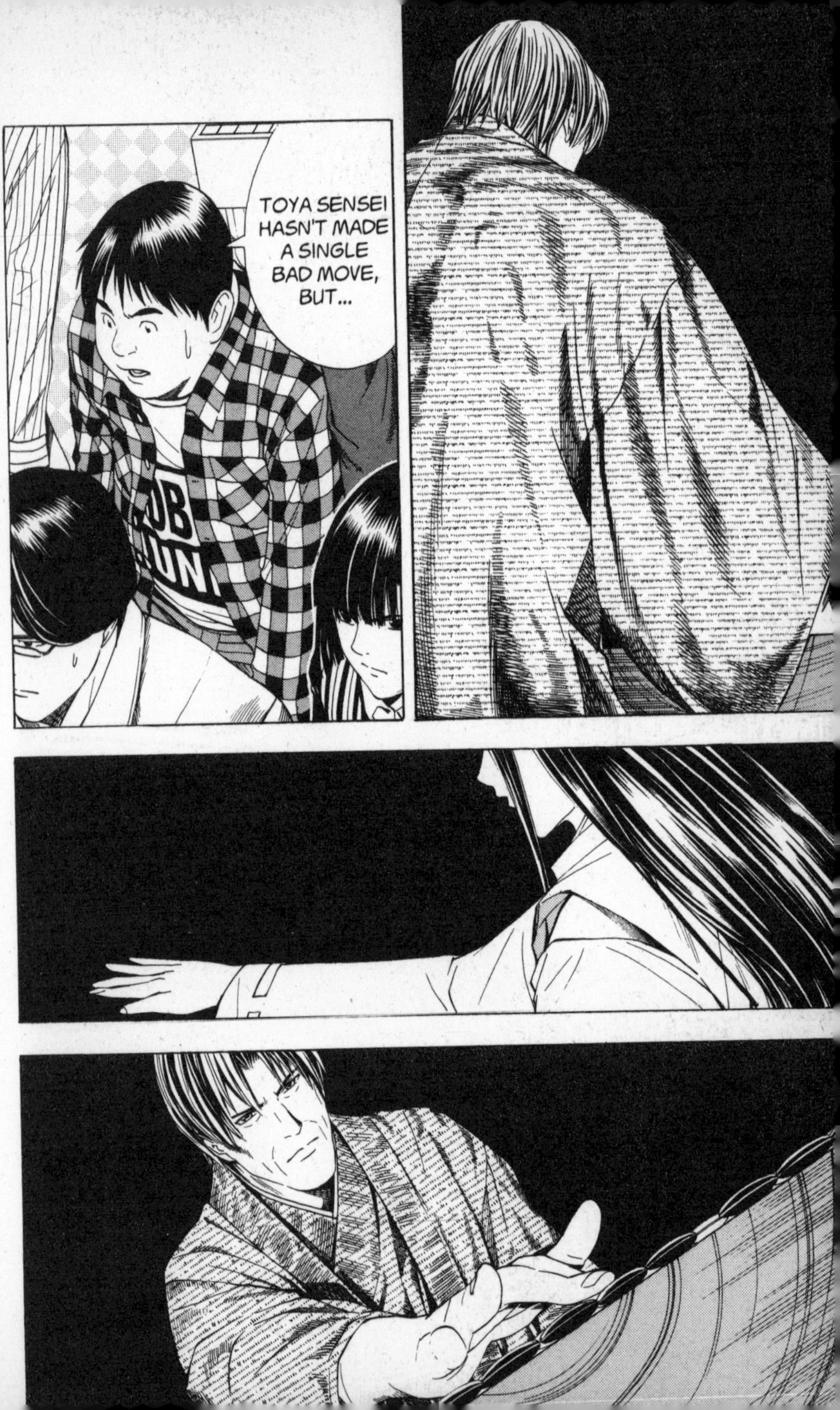
TOYA SENSEI HASN'T MADE A SINGLE BAD MOVE, BUT...

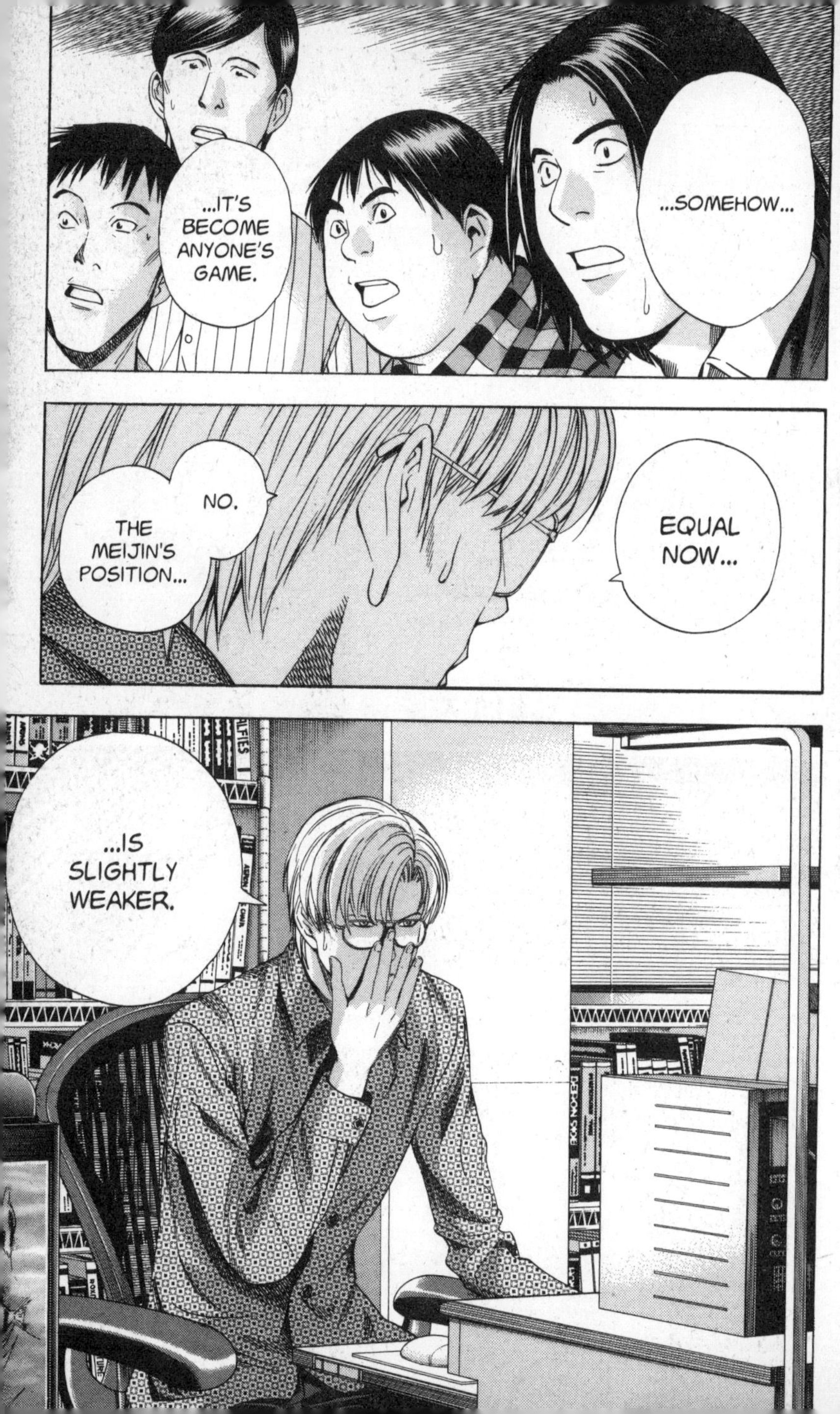
...SOMEHOW...
...IT'S BECOME ANYONE'S GAME.
EQUAL NOW...
NO.
THE MEIJIN'S POSITION...
...IS SLIGHTLY WEAKER.

A WORD ABOUT HIKARU NO GO

ALL ABOUT GO BOARDS

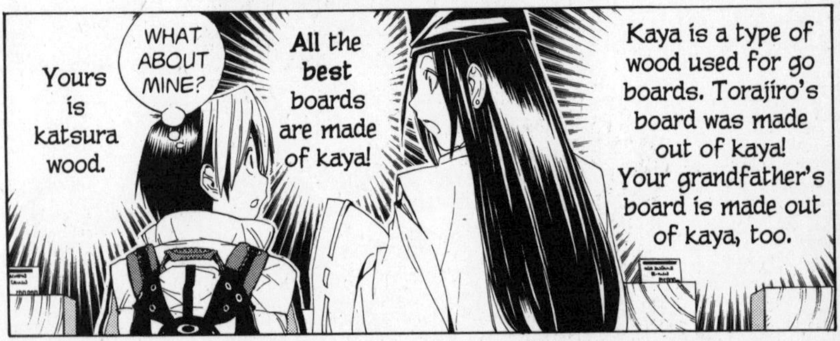
Kaya is a type of wood used for go boards. Torajiro's board was made out of kaya! Your grandfather's board is made out of kaya, too.
All the best boards are made of kaya!
WHAT ABOUT MINE?
Yours is katsura wood.

THE MOST EXPENSIVE MATERIAL IS HON-KAYA WOOD, WHICH IS GROWN IN JAPAN. NEXT IS CHINESE KAYA, SPRUCE (SHIN-KAYA), AND KATSURA WOOD.

SOME FRAUDULENT DEALERS MISREPRESENT THE TYPE OF WOOD THEIR BOARDS ARE MADE OF. IN ADDITION, THERE ARE INFERIOR PRODUCTS FOR SALE MADE OF WOOD THAT HASN'T BEEN PROPERLY DRIED.

PROFESSIONAL WOODEN GO BOARDS ARE EXPENSIVE.
IF YOU WANT TO BUY ONE, CHOOSE A REPUTABLE DEALER.

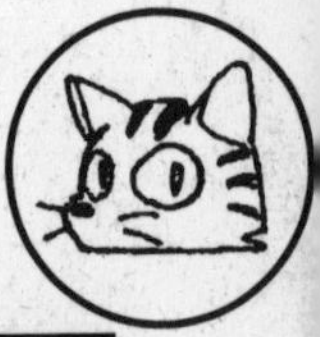

Game 116: "One Thousand Years"

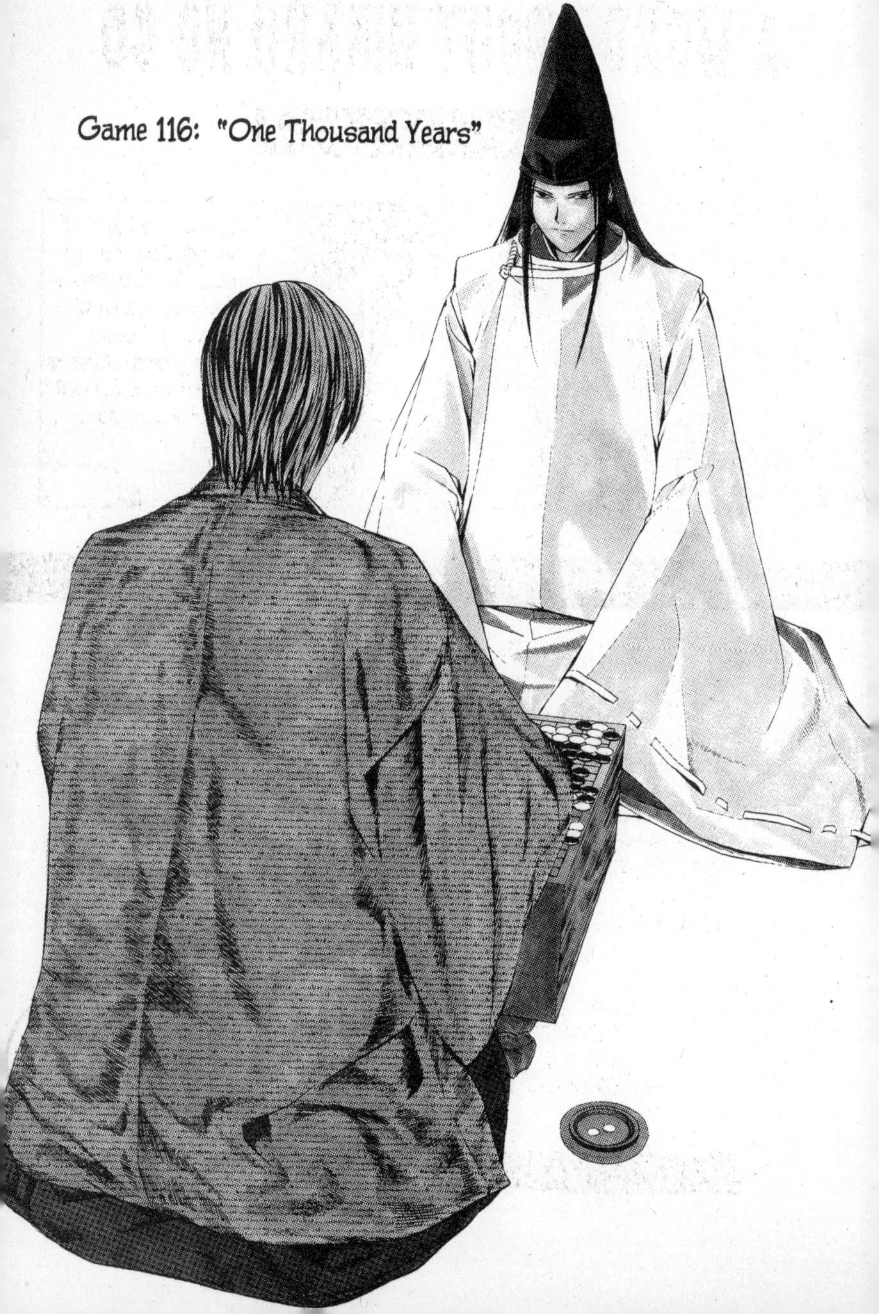

Game 116 "One Thousand Years"

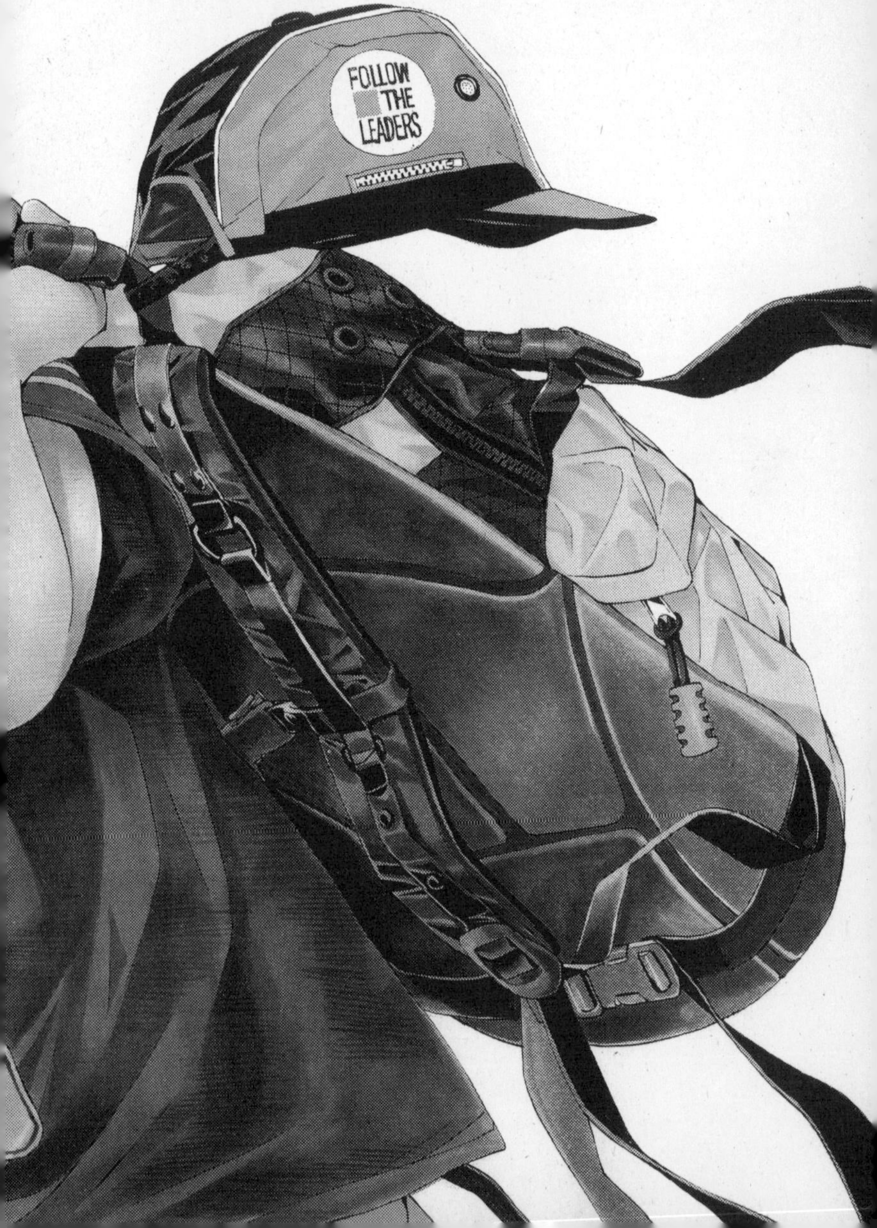
FOLLOW THE LEADERS

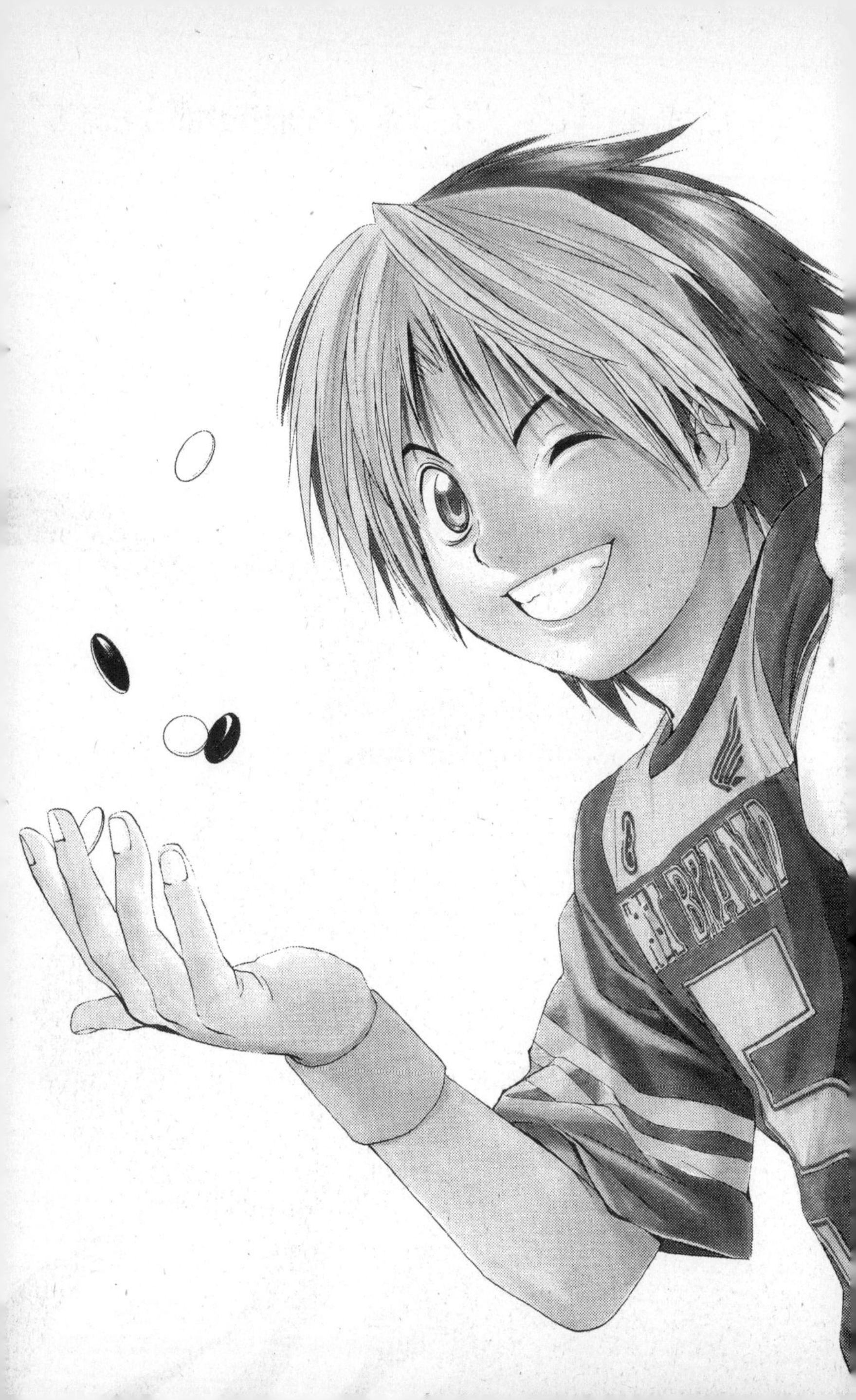
BRAND

Hikaru:
Spacesuit
Version

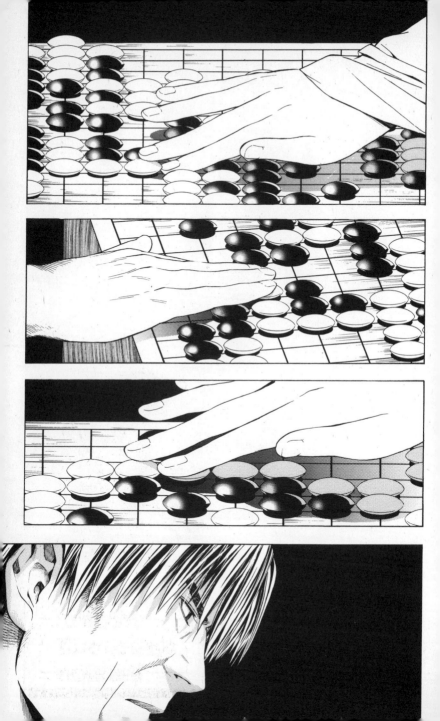

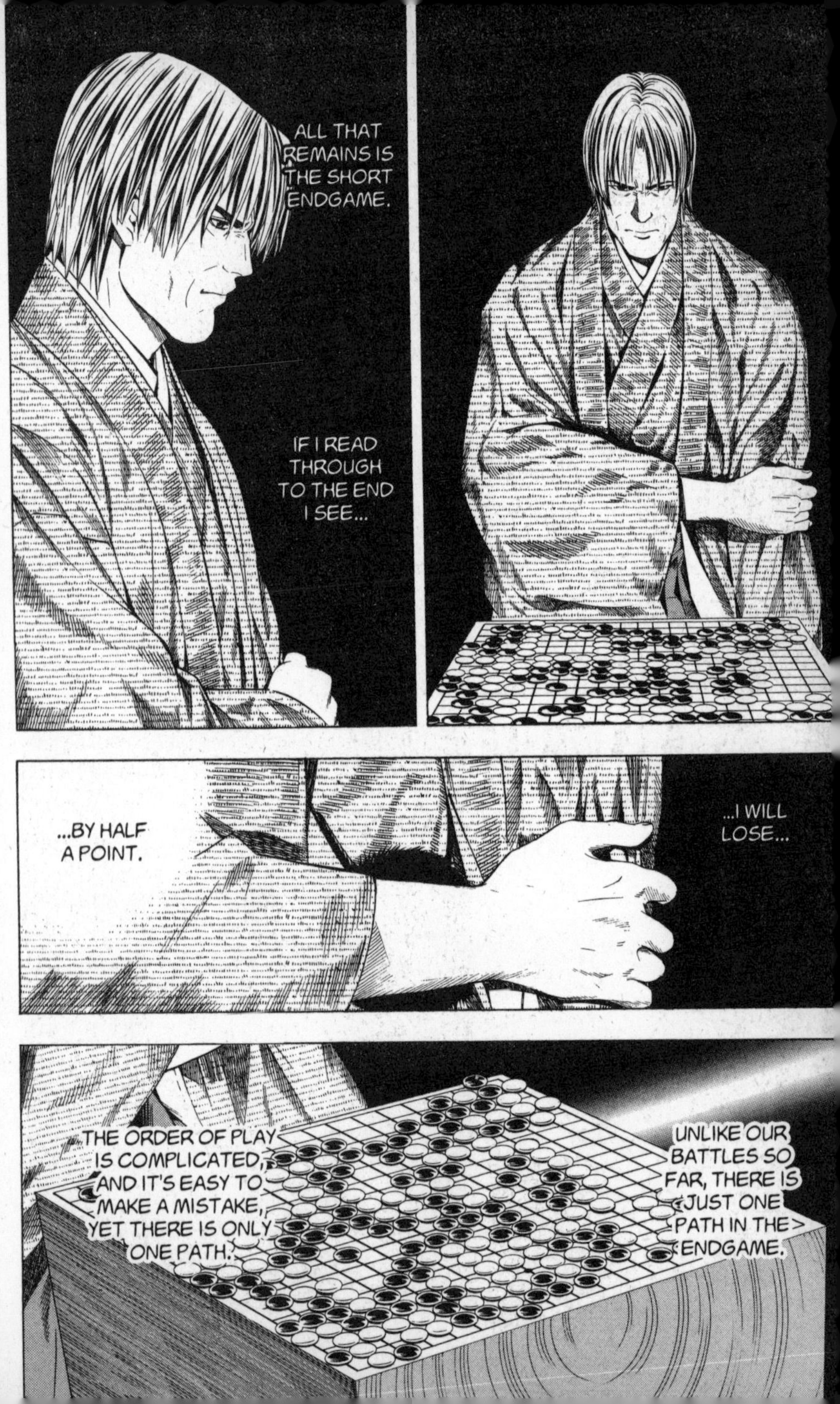
ALL THAT REMAINS IS THE SHORT ENDGAME.
IF I READ THROUGH TO THE END I SEE...
...I WILL LOSE...
...BY HALF A POINT.
UNLIKE OUR BATTLES SO FAR, THERE IS JUST ONE PATH IN THE ENDGAME.
THE ORDER OF PLAY IS COMPLICATED, AND IT'S EASY TO MAKE A MISTAKE, YET THERE IS ONLY ONE PATH.

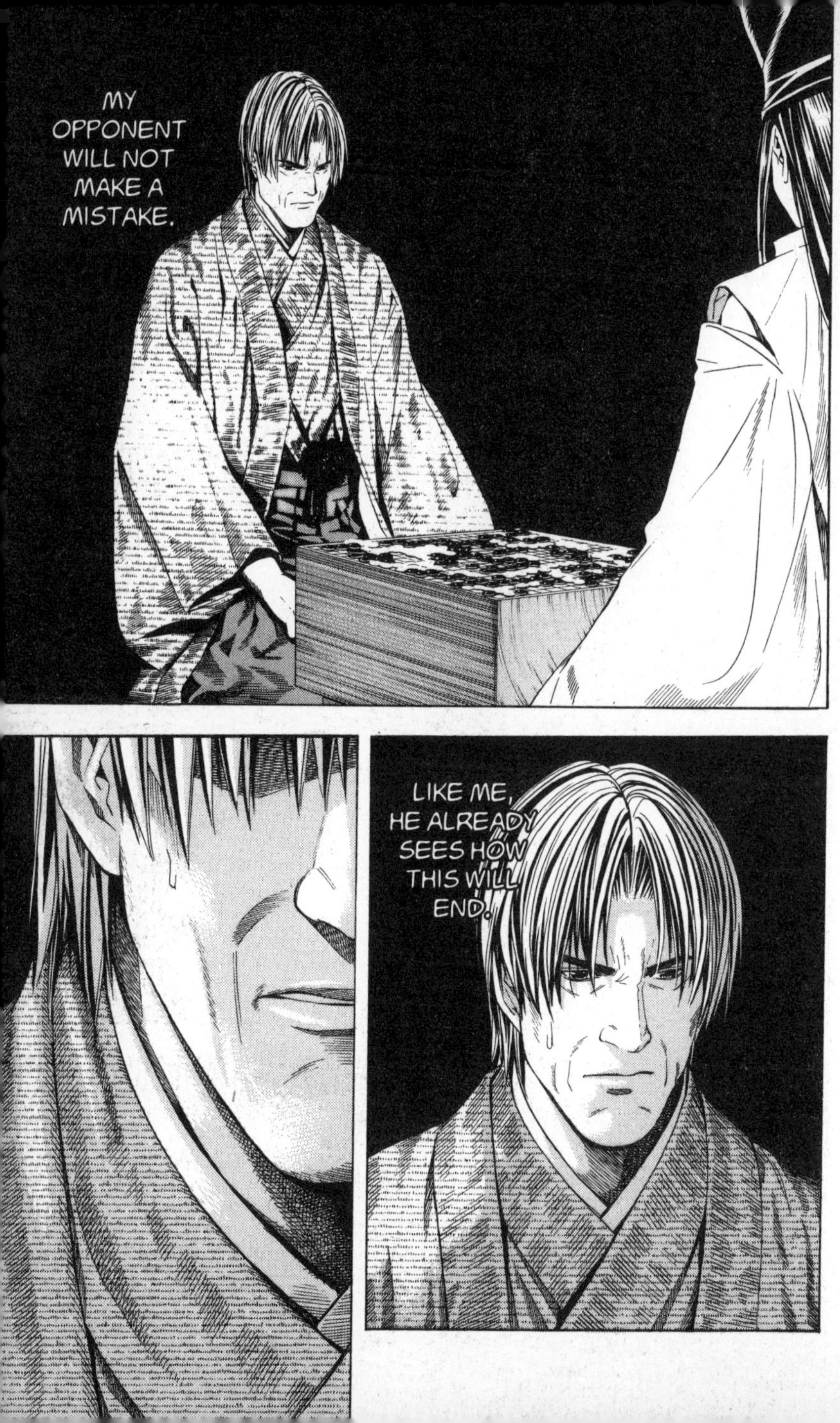
MY OPPONENT WILL NOT MAKE A MISTAKE.
LIKE ME, HE ALREADY SEES HOW THIS WILL END.

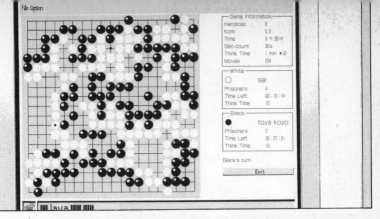

File Option

┌─ Game Information ─┐
Handicap   0
Komi   5.5
Time   3 h 00 m
Sec-count   30s
Think Time   1 min ＊10
Moves   224

┌─ White ─┐
○   sai
Prisoners   4
Time Left   00 : 13 : 14
Think Time   10

┌─ Black ─┐
●   toya koyo
Prisoners   2
Time Left   00 : 27 : 51
Think Time   10

Black's turn
              Exit

Java

Black has resigned.
White won.

Exit

WHAT?

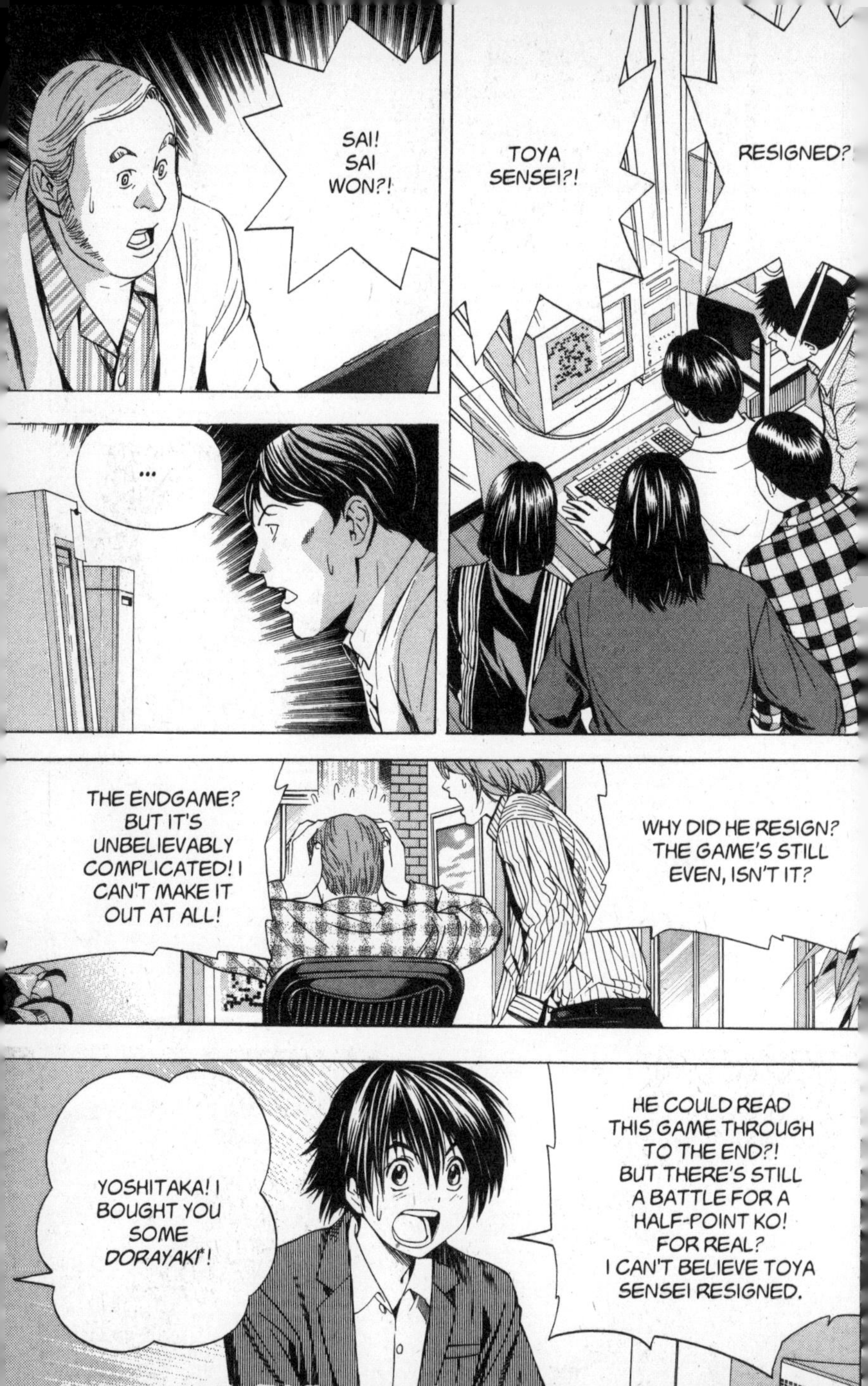
RESIGNED?
TOYA SENSEI?!
SAI! SAI WON?!
...
WHY DID HE RESIGN? THE GAME'S STILL EVEN, ISN'T IT?
THE ENDGAME? BUT IT'S UNBELIEVABLY COMPLICATED! I CAN'T MAKE IT OUT AT ALL!
HE COULD READ THIS GAME THROUGH TO THE END?! BUT THERE'S STILL A BATTLE FOR A HALF-POINT KO! FOR REAL? I CAN'T BELIEVE TOYA SENSEI RESIGNED.
YOSHITAKA! I BOUGHT YOU SOME *DORAYAKI**!

*small pancake sandwiches filled with sweet bean paste

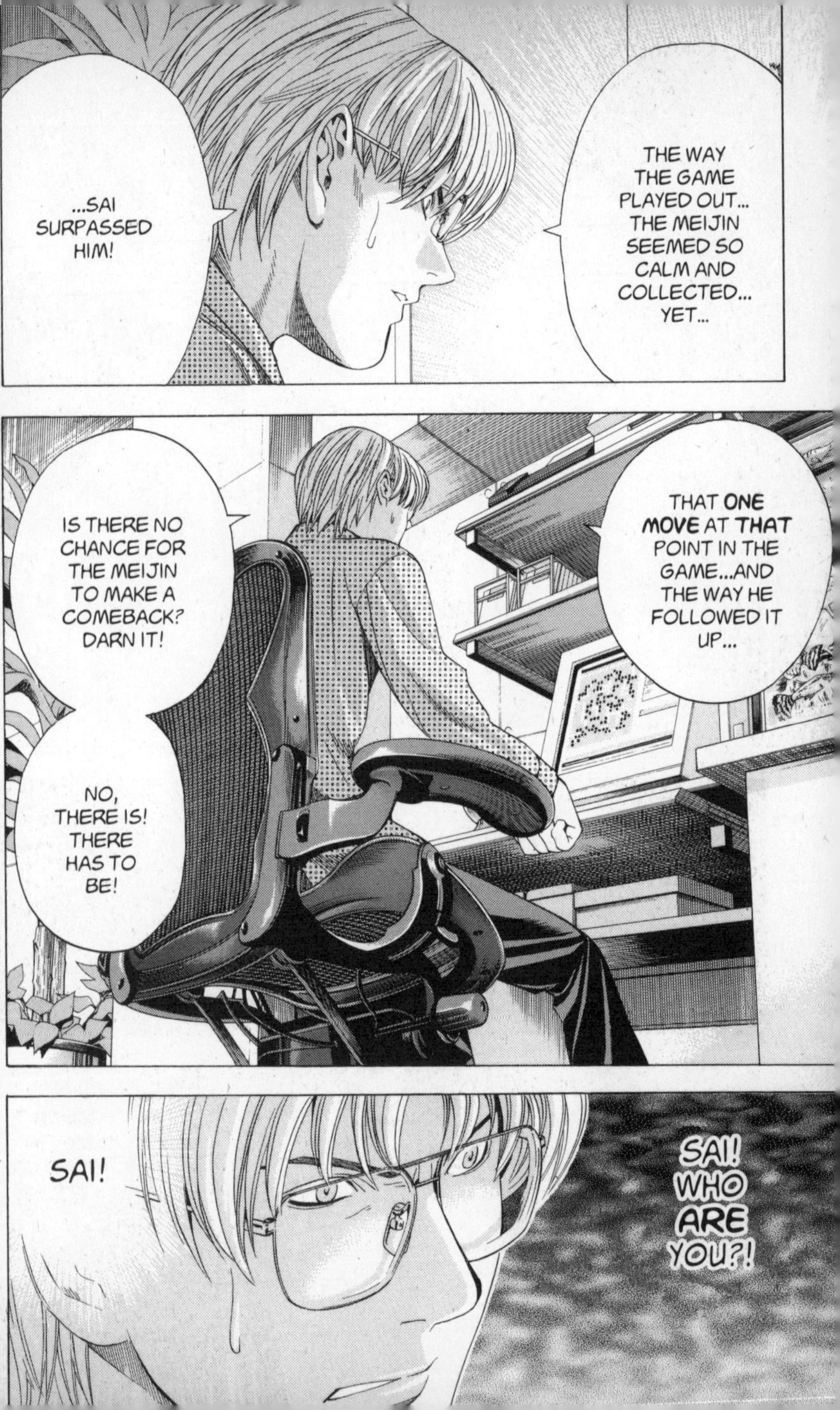
THE WAY THE GAME PLAYED OUT... THE MEIJIN SEEMED SO CALM AND COLLECTED... YET...
...SAI SURPASSED HIM!
THAT **ONE MOVE** AT **THAT** POINT IN THE GAME...AND THE WAY HE FOLLOWED IT UP...
IS THERE NO CHANCE FOR THE MEIJIN TO MAKE A COMEBACK? DARN IT!
NO, THERE IS! THERE HAS TO BE!
SAI! WHO ARE YOU?!
SAI!

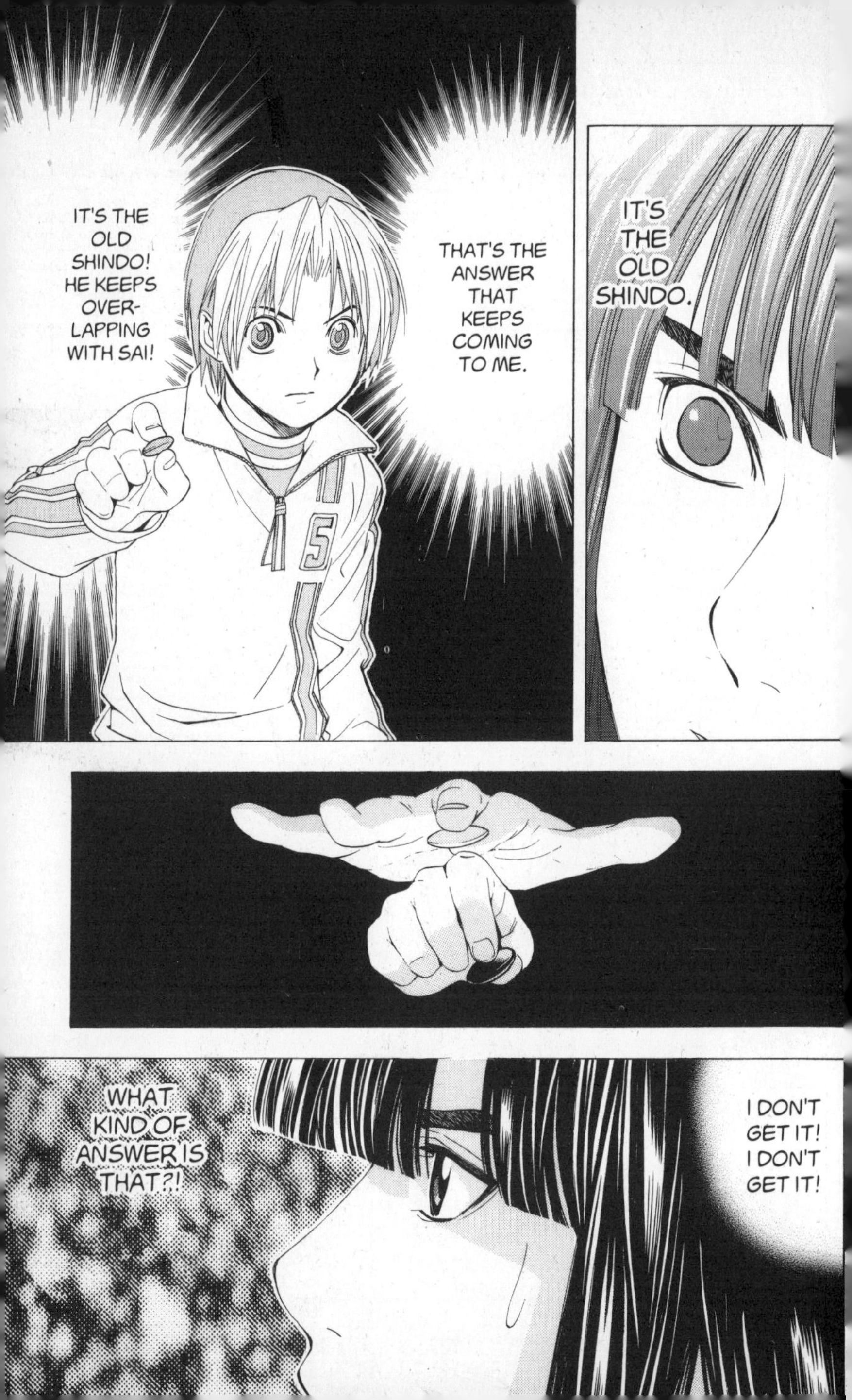
IT'S THE OLD SHINDO.
THAT'S THE ANSWER THAT KEEPS COMING TO ME.
IT'S THE OLD SHINDO! HE KEEPS OVER-LAPPING WITH SAI!
I DON'T GET IT! I DON'T GET IT!
WHAT KIND OF ANSWER IS THAT?!

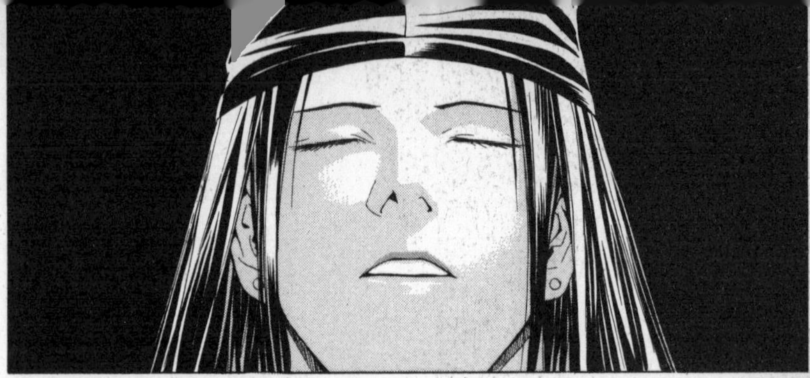
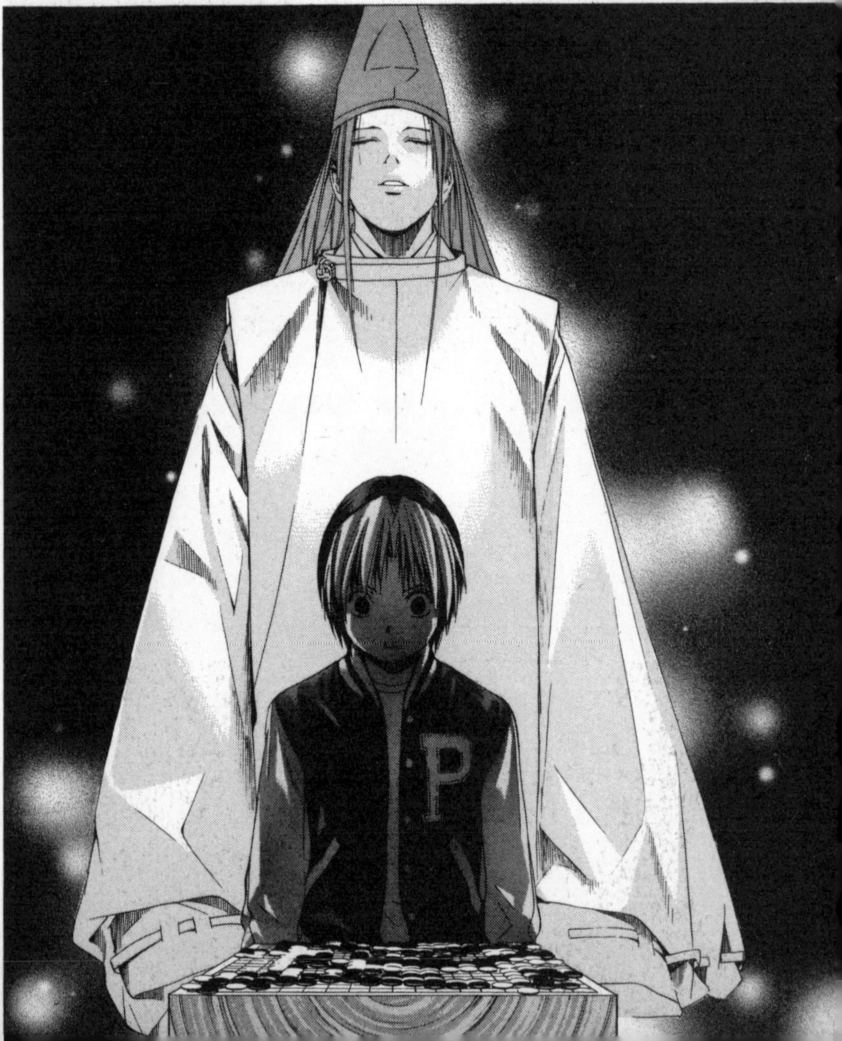

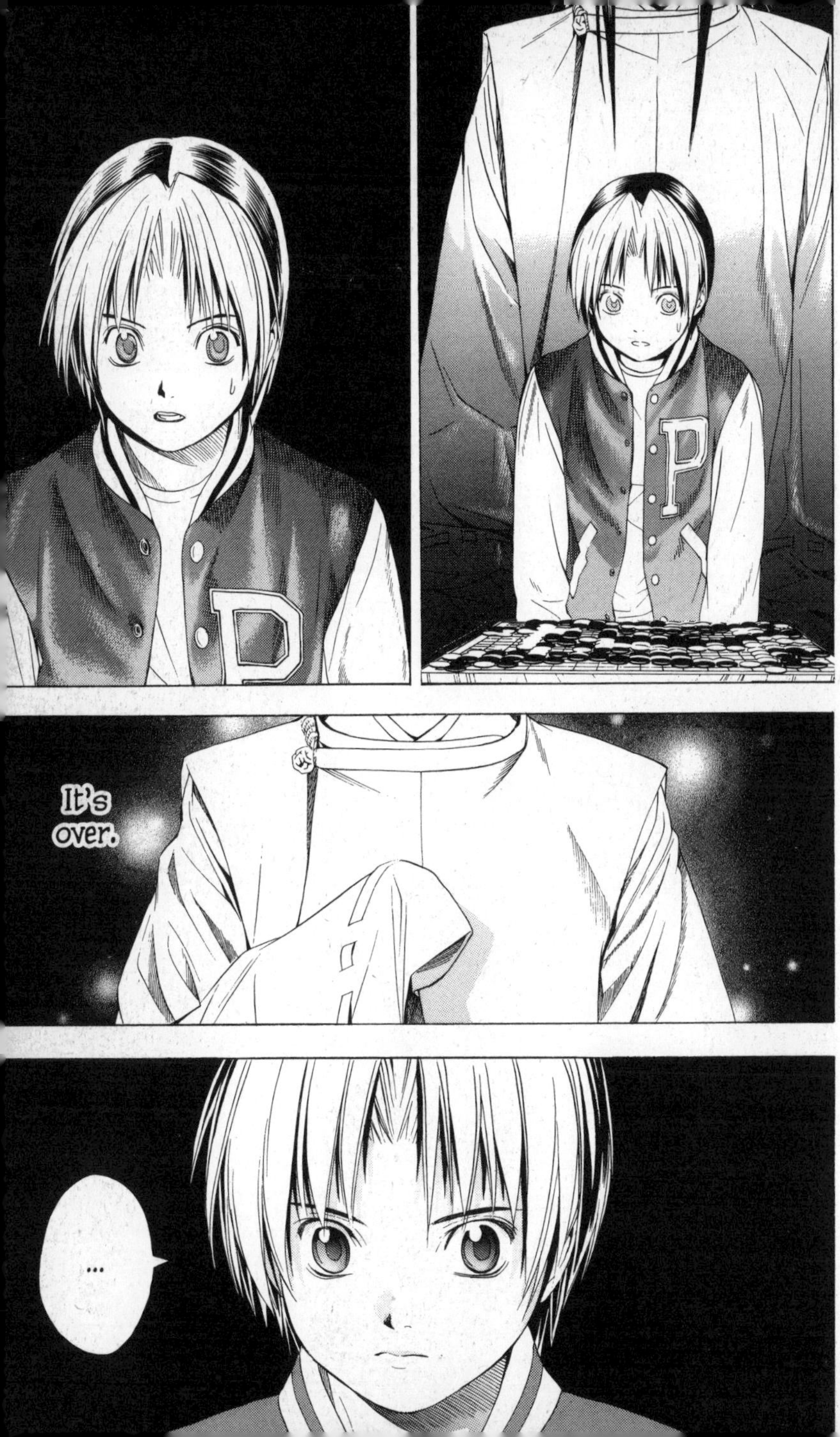
It's over.
...

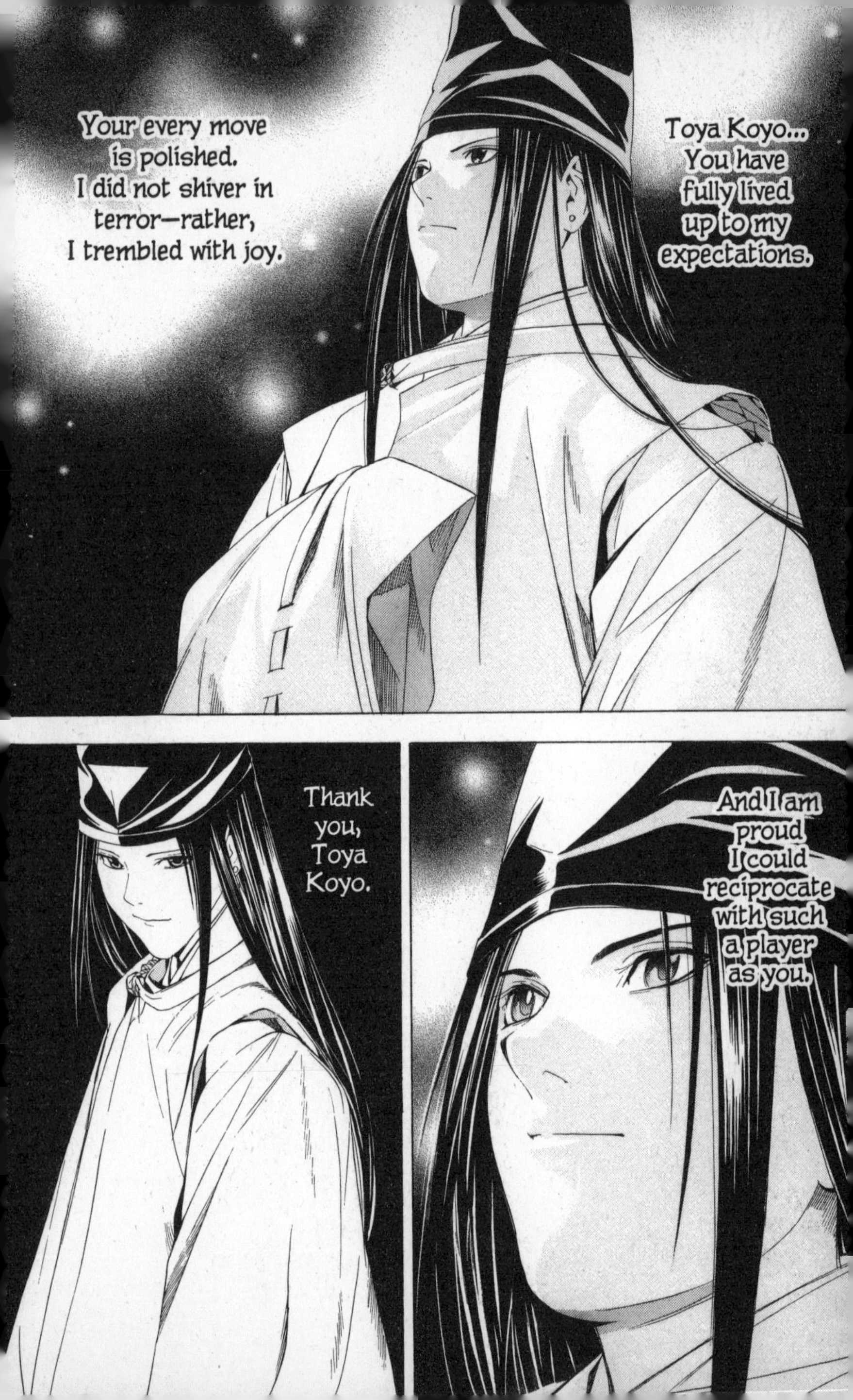
Toya Koyo... You have fully lived up to my expectations.
Your every move is polished. I did not shiver in terror—rather, I trembled with joy.
And I am proud I could reciprocate with such a player as you.
Thank you, Toya Koyo.

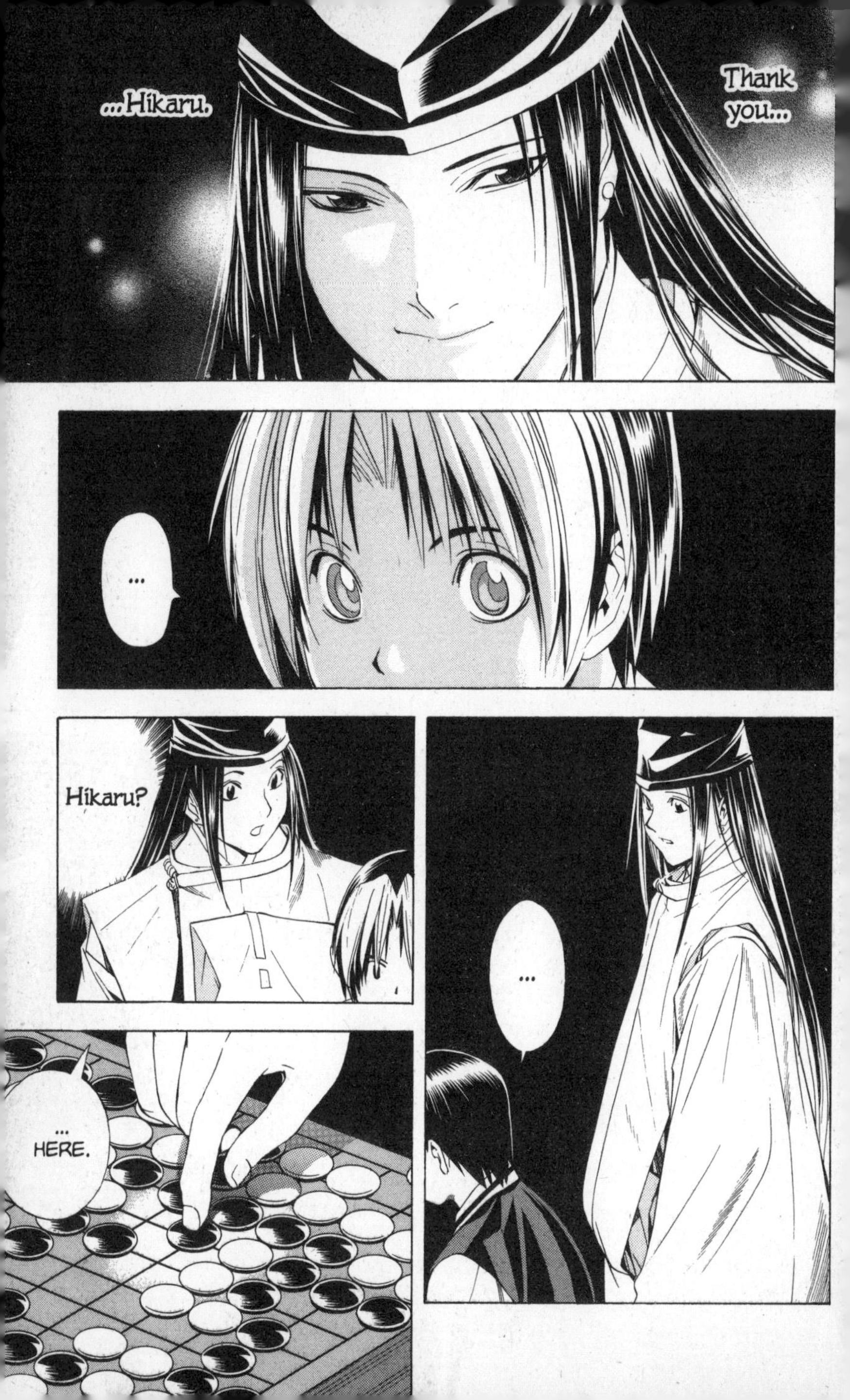
Thank you...
...Hikaru.
...
...
Hikaru?
...HERE.

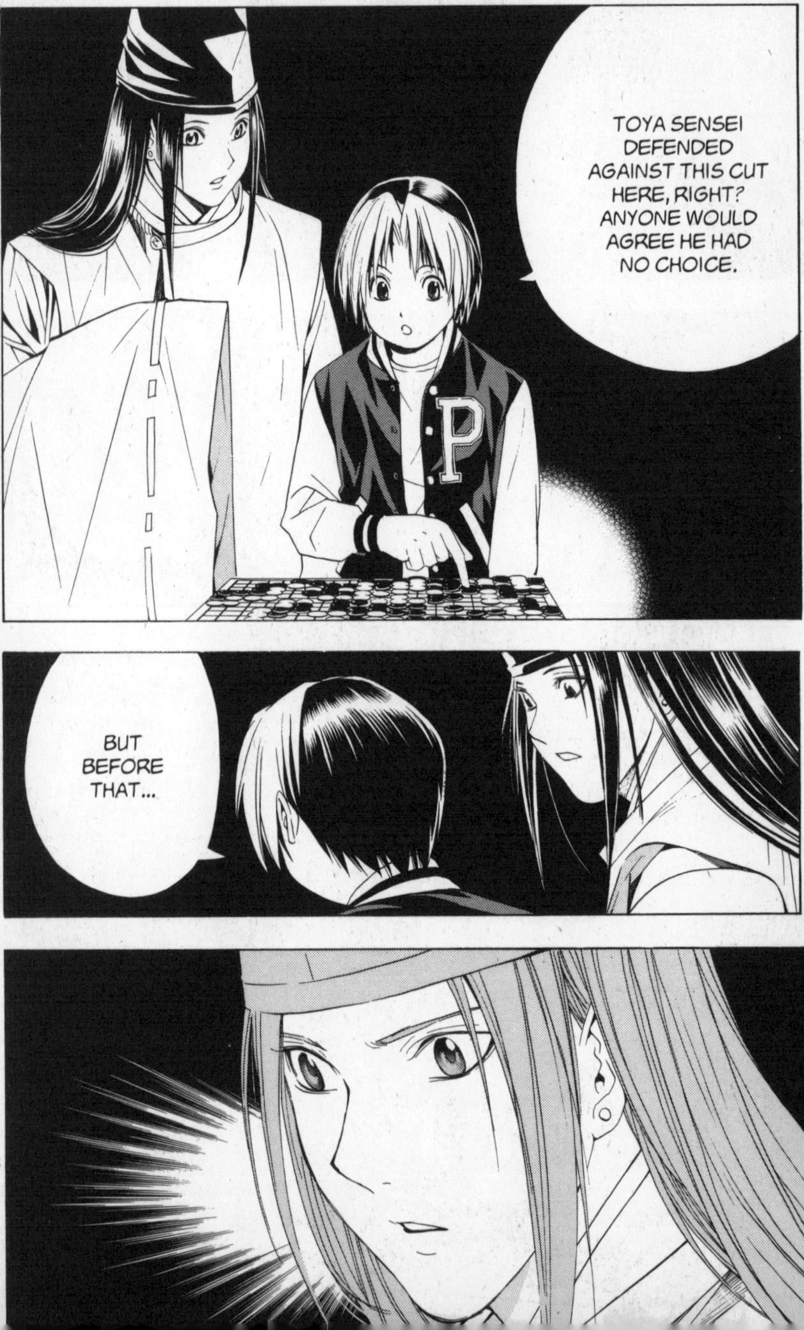
TOYA SENSEI DEFENDED AGAINST THIS CUT HERE, RIGHT? ANYONE WOULD AGREE HE HAD NO CHOICE.
BUT BEFORE THAT...

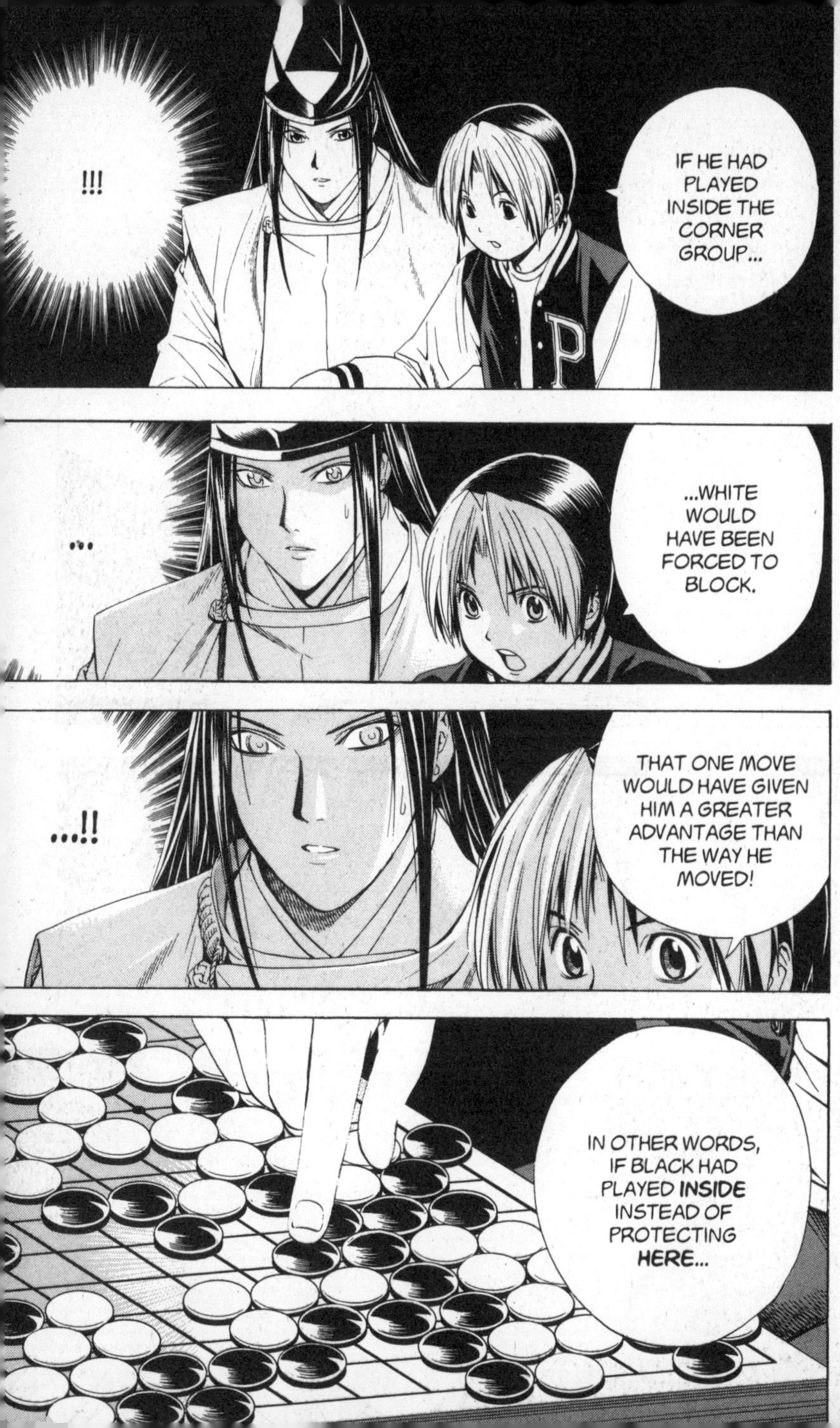
IF HE HAD PLAYED INSIDE THE CORNER GROUP...
!!!
...WHITE WOULD HAVE BEEN FORCED TO BLOCK.
...
THAT ONE MOVE WOULD HAVE GIVEN HIM A GREATER ADVANTAGE THAN THE WAY HE MOVED!
...!!
IN OTHER WORDS, IF BLACK HAD PLAYED INSIDE INSTEAD OF PROTECTING HERE...

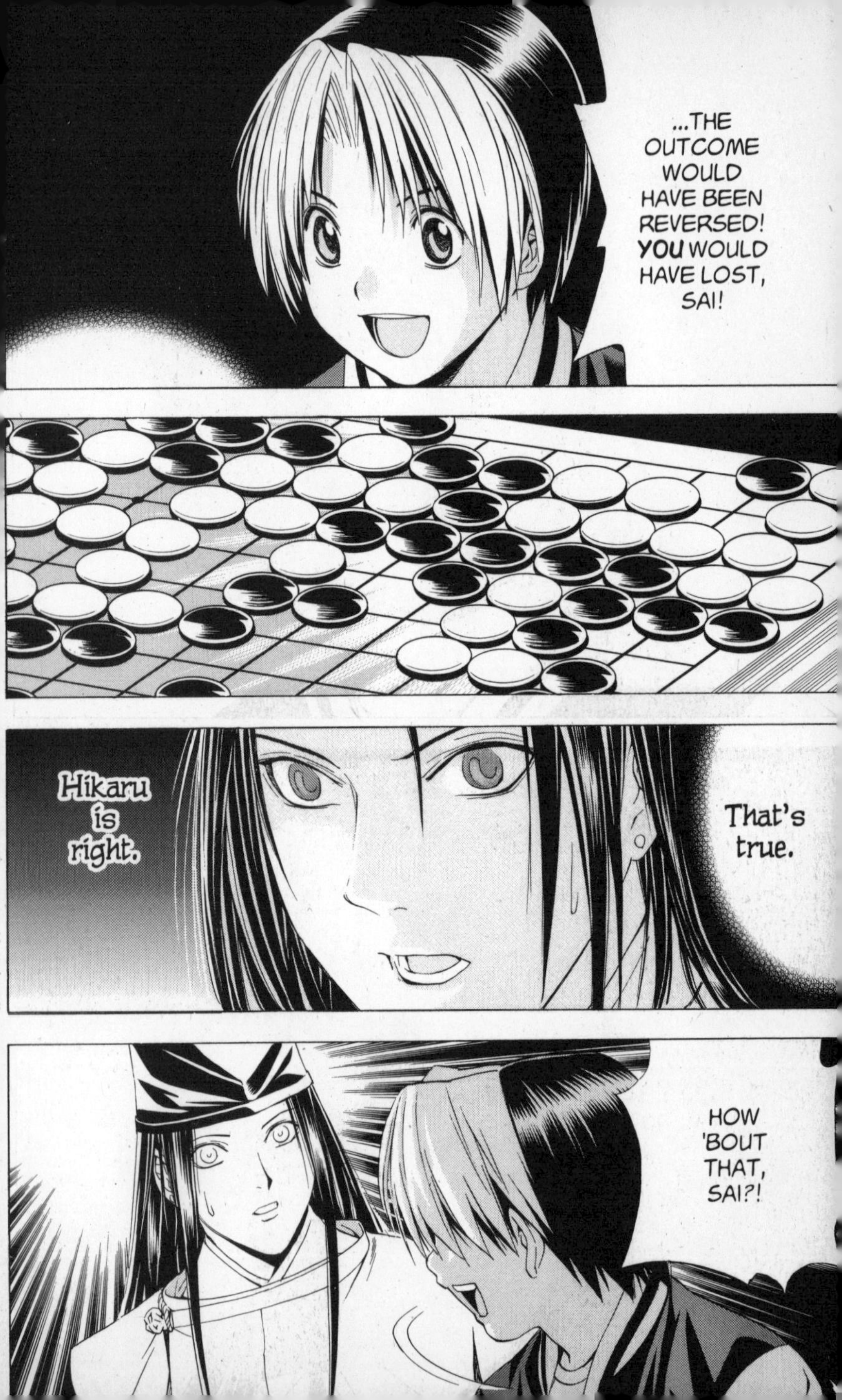
...THE OUTCOME WOULD HAVE BEEN REVERSED! YOU WOULD HAVE LOST, SAI!
That's true.
Hikaru is right.
HOW 'BOUT THAT, SAI?!

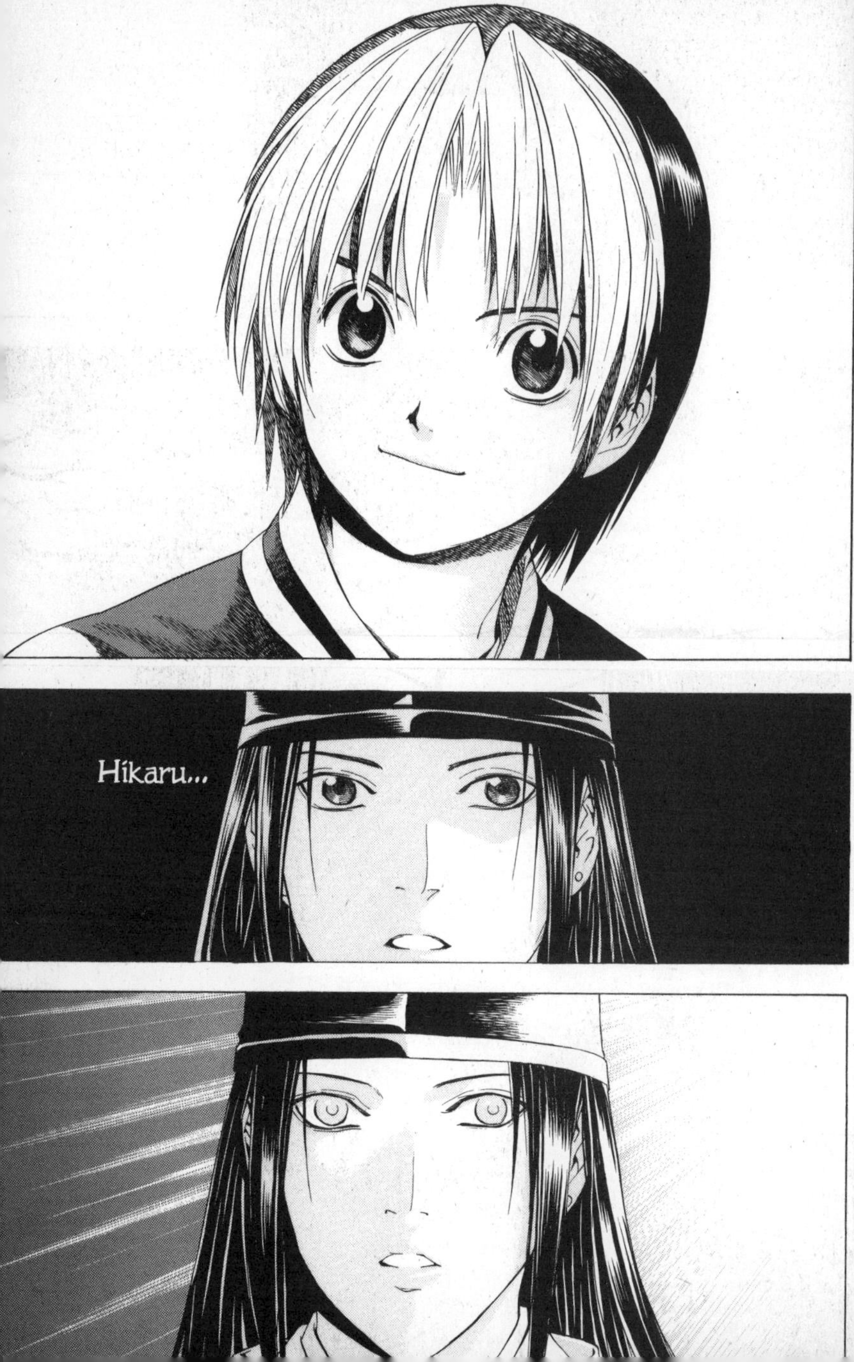
Hikaru...

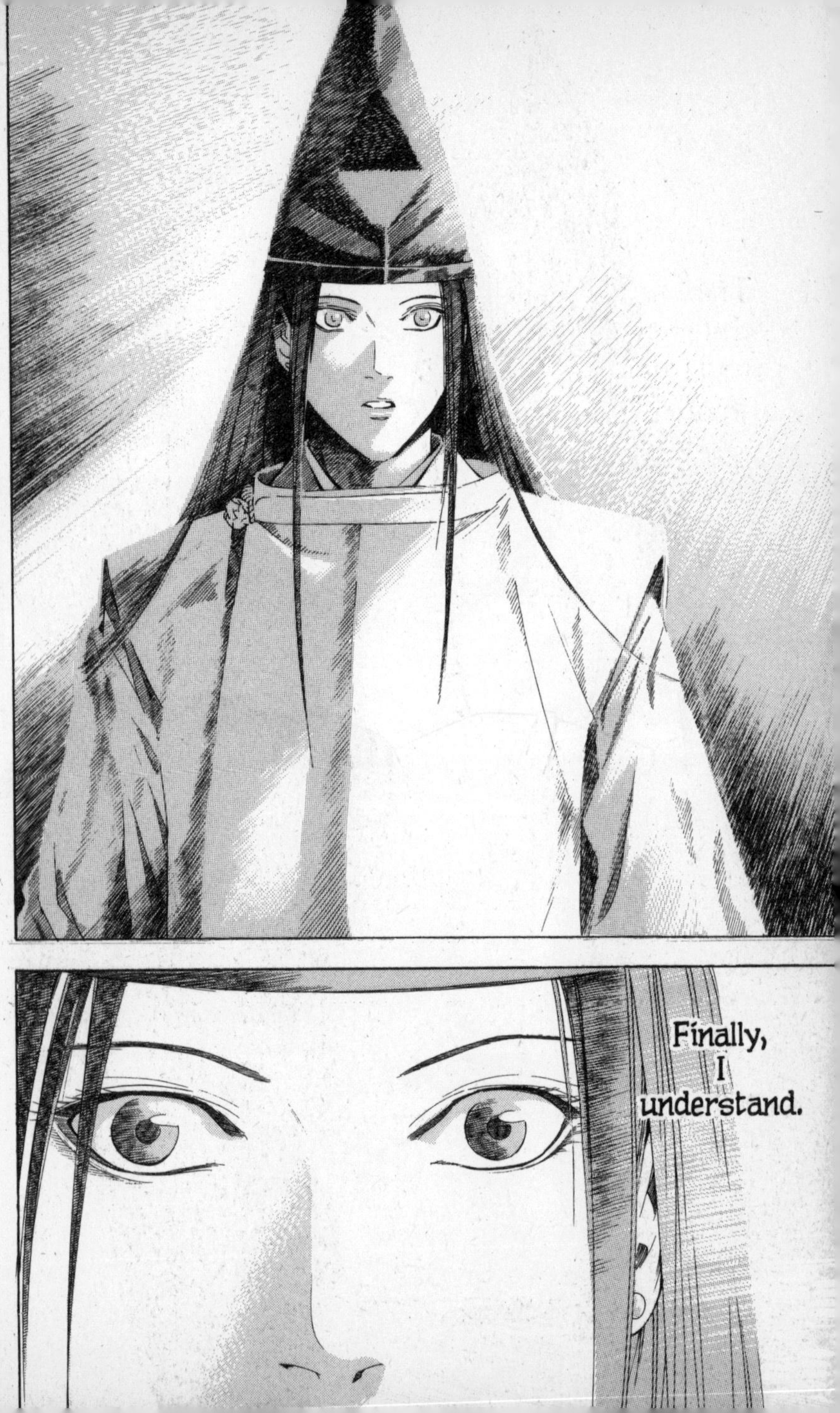
Finally, I understand.

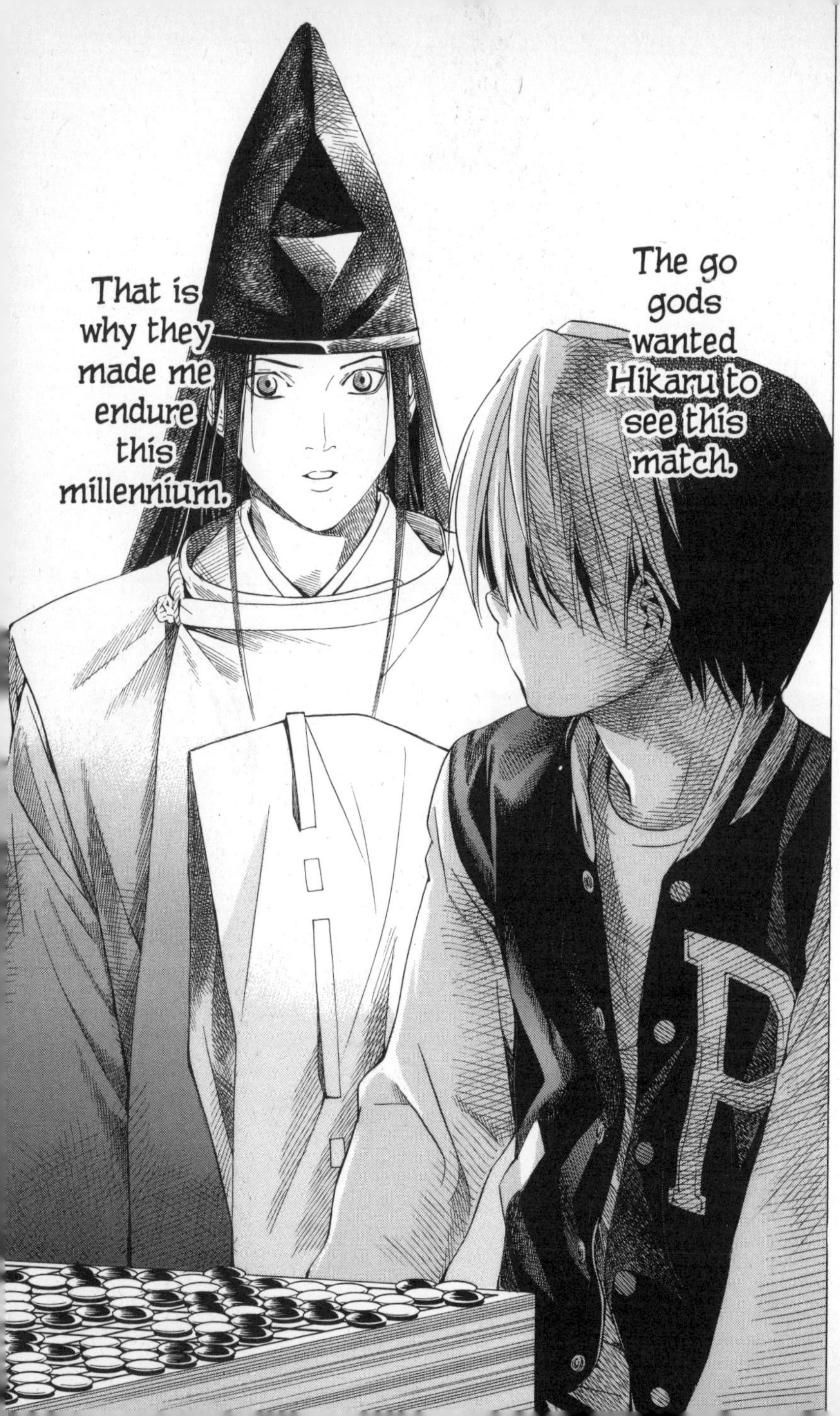
The go gods wanted Hikaru to see this match.
That is why they made me endure this millennium.

HIKARU 5 SHINDO

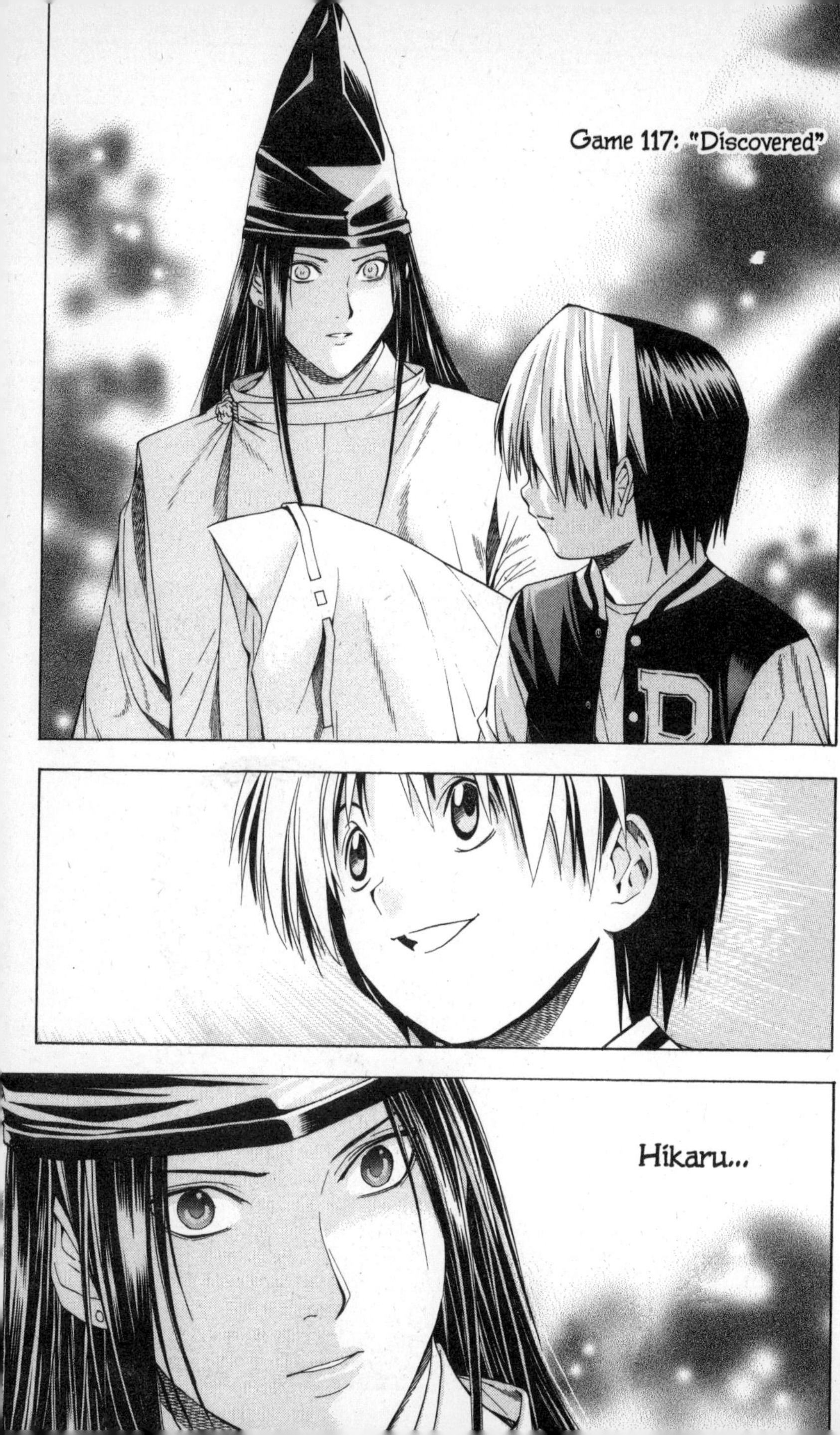
Game 117: "Discovered"
Hikaru...

Game 117 "Discovered"

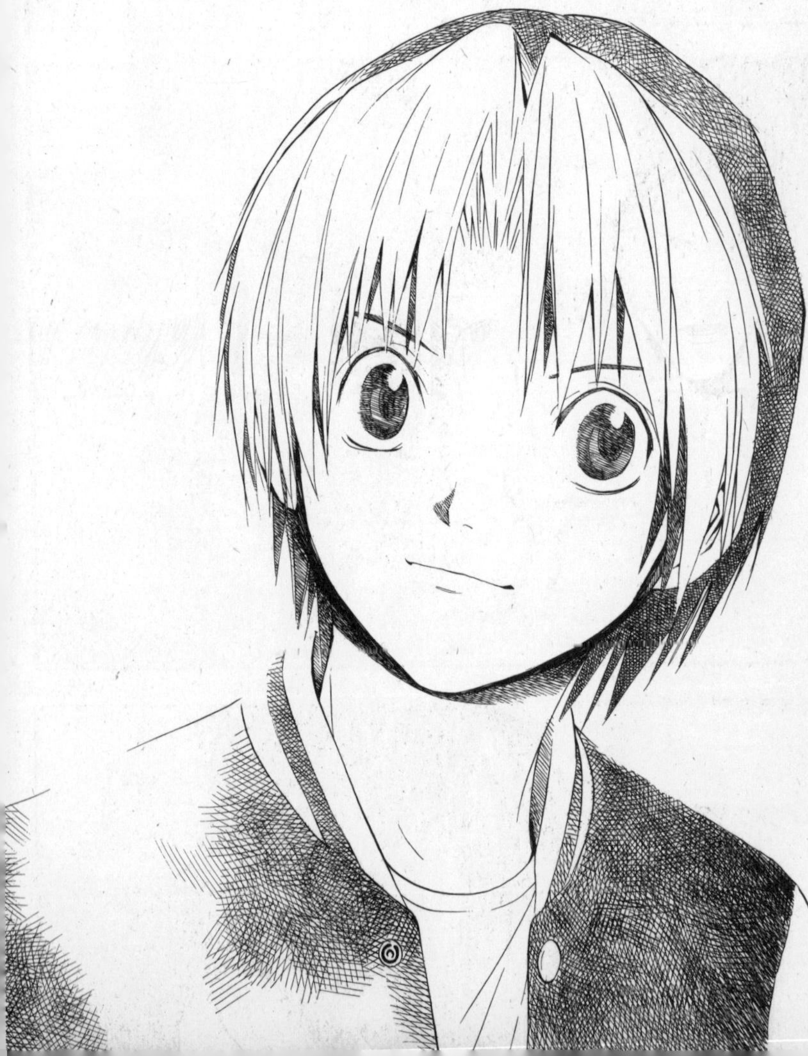

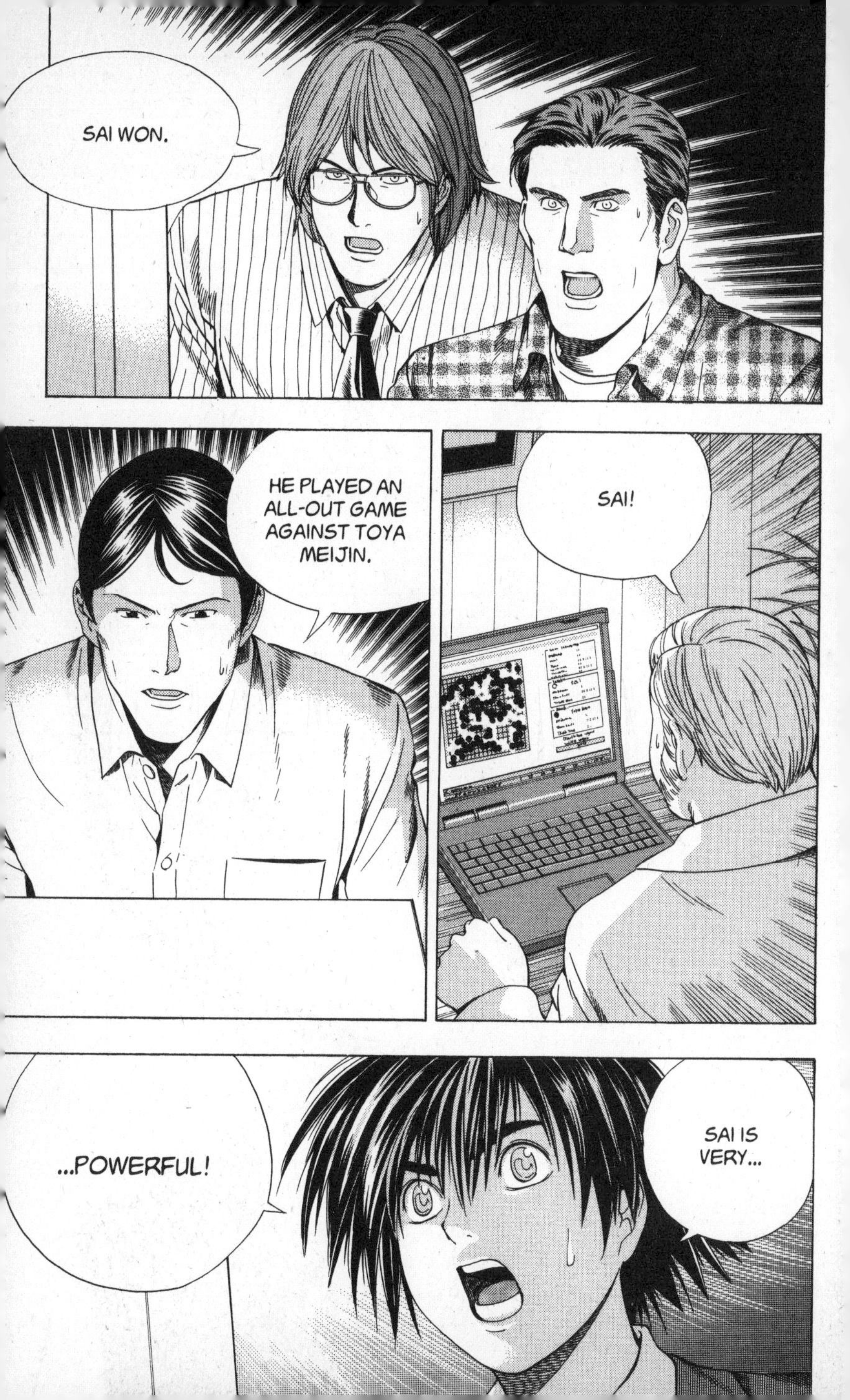
SAI WON.
SAI!
HE PLAYED AN ALL-OUT GAME AGAINST TOYA MEIJIN.
SAI IS VERY...
...POWERFUL!

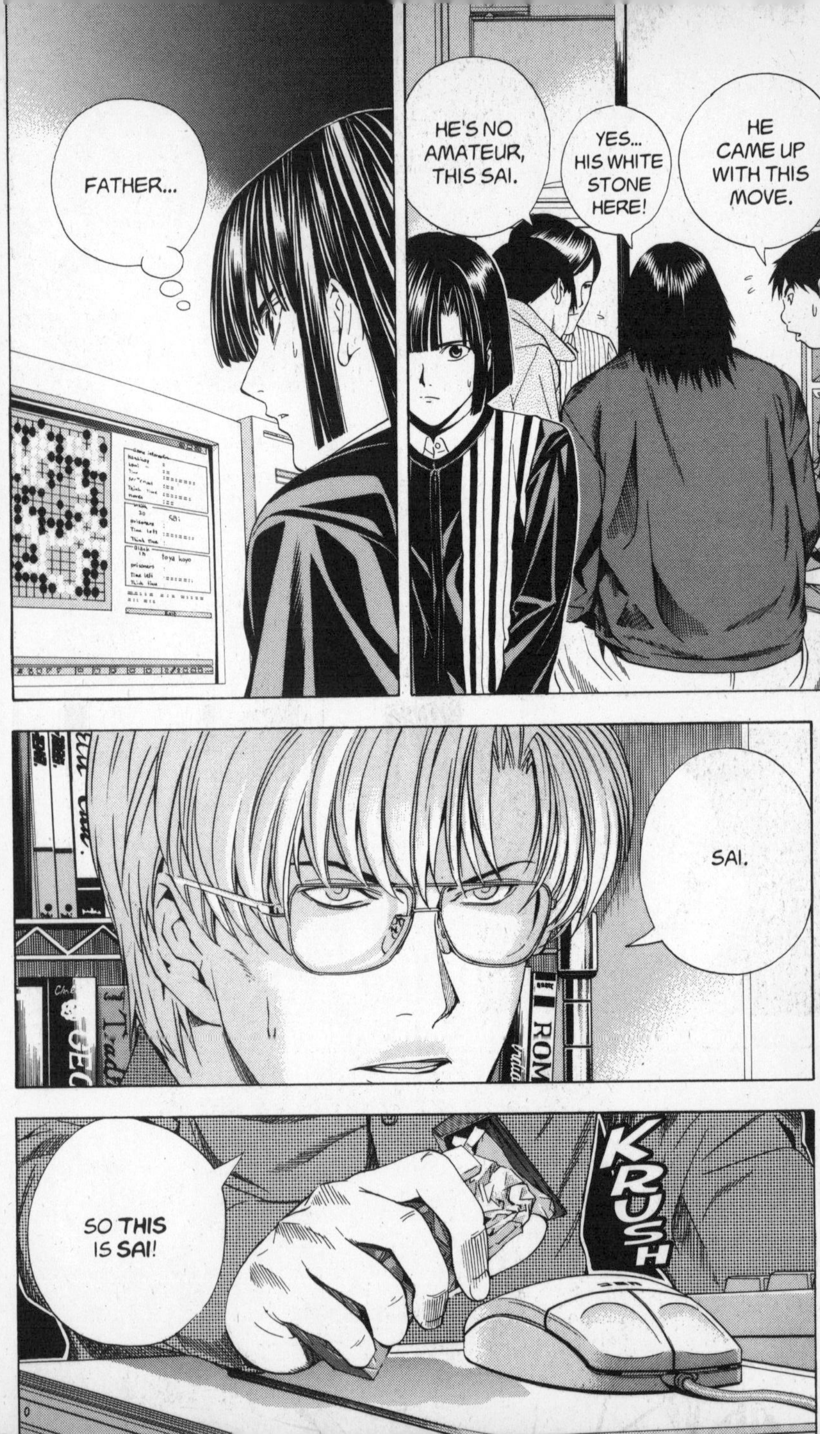
HE CAME UP WITH THIS MOVE.
YES... HIS WHITE STONE HERE!
HE'S NO AMATEUR, THIS SAI.
FATHER...
SAI.
KRUSH
SO THIS IS SAI!

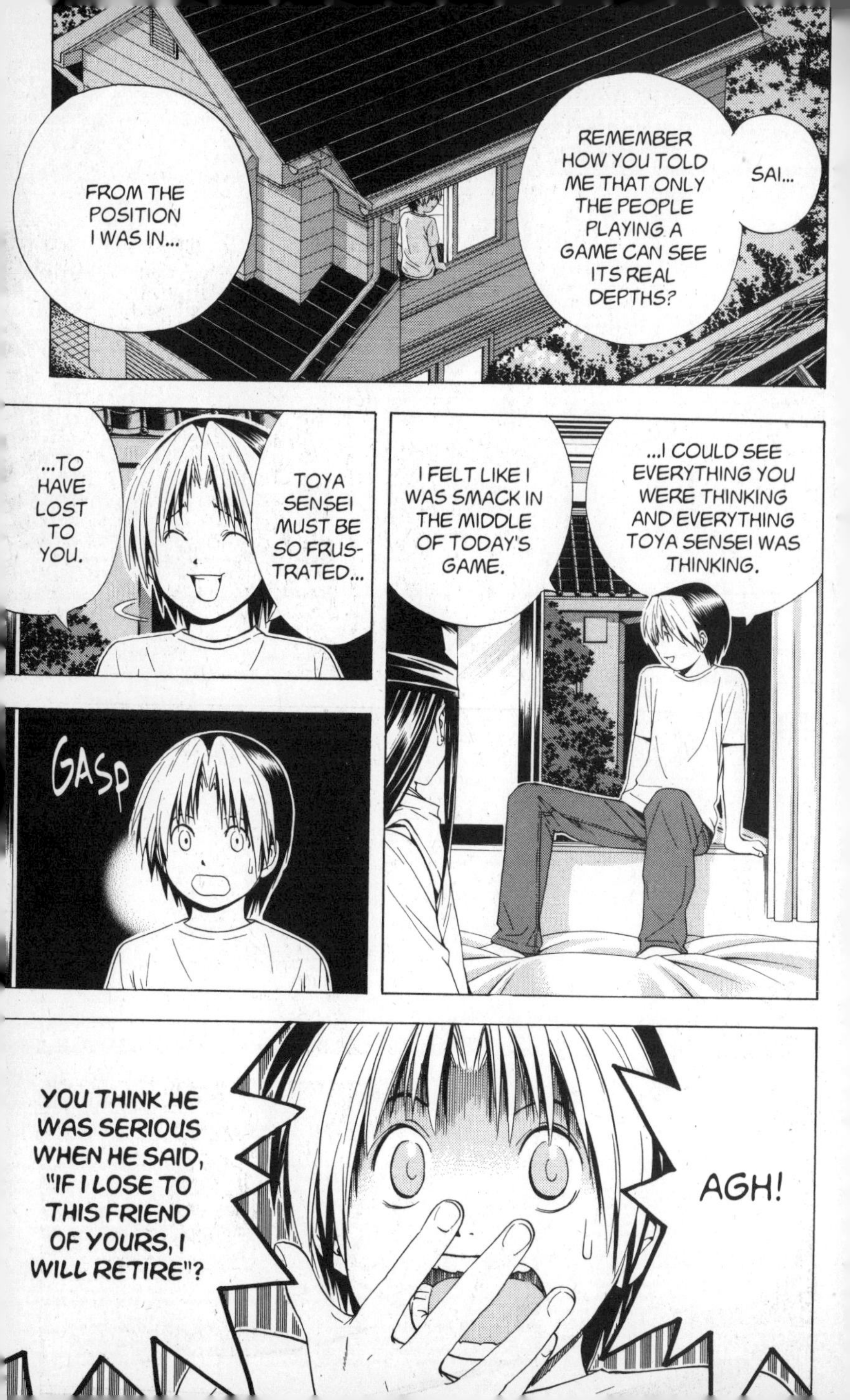
SAI...
REMEMBER HOW YOU TOLD ME THAT ONLY THE PEOPLE PLAYING A GAME CAN SEE ITS REAL DEPTHS?
FROM THE POSITION I WAS IN...
...I COULD SEE EVERYTHING YOU WERE THINKING AND EVERYTHING TOYA SENSEI WAS THINKING.
I FELT LIKE I WAS SMACK IN THE MIDDLE OF TODAY'S GAME.
TOYA SENSEI MUST BE SO FRUS-TRATED...
...TO HAVE LOST TO YOU.
GASP
AGH!
YOU THINK HE WAS SERIOUS WHEN HE SAID, "IF I LOSE TO THIS FRIEND OF YOURS, I WILL RETIRE"?

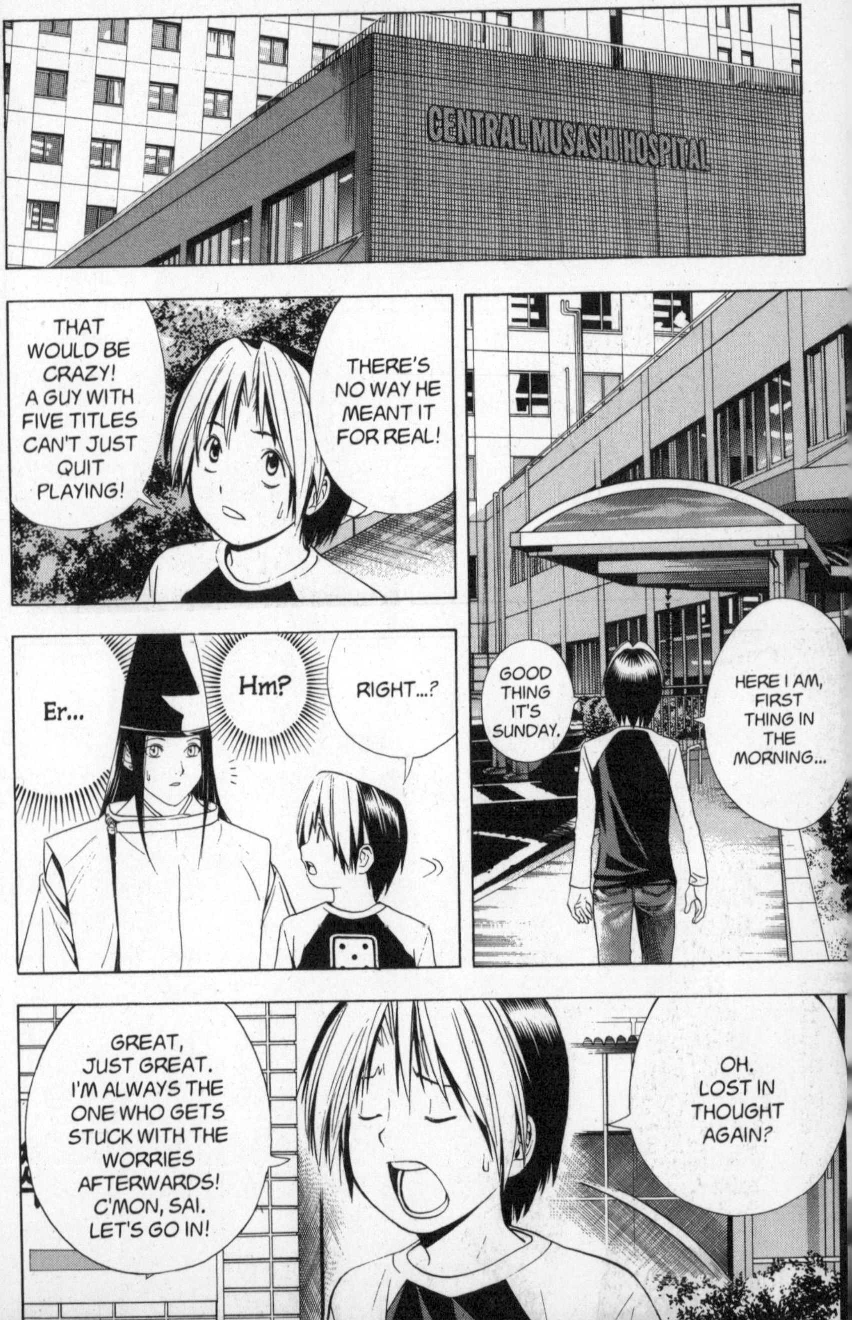
CENTRAL MUSASHI HOSPITAL
HERE I AM, FIRST THING IN THE MORNING...
GOOD THING IT'S SUNDAY.
THERE'S NO WAY HE MEANT IT FOR REAL!
THAT WOULD BE CRAZY! A GUY WITH FIVE TITLES CAN'T JUST QUIT PLAYING!
RIGHT...?
Hm?
Er...
OH. LOST IN THOUGHT AGAIN?
GREAT, JUST GREAT. I'M ALWAYS THE ONE WHO GETS STUCK WITH THE WORRIES AFTERWARDS! C'MON, SAI. LET'S GO IN!

READ THIS WAY

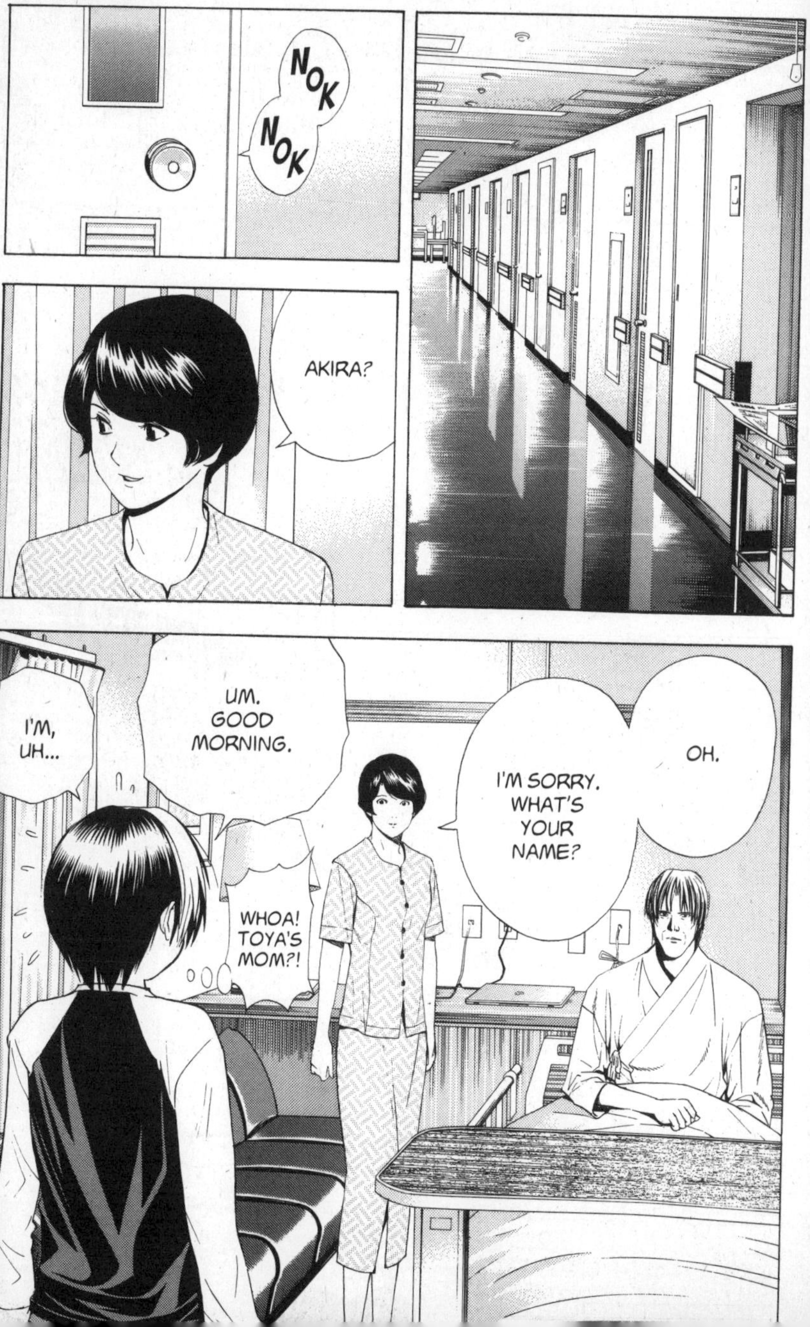
NOK NOK
AKIRA?
OH.
I'M SORRY. WHAT'S YOUR NAME?
UM. GOOD MORNING.
WHOA! TOYA'S MOM?!
I'M, UH...

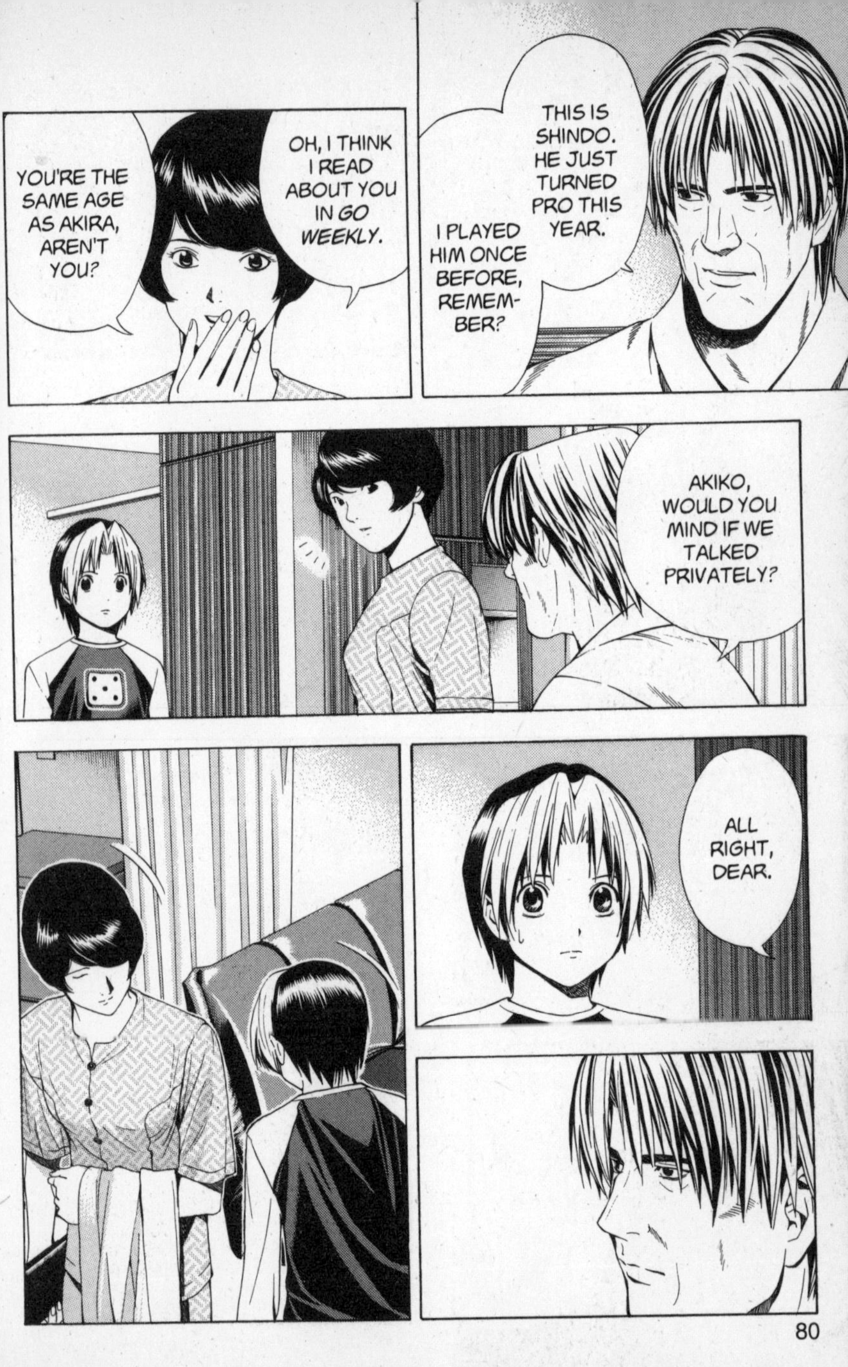
THIS IS SHINDO. HE JUST TURNED PRO THIS YEAR.
I PLAYED HIM ONCE BEFORE, REMEMBER?
OH, I THINK I READ ABOUT YOU IN *GO WEEKLY*.
YOU'RE THE SAME AGE AS AKIRA, AREN'T YOU?
AKIKO, WOULD YOU MIND IF WE TALKED PRIVATELY?
ALL RIGHT, DEAR.

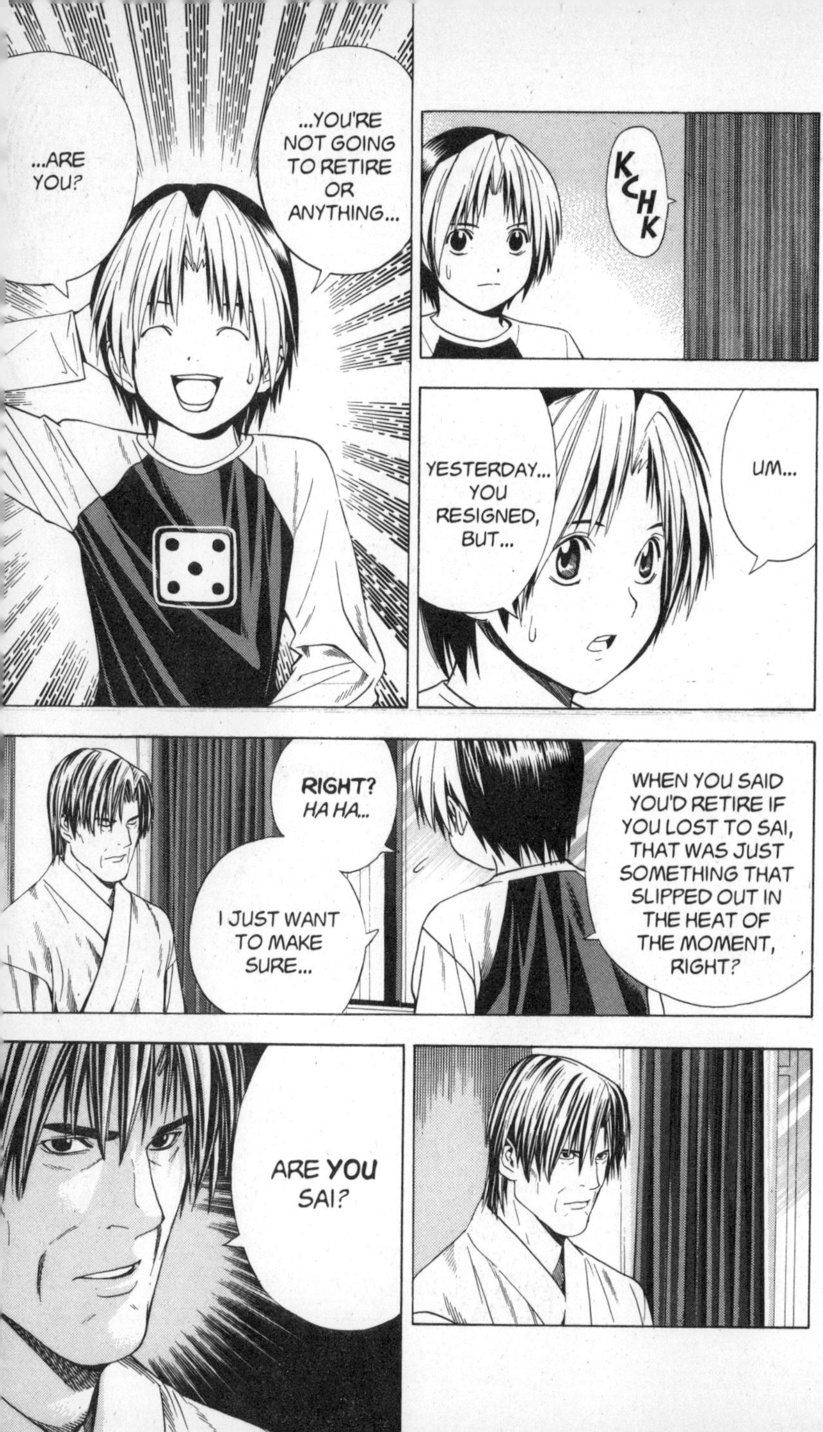
KCHK
UM...
YESTERDAY... YOU RESIGNED, BUT...
...YOU'RE NOT GOING TO RETIRE OR ANYTHING...
...ARE YOU?
WHEN YOU SAID YOU'D RETIRE IF YOU LOST TO SAI, THAT WAS JUST SOMETHING THAT SLIPPED OUT IN THE HEAT OF THE MOMENT, RIGHT?
RIGHT? HA HA...
I JUST WANT TO MAKE SURE...
ARE YOU SAI?

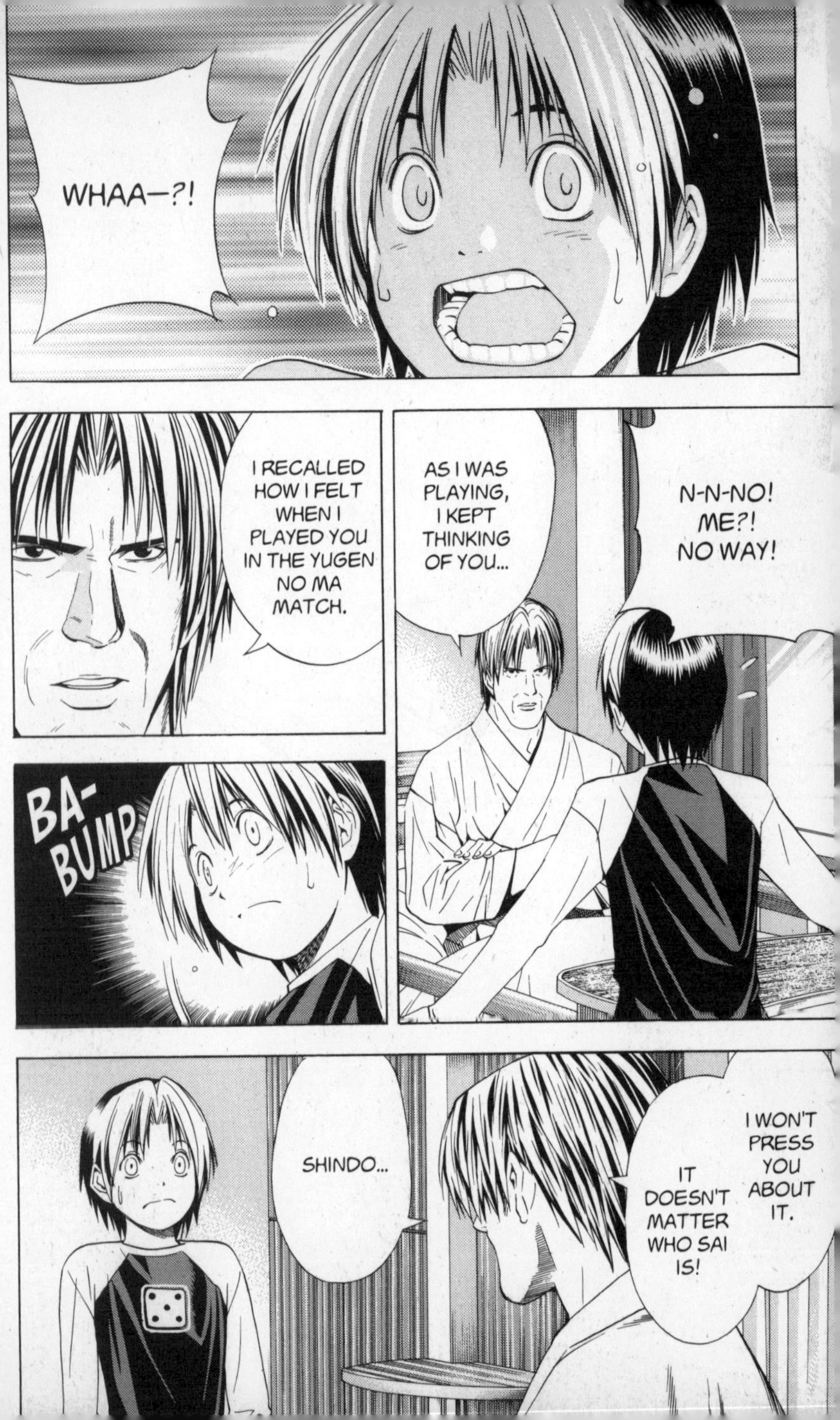
WHAA—?!
N-N-NO! ME?! NO WAY!
AS I WAS PLAYING, I KEPT THINKING OF YOU...
I RECALLED HOW I FELT WHEN I PLAYED YOU IN THE YUGEN NO MA MATCH.
BA-BUMP
I WON'T PRESS YOU ABOUT IT.
IT DOESN'T MATTER WHO SAI IS!
SHINDO...

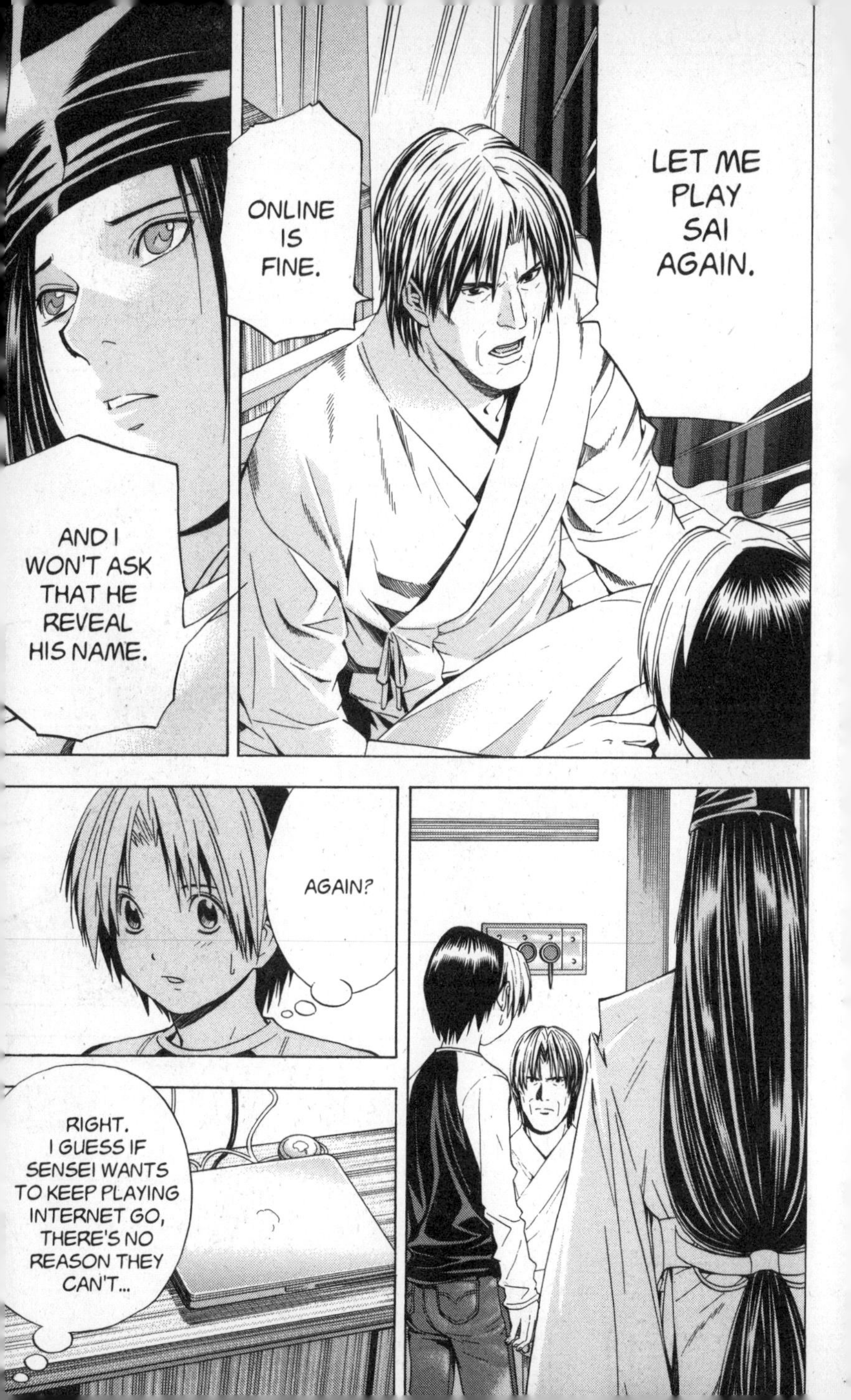
LET ME PLAY SAI AGAIN.
ONLINE IS FINE.
AND I WON'T ASK THAT HE REVEAL HIS NAME.
AGAIN?
RIGHT. I GUESS IF SENSEI WANTS TO KEEP PLAYING INTERNET GO, THERE'S NO REASON THEY CAN'T...

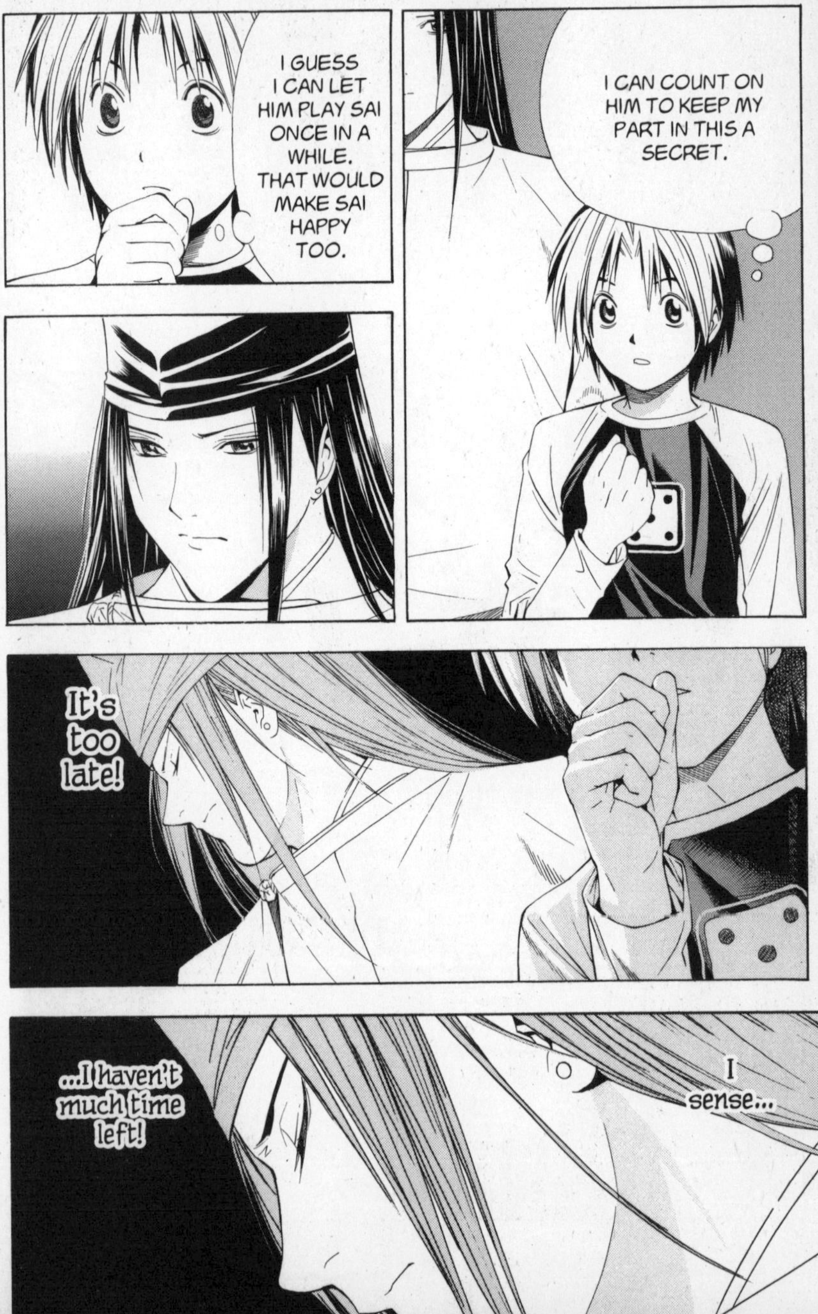

I CAN COUNT ON HIM TO KEEP MY PART IN THIS A SECRET.
I GUESS I CAN LET HIM PLAY SAI ONCE IN A WHILE. THAT WOULD MAKE SAI HAPPY TOO.
It's too late!
I sense...
...I haven't much time left!

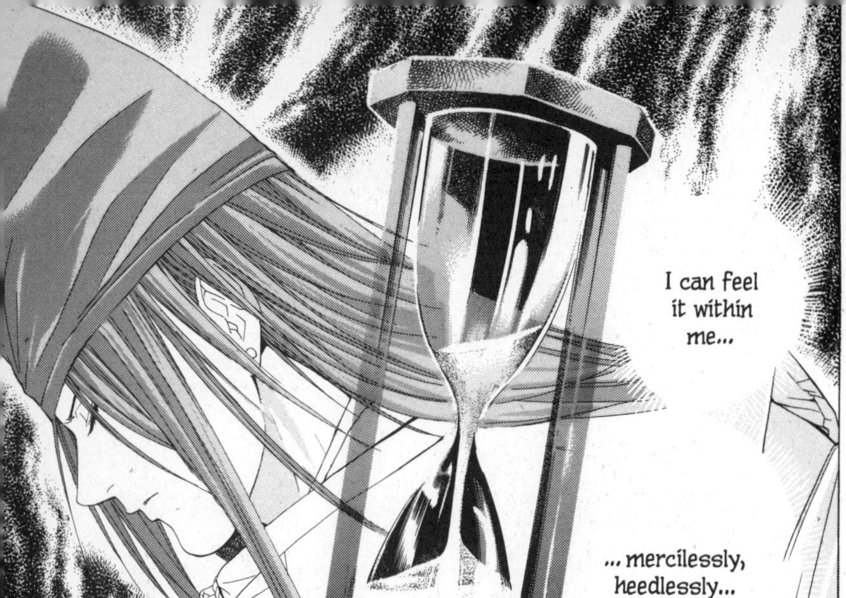
I can feel it within me...
...mercilessly, heedlessly...
...the suspended sands of time have begun to shift and fall once more.

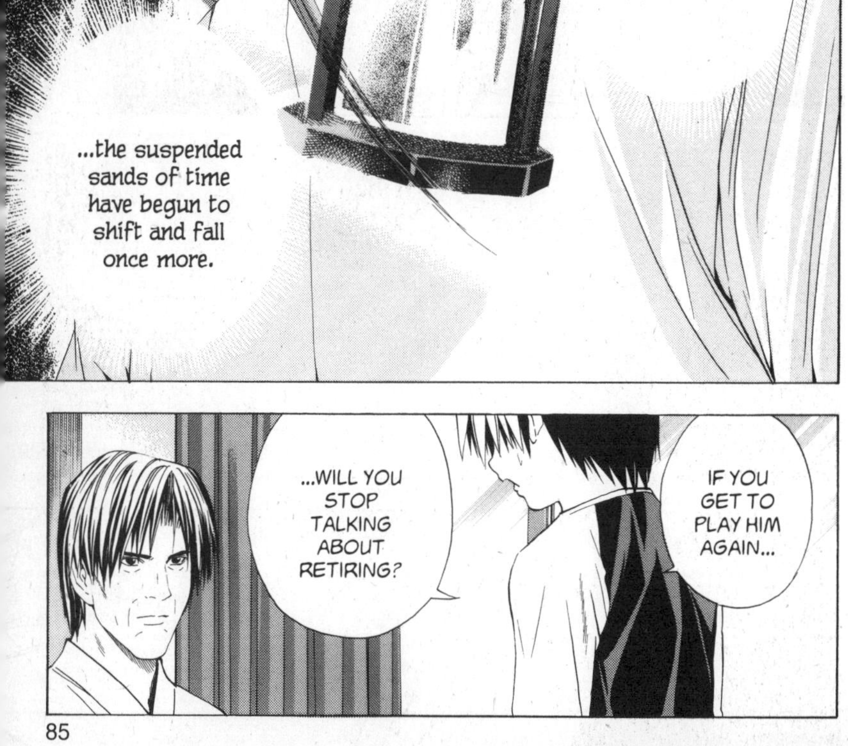
IF YOU GET TO PLAY HIM AGAIN...
...WILL YOU STOP TALKING ABOUT RETIRING?

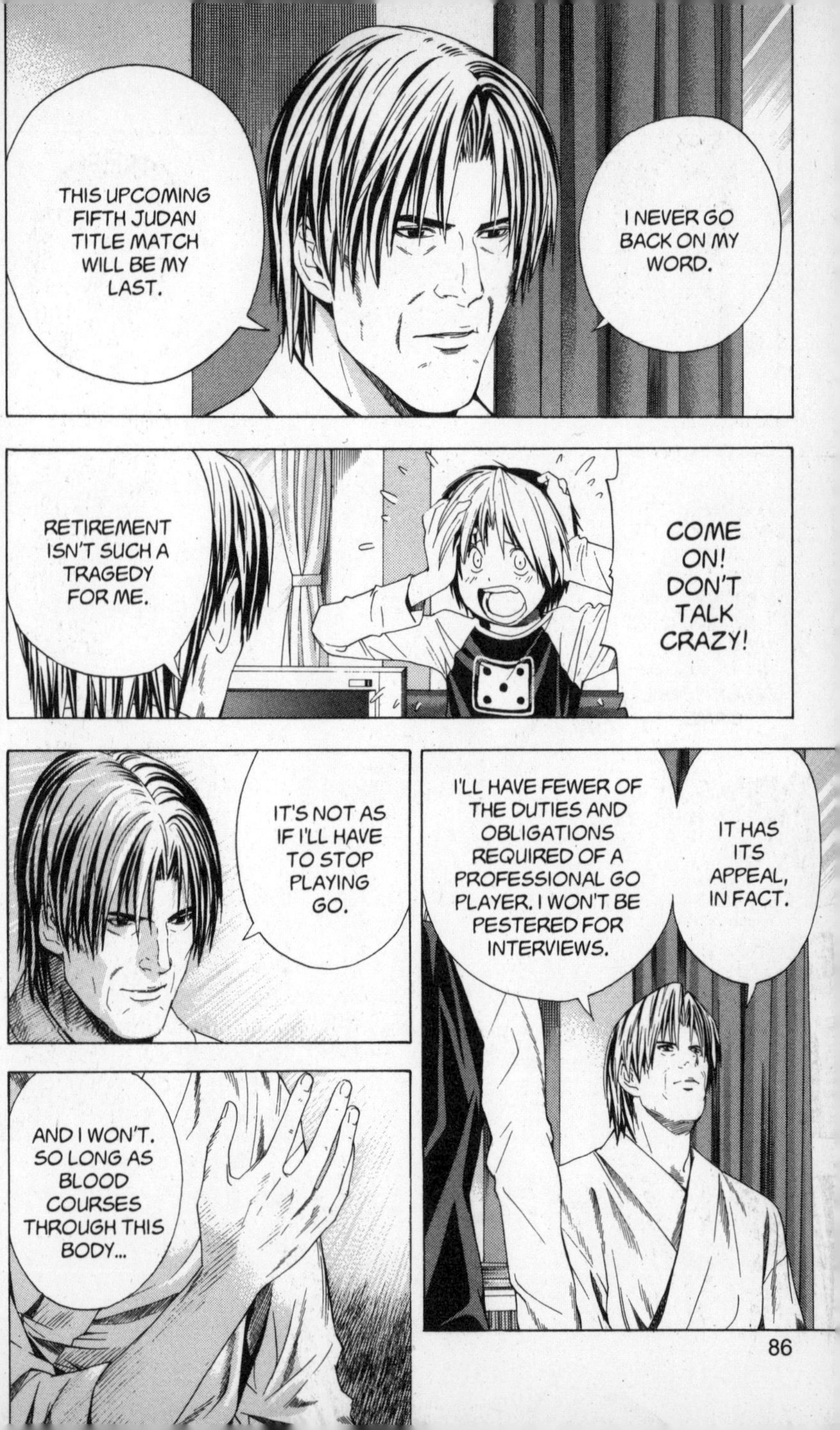
I NEVER GO BACK ON MY WORD.
THIS UPCOMING FIFTH JUDAN TITLE MATCH WILL BE MY LAST.
COME ON! DON'T TALK CRAZY!
RETIREMENT ISN'T SUCH A TRAGEDY FOR ME.
IT HAS ITS APPEAL, IN FACT.
I'LL HAVE FEWER OF THE DUTIES AND OBLIGATIONS REQUIRED OF A PROFESSIONAL GO PLAYER. I WON'T BE PESTERED FOR INTERVIEWS.
IT'S NOT AS IF I'LL HAVE TO STOP PLAYING GO.
AND I WON'T. SO LONG AS BLOOD COURSES THROUGH THIS BODY...

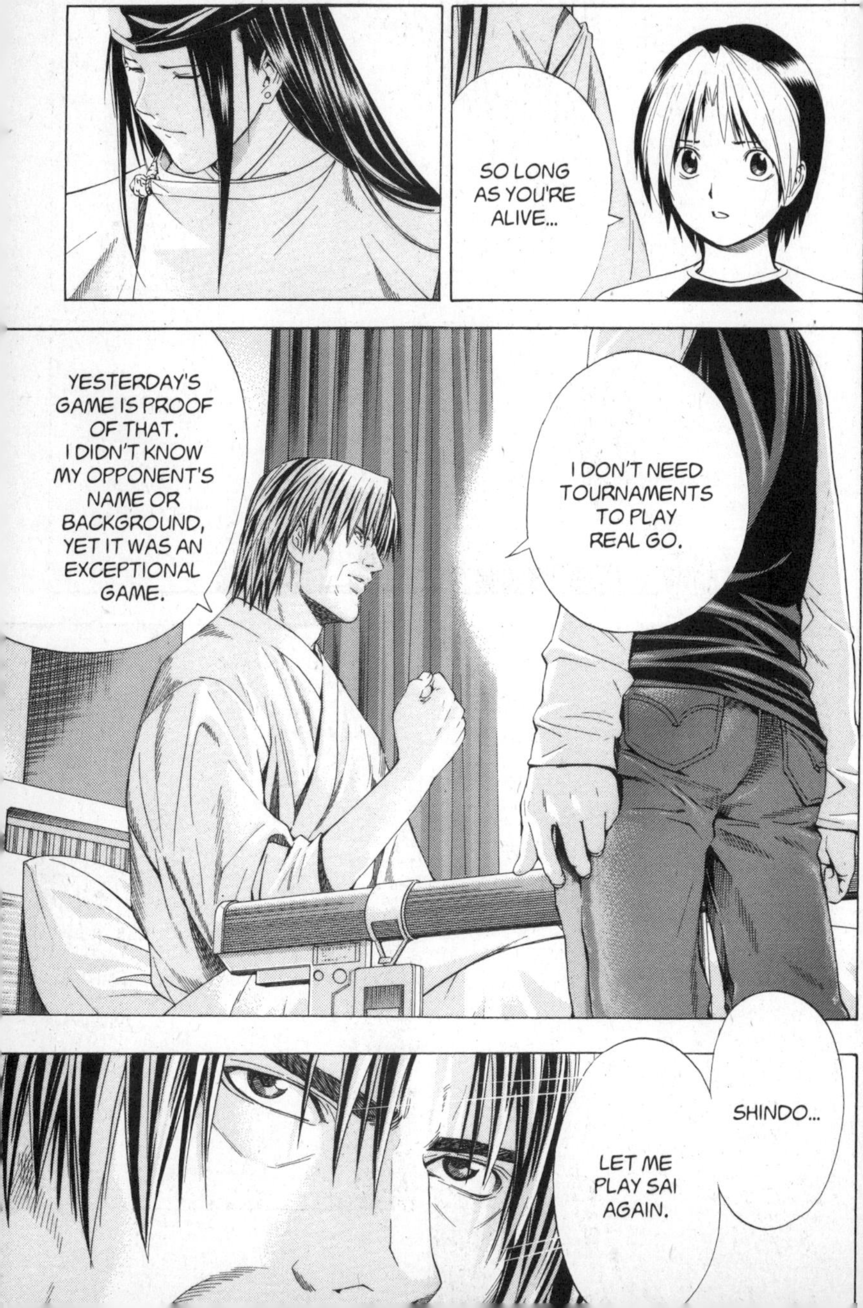
SO LONG AS YOU'RE ALIVE...
I DON'T NEED TOURNAMENTS TO PLAY REAL GO.
YESTERDAY'S GAME IS PROOF OF THAT. I DIDN'T KNOW MY OPPONENT'S NAME OR BACKGROUND, YET IT WAS AN EXCEPTIONAL GAME.
SHINDO...
LET ME PLAY SAI AGAIN.

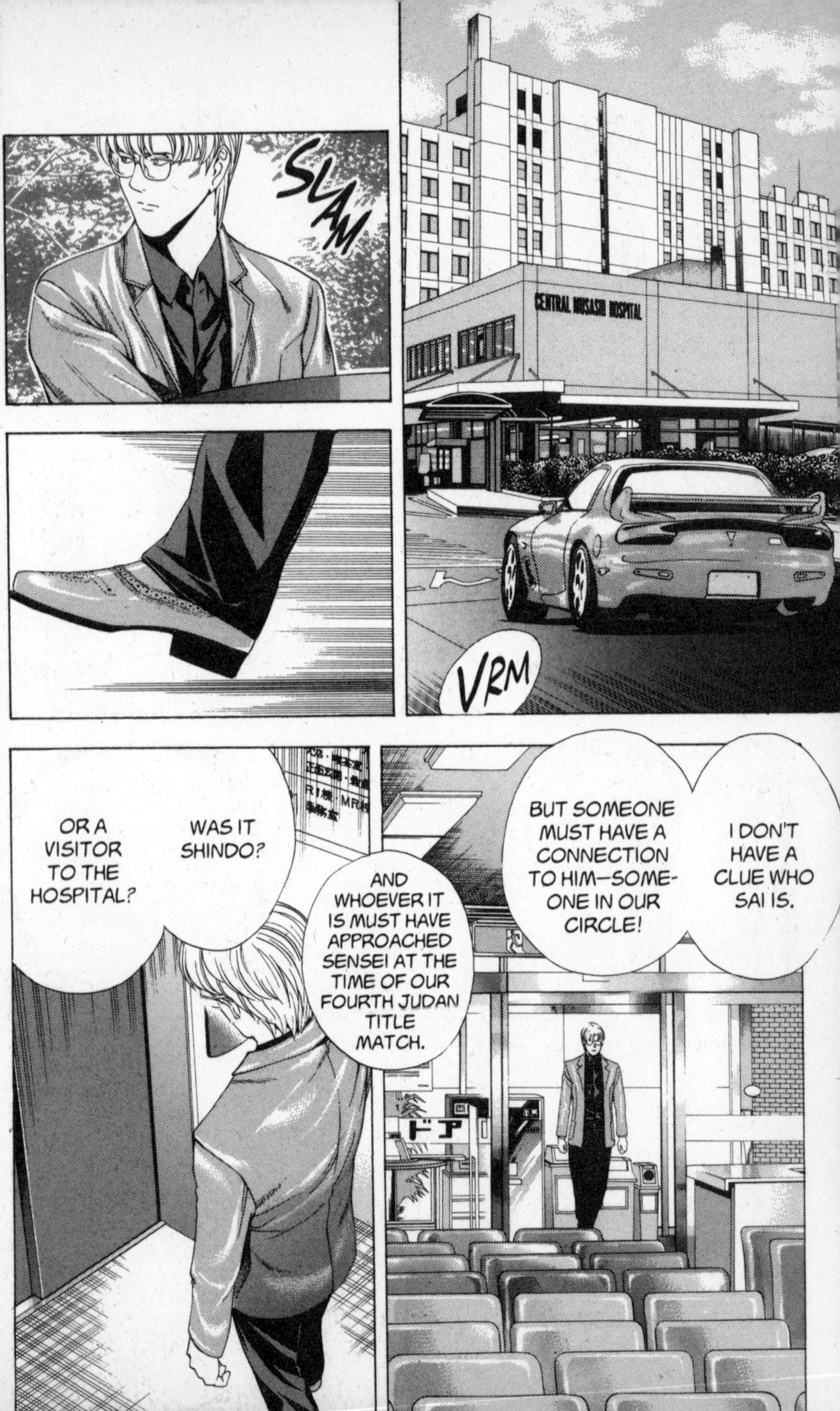
CENTRAL MUSASHI HOSPITAL
VRM
SLAM
I DON'T HAVE A CLUE WHO SAI IS.
BUT SOMEONE MUST HAVE A CONNECTION TO HIM—SOMEONE IN OUR CIRCLE!
AND WHOEVER IT IS MUST HAVE APPROACHED SENSEI AT THE TIME OF OUR FOURTH JUDAN TITLE MATCH.
WAS IT SHINDO?
OR A VISITOR TO THE HOSPITAL?

...SOMEBODY MUST HAVE HEARD THAT THE MEIJIN STARTED PLAYING INTERNET GO AND APPROACHED HIM TO SET UP THE GAME.

IN ANY CASE...

THE ONLY SURE WAY TO FIND OUT IS...

...TO ASK TOYA SENSEI! HE KNOWS!

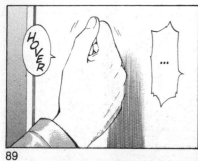

HOVER

...

89

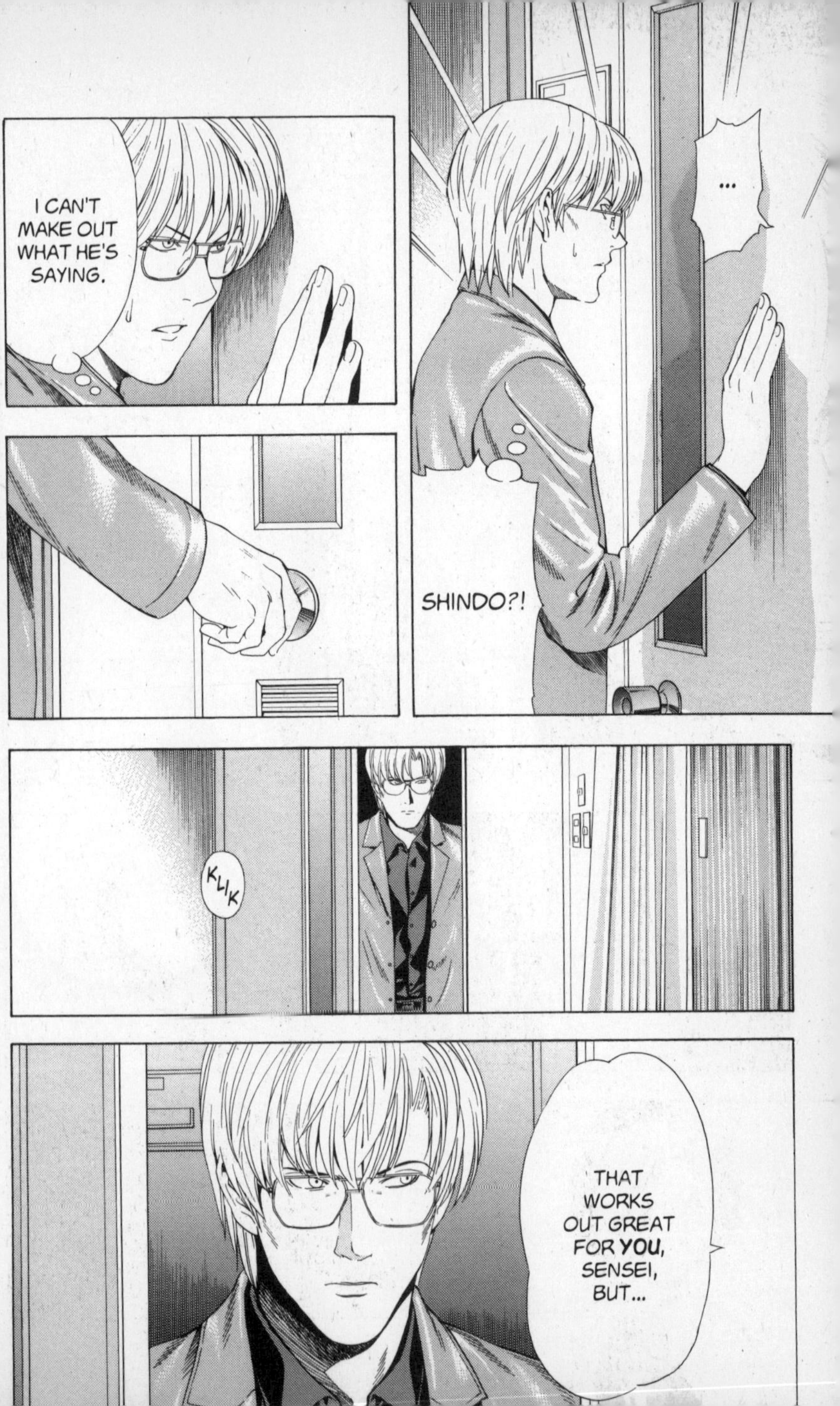
...
SHINDO?!
I CAN'T MAKE OUT WHAT HE'S SAYING.
KLIK
THAT WORKS OUT GREAT FOR **YOU**, SENSEI, BUT...

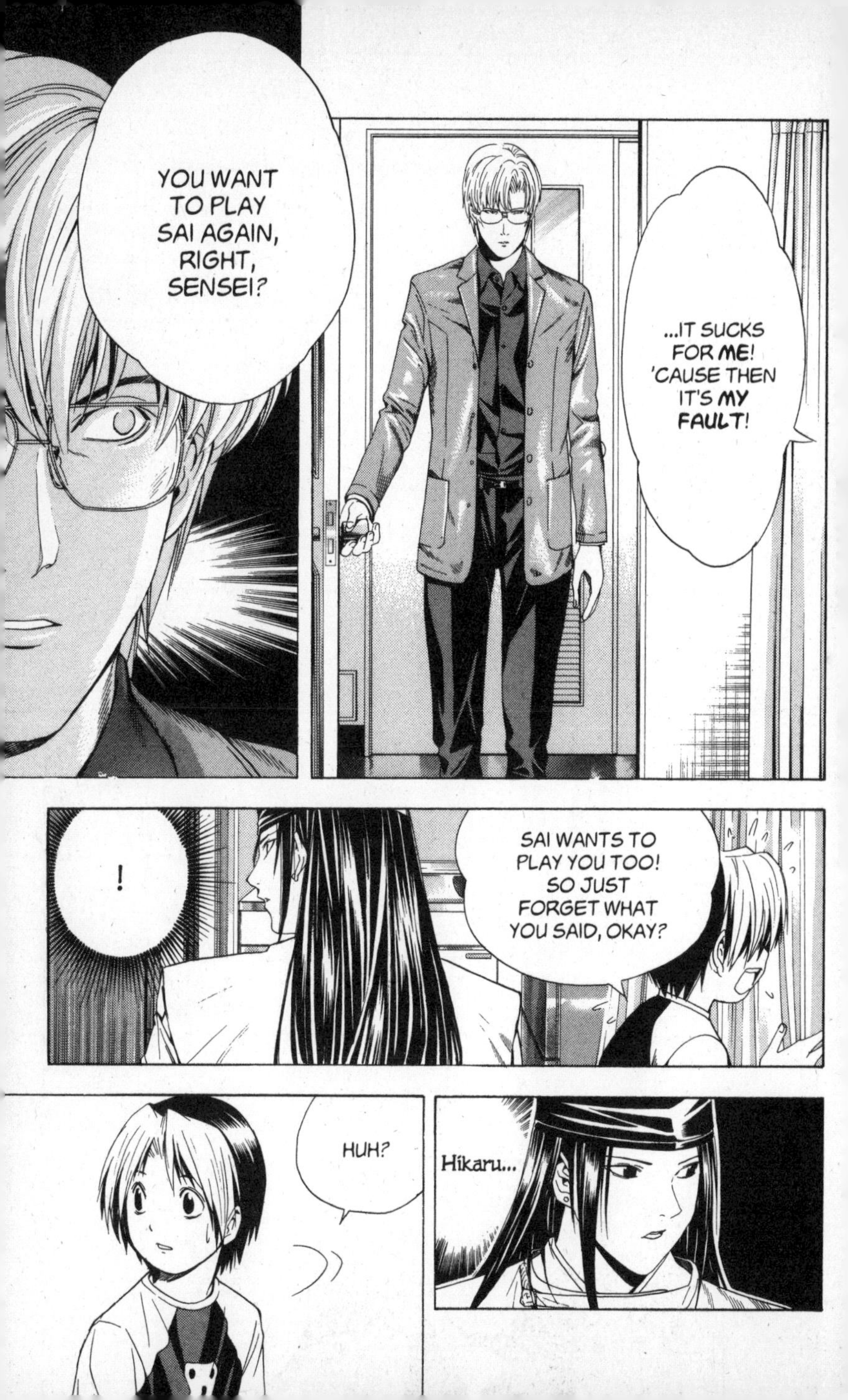
...IT SUCKS FOR ME! 'CAUSE THEN IT'S MY FAULT!
YOU WANT TO PLAY SAI AGAIN, RIGHT, SENSEI?
SAI WANTS TO PLAY YOU TOO! SO JUST FORGET WHAT YOU SAID, OKAY?
!
Hikaru...
HUH?

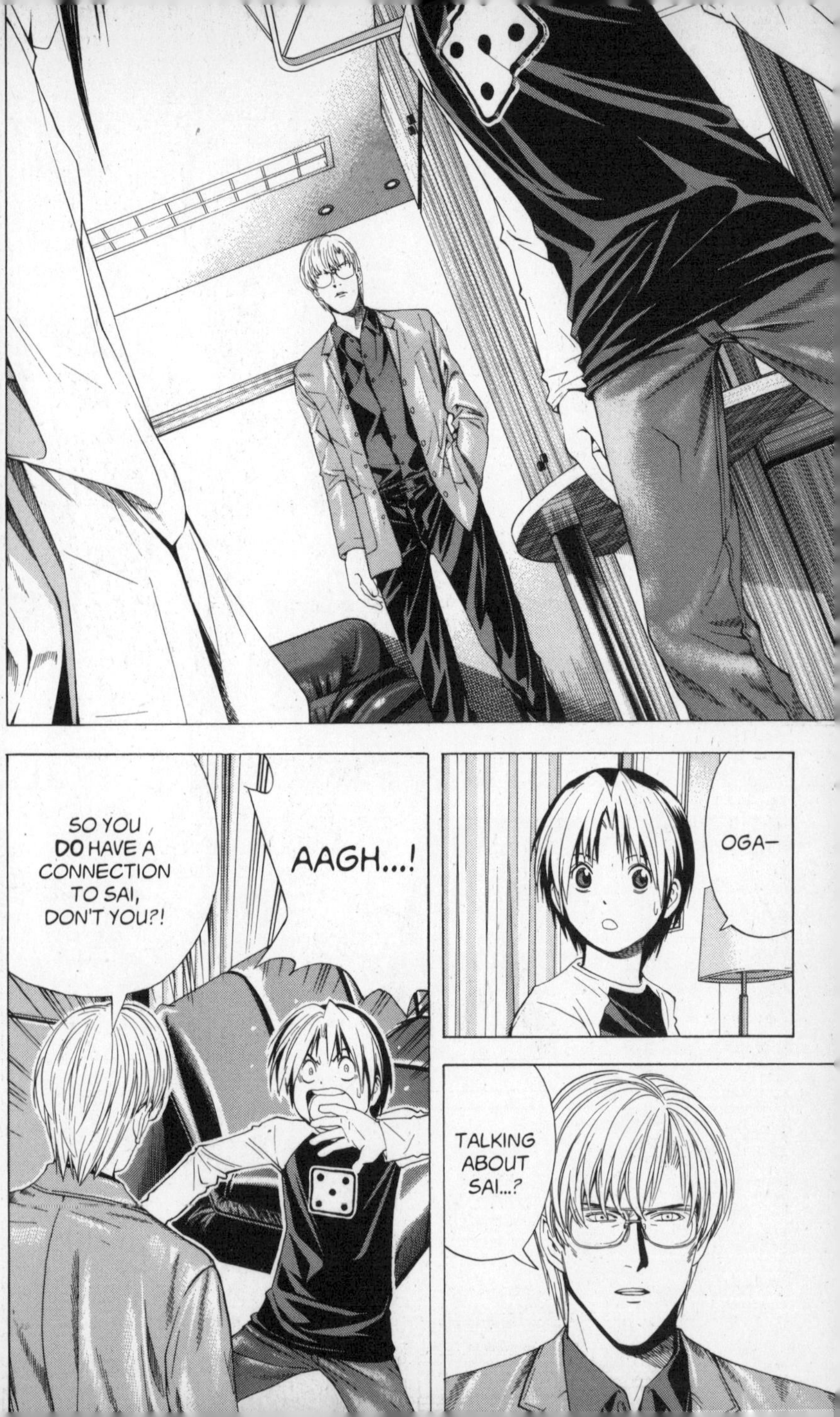
OGA-
TALKING ABOUT SAI...?
SO YOU DO HAVE A CONNECTION TO SAI, DON'T YOU?!
AAGH...!

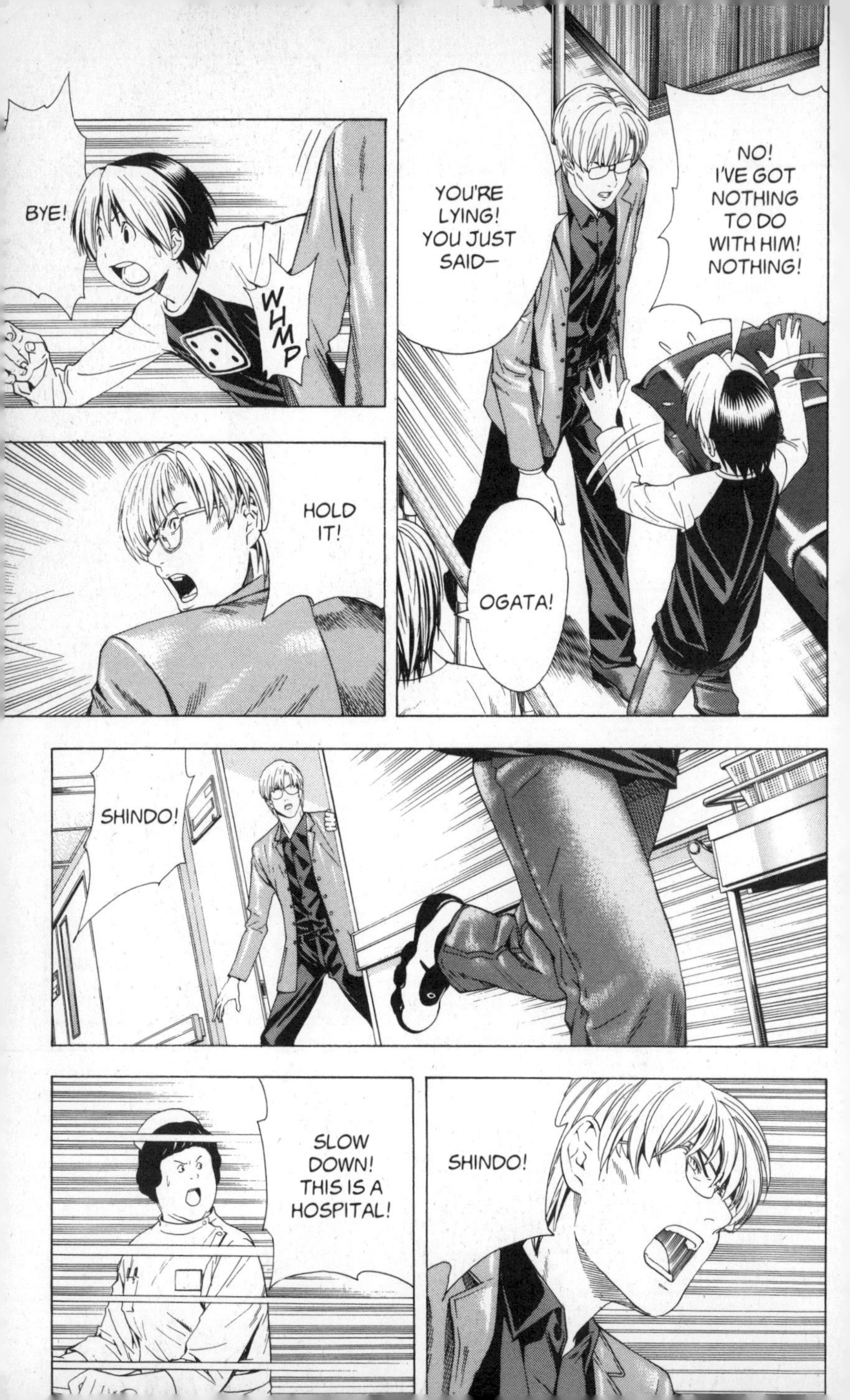
NO! I'VE GOT NOTHING TO DO WITH HIM! NOTHING!
YOU'RE LYING! YOU JUST SAID—
OGATA!
BYE!
WHMP
HOLD IT!
SHINDO!
SHINDO!
SLOW DOWN! THIS IS A HOSPITAL!

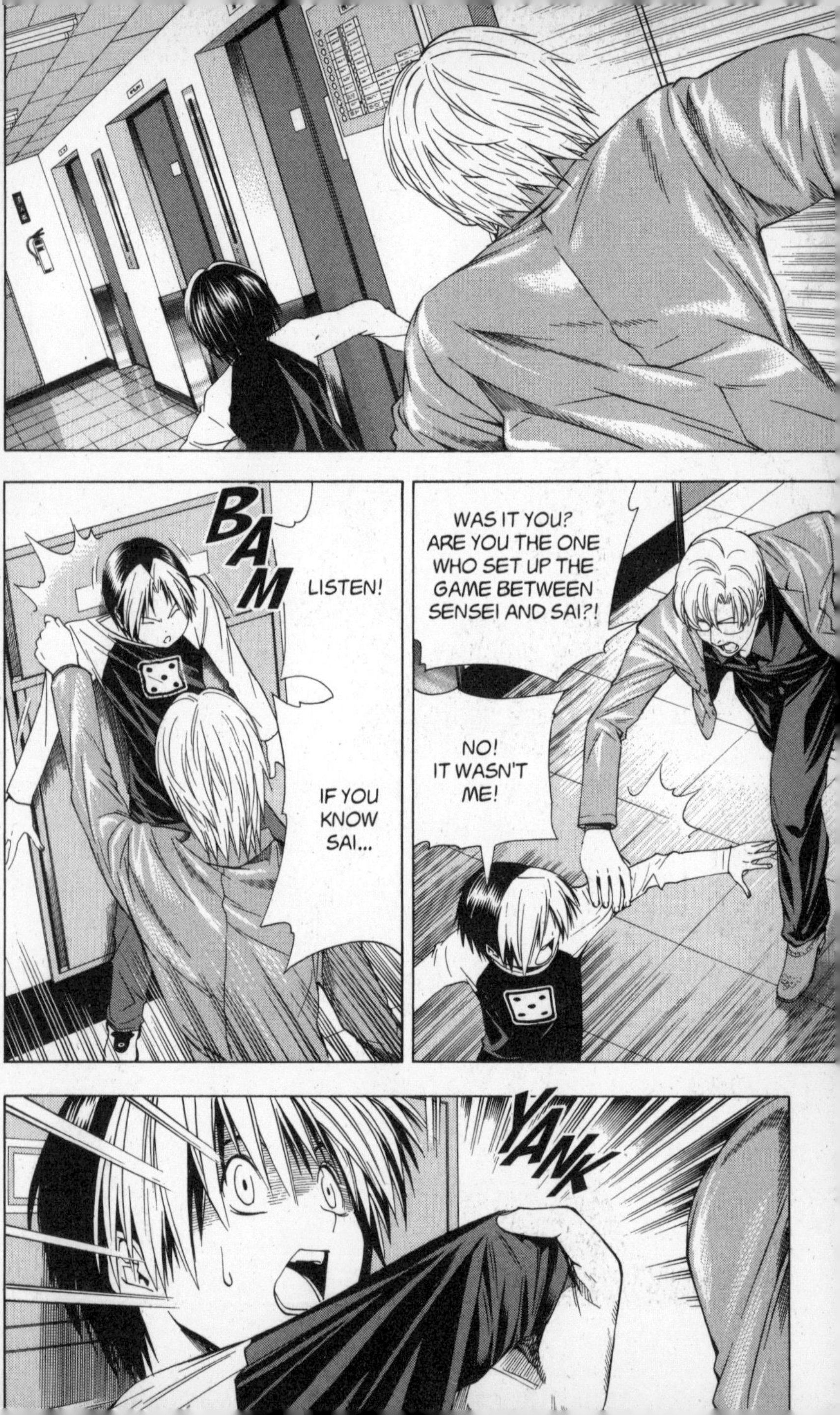
WAS IT YOU? ARE YOU THE ONE WHO SET UP THE GAME BETWEEN SENSEI AND SAI?!
NO! IT WASN'T ME!
BAM
LISTEN!
IF YOU KNOW SAI...
YANK

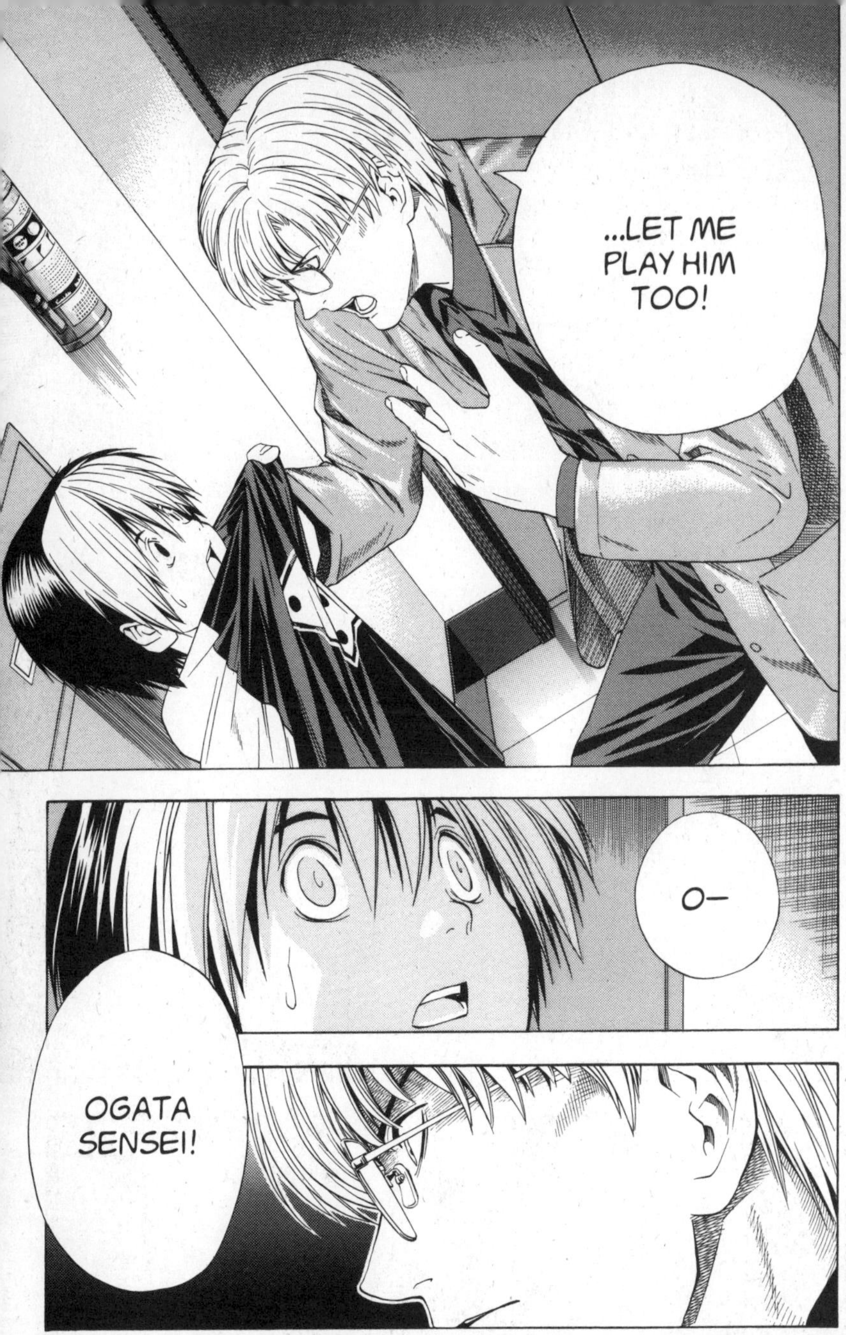
...LET ME PLAY HIM TOO!
O—
OGATA SENSEI!

HIKARU NO 5*

CLOTHING COLLECTION

*The number 5 is pronounced "go" in Japanese

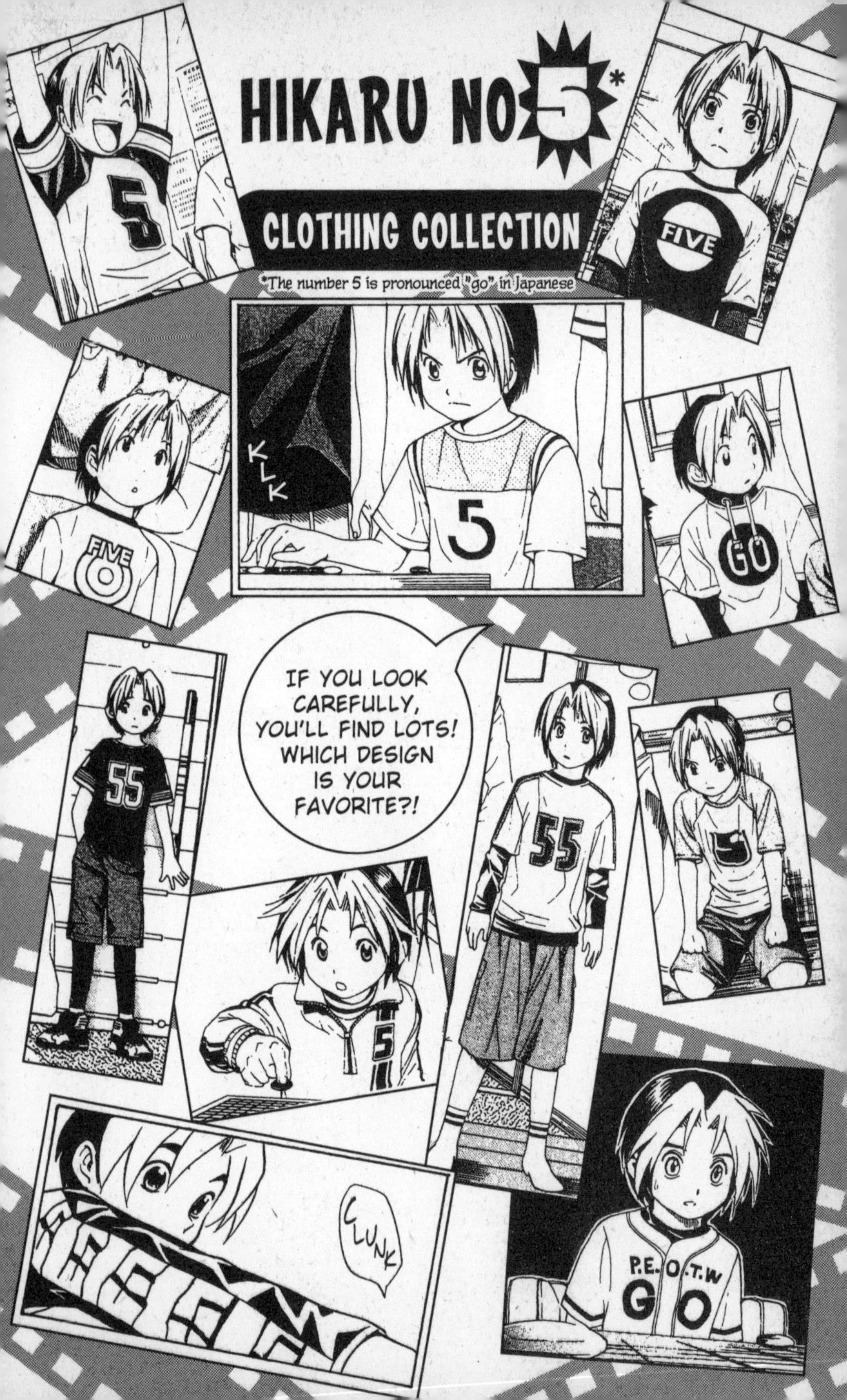
KLK
IF YOU LOOK CAREFULLY, YOU'LL FIND LOTS! WHICH DESIGN IS YOUR FAVORITE?!
CLUNK

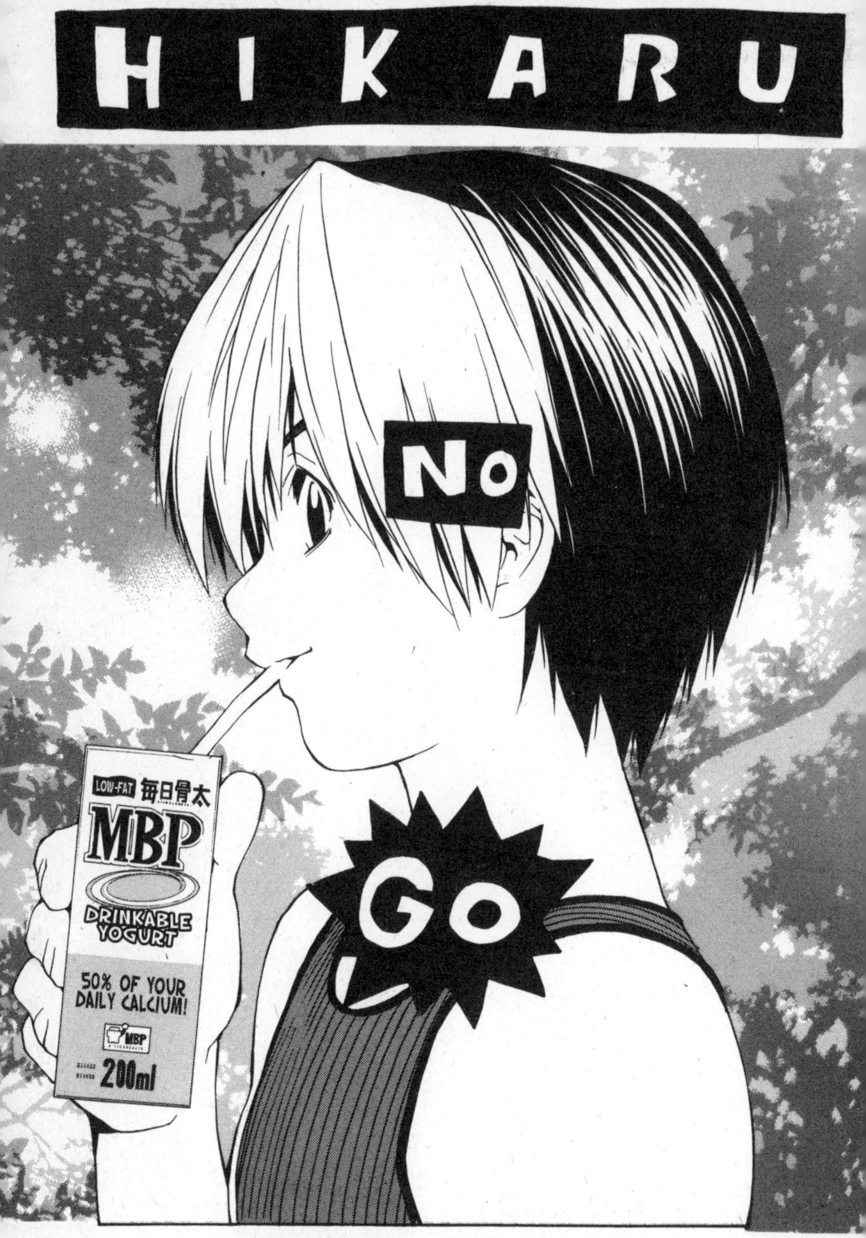
HIKARU
NO
GO
LOW-FAT 毎日骨太
MBP
DRINKABLE YOGURT
50% OF YOUR DAILY CALCIUM!
MBP
200ml

Game 118 "Pursued"

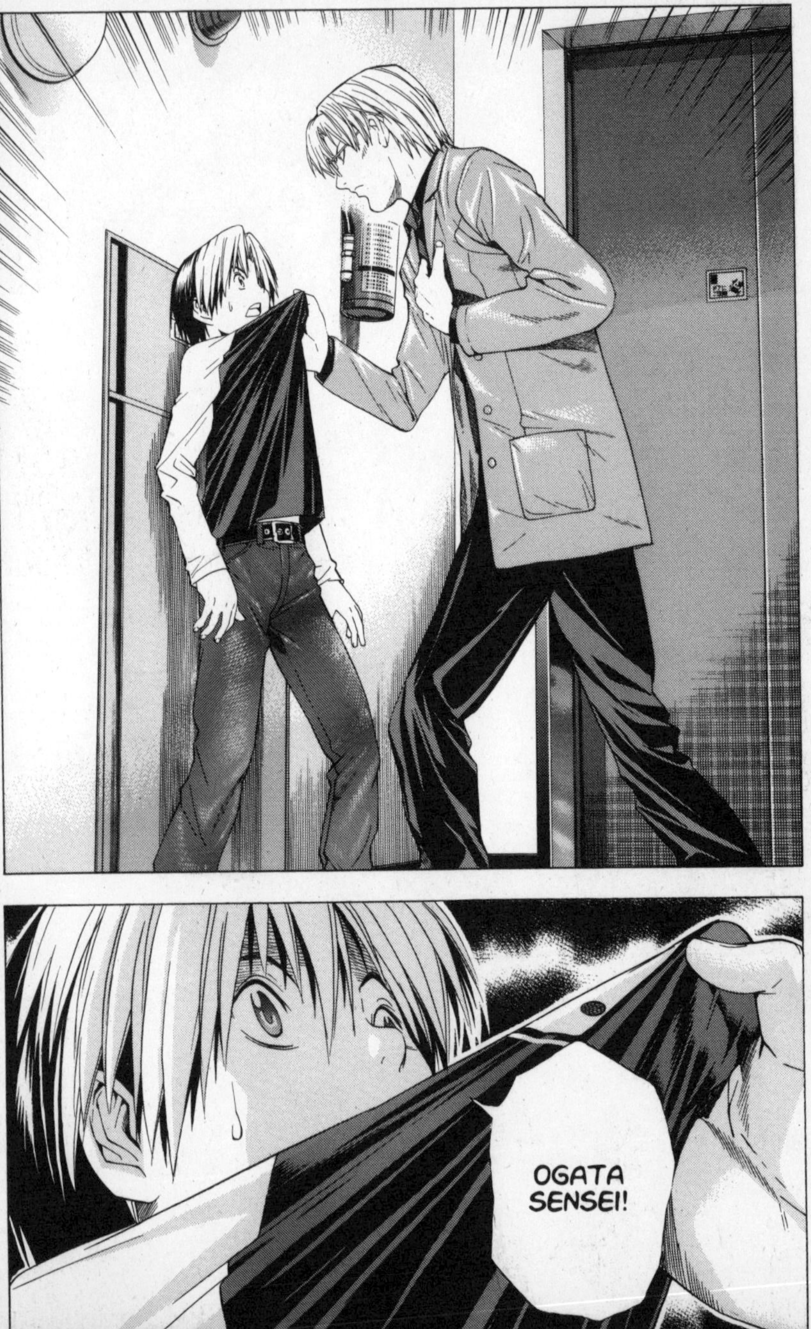
OGATA SENSEI!

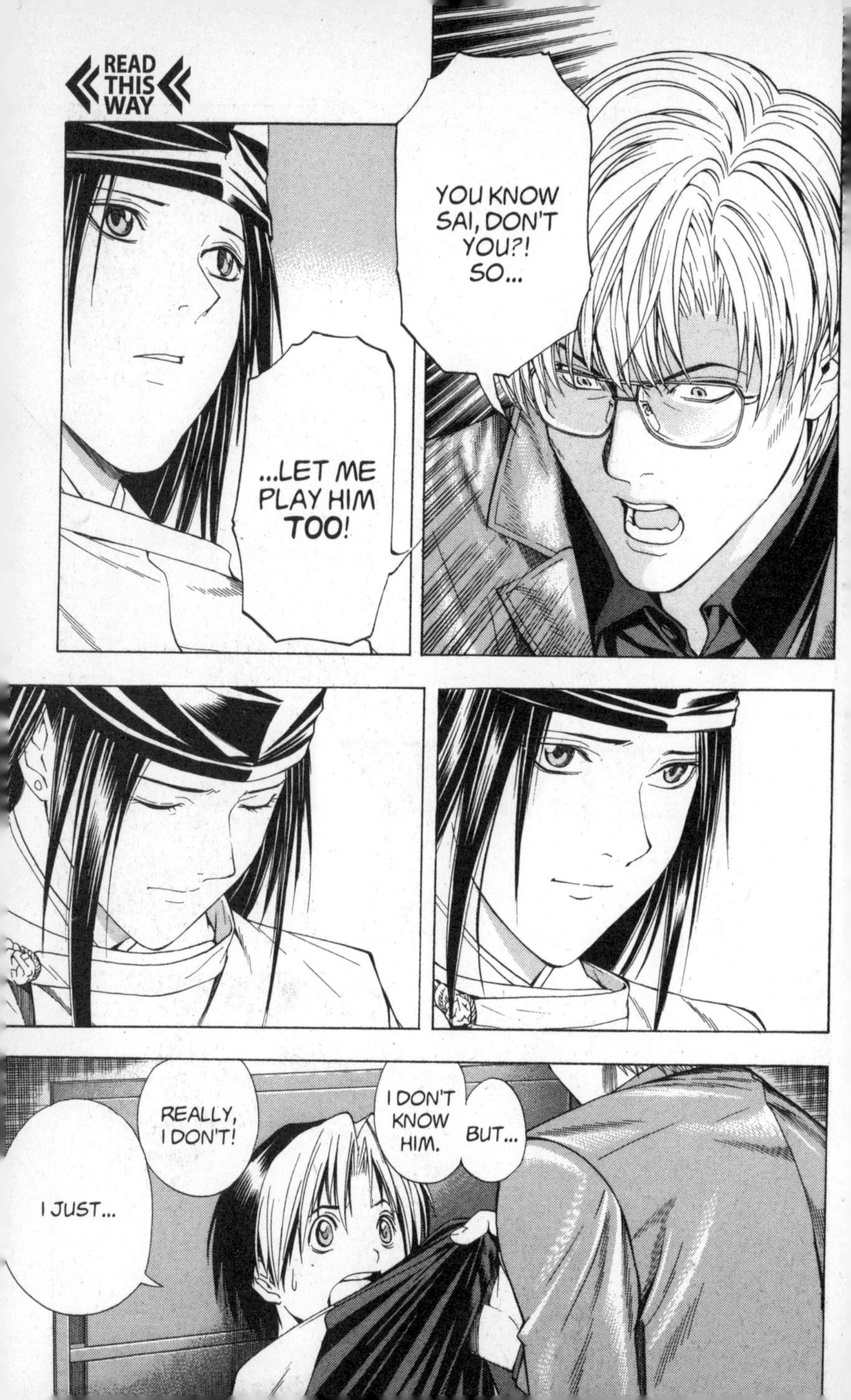
READ THIS WAY
YOU KNOW SAI, DON'T YOU?! SO...
...LET ME PLAY HIM TOO!
I DON'T KNOW HIM.
BUT...
REALLY, I DON'T!
I JUST...

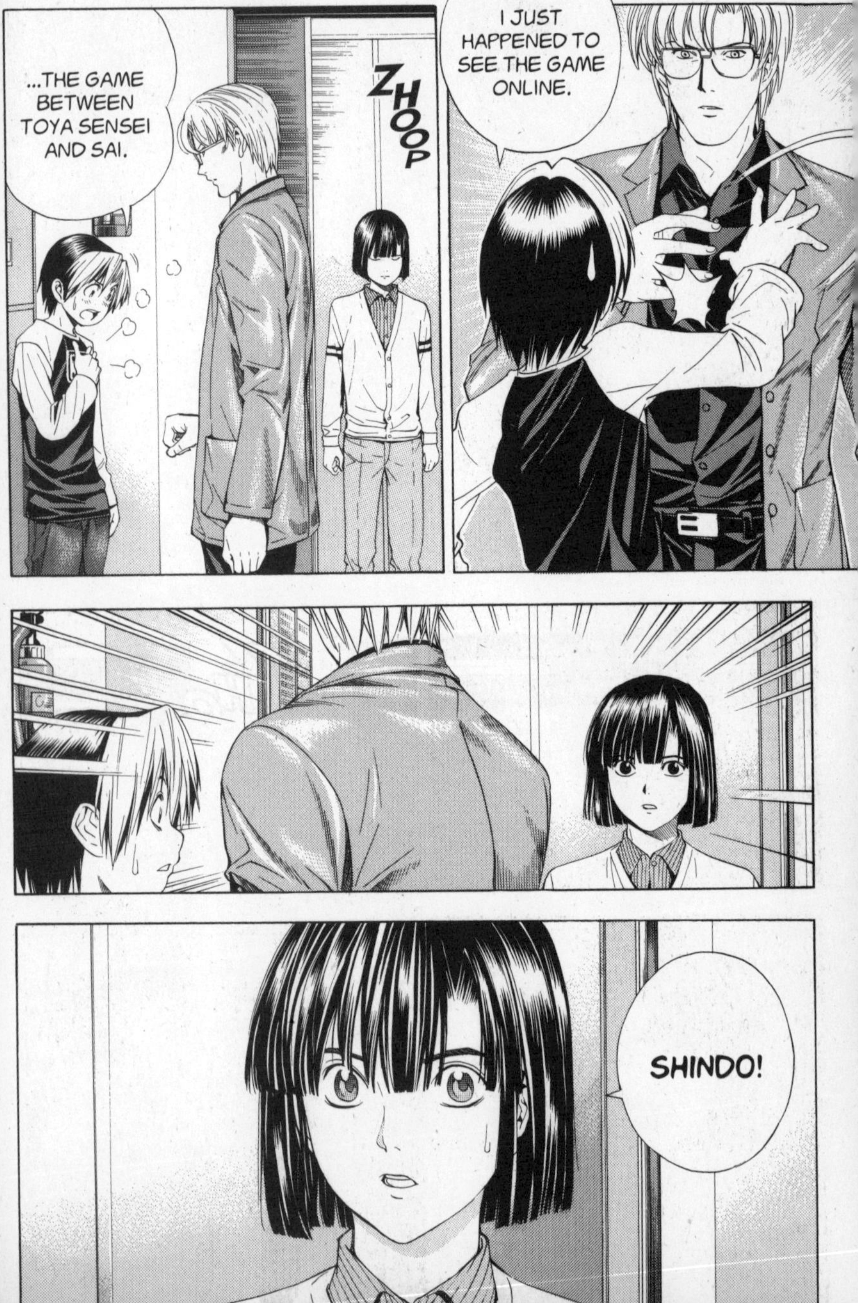
I JUST HAPPENED TO SEE THE GAME ONLINE.
...THE GAME BETWEEN TOYA SENSEI AND SAI.
ZHOOP
SHINDO!

FWMP

TOYA!

ONE AFTER ANOTHER!

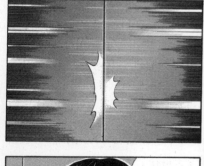

OGATA?!

ZHOOP

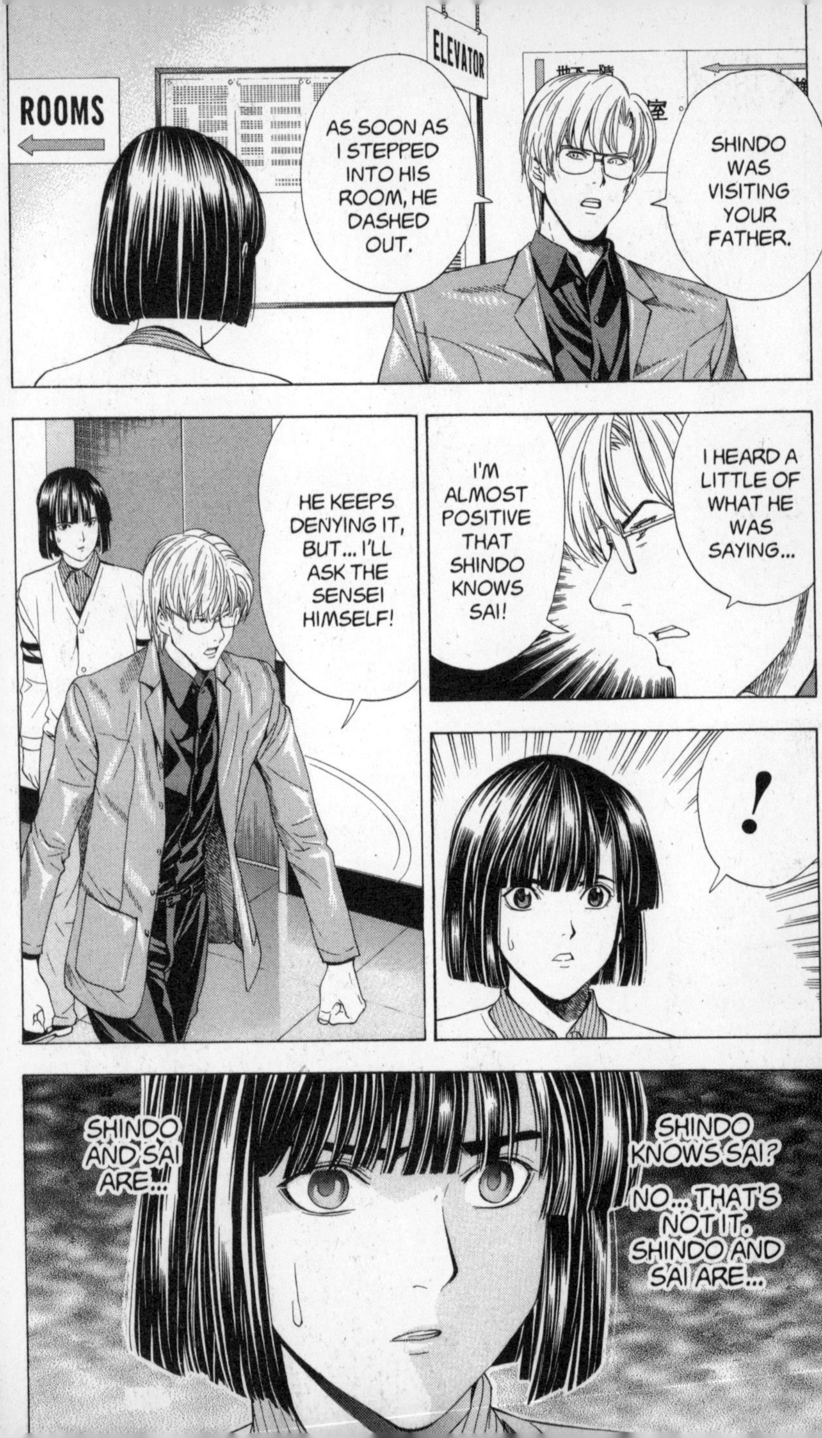
ELEVATOR
ROOMS
SHINDO WAS VISITING YOUR FATHER.
AS SOON AS I STEPPED INTO HIS ROOM, HE DASHED OUT.
I HEARD A LITTLE OF WHAT HE WAS SAYING...
I'M ALMOST POSITIVE THAT SHINDO KNOWS SAI!
!
HE KEEPS DENYING IT, BUT... I'LL ASK THE SENSEI HIMSELF!
SHINDO KNOWS SAI?
NO... THAT'S NOT IT. SHINDO AND SAI ARE...
SHINDO AND SAI ARE...

READ THIS WAY

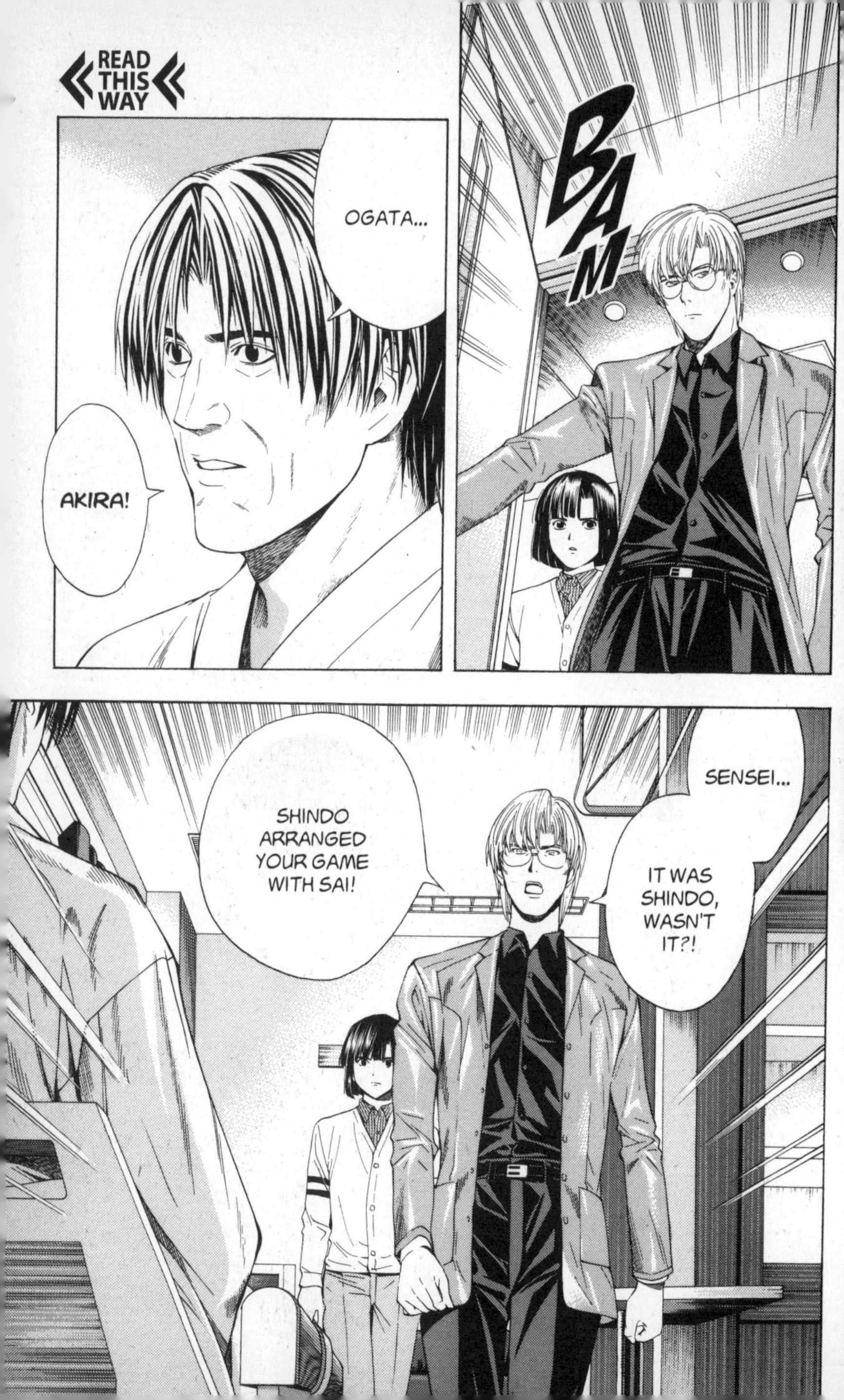
BAM
OGATA...
AKIRA!
SENSEI...
IT WAS SHINDO, WASN'T IT?!
SHINDO ARRANGED YOUR GAME WITH SAI!

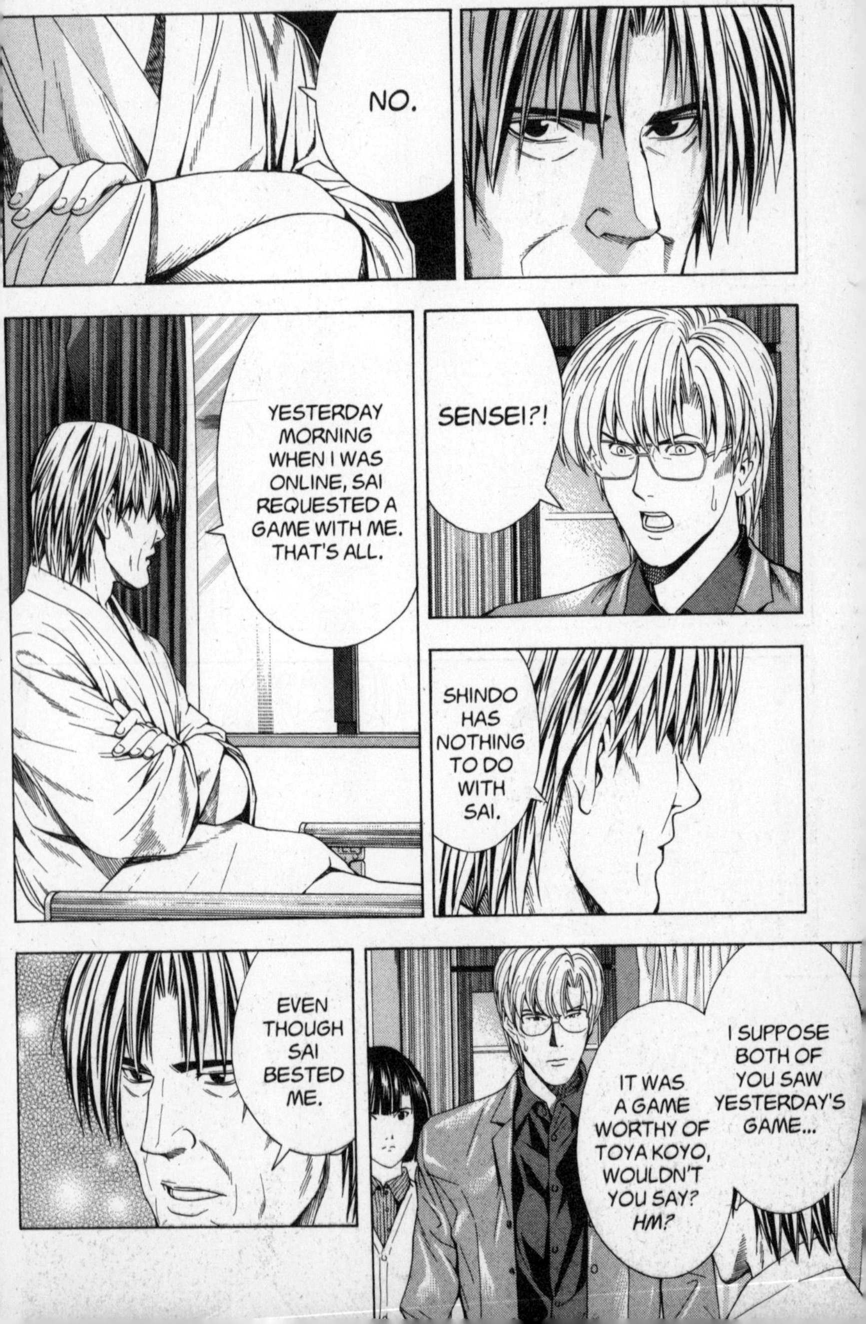
NO.
SENSEI?!
SHINDO HAS NOTHING TO DO WITH SAI.
YESTERDAY MORNING WHEN I WAS ONLINE, SAI REQUESTED A GAME WITH ME. THAT'S ALL.
I SUPPOSE BOTH OF YOU SAW YESTERDAY'S GAME...
IT WAS A GAME WORTHY OF TOYA KOYO, WOULDN'T YOU SAY? HM?
EVEN THOUGH SAI BESTED ME.

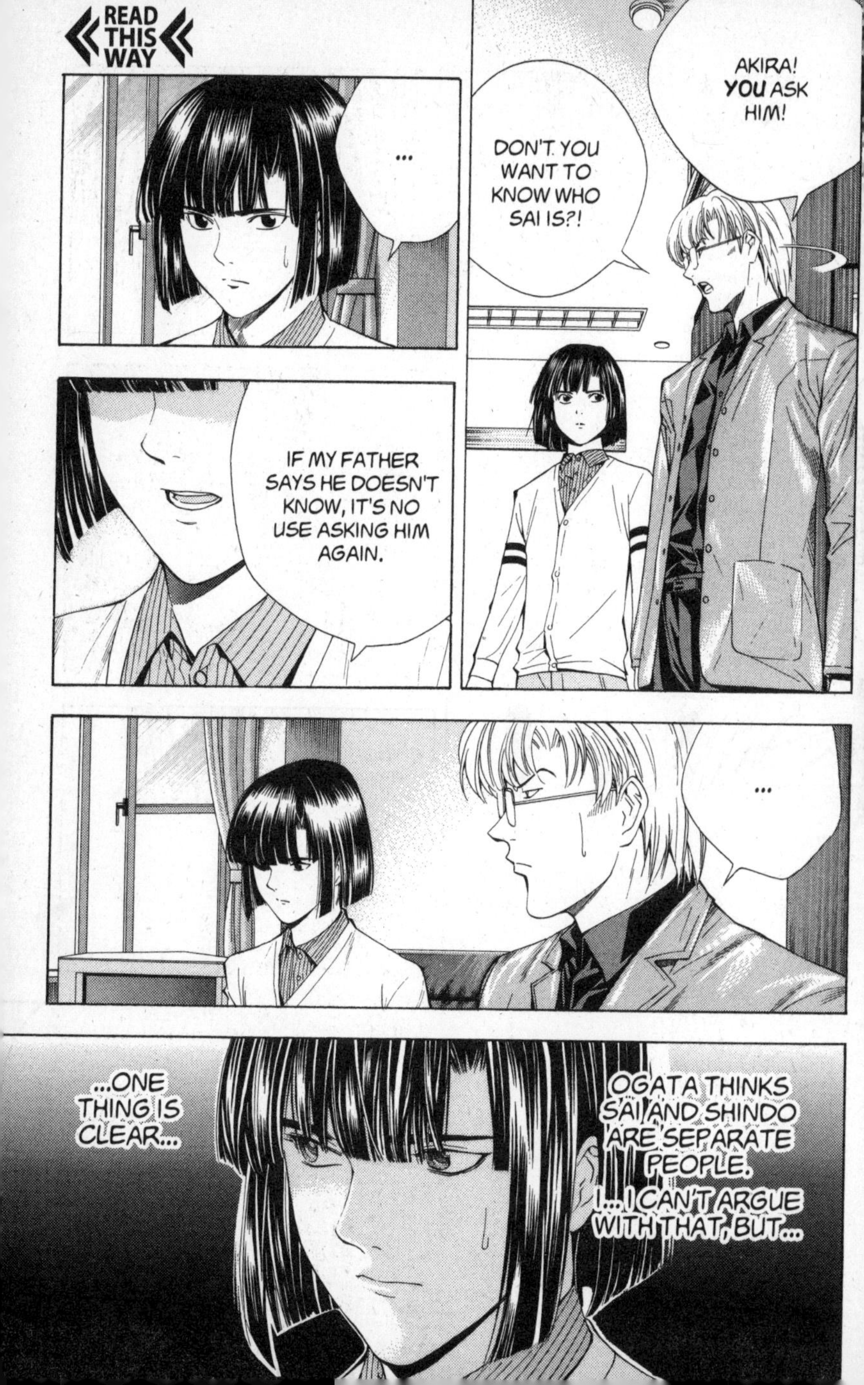
READ THIS WAY
AKIRA! YOU ASK HIM!
DON'T YOU WANT TO KNOW WHO SAI IS?!
...
IF MY FATHER SAYS HE DOESN'T KNOW, IT'S NO USE ASKING HIM AGAIN.
...
OGATA THINKS SAI AND SHINDO ARE SEPARATE PEOPLE. I... I CAN'T ARGUE WITH THAT, BUT...
...ONE THING IS CLEAR...

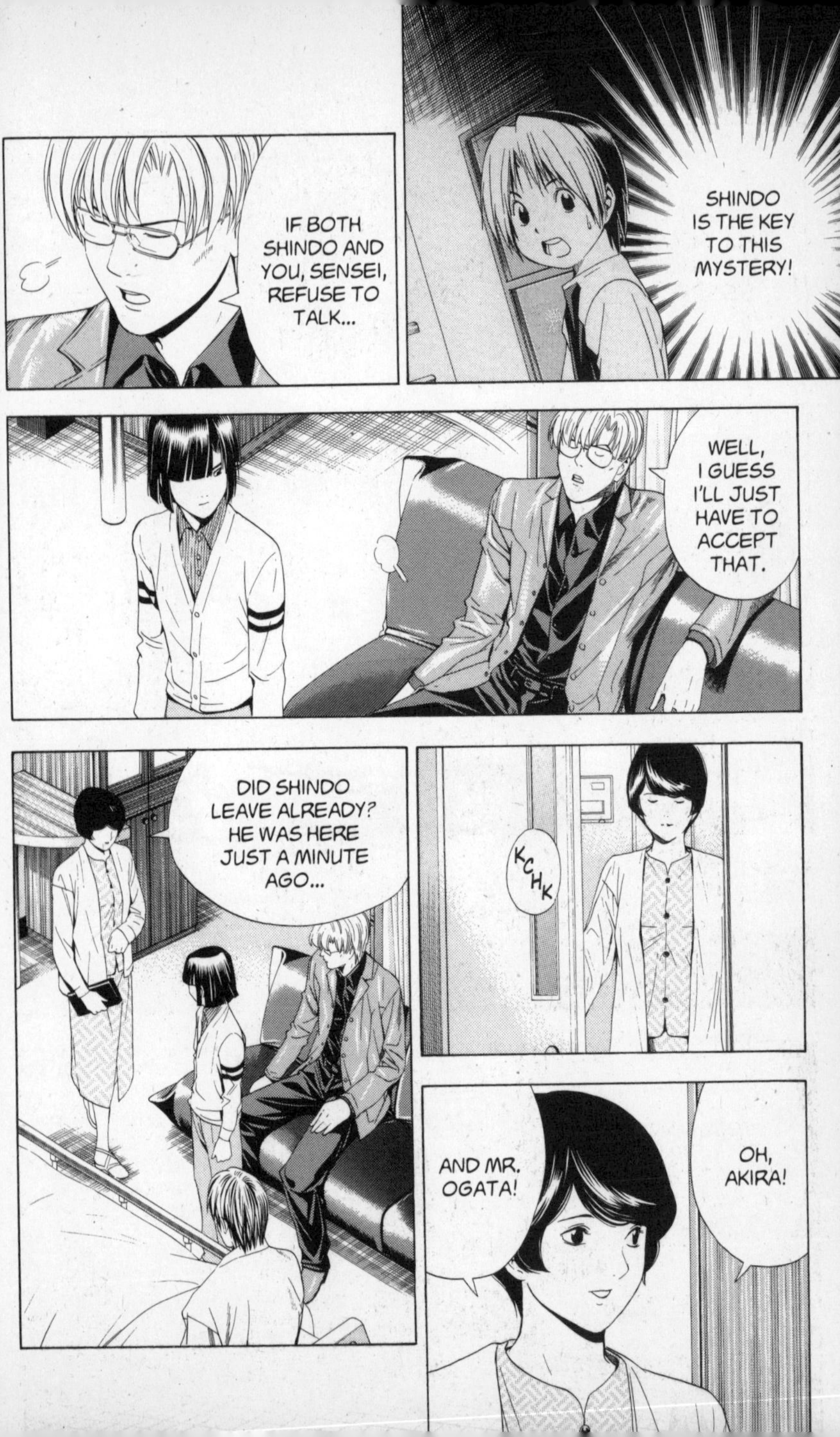
SHINDO IS THE KEY TO THIS MYSTERY!
IF BOTH SHINDO AND YOU, SENSEI, REFUSE TO TALK...
WELL, I GUESS I'LL JUST HAVE TO ACCEPT THAT.
KCHK
OH, AKIRA!
AND MR. OGATA!
DID SHINDO LEAVE ALREADY? HE WAS HERE JUST A MINUTE AGO...

READ THIS WAY

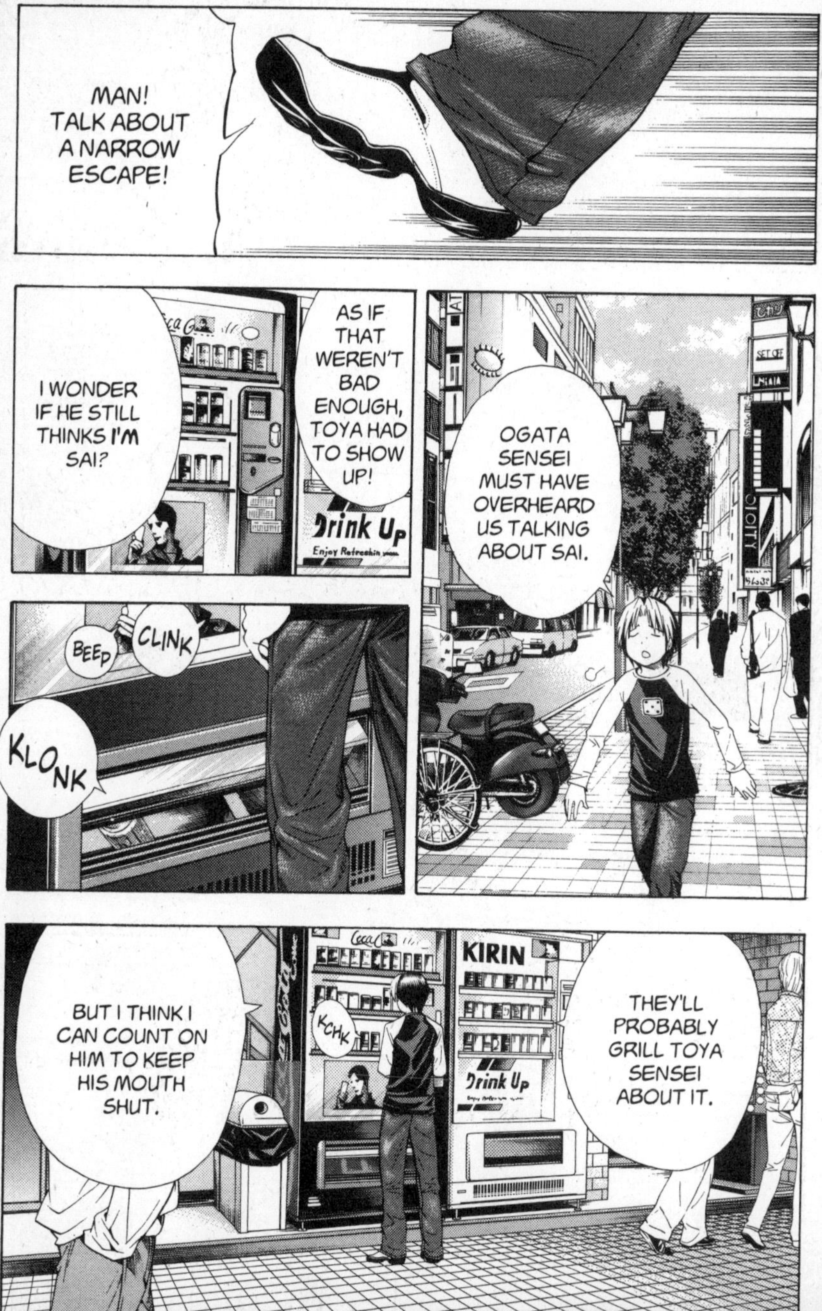
MAN! TALK ABOUT A NARROW ESCAPE!
OGATA SENSEI MUST HAVE OVERHEARD US TALKING ABOUT SAI.
AS IF THAT WEREN'T BAD ENOUGH, TOYA HAD TO SHOW UP!
I WONDER IF HE STILL THINKS I'M SAI?
Drink Up
CLINK
BEEP
KLONK
THEY'LL PROBABLY GRILL TOYA SENSEI ABOUT IT.
KIRIN
Drink Up
KCHK
BUT I THINK I CAN COUNT ON HIM TO KEEP HIS MOUTH SHUT.

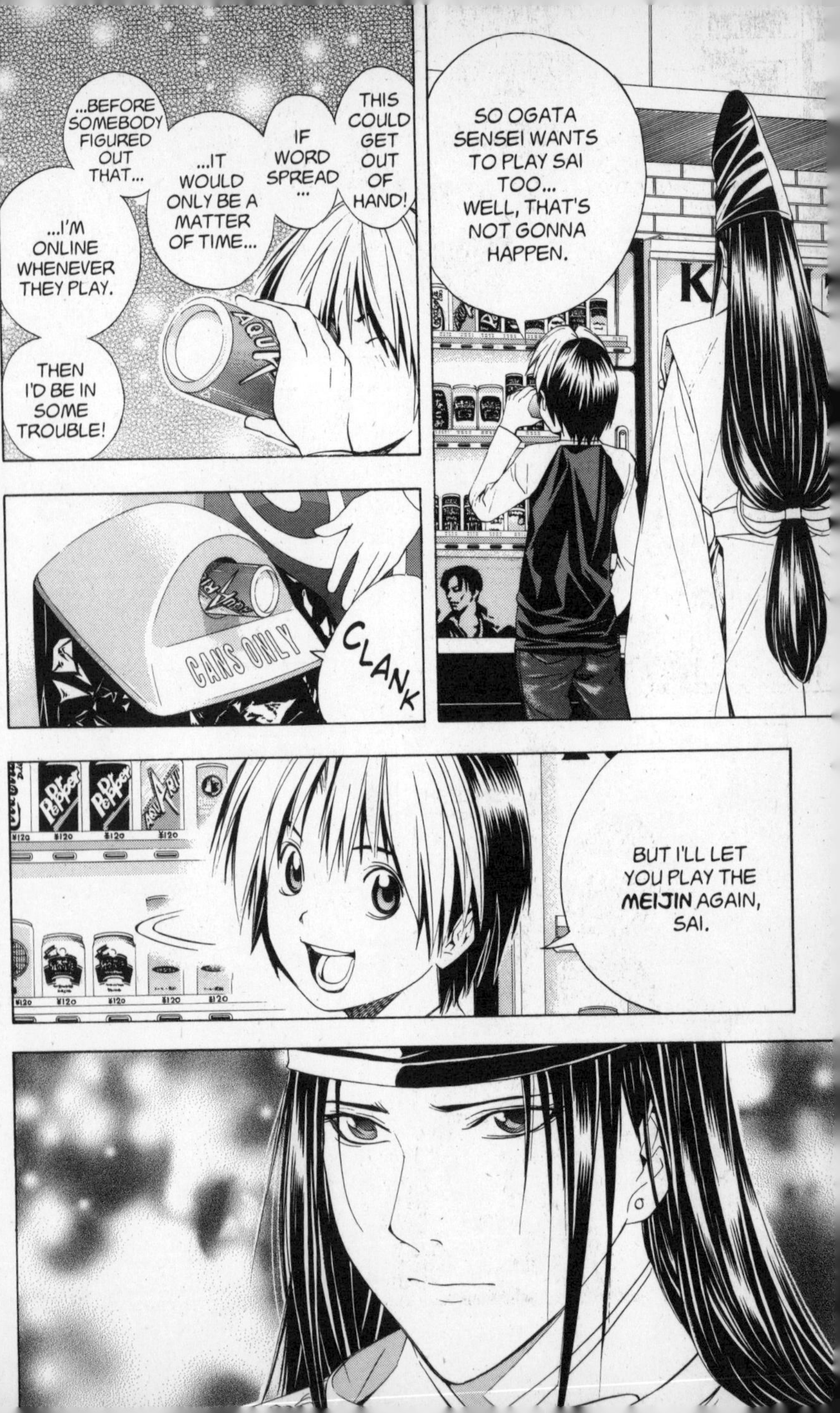
SO OGATA SENSEI WANTS TO PLAY SAI TOO... WELL, THAT'S NOT GONNA HAPPEN.
THIS COULD GET OUT OF HAND!
IF WORD SPREAD...
...IT WOULD ONLY BE A MATTER OF TIME...
...BEFORE SOMEBODY FIGURED OUT THAT...
...I'M ONLINE WHENEVER THEY PLAY.
THEN I'D BE IN SOME TROUBLE!
CANS ONLY
CLANK
BUT I'LL LET YOU PLAY THE **MEIJIN** AGAIN, SAI.

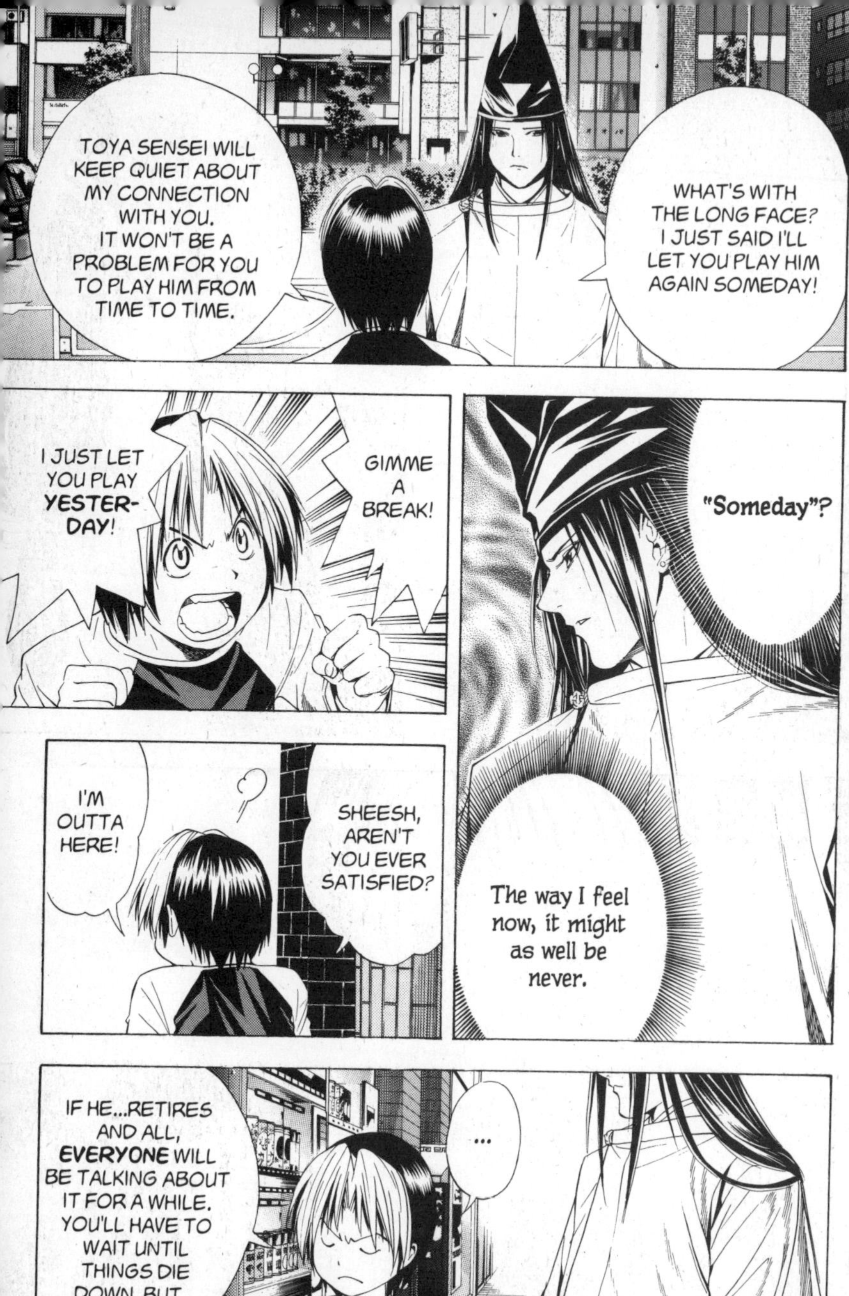
WHAT'S WITH THE LONG FACE? I JUST SAID I'LL LET YOU PLAY HIM AGAIN SOMEDAY!
TOYA SENSEI WILL KEEP QUIET ABOUT MY CONNECTION WITH YOU. IT WON'T BE A PROBLEM FOR YOU TO PLAY HIM FROM TIME TO TIME.
"Someday"?
The way I feel now, it might as well be never.
GIMME A BREAK!
I JUST LET YOU PLAY **YESTER-DAY**!
SHEESH, AREN'T YOU EVER SATISFIED?
I'M OUTTA HERE!
...
IF HE...RETIRES AND ALL, **EVERYONE** WILL BE TALKING ABOUT IT FOR A WHILE. YOU'LL HAVE TO WAIT UNTIL THINGS DIE DOWN, BUT...

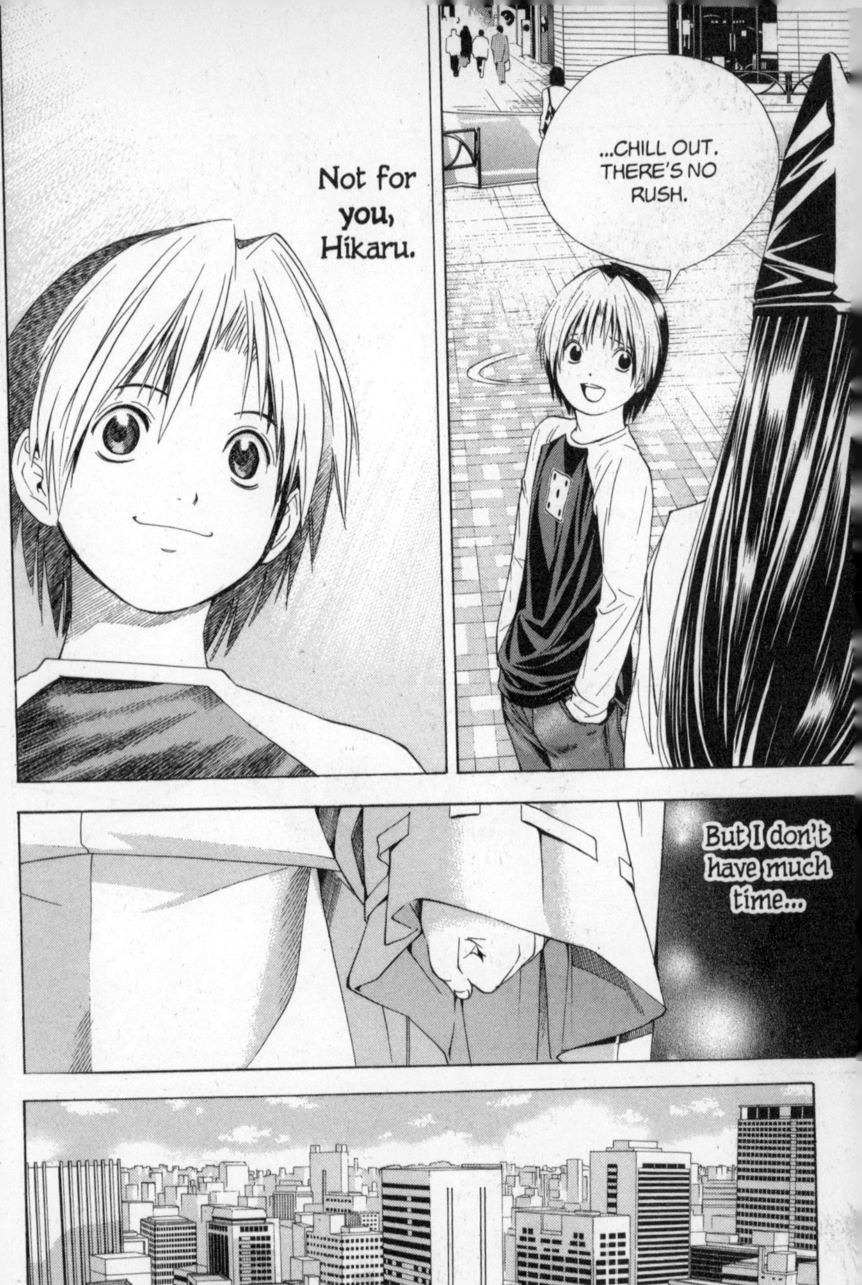
...CHILL OUT. THERE'S NO RUSH.
Not for you, Hikaru.
But I don't have much time...

READ THIS WAY

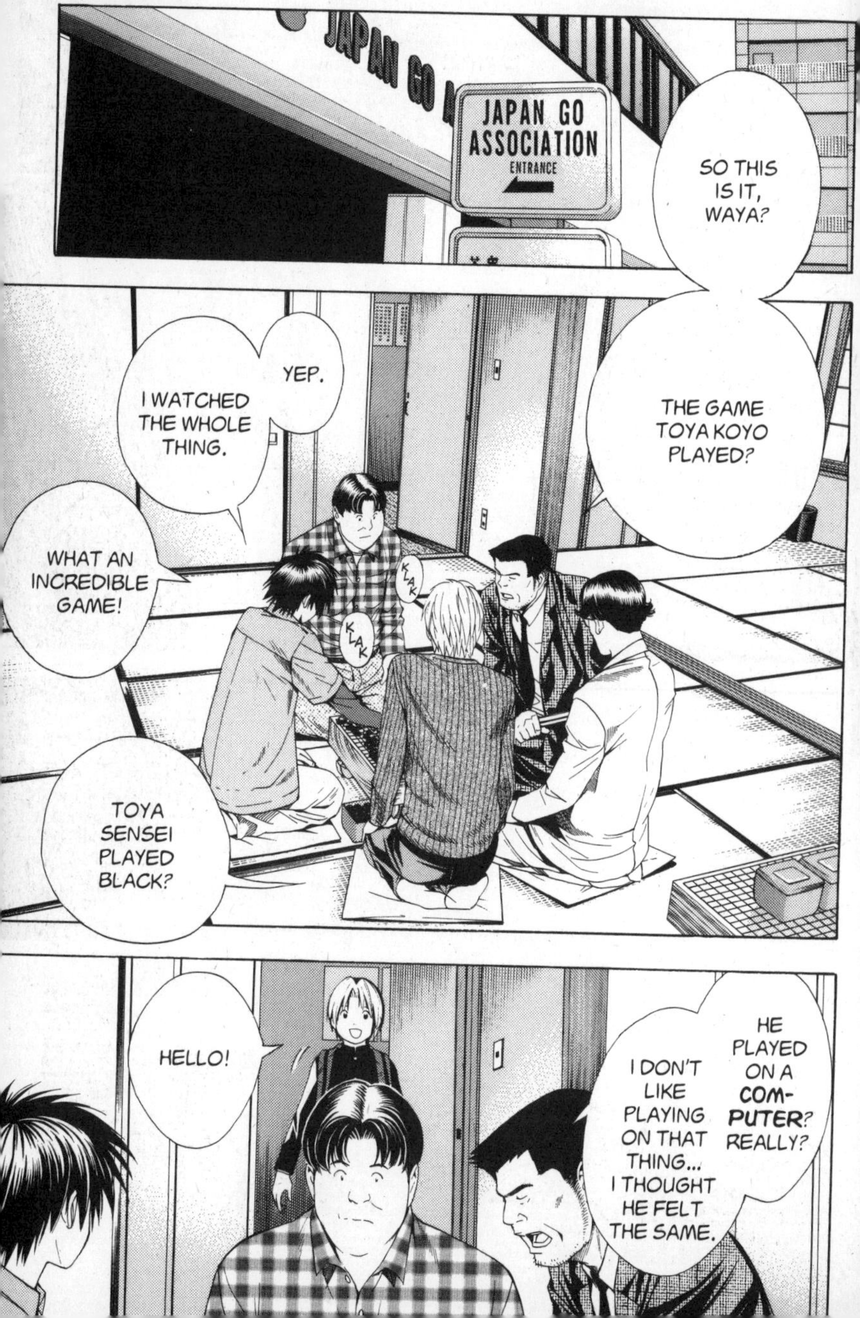
JAPAN GO ASSOCIATION
ENTRANCE
SO THIS IS IT, WAYA?
THE GAME TOYA KOYO PLAYED?
YEP.
I WATCHED THE WHOLE THING.
WHAT AN INCREDIBLE GAME!
KLAK
KLAK
TOYA SENSEI PLAYED BLACK?
HE PLAYED ON A **COMPUTER**? REALLY?
I DON'T LIKE PLAYING ON THAT THING... I THOUGHT HE FELT THE SAME.
HELLO!

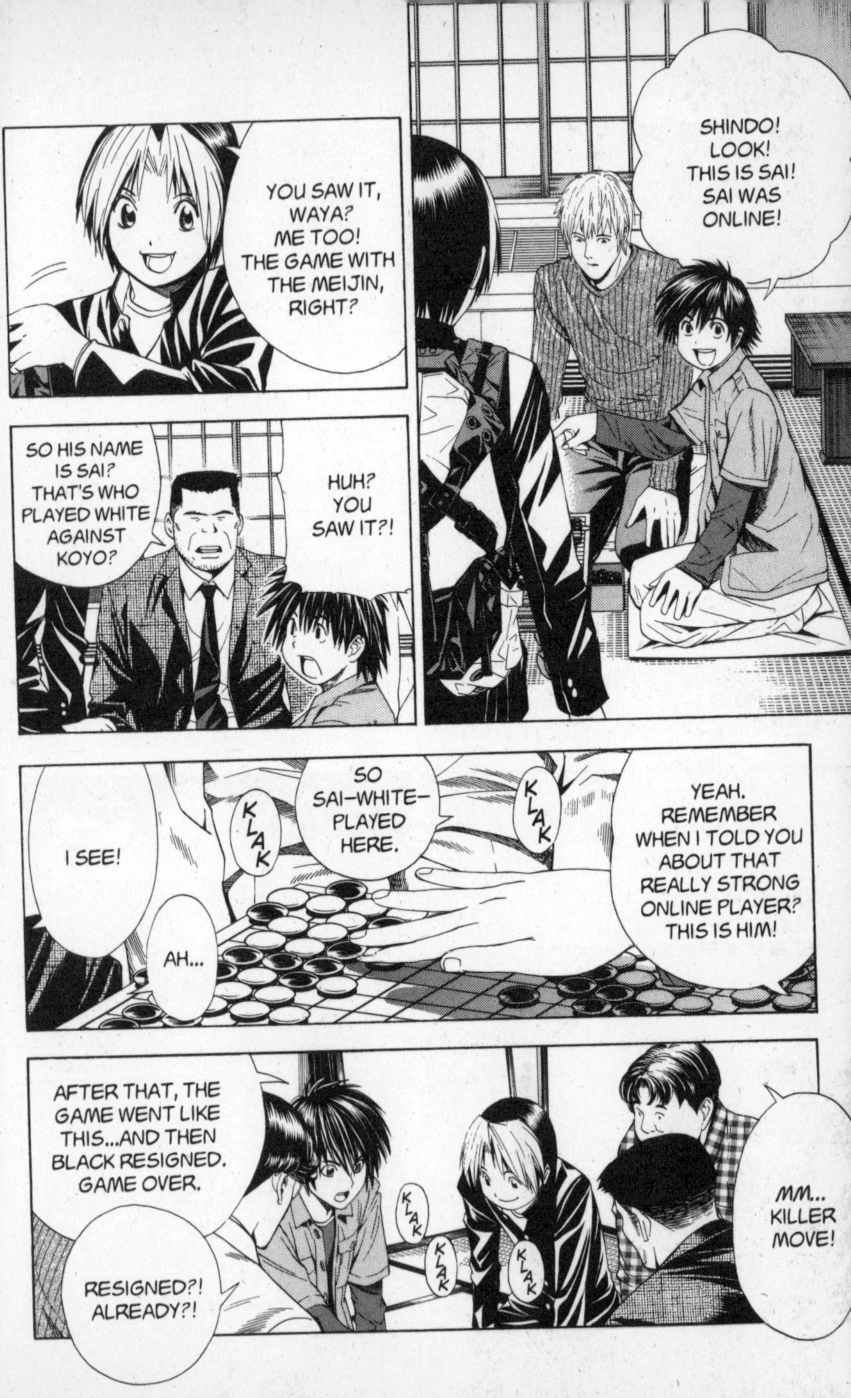
SHINDO! LOOK! THIS IS SAI! SAI WAS ONLINE!
YOU SAW IT, WAYA? ME TOO! THE GAME WITH THE MEIJIN, RIGHT?
HUH? YOU SAW IT?!
SO HIS NAME IS SAI? THAT'S WHO PLAYED WHITE AGAINST KOYO?
YEAH. REMEMBER WHEN I TOLD YOU ABOUT THAT REALLY STRONG ONLINE PLAYER? THIS IS HIM!
KLAK
SO SAI—WHITE—PLAYED HERE.
KLAK
I SEE!
AH...
MM... KILLER MOVE!
KLAK
KLAK
KLAK
AFTER THAT, THE GAME WENT LIKE THIS...AND THEN BLACK RESIGNED. GAME OVER.
RESIGNED?! ALREADY?!

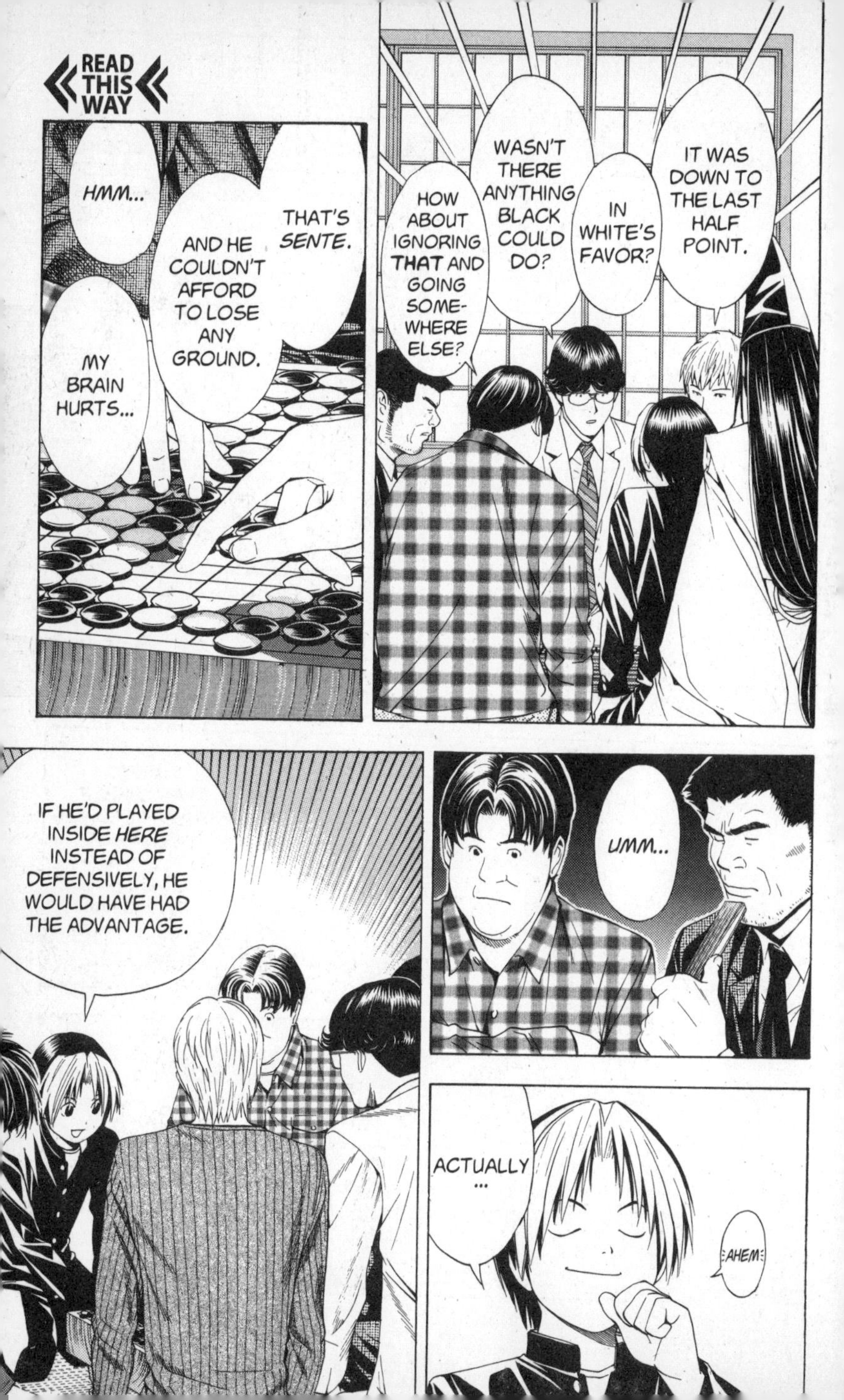
READ THIS WAY
IT WAS DOWN TO THE LAST HALF POINT.
IN WHITE'S FAVOR?
WASN'T THERE ANYTHING BLACK COULD DO?
HOW ABOUT IGNORING THAT AND GOING SOMEWHERE ELSE?
THAT'S SENTE.
AND HE COULDN'T AFFORD TO LOSE ANY GROUND.
HMM...
MY BRAIN HURTS...
UMM...
AHEM
ACTUALLY ...
IF HE'D PLAYED INSIDE HERE INSTEAD OF DEFENSIVELY, HE WOULD HAVE HAD THE ADVANTAGE.

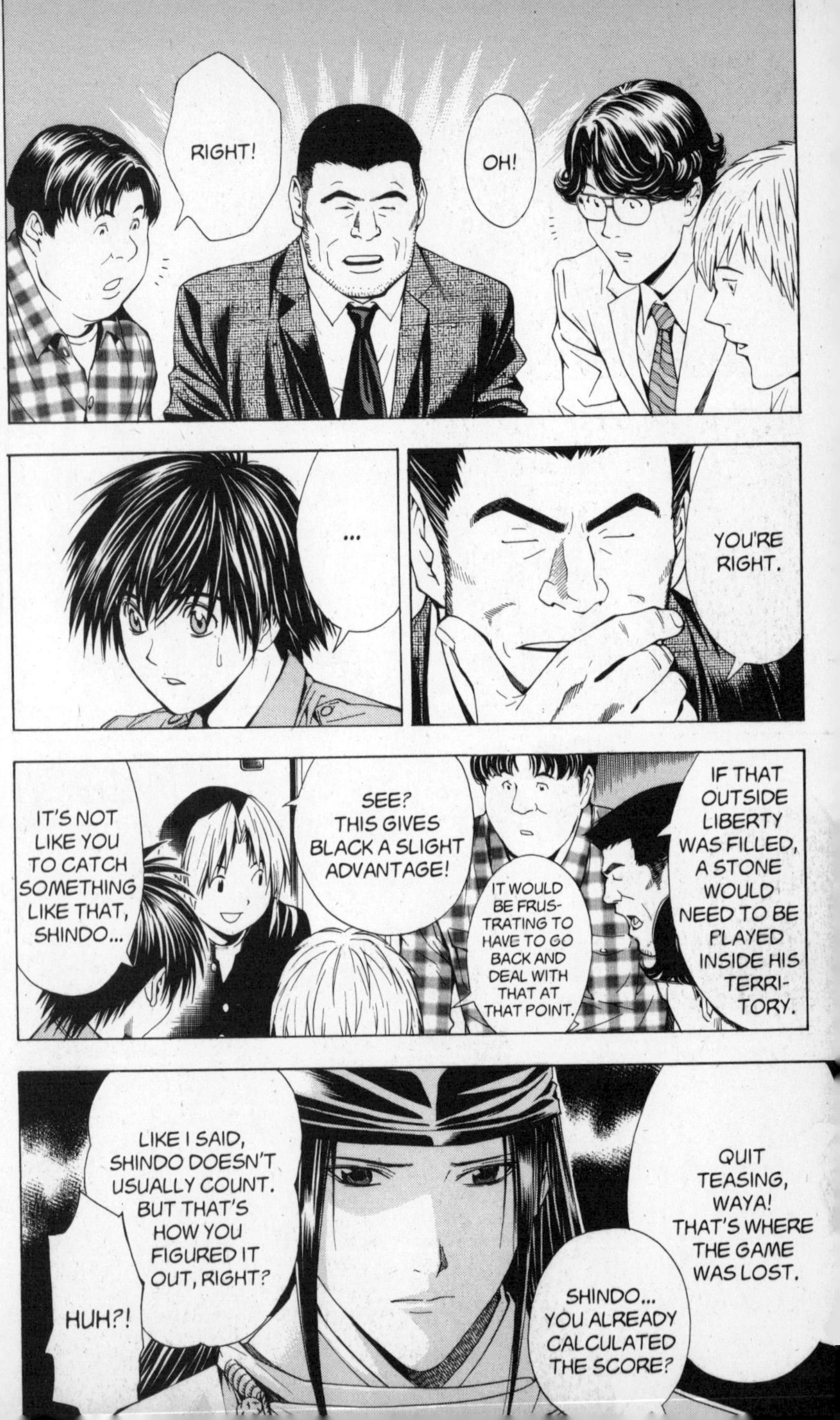
OH!
RIGHT!
YOU'RE RIGHT.
...
IF THAT OUTSIDE LIBERTY WAS FILLED, A STONE WOULD NEED TO BE PLAYED INSIDE HIS TERRITORY.
IT WOULD BE FRUS-TRATING TO HAVE TO GO BACK AND DEAL WITH THAT AT THAT POINT.
SEE? THIS GIVES BLACK A SLIGHT ADVANTAGE!
IT'S NOT LIKE YOU TO CATCH SOMETHING LIKE THAT, SHINDO...
SHINDO... YOU ALREADY CALCULATED THE SCORE?
HUH?!
LIKE I SAID, SHINDO DOESN'T USUALLY COUNT. BUT THAT'S HOW YOU FIGURED IT OUT, RIGHT?
QUIT TEASING, WAYA! THAT'S WHERE THE GAME WAS LOST.

READ THIS WAY

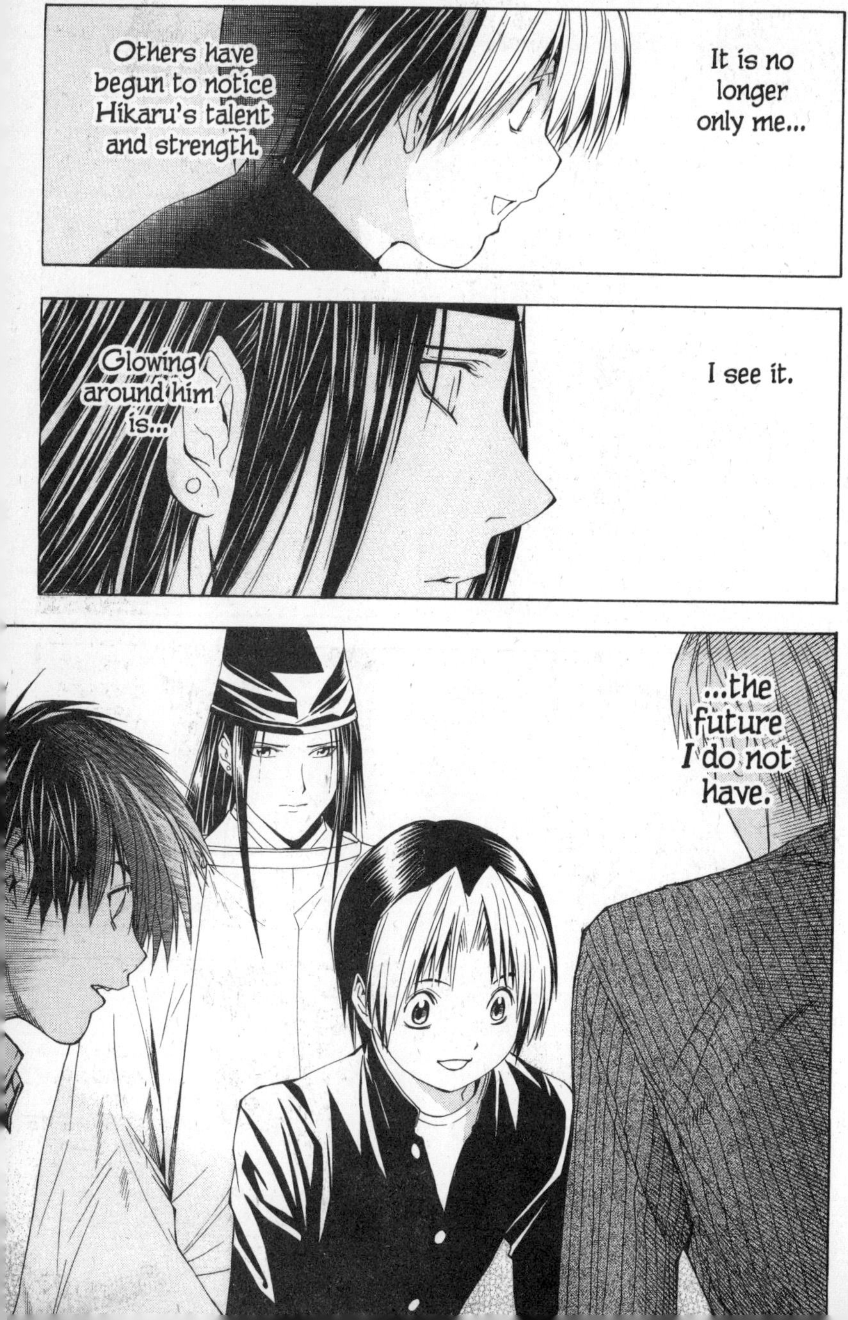
It is no longer only me...
Others have begun to notice Hikaru's talent and strength.
I see it.
Glowing around him is...
...the future I do not have.

A WORD ABOUT HIKARU NO GO

ANIME SCRIPTS

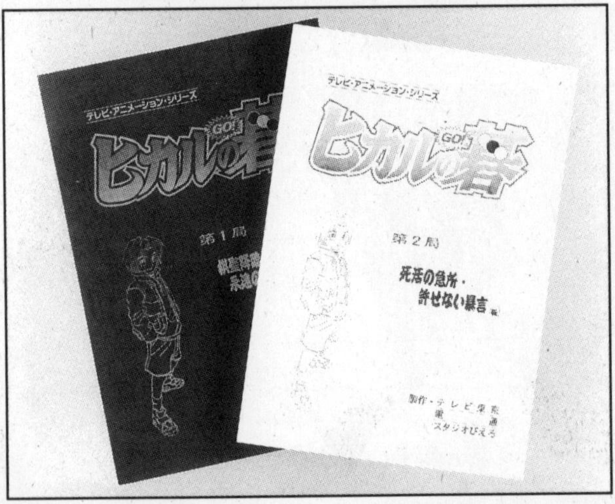
テレビ・アニメーション・シリーズ
ヒカルの碁
第1局
テレビ・アニメーション・シリーズ
ヒカルの碁
第2局
死活の急所・
許せない暴言
スタジオぴえろ

PICTURED ABOVE ARE THE SCRIPTS FOR EPISODES 1 AND 2 OF THE HIKARU NO GO ANIME. THE COVERS ALTERNATE BETWEEN BLACK AND WHITE THROUGHOUT THE EPISODES.

PERFECT STYLE FOR A GO ANIME!

THE VOICE ACTORS HOLD THESE IN THEIR HANDS DURING THEIR RECORDING SESSIONS.

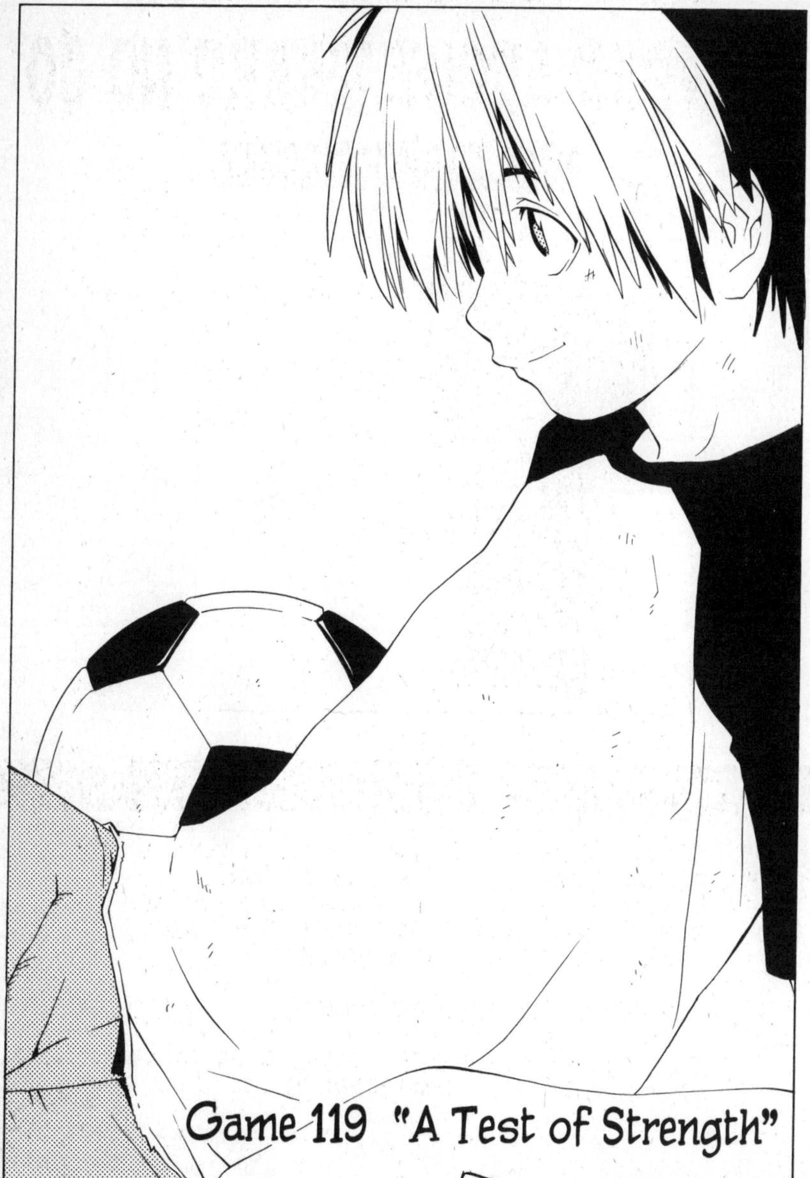
Game 119 "A Test of Strength"

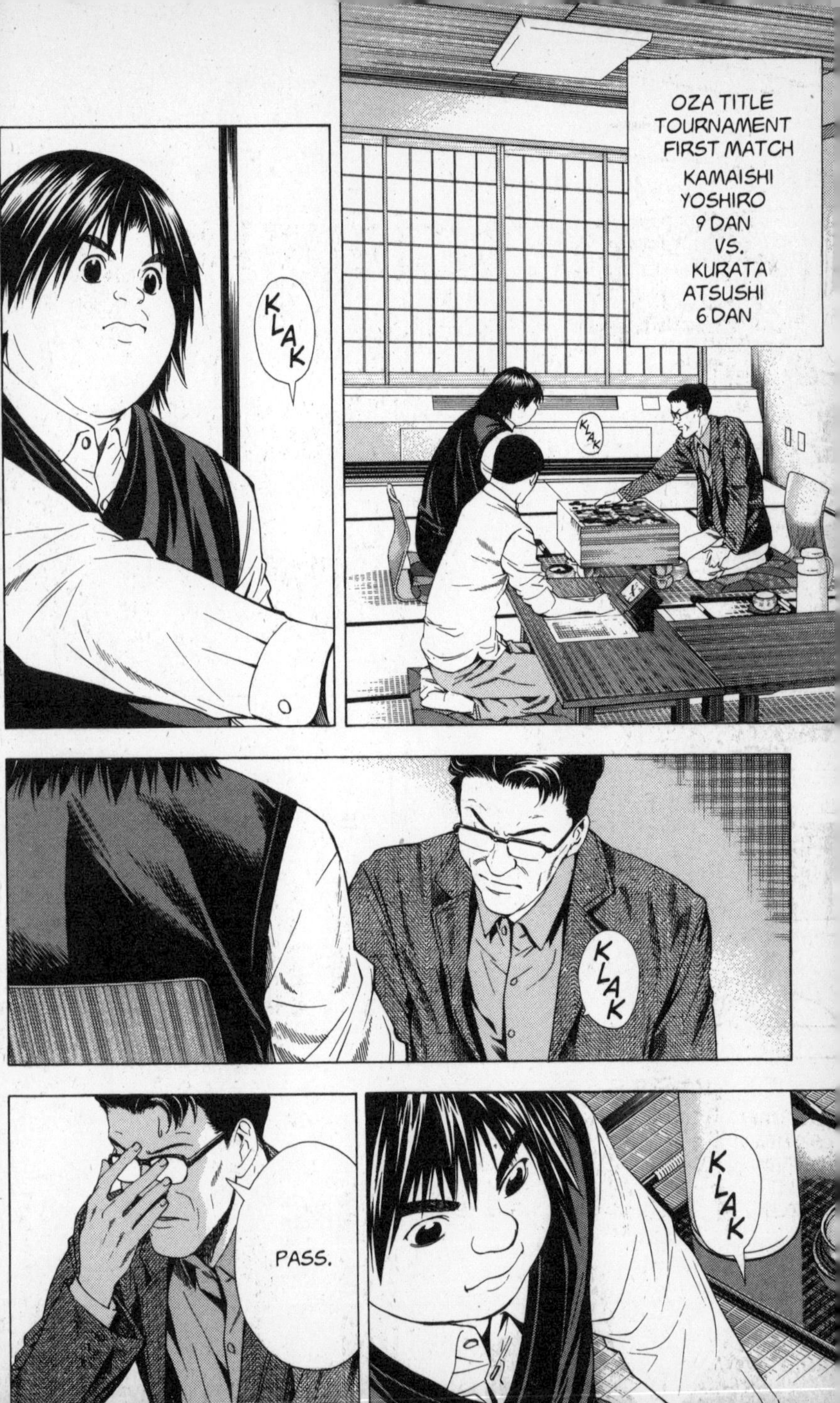
OZA TITLE TOURNAMENT FIRST MATCH
KAMAISHI YOSHIRO 9 DAN VS. KURATA ATSUSHI 6 DAN
KLAK
KLAK
KLAK
KLAK
PASS.

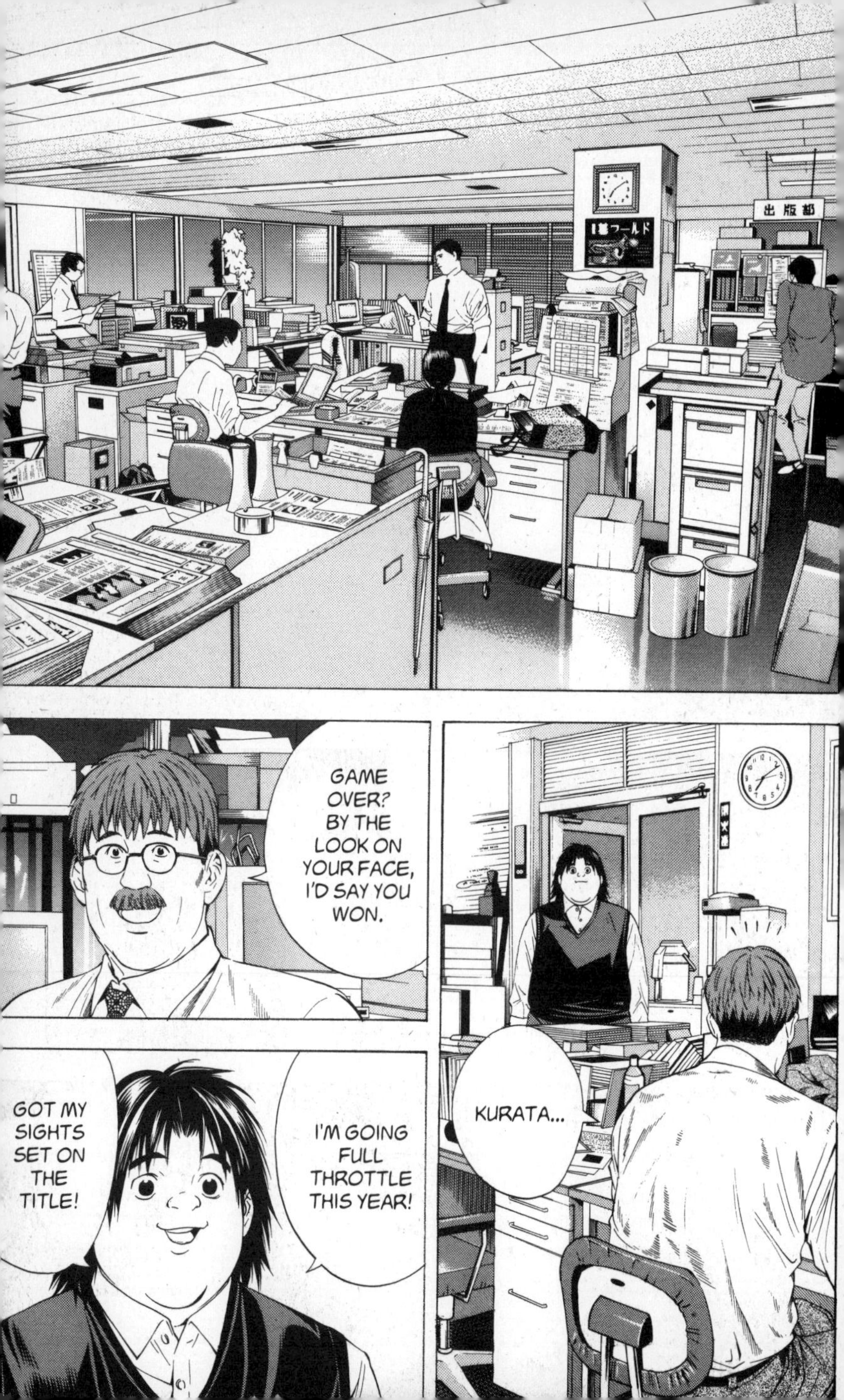
出版部
KURATA...
GAME OVER? BY THE LOOK ON YOUR FACE, I'D SAY YOU WON.
I'M GOING FULL THROTTLE THIS YEAR!
GOT MY SIGHTS SET ON THE TITLE!

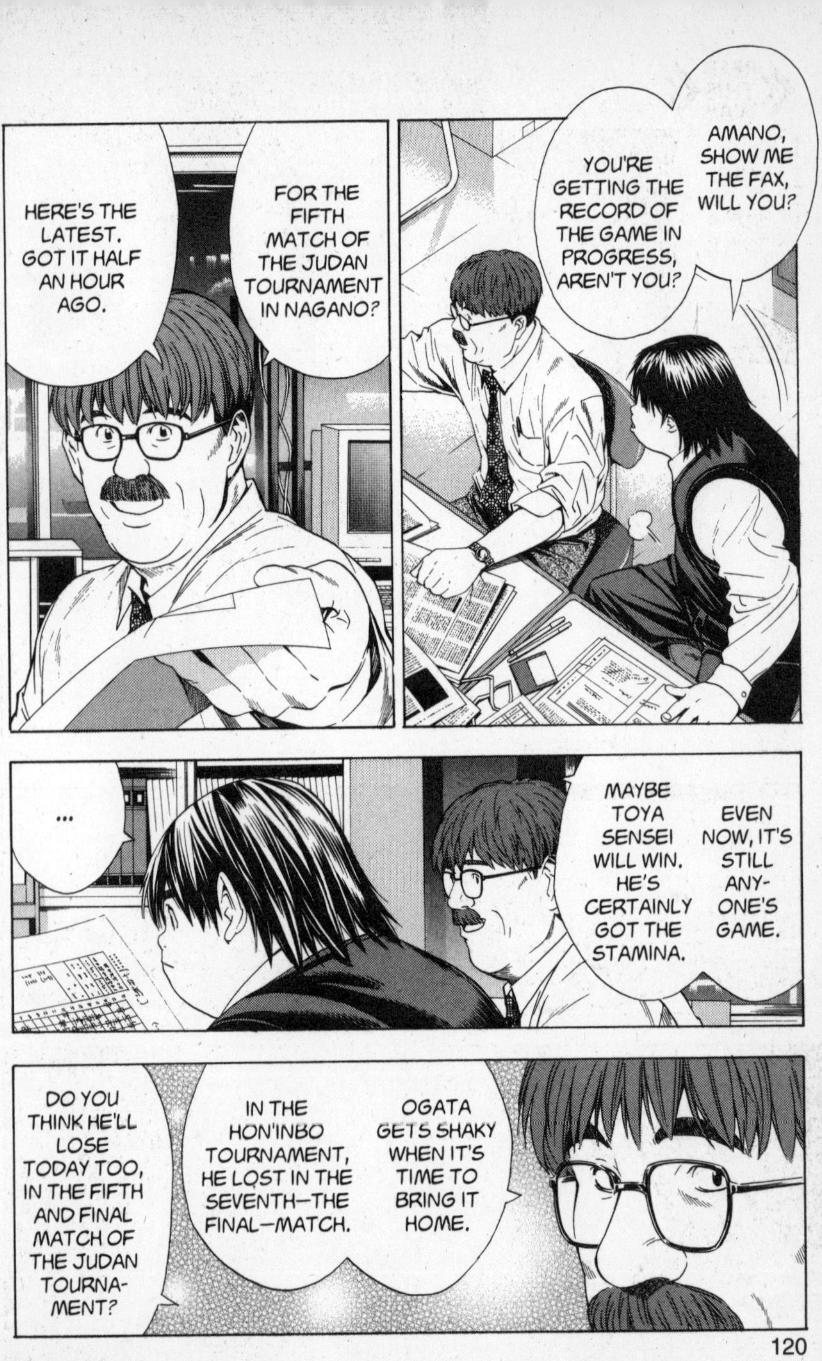
AMANO, SHOW ME THE FAX, WILL YOU?
YOU'RE GETTING THE RECORD OF THE GAME IN PROGRESS, AREN'T YOU?
FOR THE FIFTH MATCH OF THE JUDAN TOURNAMENT IN NAGANO?
HERE'S THE LATEST. GOT IT HALF AN HOUR AGO.
EVEN NOW, IT'S STILL ANY-ONE'S GAME.
MAYBE TOYA SENSEI WILL WIN. HE'S CERTAINLY GOT THE STAMINA.
...
OGATA GETS SHAKY WHEN IT'S TIME TO BRING IT HOME.
IN THE HON'INBO TOURNAMENT, HE LOST IN THE SEVENTH—THE FINAL—MATCH.
DO YOU THINK HE'LL LOSE TODAY TOO, IN THE FIFTH AND FINAL MATCH OF THE JUDAN TOURNA-MENT?

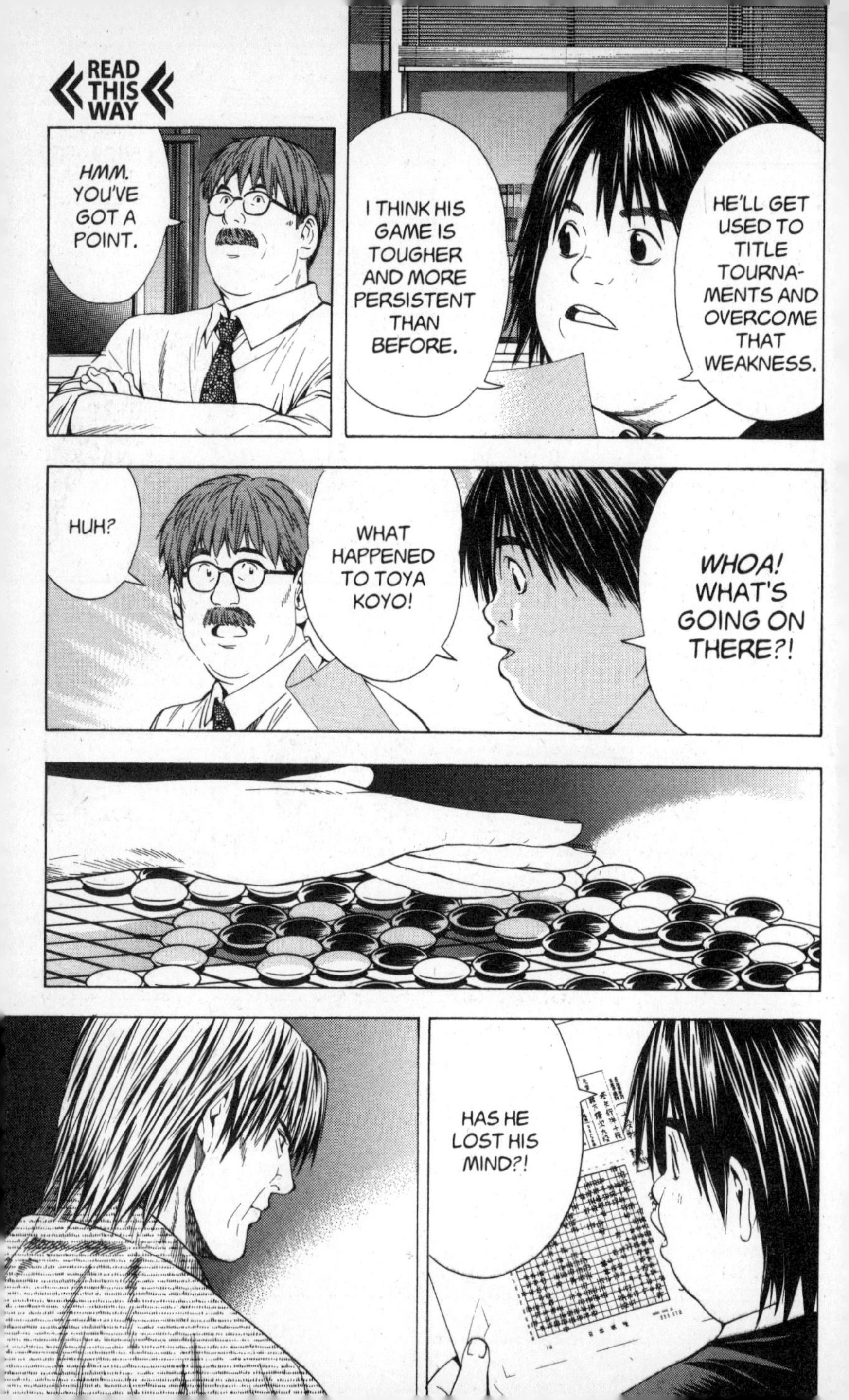
READ THIS WAY
HE'LL GET USED TO TITLE TOURNA-MENTS AND OVERCOME THAT WEAKNESS.
I THINK HIS GAME IS TOUGHER AND MORE PERSISTENT THAN BEFORE.
HMM. YOU'VE GOT A POINT.
WHOA! WHAT'S GOING ON THERE?!
WHAT HAPPENED TO TOYA KOYO!
HUH?
HAS HE LOST HIS MIND?!

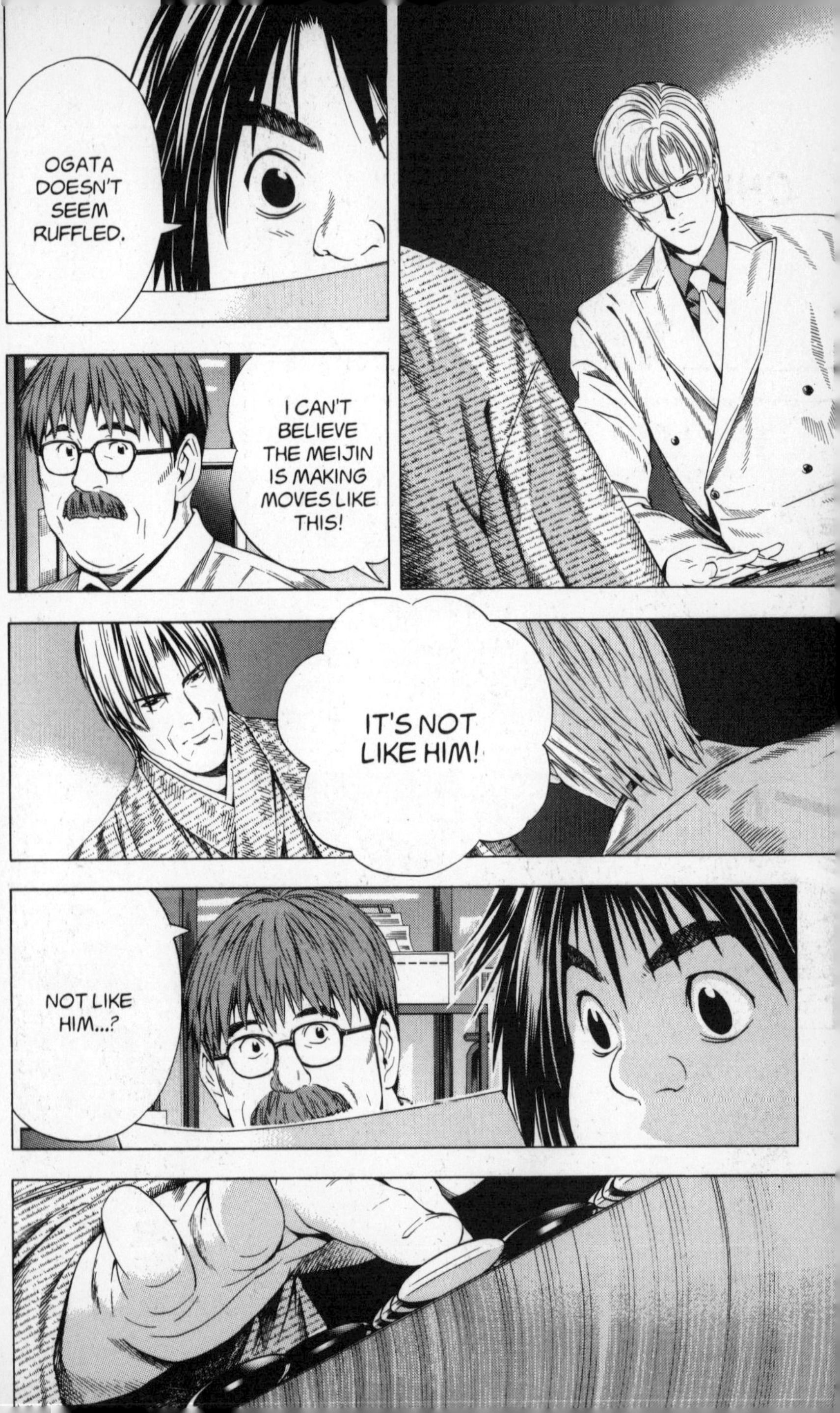
OGATA DOESN'T SEEM RUFFLED.
I CAN'T BELIEVE THE MEIJIN IS MAKING MOVES LIKE THIS!
IT'S NOT LIKE HIM!
NOT LIKE HIM...?

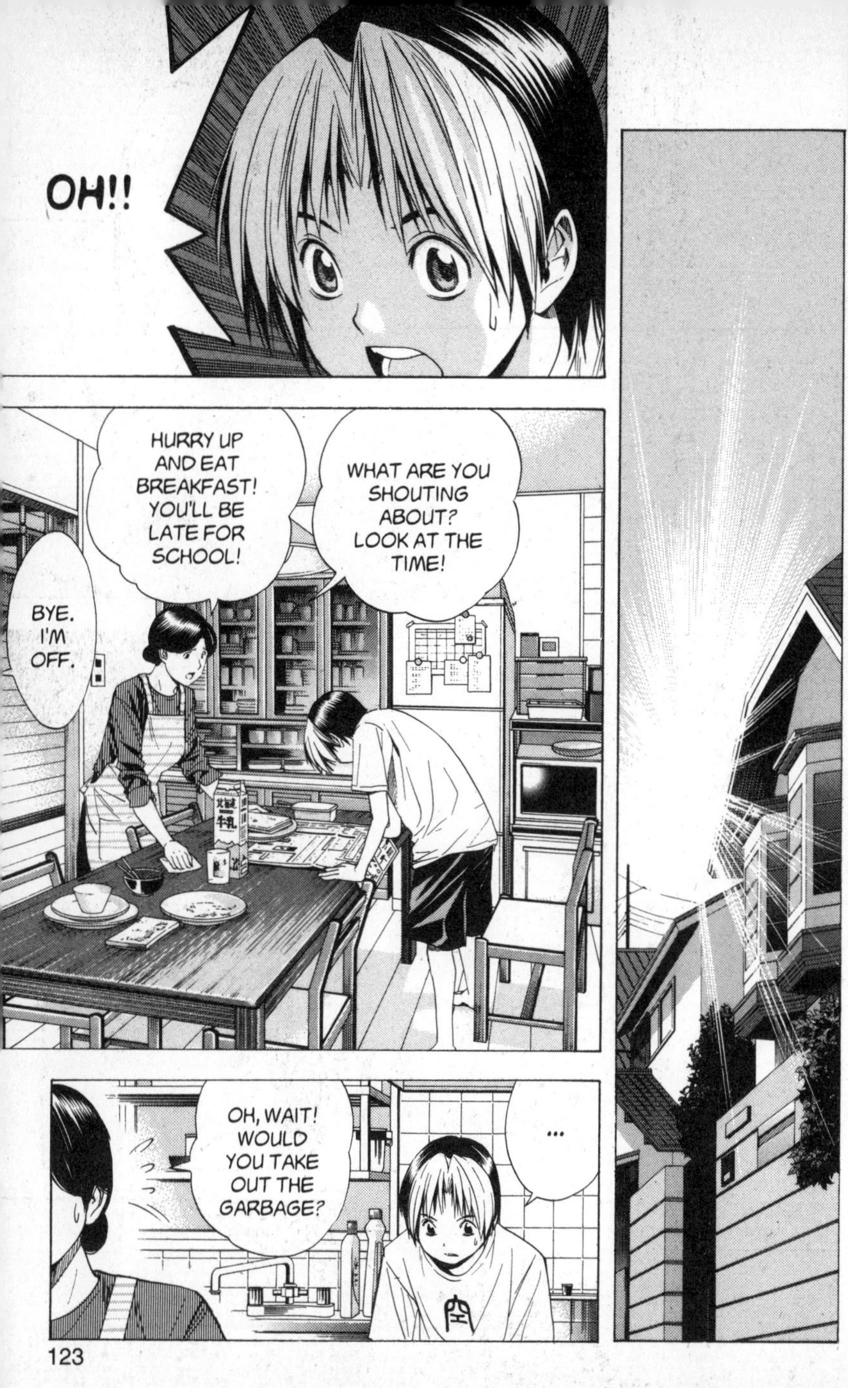
OH!!
WHAT ARE YOU SHOUTING ABOUT? LOOK AT THE TIME!
HURRY UP AND EAT BREAKFAST! YOU'LL BE LATE FOR SCHOOL!
BYE. I'M OFF.
...
OH, WAIT! WOULD YOU TAKE OUT THE GARBAGE?

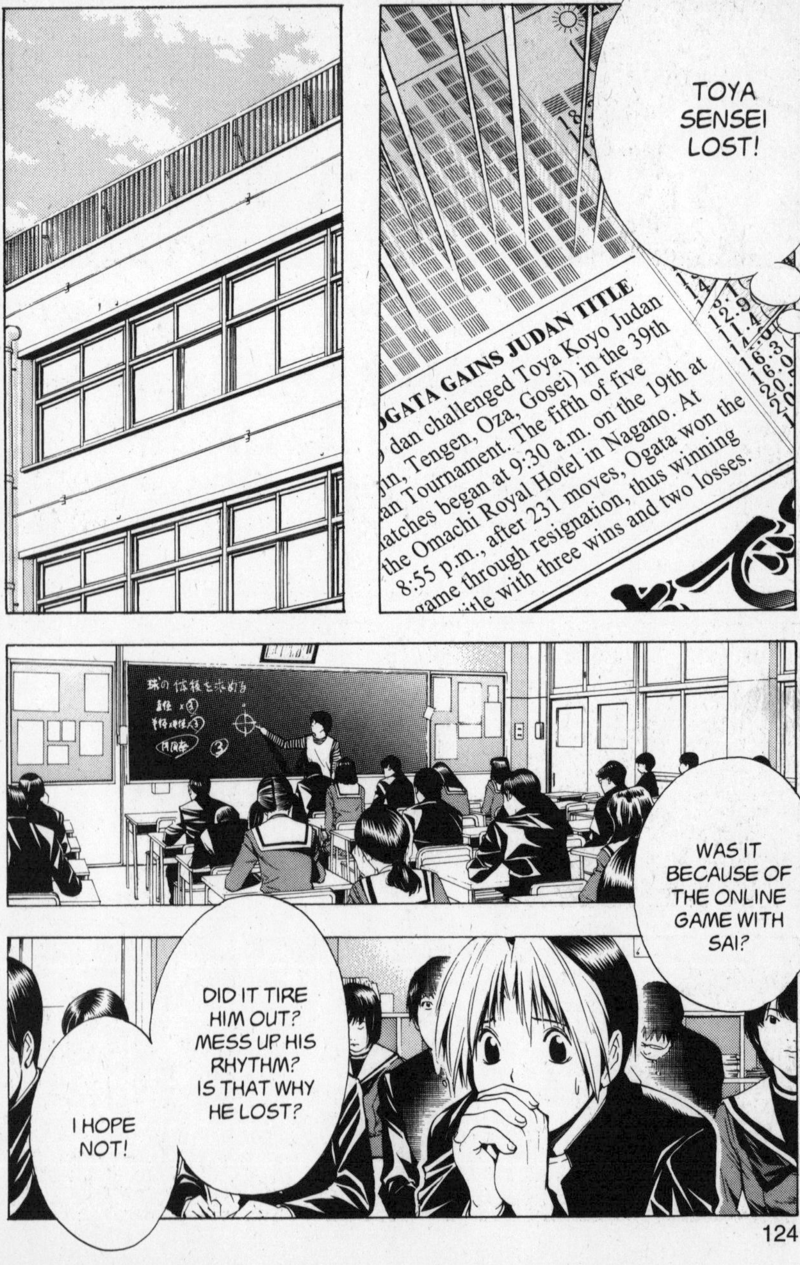
TOYA SENSEI LOST!
OGATA GAINS JUDAN TITLE
dan challenged Toya Koyo Judan
n, Tengen, Oza, Gosei) in the 39th
an Tournament. The fifth of five
atches began at 9:30 a.m. on the 19th at
the Omachi Royal Hotel in Nagano. At
8:55 p.m., after 231 moves, Ogata won the
game through resignation, thus winning
itle with three wins and two losses.
WAS IT BECAUSE OF THE ONLINE GAME WITH SAI?
DID IT TIRE HIM OUT? MESS UP HIS RHYTHM? IS THAT WHY HE LOST?
I HOPE NOT!

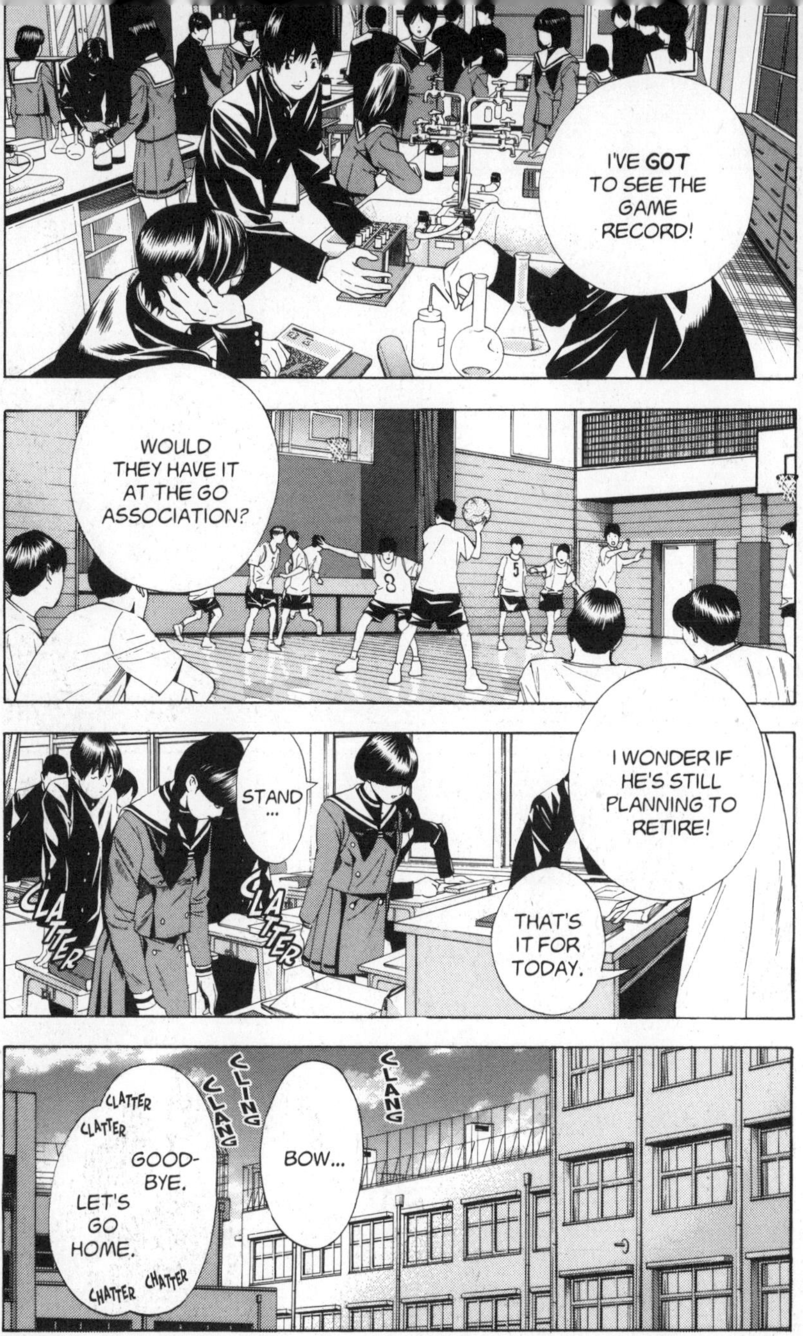
I'VE GOT TO SEE THE GAME RECORD!
WOULD THEY HAVE IT AT THE GO ASSOCIATION?
I WONDER IF HE'S STILL PLANNING TO RETIRE!
THAT'S IT FOR TODAY.
STAND ...
CLATTER
CLATTER
CLANG
BOW...
CLING
CLANG
GOOD-BYE.
LET'S GO HOME.
CLATTER
CLATTER
CHATTER
CHATTER

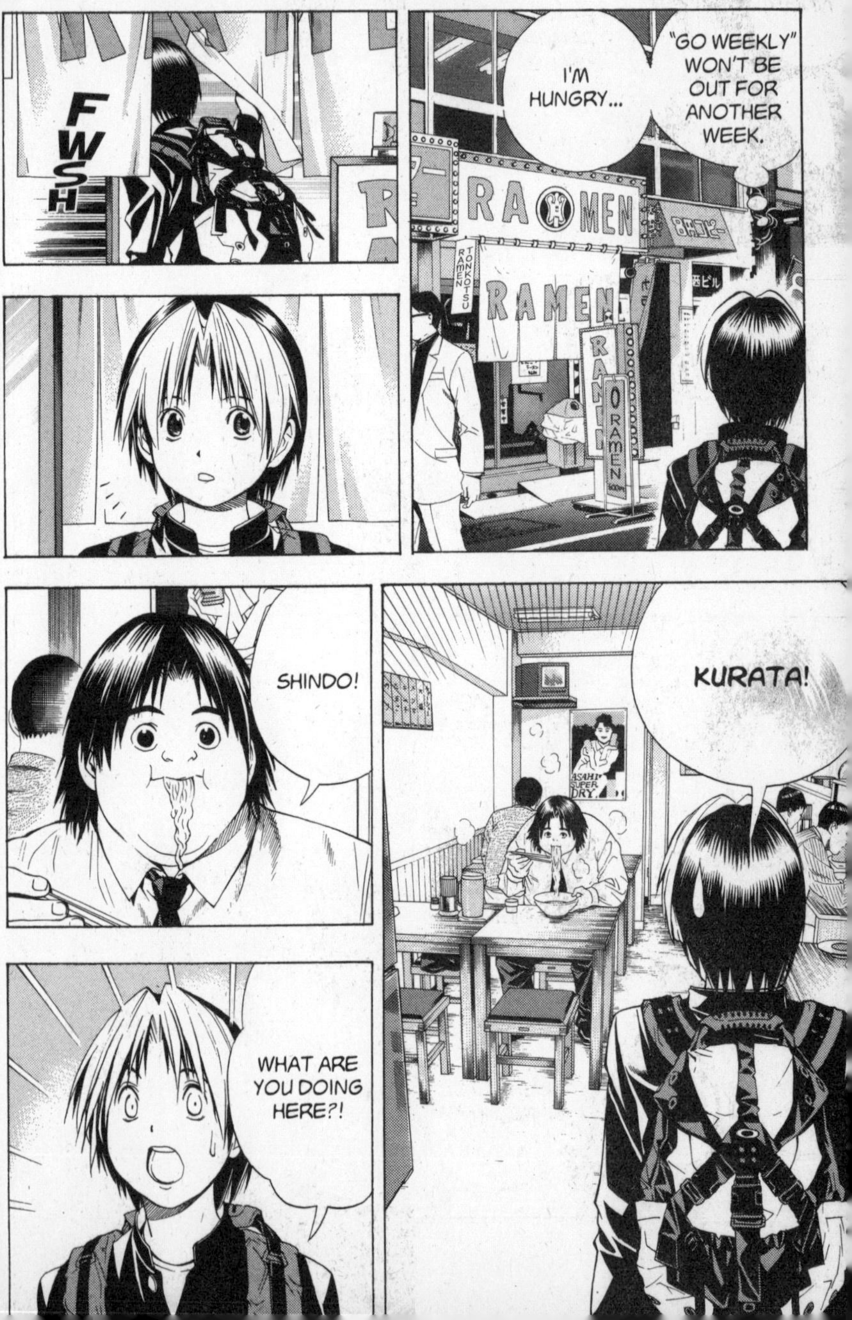
"GO WEEKLY" WON'T BE OUT FOR ANOTHER WEEK.
I'M HUNGRY...
RA MEN
TONKOTSU RAMEN
RAMEN
RAMEN
FWSH
KURATA!
ASAHI SUPER DRY
SHINDO!
WHAT ARE YOU DOING HERE?!

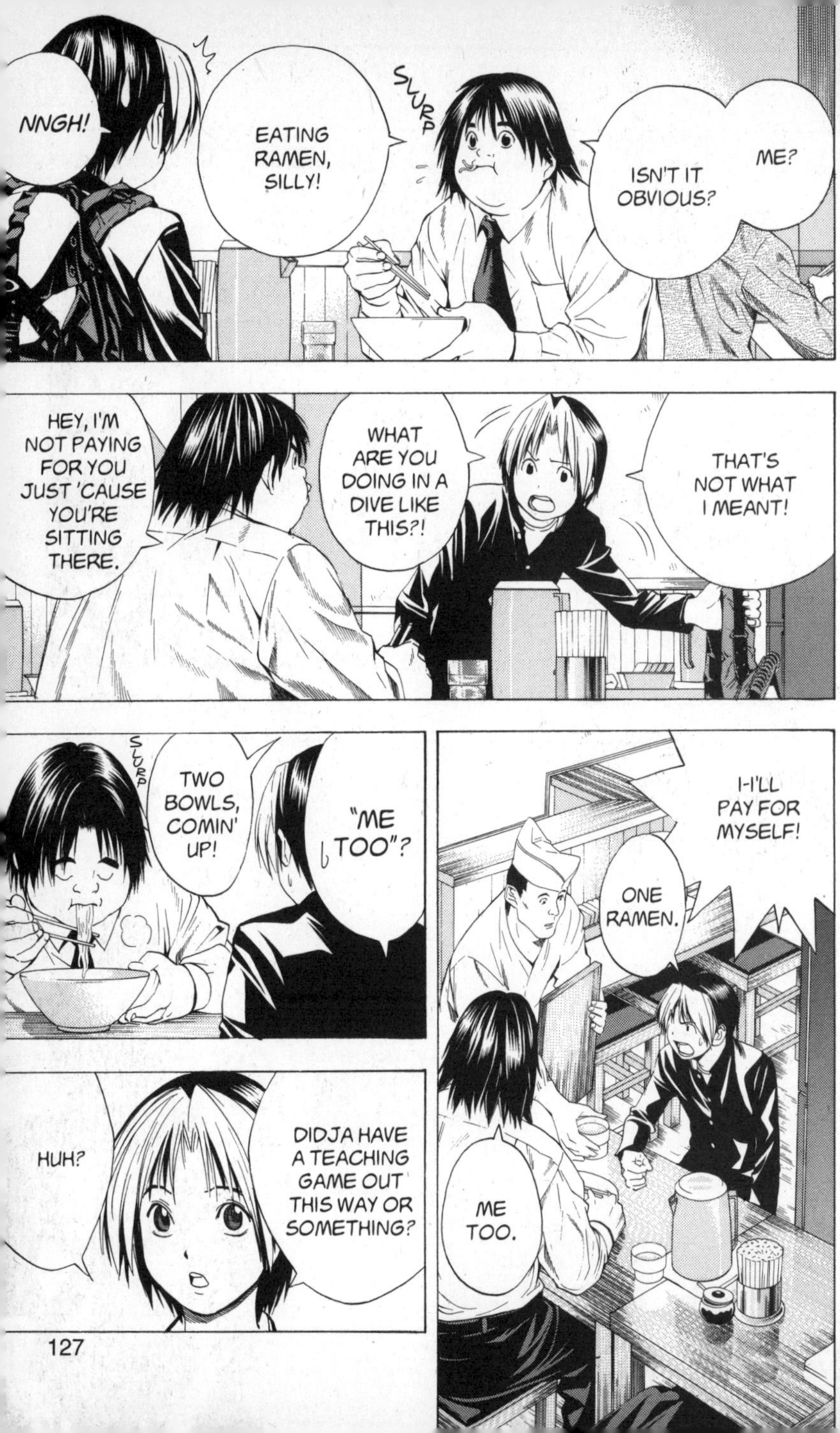
ME?
ISN'T IT OBVIOUS?
SLURP
EATING RAMEN, SILLY!
NNGH!
THAT'S NOT WHAT I MEANT!
WHAT ARE YOU DOING IN A DIVE LIKE THIS?!
HEY, I'M NOT PAYING FOR YOU JUST 'CAUSE YOU'RE SITTING THERE.
I-I'LL PAY FOR MYSELF!
ONE RAMEN.
ME TOO.
"ME TOO"?
TWO BOWLS, COMIN' UP!
SLURP
DIDJA HAVE A TEACHING GAME OUT THIS WAY OR SOMETHING?
HUH?

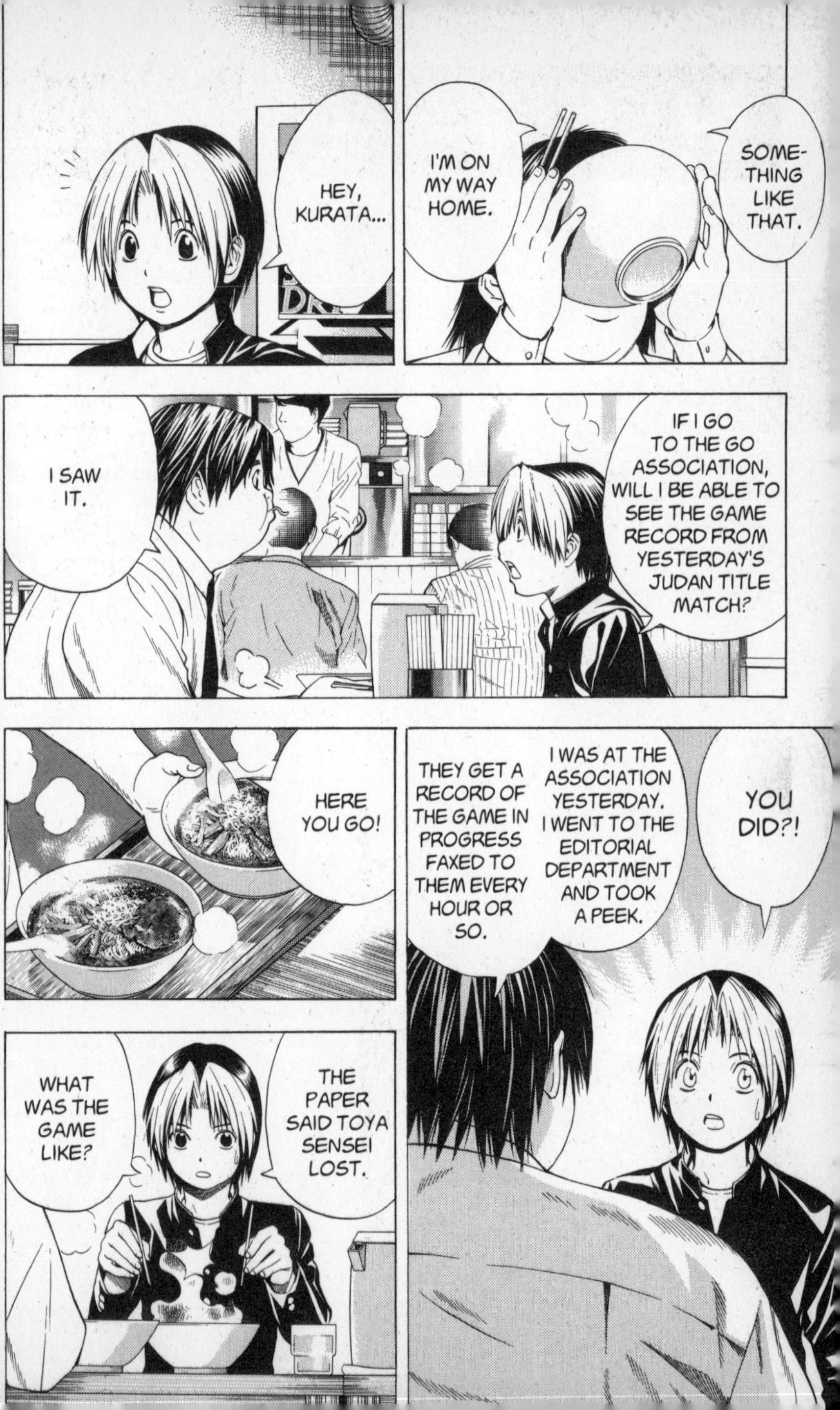
SOME-THING LIKE THAT.
I'M ON MY WAY HOME.
HEY, KURATA...
IF I GO TO THE GO ASSOCIATION, WILL I BE ABLE TO SEE THE GAME RECORD FROM YESTERDAY'S JUDAN TITLE MATCH?
I SAW IT.
YOU DID?!
I WAS AT THE ASSOCIATION YESTERDAY. I WENT TO THE EDITORIAL DEPARTMENT AND TOOK A PEEK.
THEY GET A RECORD OF THE GAME IN PROGRESS FAXED TO THEM EVERY HOUR OR SO.
HERE YOU GO!
THE PAPER SAID TOYA SENSEI LOST.
WHAT WAS THE GAME LIKE?

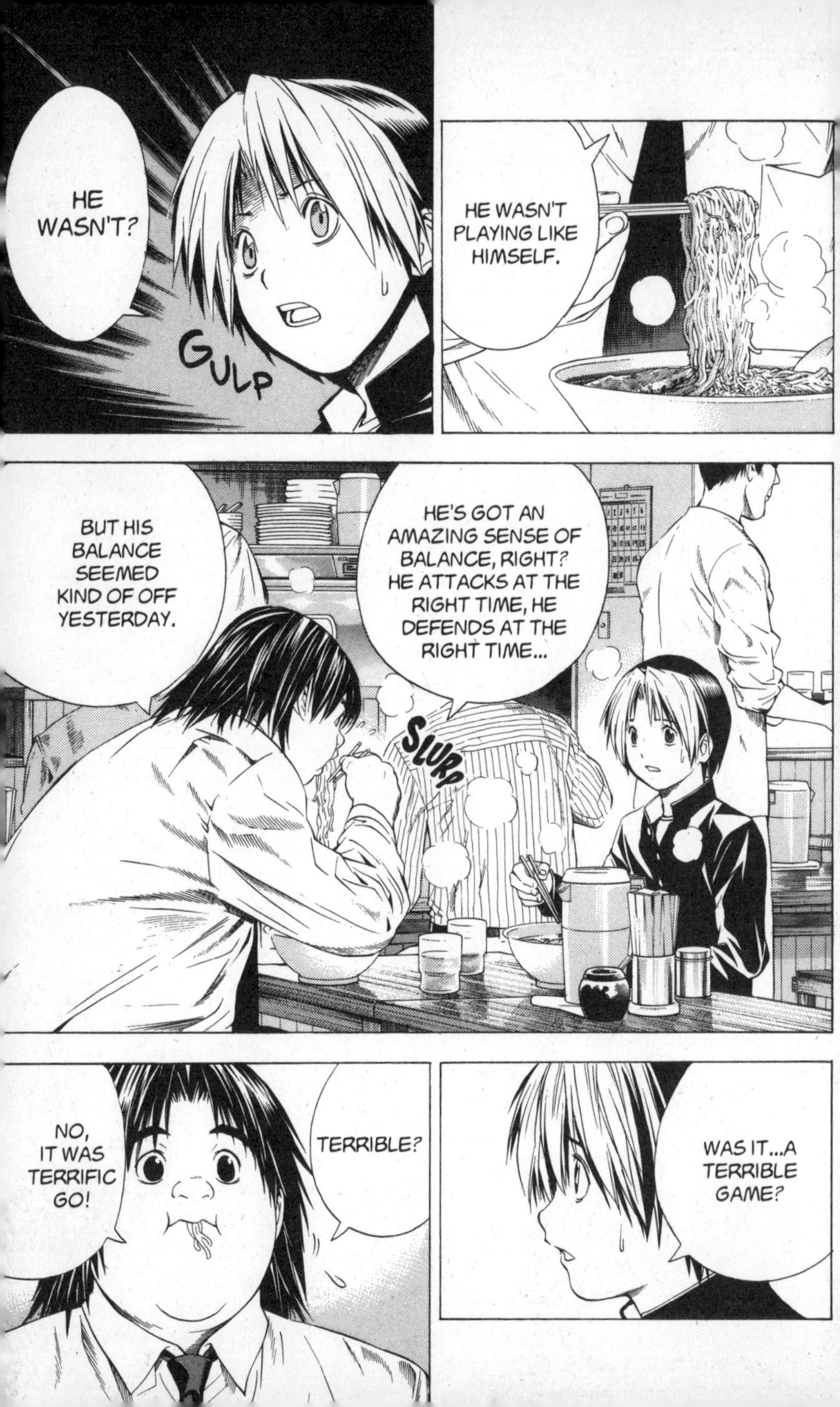
HE WASN'T PLAYING LIKE HIMSELF.
HE WASN'T?
GULP
HE'S GOT AN AMAZING SENSE OF BALANCE, RIGHT? HE ATTACKS AT THE RIGHT TIME, HE DEFENDS AT THE RIGHT TIME...
BUT HIS BALANCE SEEMED KIND OF OFF YESTERDAY.
SLURP
WAS IT...A TERRIBLE GAME?
TERRIBLE?
NO, IT WAS TERRIFIC GO!

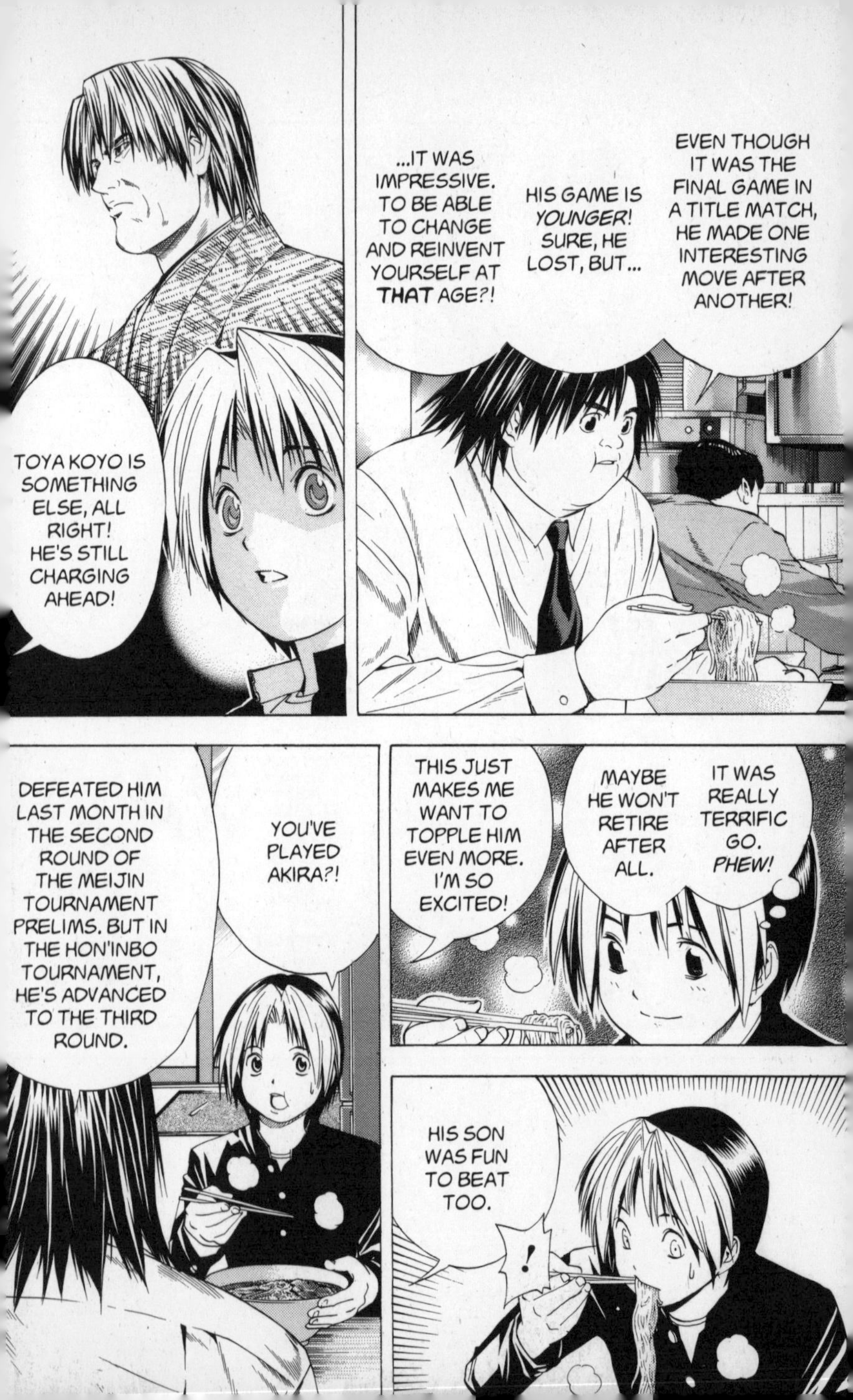
EVEN THOUGH IT WAS THE FINAL GAME IN A TITLE MATCH, HE MADE ONE INTERESTING MOVE AFTER ANOTHER!
HIS GAME IS *YOUNGER*! SURE, HE LOST, BUT...
...IT WAS IMPRESSIVE. TO BE ABLE TO CHANGE AND REINVENT YOURSELF AT **THAT** AGE?!
TOYA KOYO IS SOMETHING ELSE, ALL RIGHT! HE'S STILL CHARGING AHEAD!
IT WAS REALLY TERRIFIC GO. *PHEW!*
MAYBE HE WON'T RETIRE AFTER ALL.
THIS JUST MAKES ME WANT TO TOPPLE HIM EVEN MORE. I'M SO EXCITED!
HIS SON WAS FUN TO BEAT TOO.
!
YOU'VE PLAYED AKIRA?!
DEFEATED HIM LAST MONTH IN THE SECOND ROUND OF THE MEIJIN TOURNAMENT PRELIMS. BUT IN THE HON'INBO TOURNAMENT, HE'S ADVANCED TO THE THIRD ROUND.

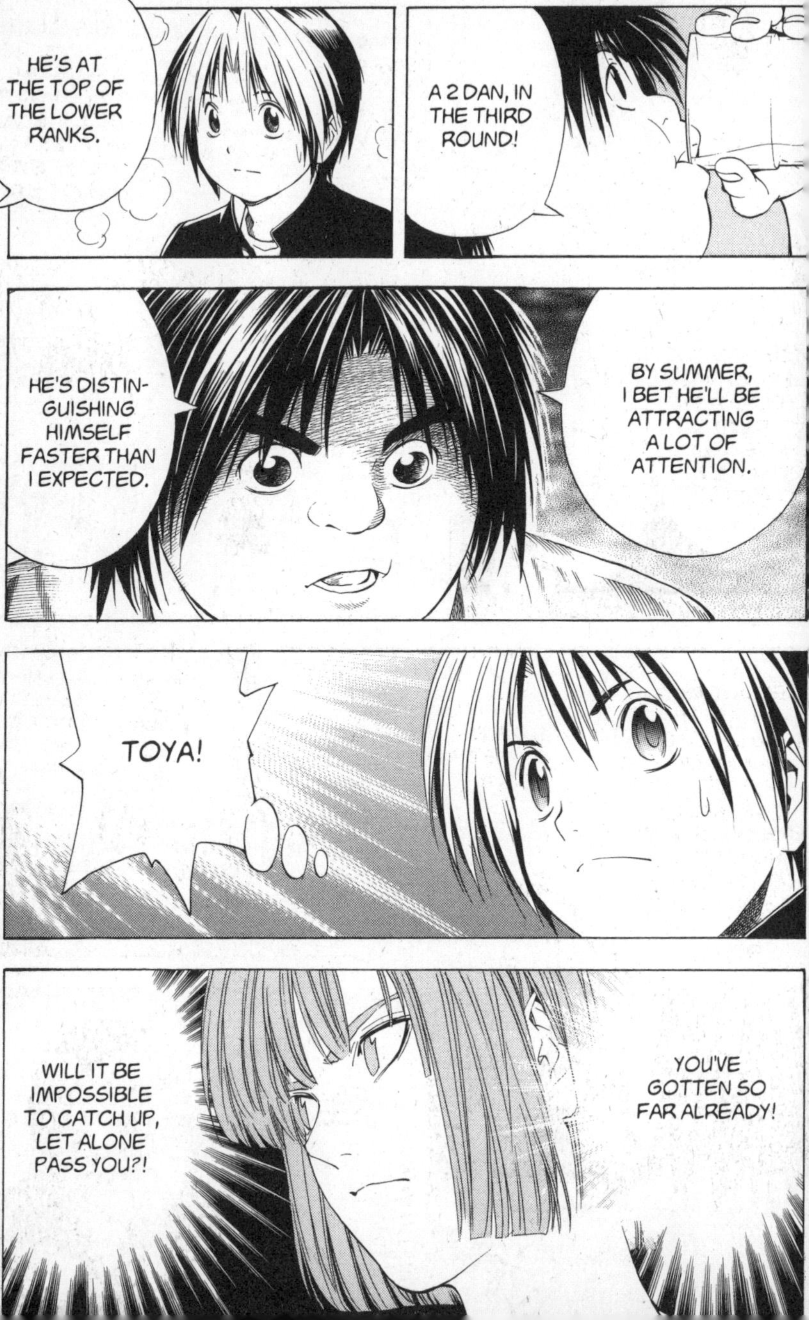
A 2 DAN, IN THE THIRD ROUND!
HE'S AT THE TOP OF THE LOWER RANKS.
BY SUMMER, I BET HE'LL BE ATTRACTING A LOT OF ATTENTION.
HE'S DISTIN-GUISHING HIMSELF FASTER THAN I EXPECTED.
TOYA!
YOU'VE GOTTEN SO FAR ALREADY!
WILL IT BE IMPOSSIBLE TO CATCH UP, LET ALONE PASS YOU?!

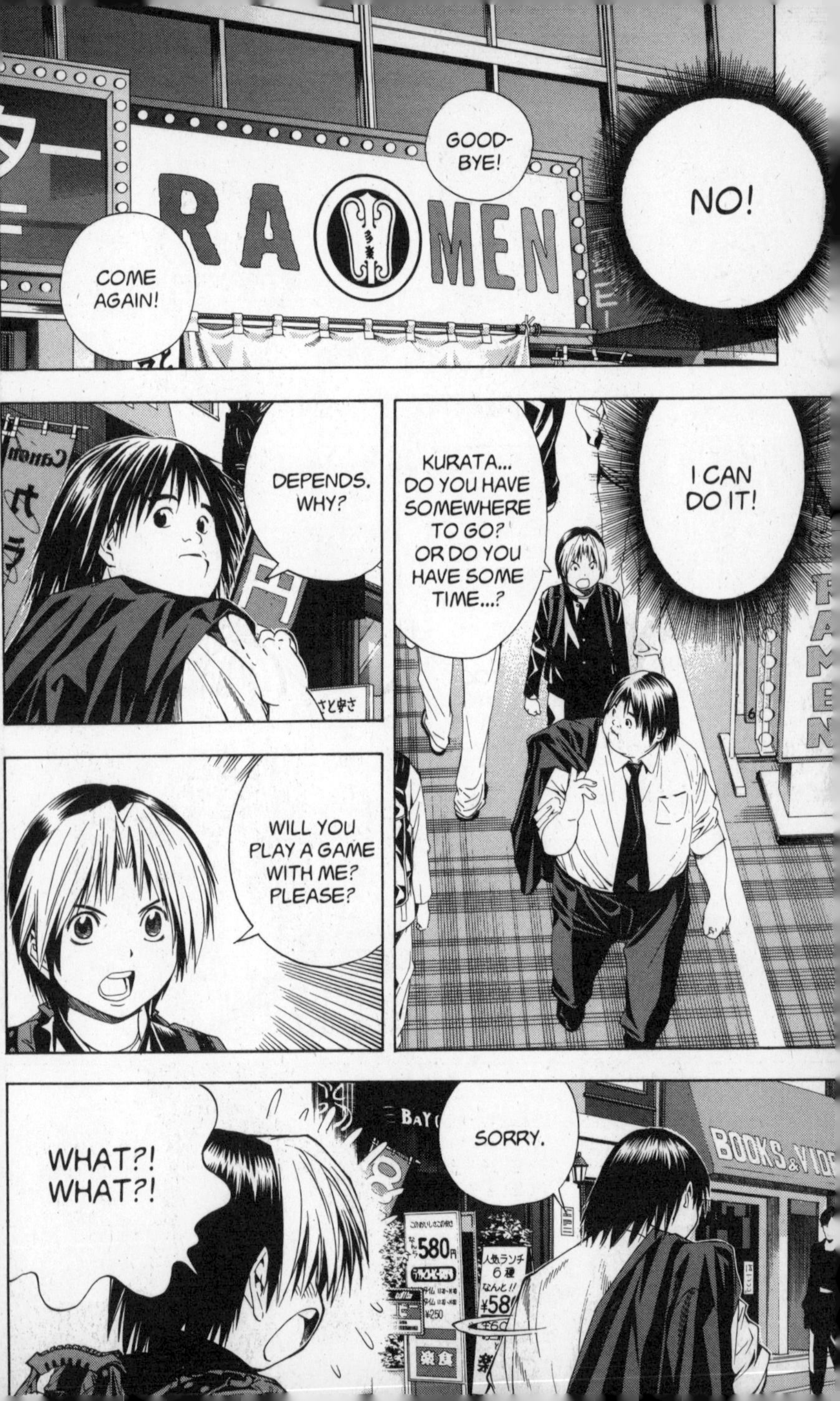
NO!
GOOD-BYE!
COME AGAIN!
I CAN DO IT!
KURATA... DO YOU HAVE SOMEWHERE TO GO? OR DO YOU HAVE SOME TIME...?
DEPENDS. WHY?
WILL YOU PLAY A GAME WITH ME? PLEASE?
SORRY.
WHAT?! WHAT?!

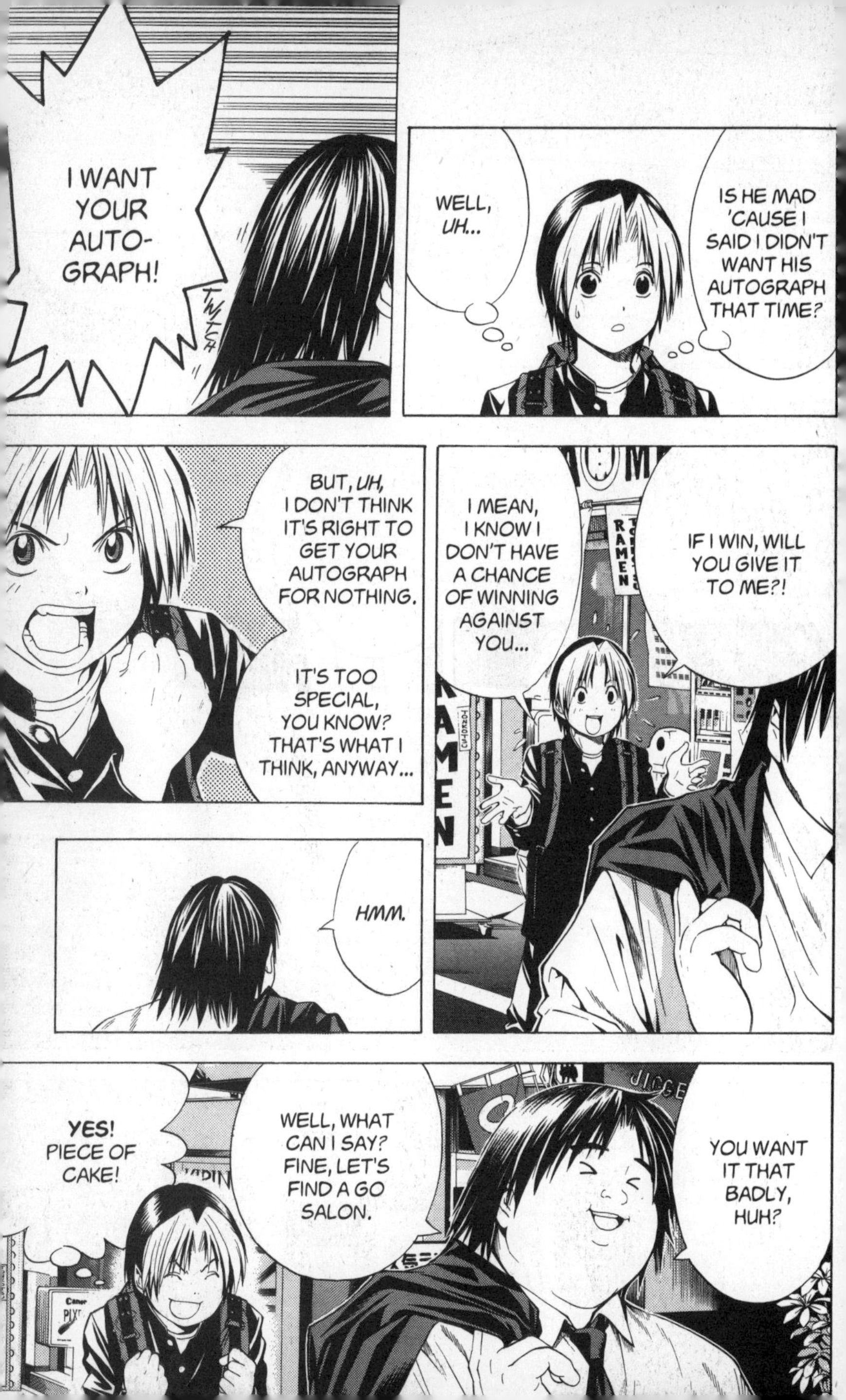
IS HE MAD 'CAUSE I SAID I DIDN'T WANT HIS AUTOGRAPH THAT TIME?
WELL, UH...
I WANT YOUR AUTO-GRAPH!
TWITCH
IF I WIN, WILL YOU GIVE IT TO ME?!
I MEAN, I KNOW I DON'T HAVE A CHANCE OF WINNING AGAINST YOU...
RAMEN
RAMEN
BUT, UH, I DON'T THINK IT'S RIGHT TO GET YOUR AUTOGRAPH FOR NOTHING.
IT'S TOO SPECIAL, YOU KNOW? THAT'S WHAT I THINK, ANYWAY...
HMM.
YOU WANT IT THAT BADLY, HUH?
WELL, WHAT CAN I SAY? FINE, LET'S FIND A GO SALON.
YES! PIECE OF CAKE!

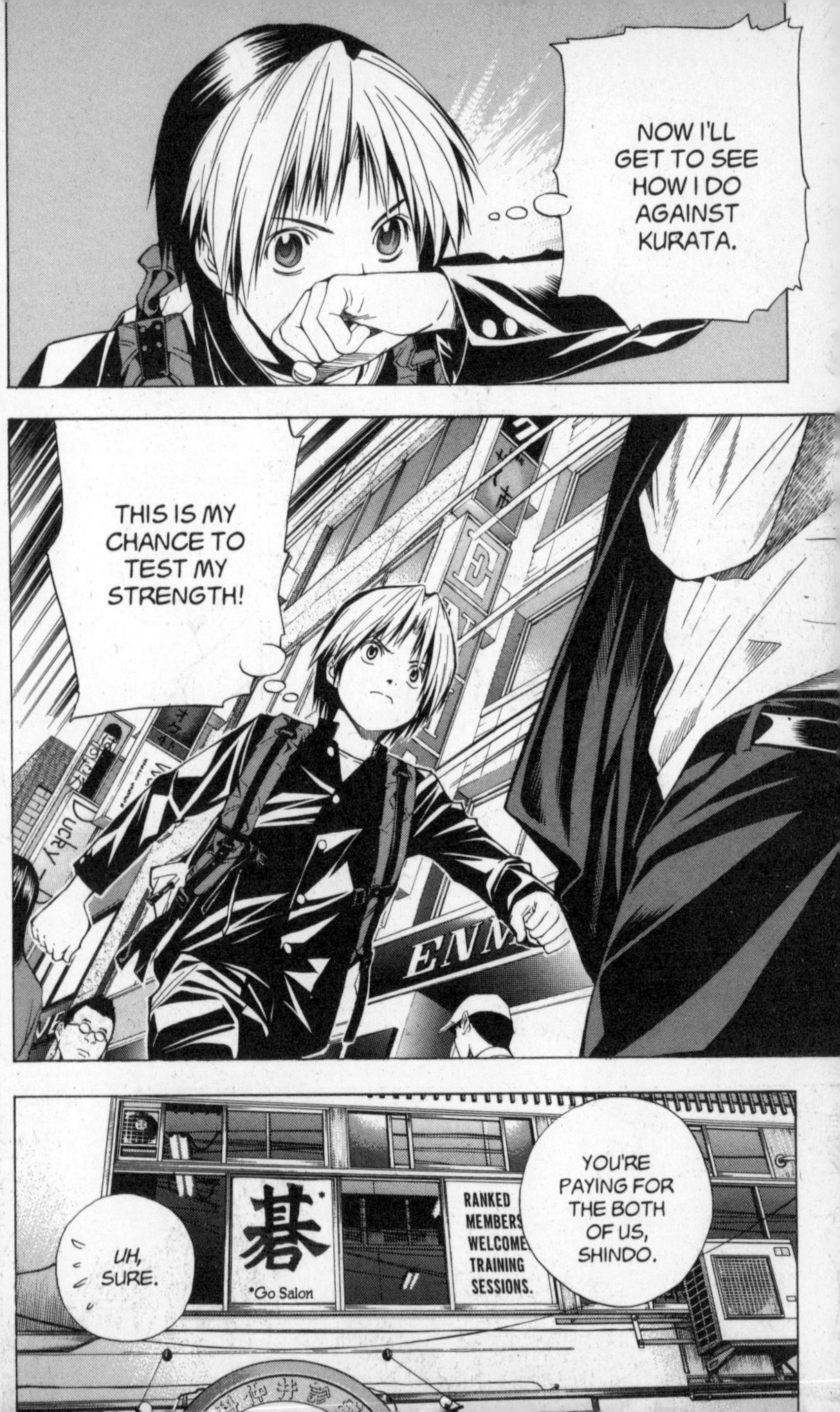
NOW I'LL GET TO SEE HOW I DO AGAINST KURATA.
THIS IS MY CHANCE TO TEST MY STRENGTH!
YOU'RE PAYING FOR THE BOTH OF US, SHINDO.
RANKED MEMBERS WELCOME TRAINING SESSIONS.
碁*
*Go Salon
UH, SURE.

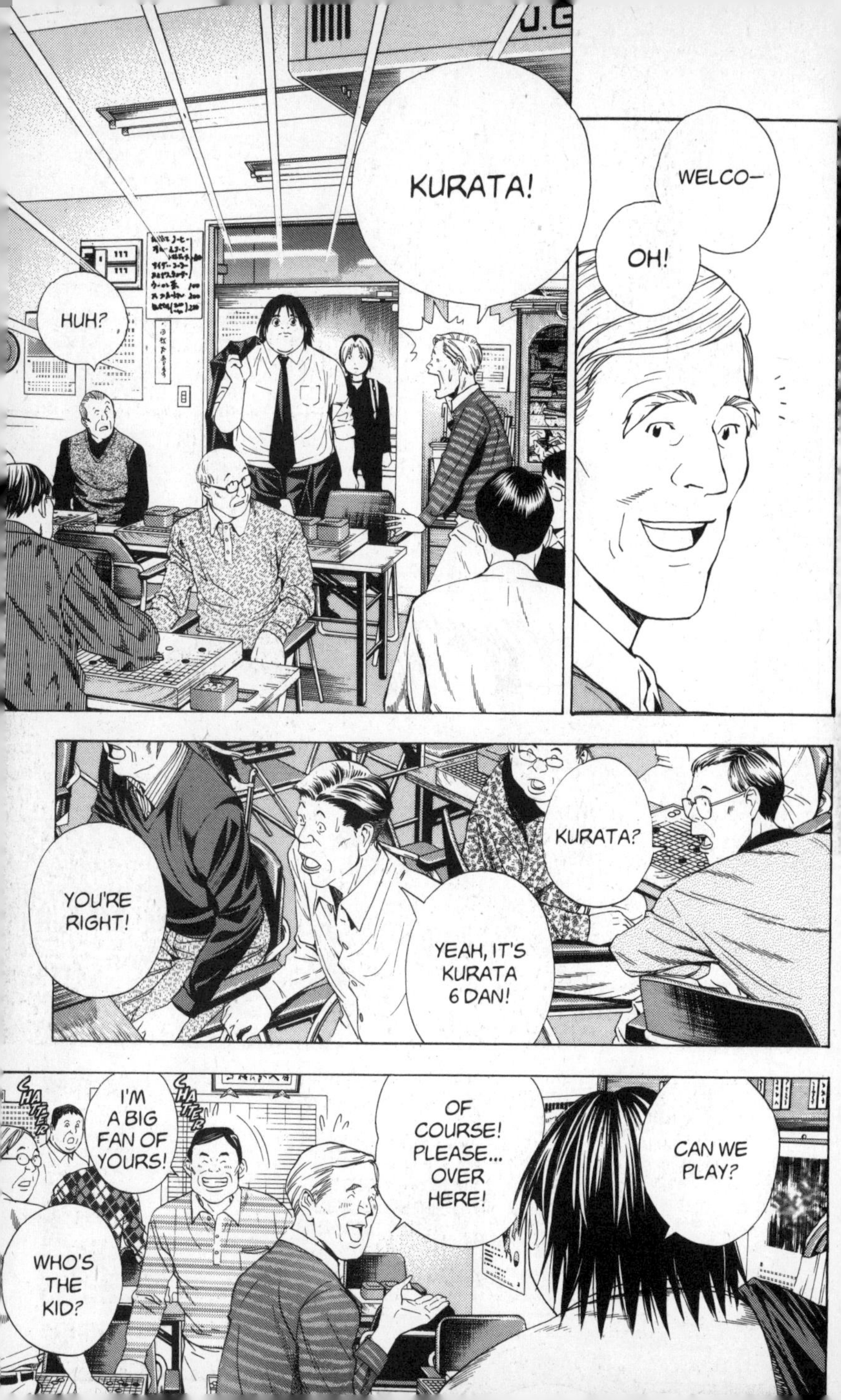
WELCO—
OH!
KURATA!
HUH?
KURATA?
YEAH, IT'S KURATA 6 DAN!
YOU'RE RIGHT!
CAN WE PLAY?
OF COURSE! PLEASE... OVER HERE!
CHATTER
I'M A BIG FAN OF YOURS!
CHATTER
WHO'S THE KID?

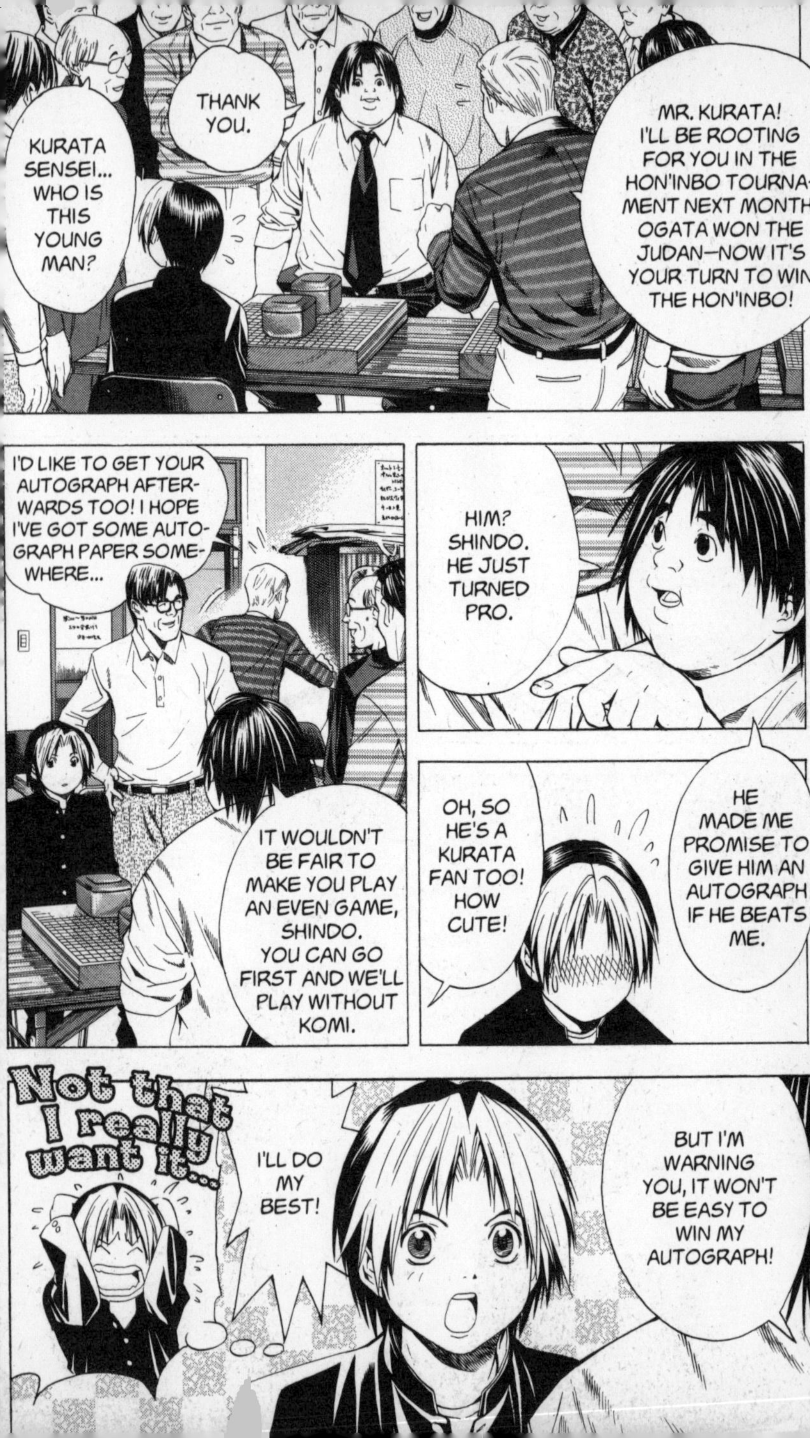
MR. KURATA! I'LL BE ROOTING FOR YOU IN THE HON'INBO TOURNAMENT NEXT MONTH! OGATA WON THE JUDAN—NOW IT'S YOUR TURN TO WIN THE HON'INBO!
THANK YOU.
KURATA SENSEI... WHO IS THIS YOUNG MAN?
HIM? SHINDO. HE JUST TURNED PRO.
HE MADE ME PROMISE TO GIVE HIM AN AUTOGRAPH IF HE BEATS ME.
OH, SO HE'S A KURATA FAN TOO! HOW CUTE!
I'D LIKE TO GET YOUR AUTOGRAPH AFTERWARDS TOO! I HOPE I'VE GOT SOME AUTOGRAPH PAPER SOMEWHERE...
IT WOULDN'T BE FAIR TO MAKE YOU PLAY AN EVEN GAME, SHINDO. YOU CAN GO FIRST AND WE'LL PLAY WITHOUT KOMI.
BUT I'M WARNING YOU, IT WON'T BE EASY TO WIN MY AUTOGRAPH!
I'LL DO MY BEST!
Not that I really want it...

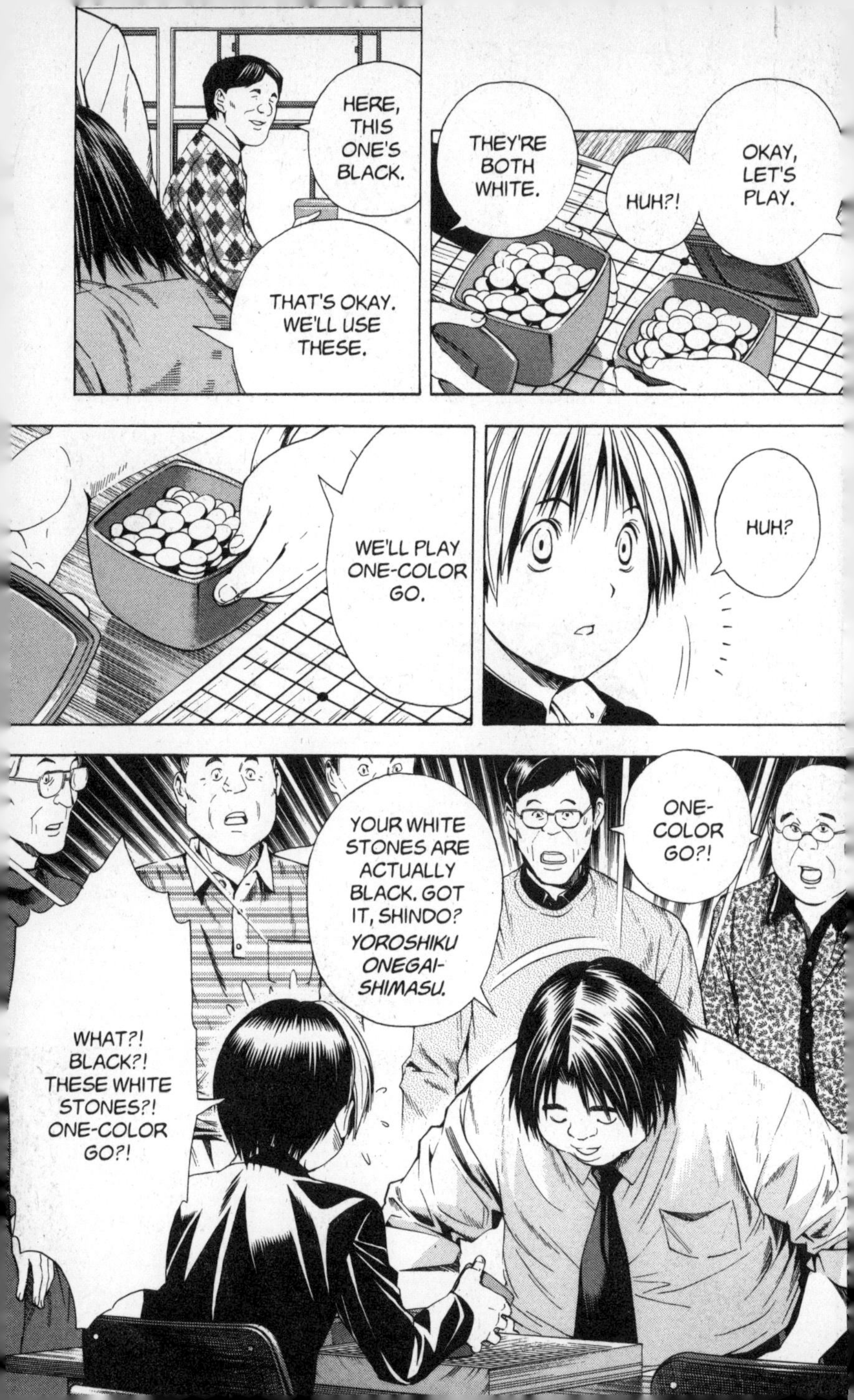
OKAY, LET'S PLAY.
HUH?!
THEY'RE BOTH WHITE.
HERE, THIS ONE'S BLACK.
THAT'S OKAY. WE'LL USE THESE.
HUH?
WE'LL PLAY ONE-COLOR GO.
ONE-COLOR GO?!
YOUR WHITE STONES ARE ACTUALLY BLACK. GOT IT, SHINDO? *YOROSHIKU ONEGAI-SHIMASU.*
WHAT?! BLACK?! THESE WHITE STONES?! ONE-COLOR GO?!

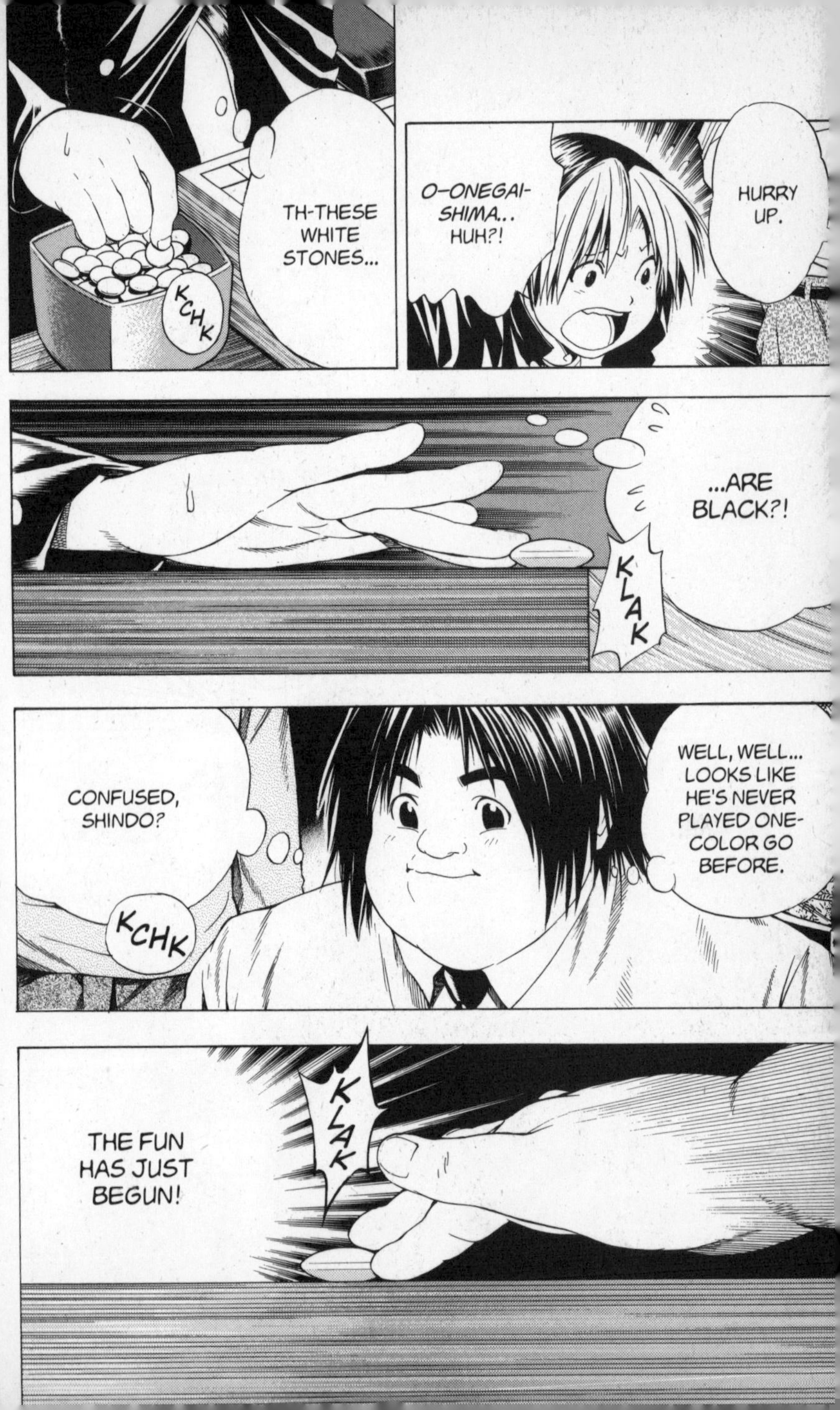
HURRY UP.
O-ONEGAI-SHIMA... HUH?!
TH-THESE WHITE STONES...
KCHK
...ARE BLACK?!
KLAK
WELL, WELL... LOOKS LIKE HE'S NEVER PLAYED ONE-COLOR GO BEFORE.
CONFUSED, SHINDO?
KCHK
KLAK
THE FUN HAS JUST BEGUN!

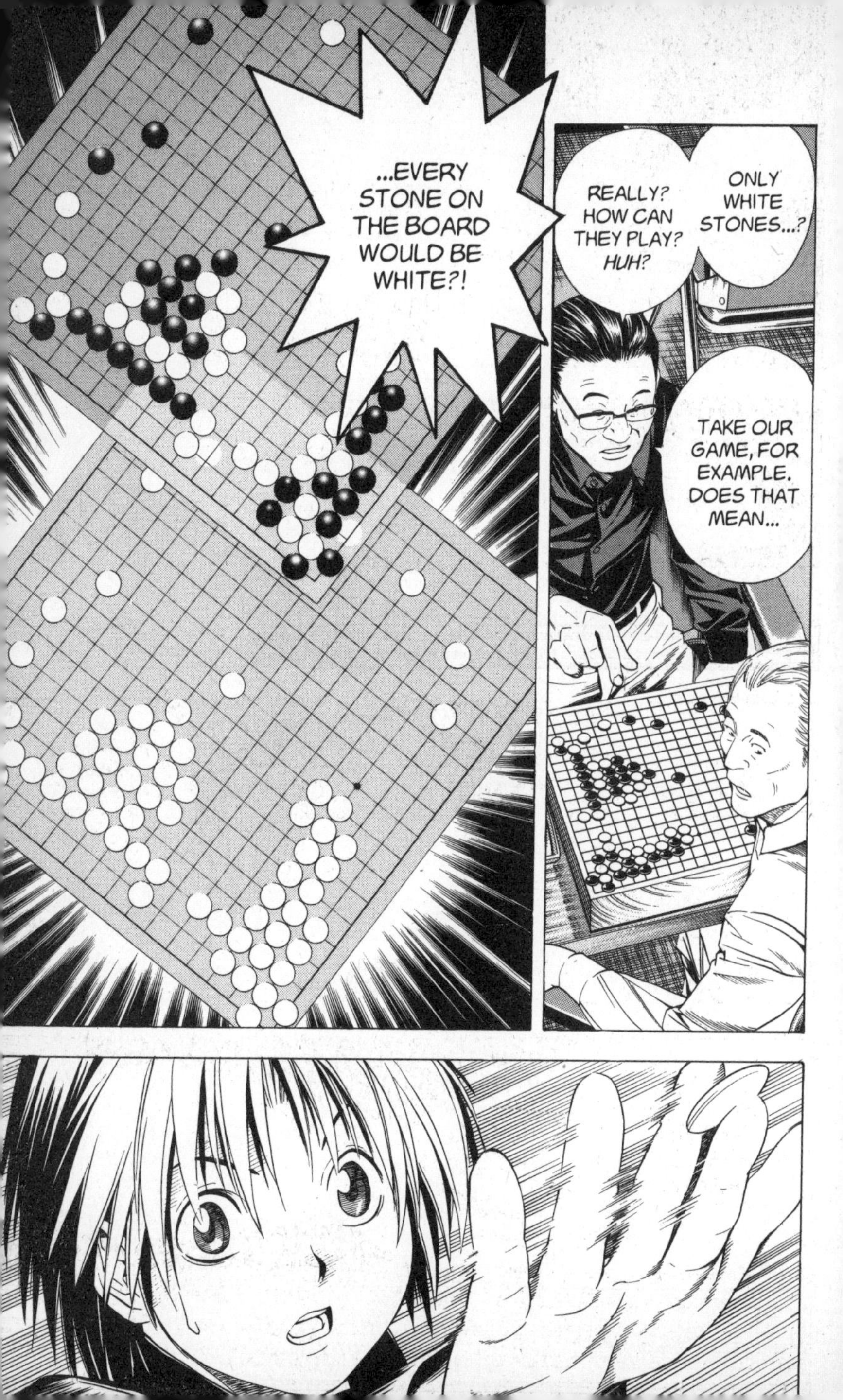
ONLY WHITE STONES...?
REALLY? HOW CAN THEY PLAY? HUH?
TAKE OUR GAME, FOR EXAMPLE. DOES THAT MEAN...
...EVERY STONE ON THE BOARD WOULD BE WHITE?!

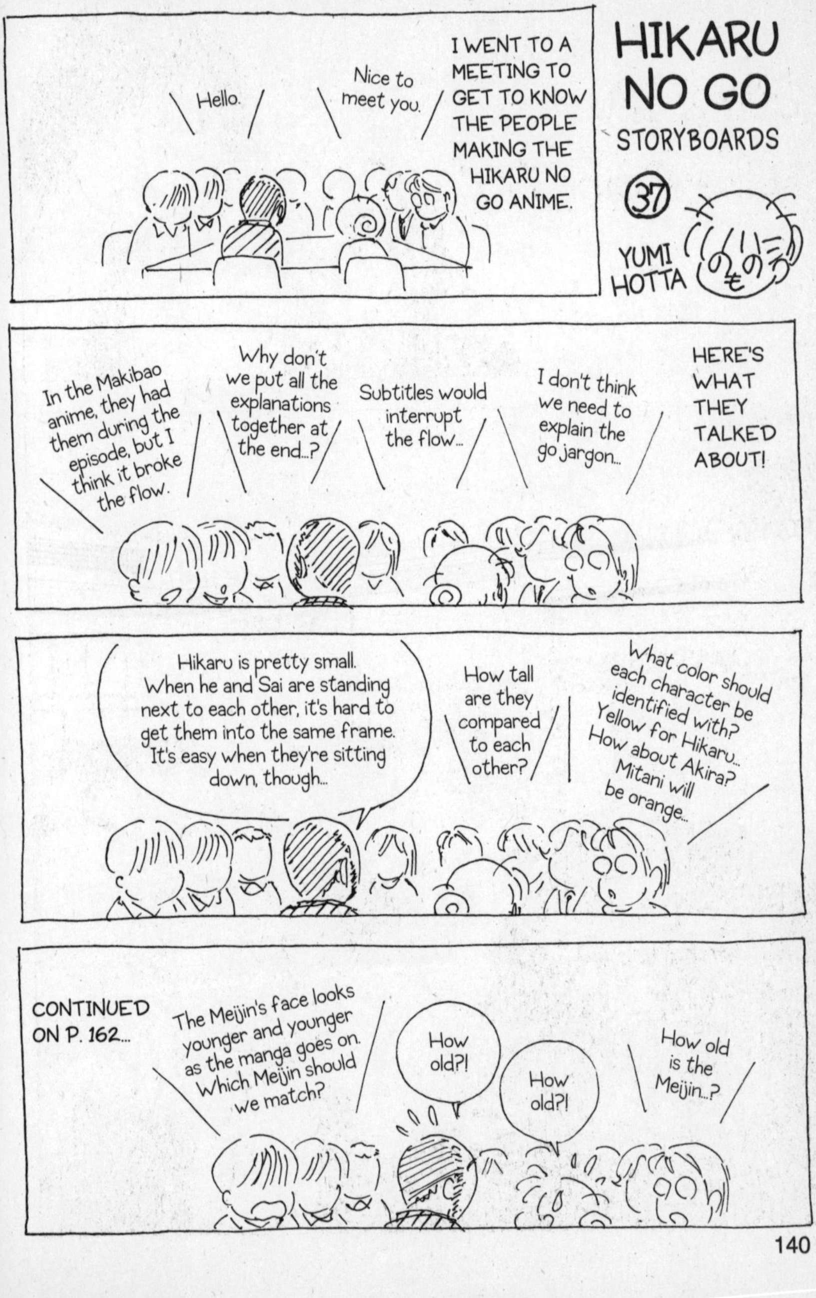
HIKARU NO GO STORYBOARDS
37
YUMI HOTTA
I WENT TO A MEETING TO GET TO KNOW THE PEOPLE MAKING THE HIKARU NO GO ANIME.
Nice to meet you.
Hello.
HERE'S WHAT THEY TALKED ABOUT!
I don't think we need to explain the go jargon...
Subtitles would interrupt the flow...
Why don't we put all the explanations together at the end...?
In the Makibao anime, they had them during the episode, but I think it broke the flow.
What color should each character be identified with? Yellow for Hikaru... How about Akira? Mitani will be orange...
How tall are they compared to each other?
Hikaru is pretty small. When he and Sai are standing next to each other, it's hard to get them into the same frame. It's easy when they're sitting down, though...
How old is the Meijin...?
How old?!
How old?!
The Meijin's face looks younger and younger as the manga goes on. Which Meijin should we match?
CONTINUED ON P. 162...

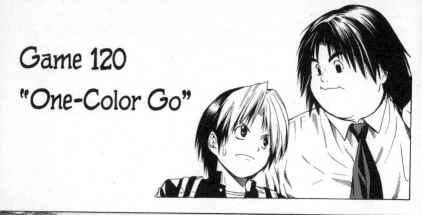

Game 120
"One-Color Go"

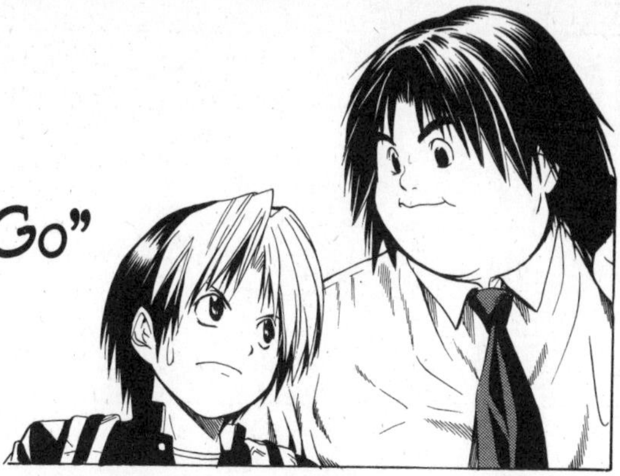

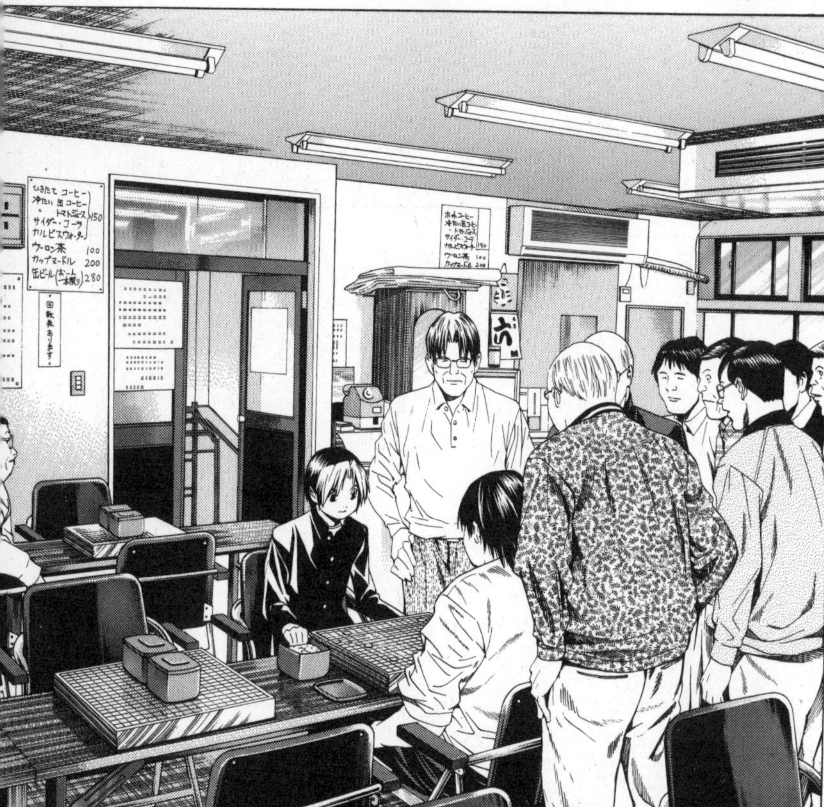

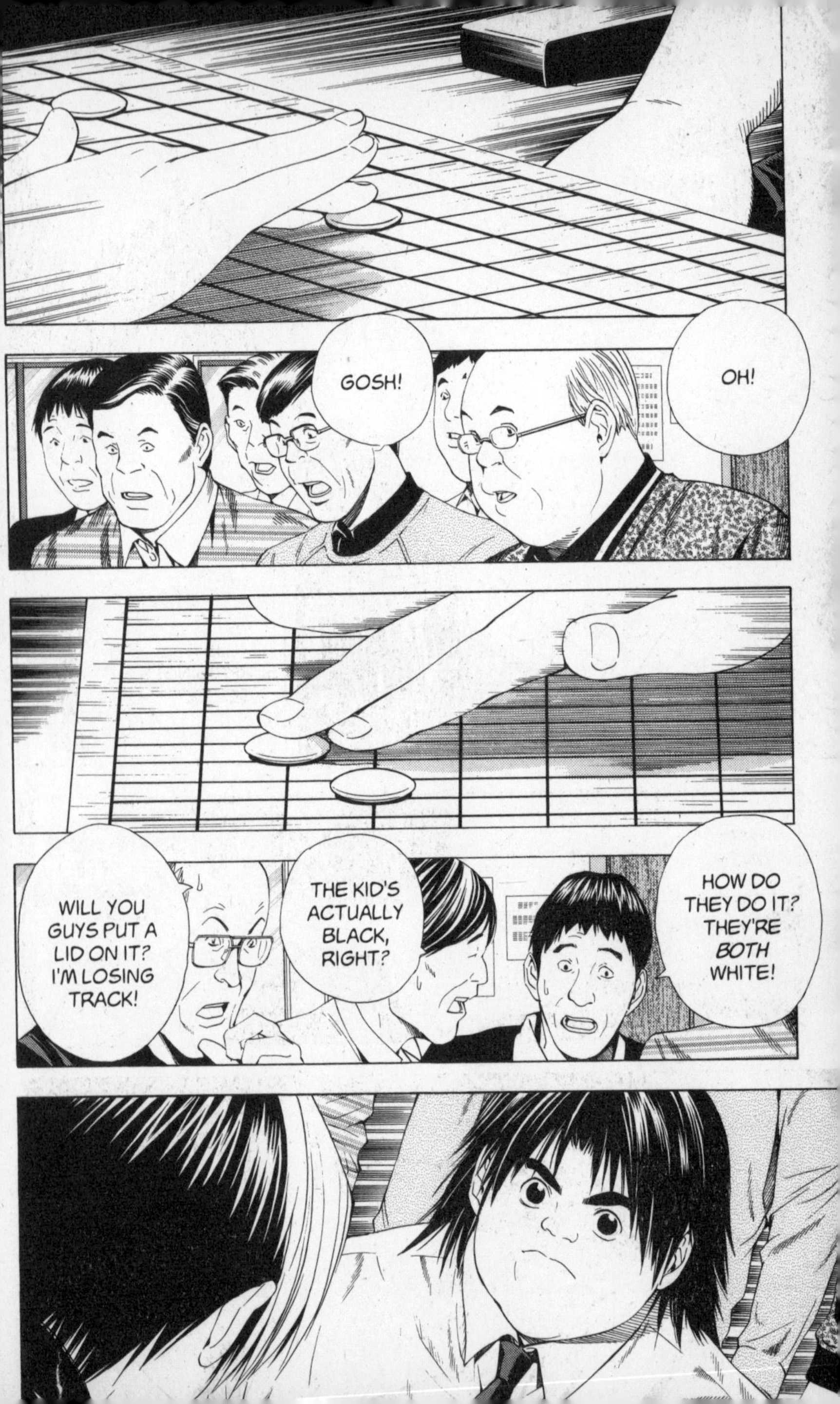
OH!
GOSH!
HOW DO THEY DO IT? THEY'RE *BOTH* WHITE!
THE KID'S ACTUALLY BLACK, RIGHT?
WILL YOU GUYS PUT A LID ON IT? I'M LOSING TRACK!

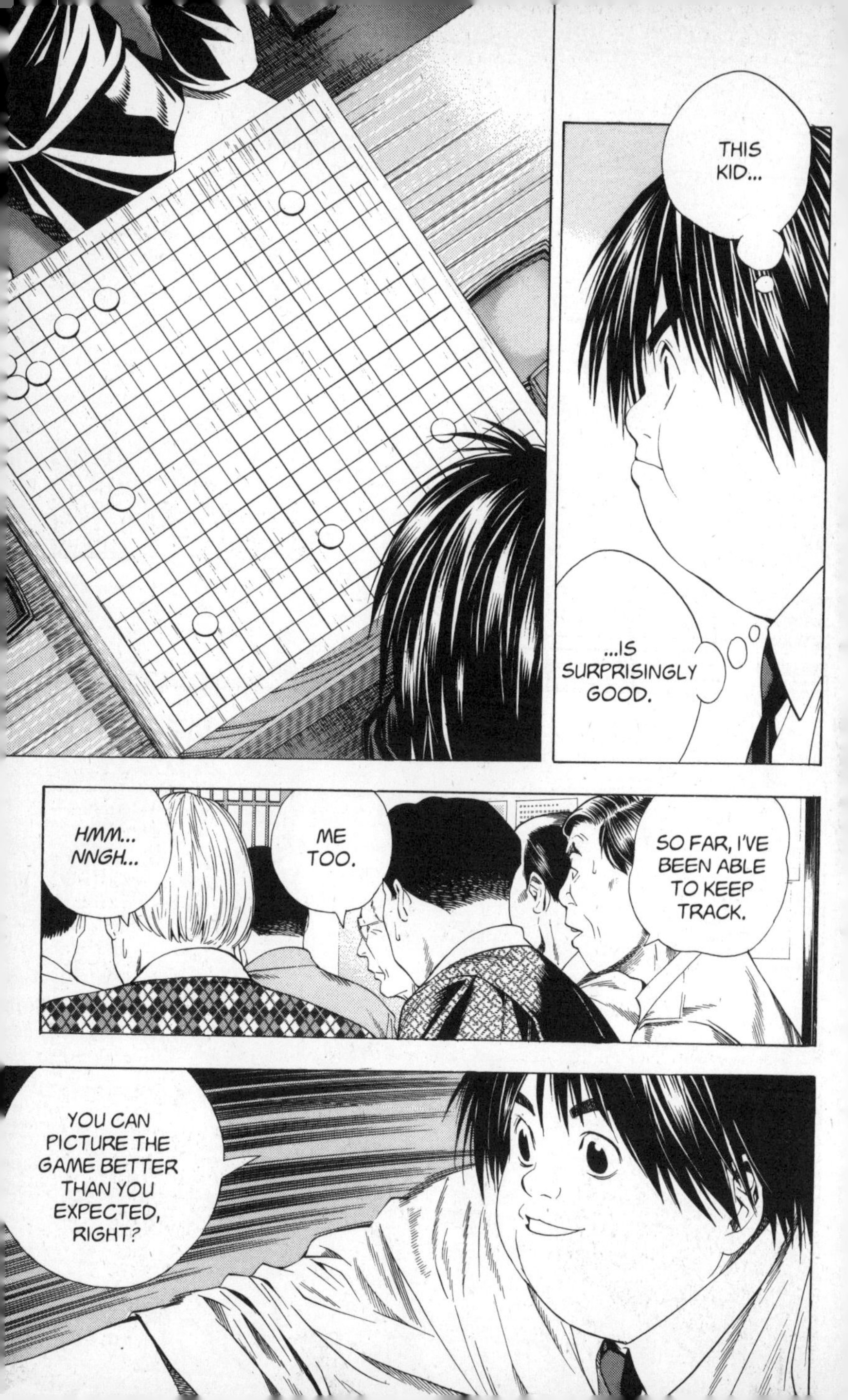
THIS KID...
...IS SURPRISINGLY GOOD.
SO FAR, I'VE BEEN ABLE TO KEEP TRACK.
ME TOO.
HMM... NNGH...
YOU CAN PICTURE THE GAME BETTER THAN YOU EXPECTED, RIGHT?

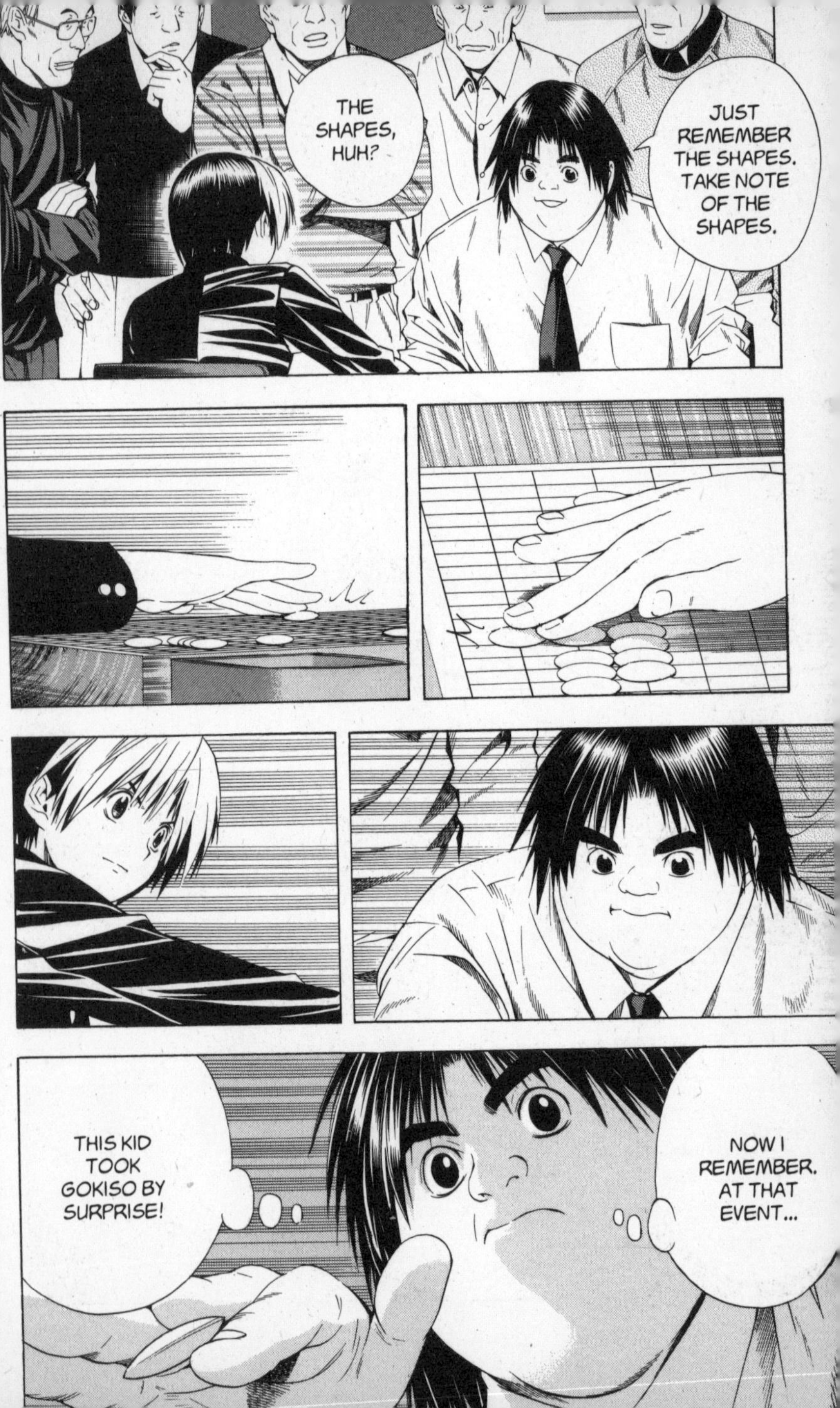
JUST REMEMBER THE SHAPES. TAKE NOTE OF THE SHAPES.
THE SHAPES, HUH?
NOW I REMEMBER. AT THAT EVENT...
THIS KID TOOK GOKISO BY SURPRISE!

READ THIS WAY

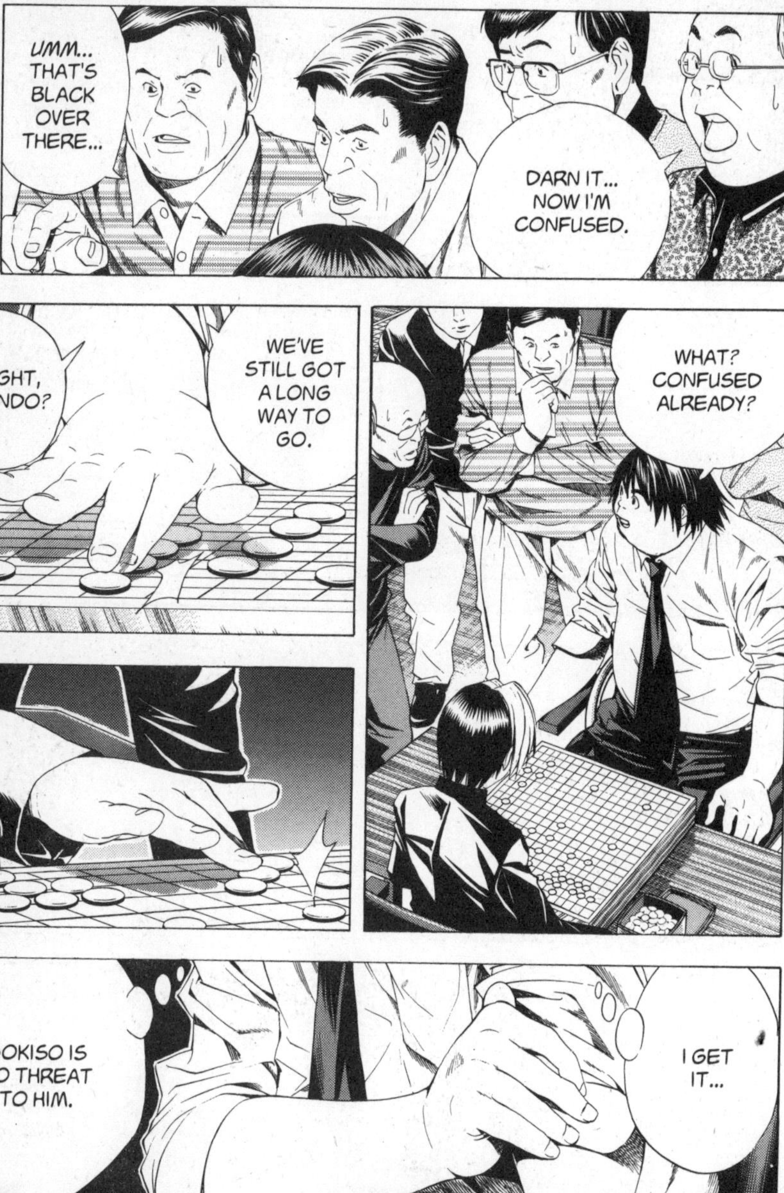
DARN IT... NOW I'M CONFUSED.
UMM... THAT'S BLACK OVER THERE...
WHAT? CONFUSED ALREADY?
WE'VE STILL GOT A LONG WAY TO GO.
RIGHT, SHINDO?
I GET IT...
GOKISO IS NO THREAT TO HIM.

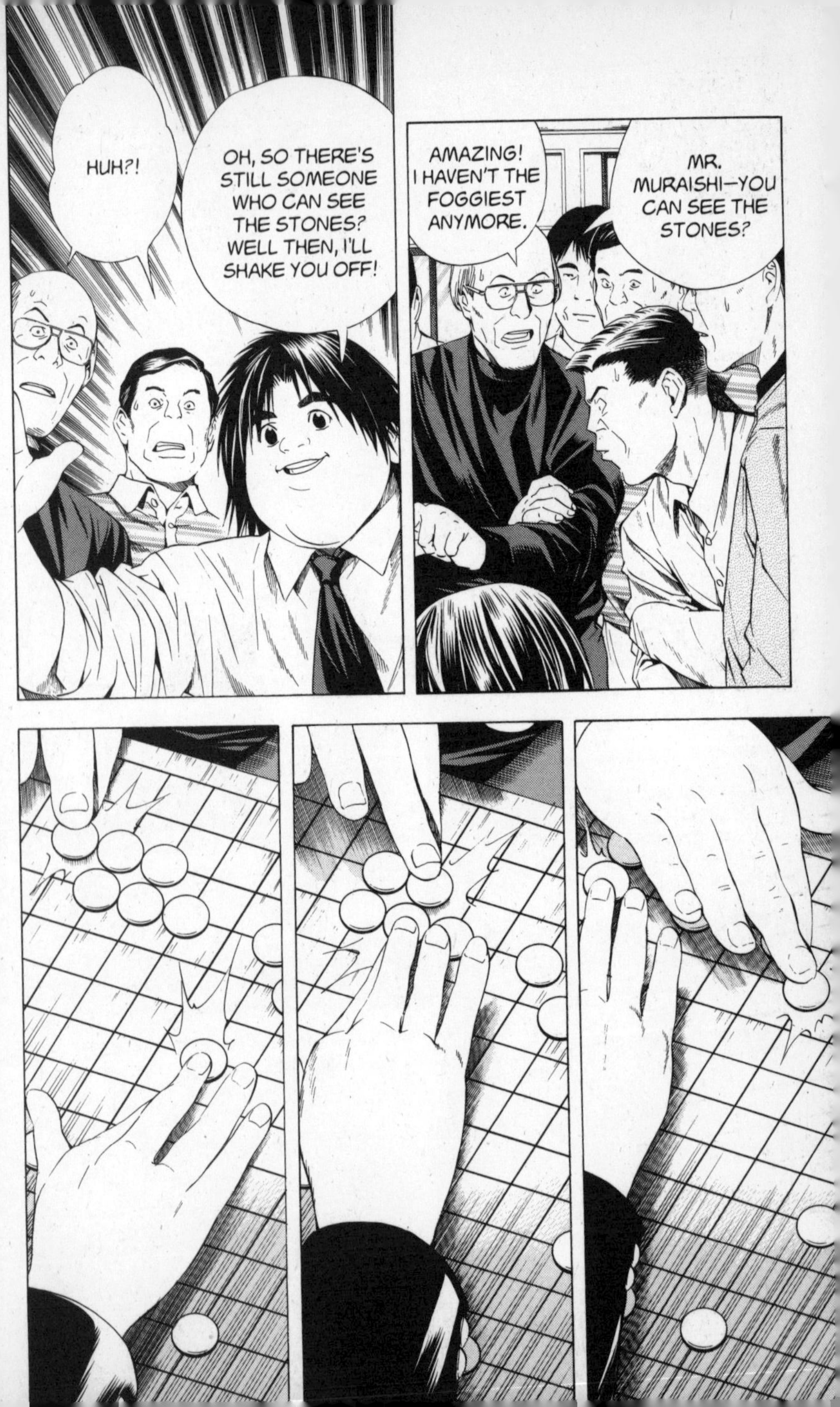
MR. MURAISHI—YOU CAN SEE THE STONES?
AMAZING! I HAVEN'T THE FOGGIEST ANYMORE.
OH, SO THERE'S STILL SOMEONE WHO CAN SEE THE STONES? WELL THEN, I'LL SHAKE YOU OFF!
HUH?!

READ THIS WAY

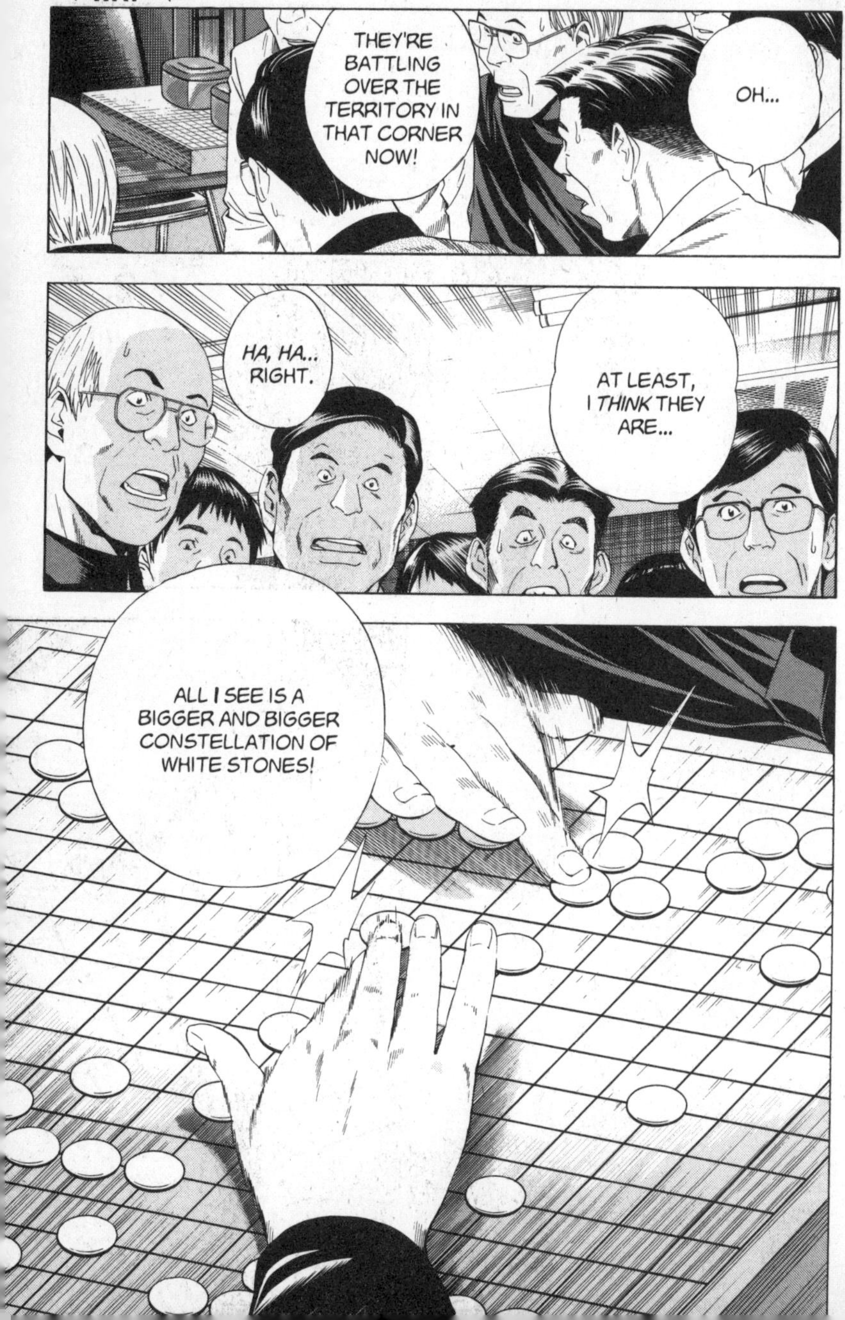
OH...
THEY'RE BATTLING OVER THE TERRITORY IN THAT CORNER NOW!
AT LEAST, I *THINK* THEY ARE...
HA, HA... RIGHT.
ALL I SEE IS A BIGGER AND BIGGER CONSTELLATION OF WHITE STONES!

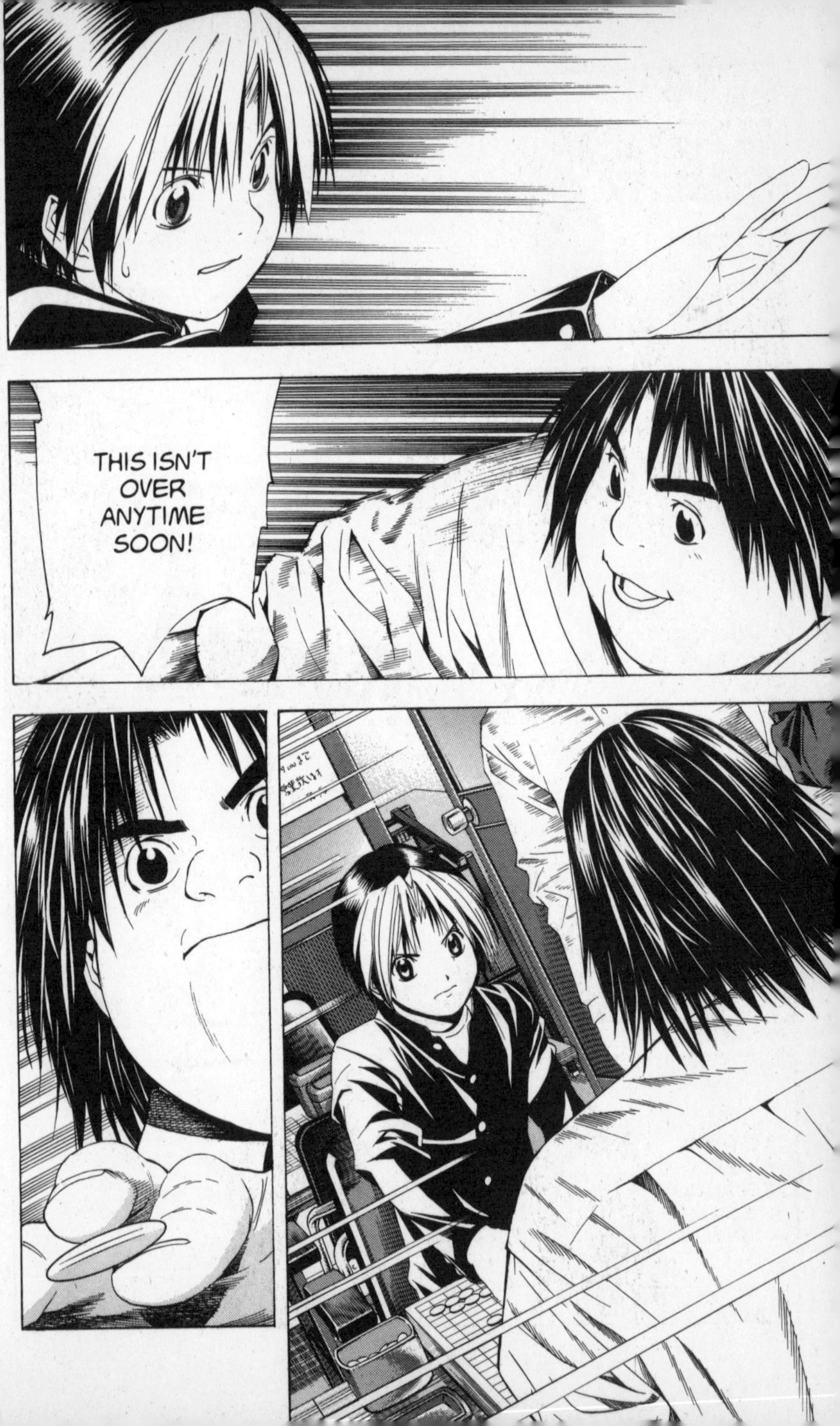
THIS ISN'T OVER ANYTIME SOON!

READ THIS WAY

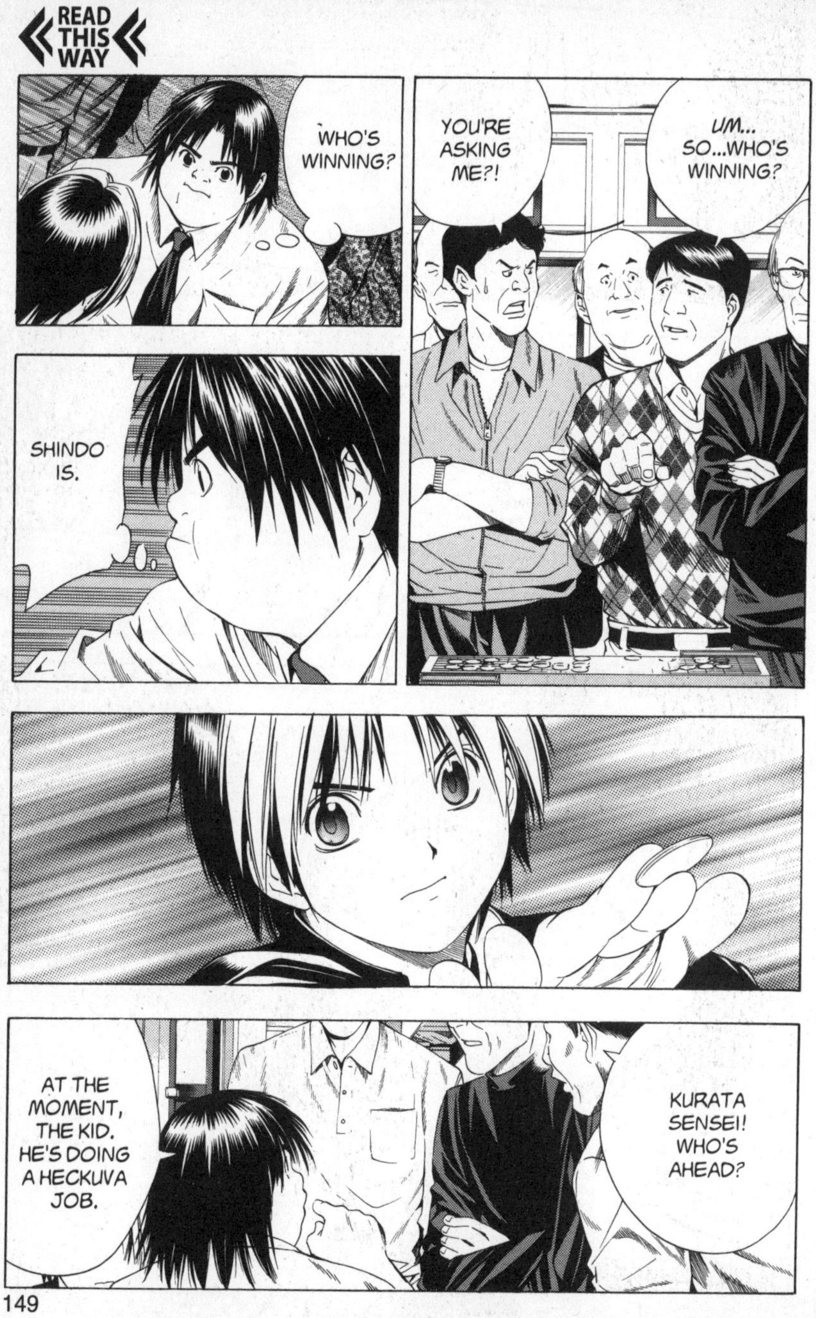
UM... SO...WHO'S WINNING?
YOU'RE ASKING ME?!
WHO'S WINNING?
SHINDO IS.
KURATA SENSEI! WHO'S AHEAD?
AT THE MOMENT, THE KID. HE'S DOING A HECKUVA JOB.

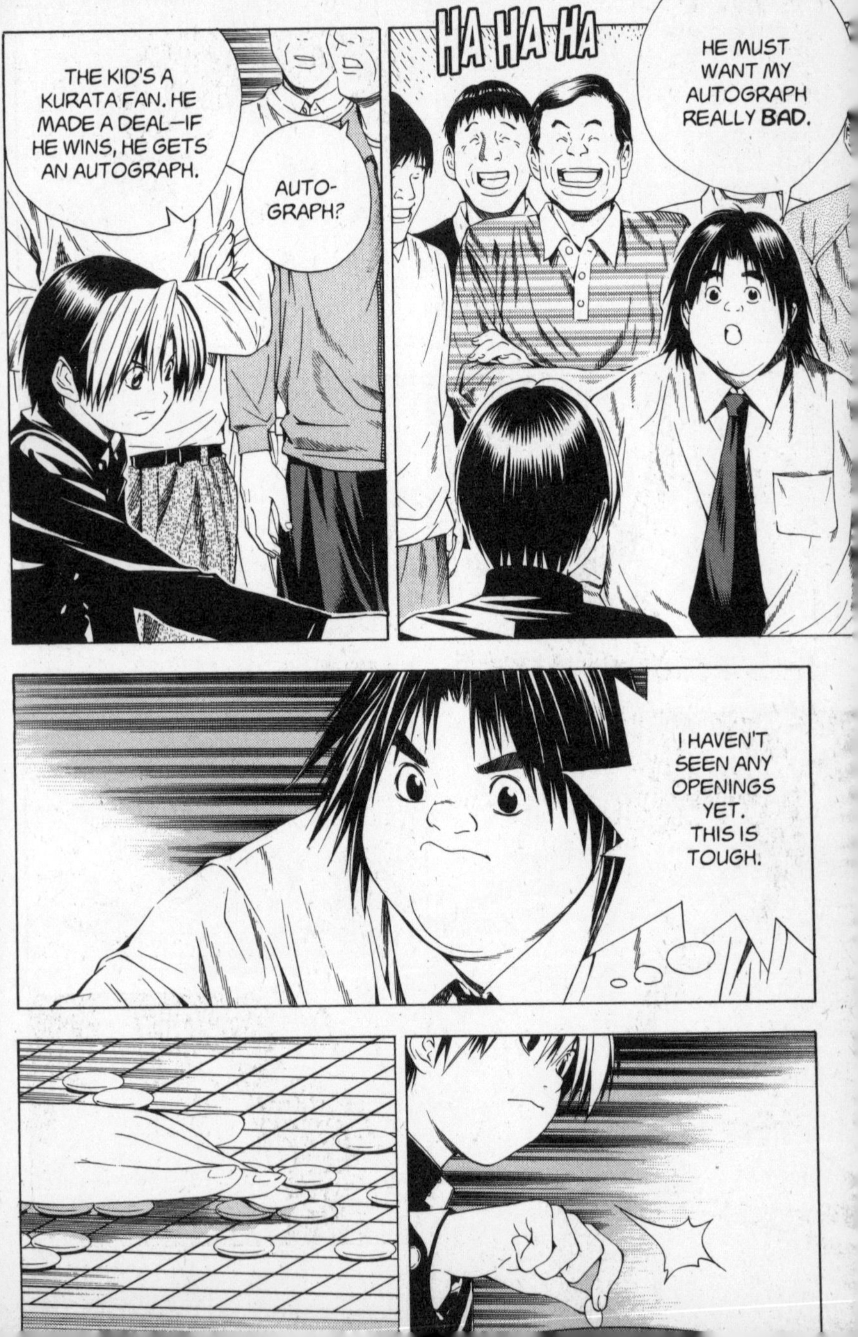
HA HA HA
HE MUST WANT MY AUTOGRAPH REALLY BAD.
THE KID'S A KURATA FAN. HE MADE A DEAL—IF HE WINS, HE GETS AN AUTOGRAPH.
AUTO-GRAPH?
I HAVEN'T SEEN ANY OPENINGS YET. THIS IS TOUGH.

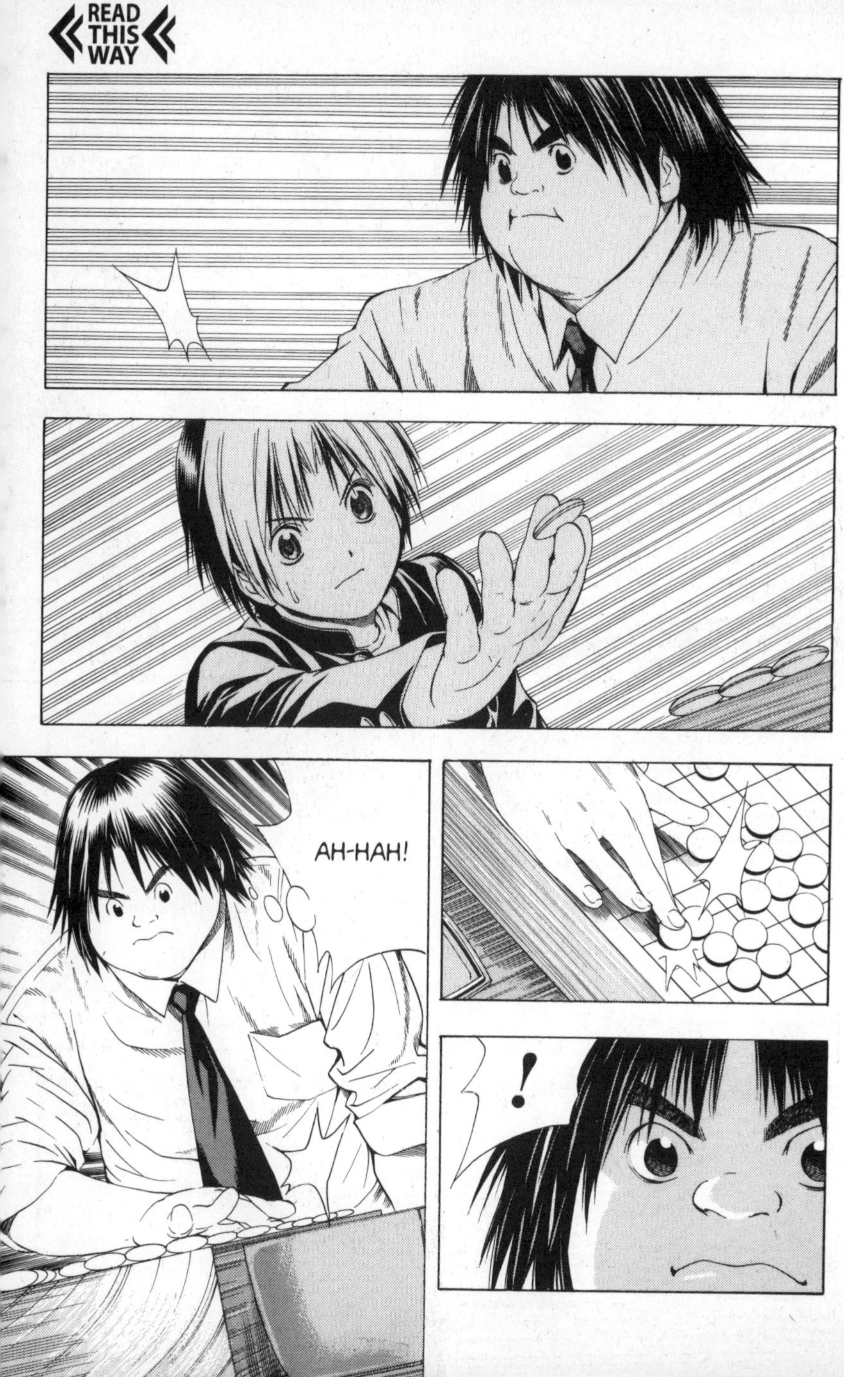
READ THIS WAY
AH-HAH!
!

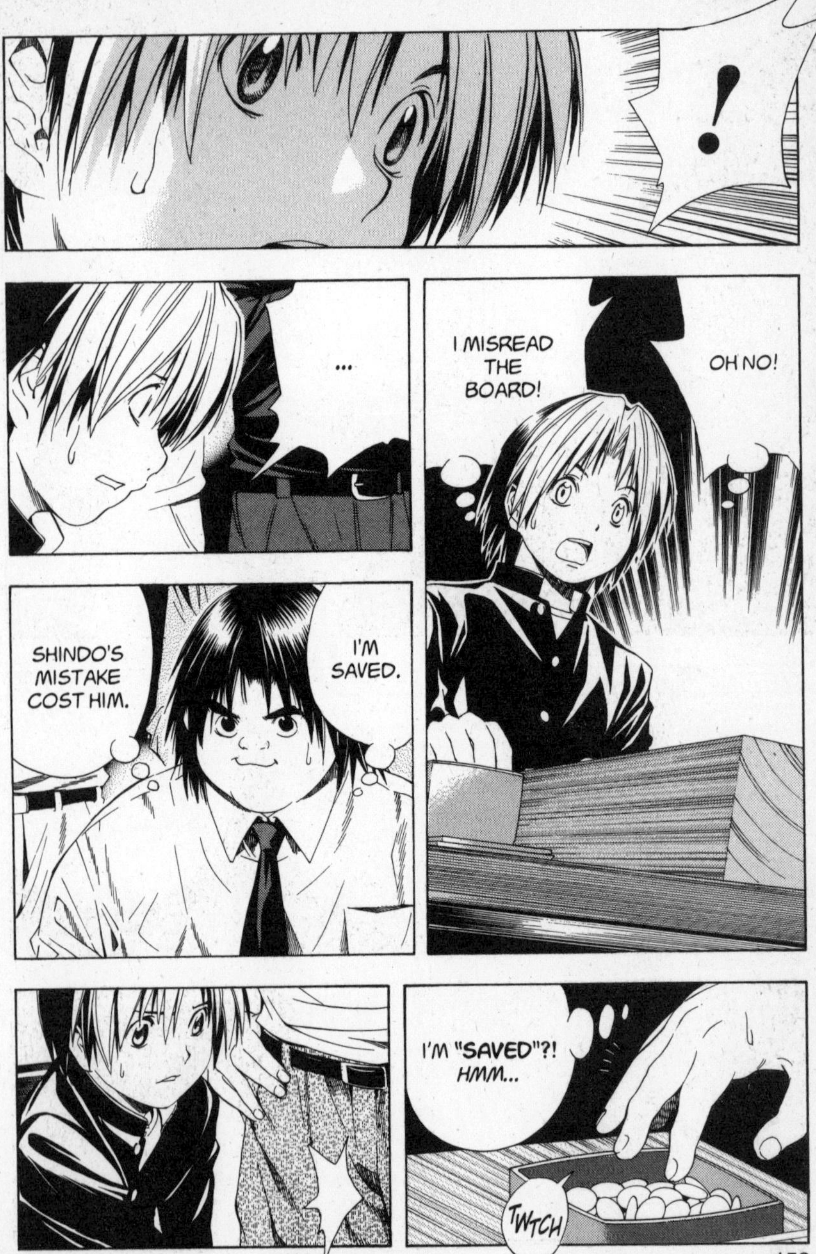
!
OH NO!
I MISREAD THE BOARD!
...
I'M SAVED.
SHINDO'S MISTAKE COST HIM.
I'M "SAVED"?! HMM...
TWITCH

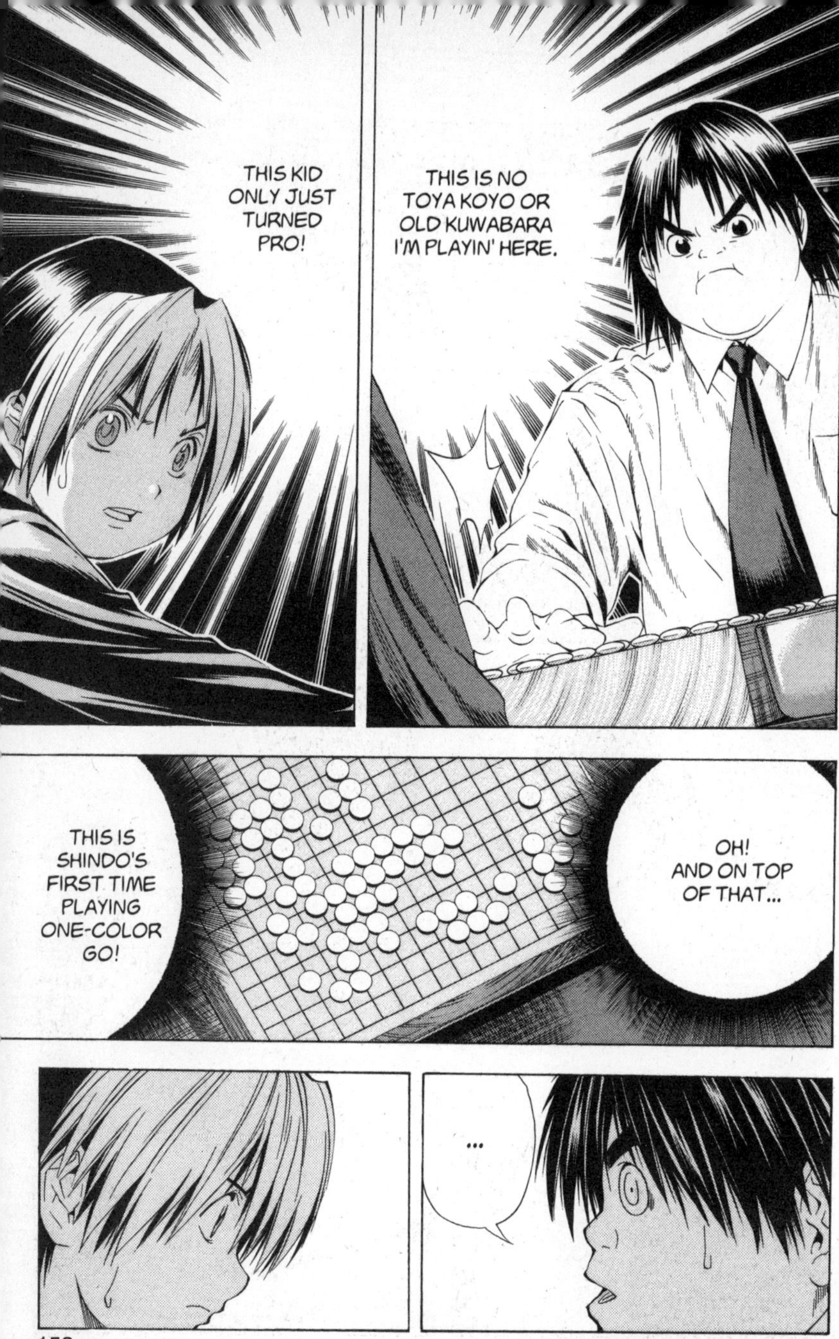
THIS IS NO TOYA KOYO OR OLD KUWABARA I'M PLAYIN' HERE.
THIS KID ONLY JUST TURNED PRO!
OH! AND ON TOP OF THAT...
THIS IS SHINDO'S FIRST TIME PLAYING ONE-COLOR GO!
...

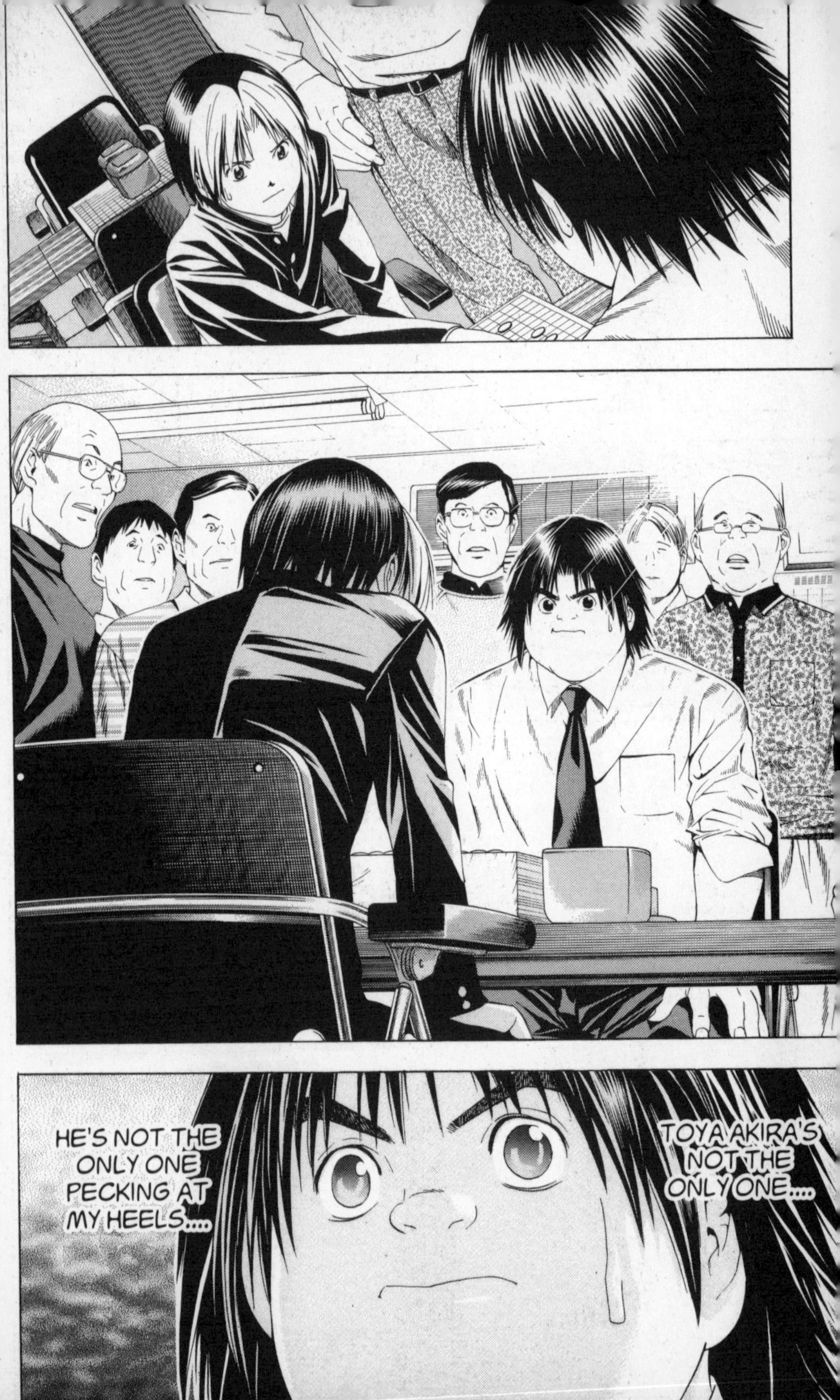
TOYA AKIRA'S NOT THE ONLY ONE....
HE'S NOT THE ONLY ONE PECKING AT MY HEELS....

READ THIS WAY

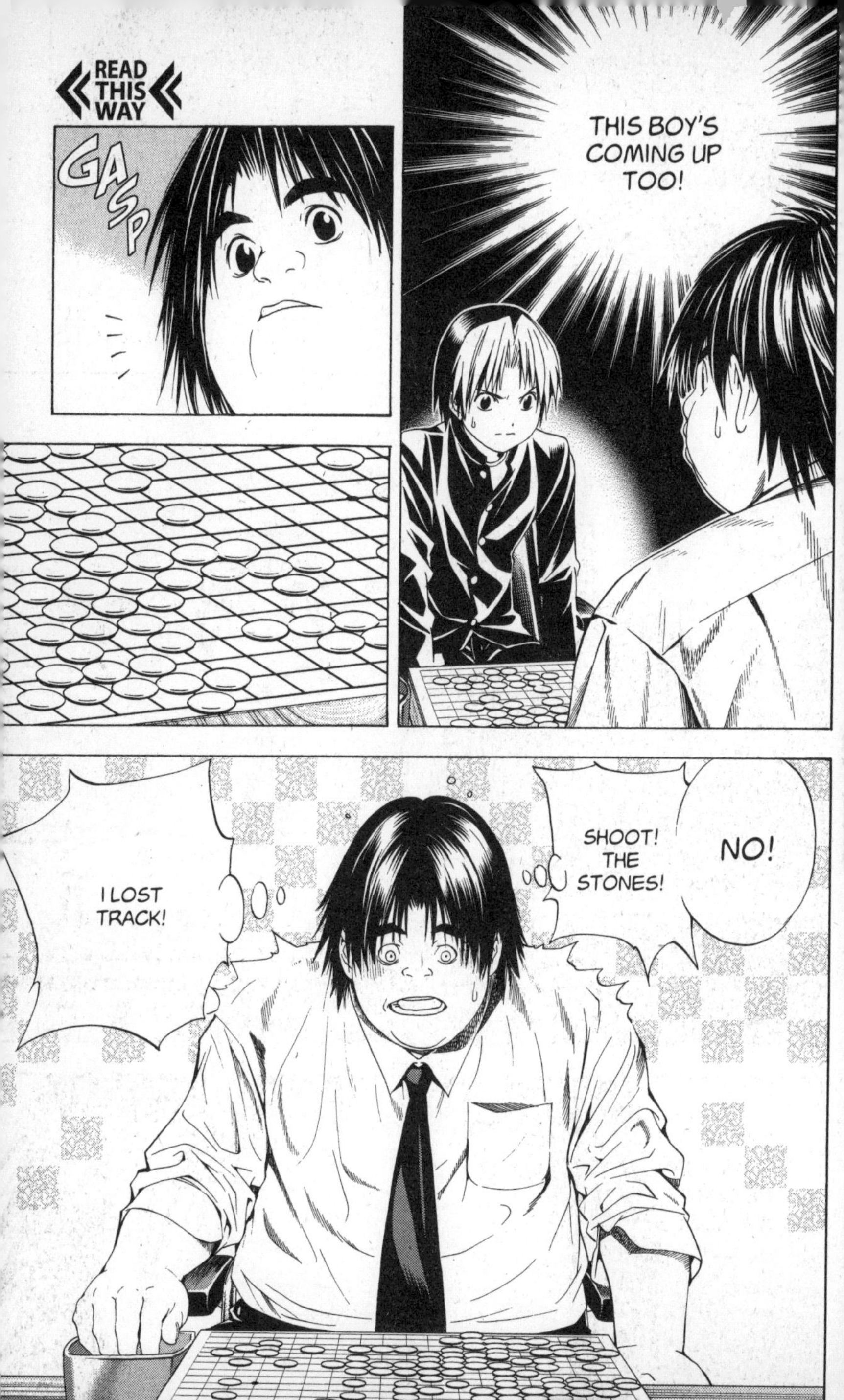
THIS BOY'S COMING UP TOO!
GASP
NO!
SHOOT! THE STONES!
I LOST TRACK!

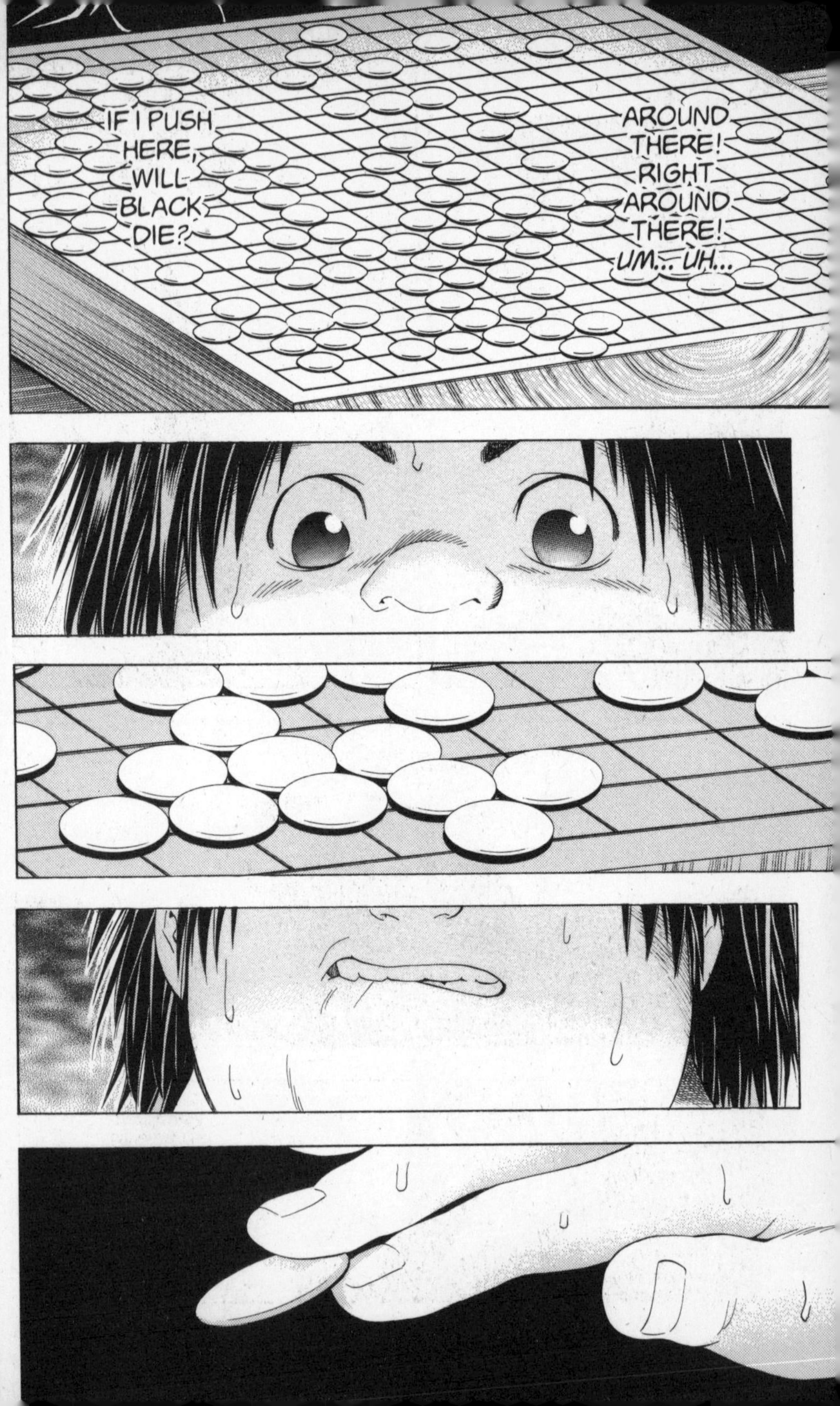
AROUND THERE! RIGHT AROUND THERE! UM... UH...
IF I PUSH HERE, WILL BLACK DIE?

READ THIS WAY

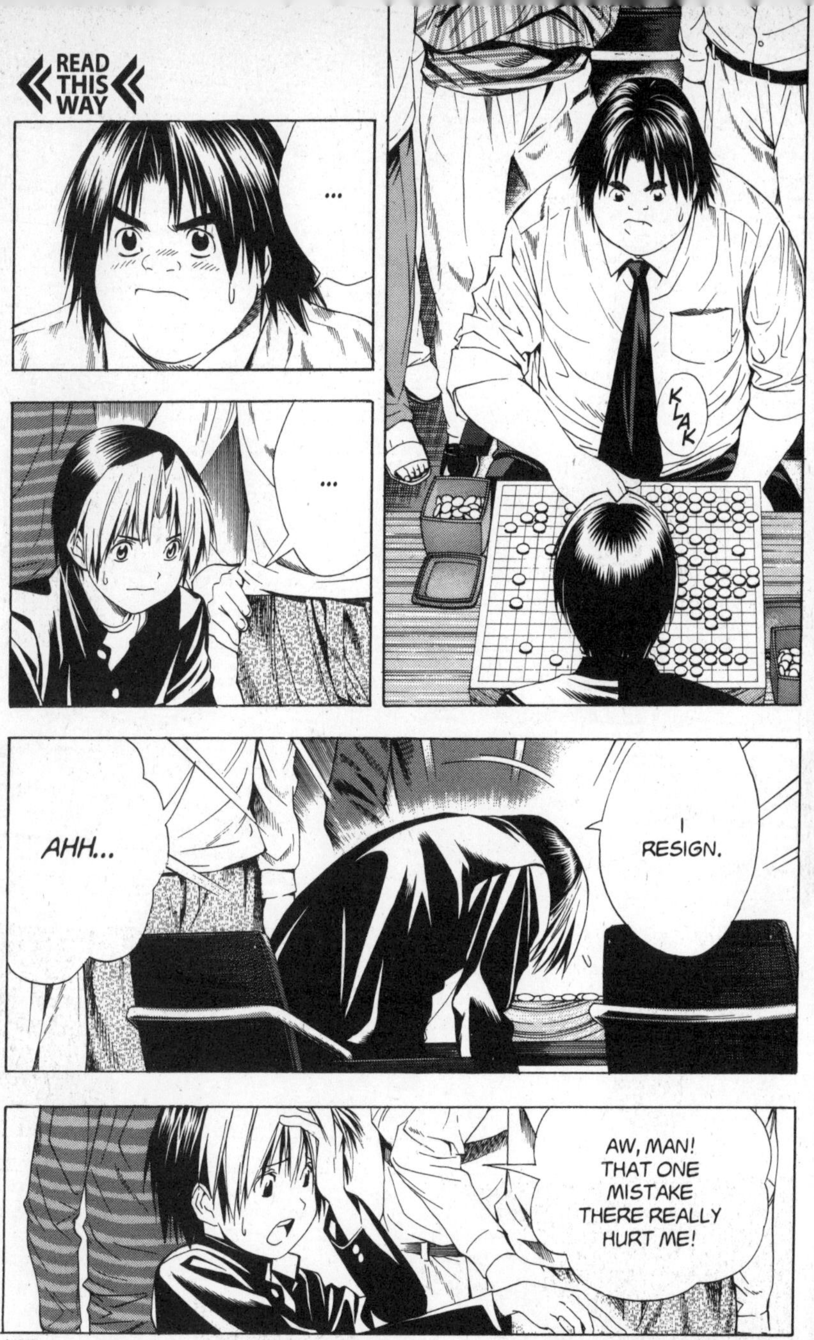
KLAK
...
...
I RESIGN.
AHH...
AW, MAN! THAT ONE MISTAKE THERE REALLY HURT ME!

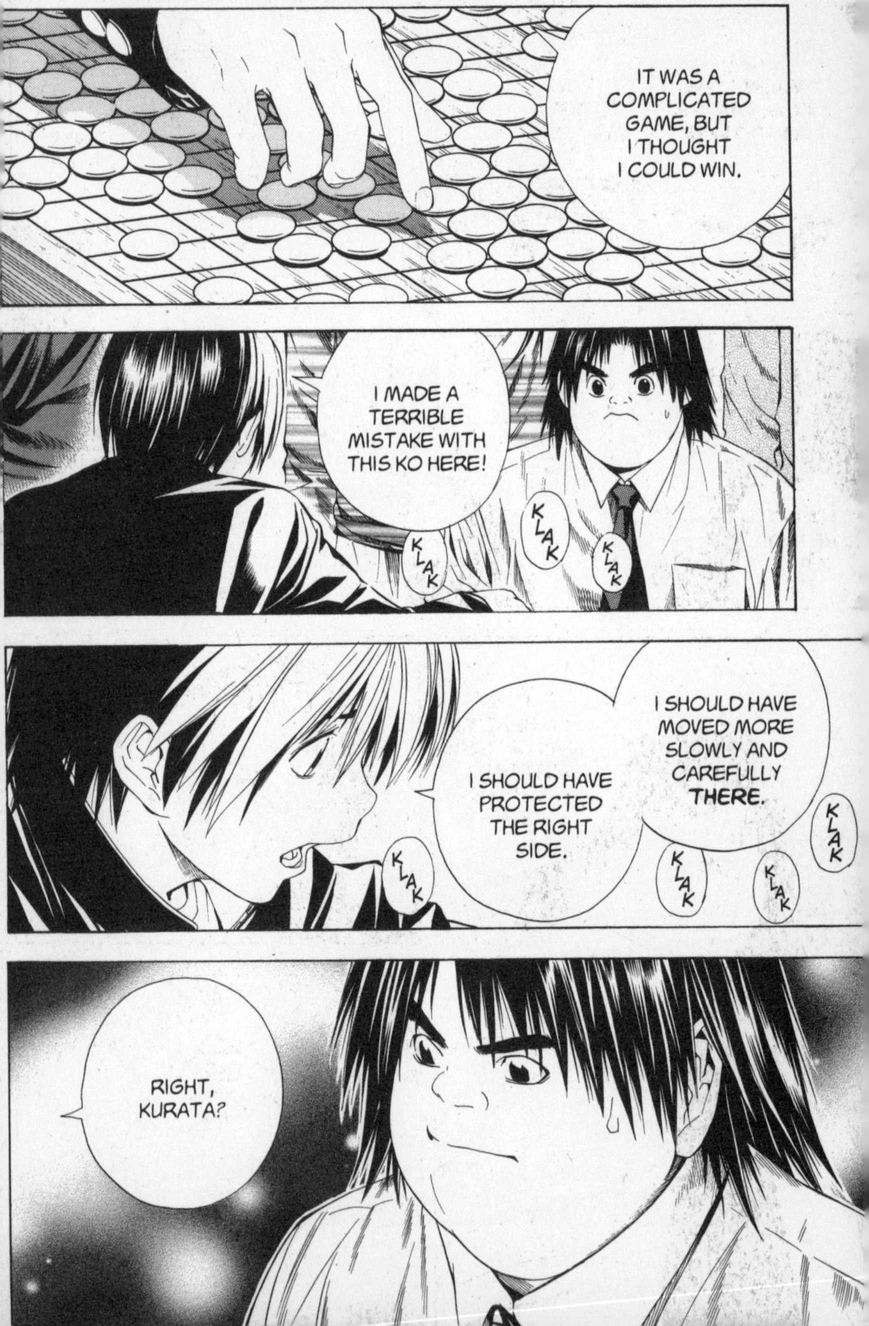
IT WAS A COMPLICATED GAME, BUT I THOUGHT I COULD WIN.
I MADE A TERRIBLE MISTAKE WITH THIS KO HERE!
KLAK
KLAK
KLAK
I SHOULD HAVE MOVED MORE SLOWLY AND CAREFULLY THERE.
I SHOULD HAVE PROTECTED THE RIGHT SIDE.
KLAK
KLAK
KLAK
KLAK
RIGHT, KURATA?

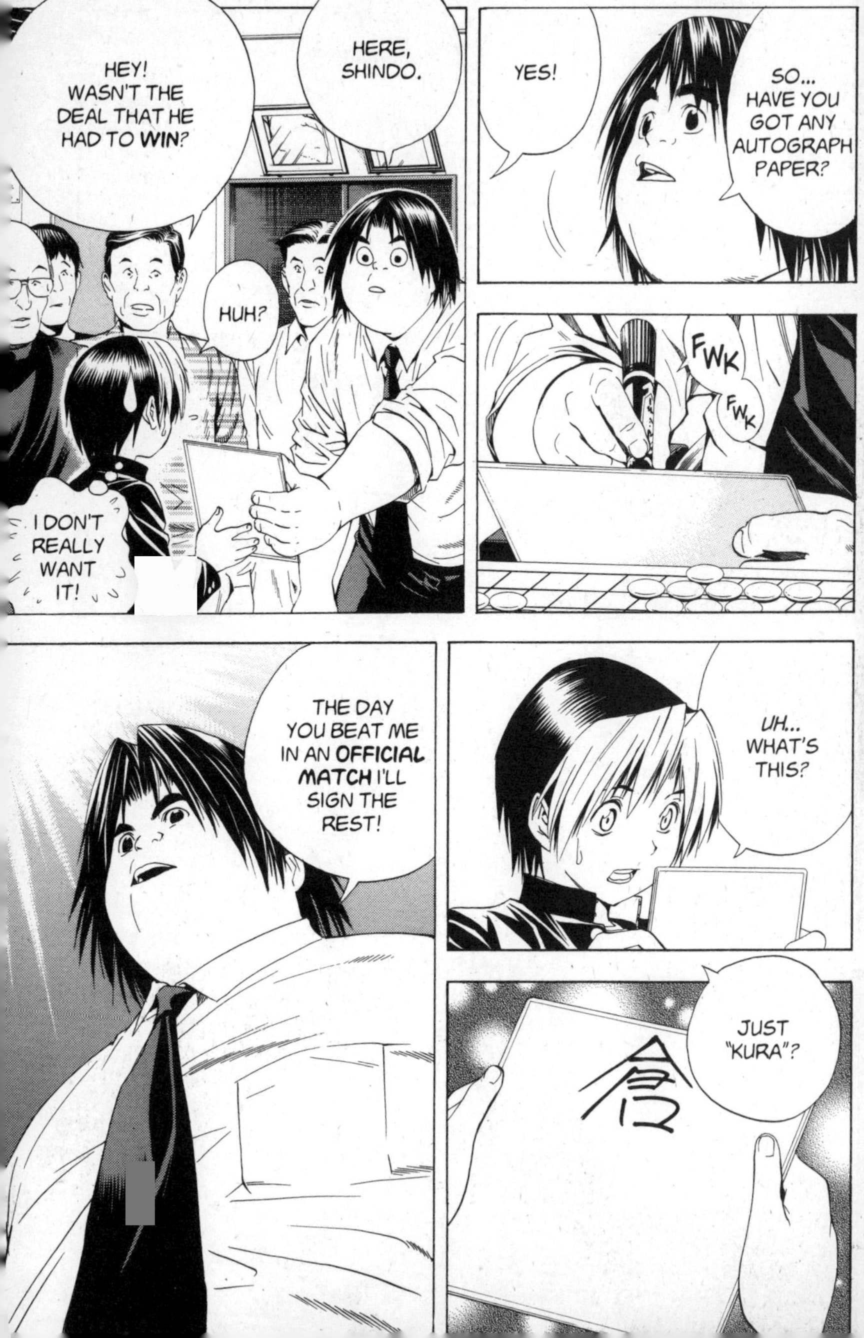
SO... HAVE YOU GOT ANY AUTOGRAPH PAPER?
YES!
FWK
FWK
HERE, SHINDO.
HEY! WASN'T THE DEAL THAT HE HAD TO WIN?
HUH?
I DON'T REALLY WANT IT!
UH... WHAT'S THIS?
JUST "KURA"?
THE DAY YOU BEAT ME IN AN OFFICIAL MATCH I'LL SIGN THE REST!

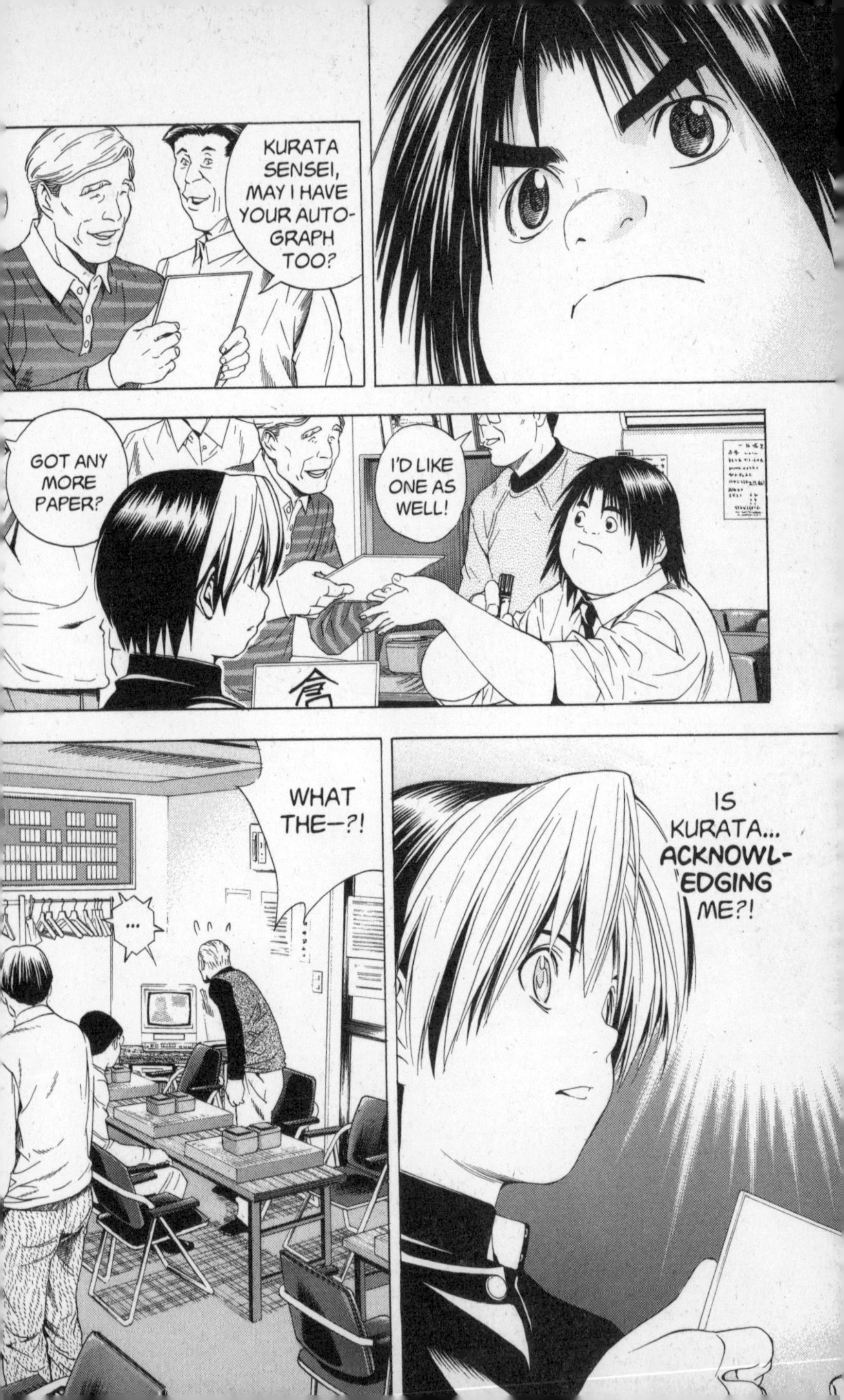
KURATA SENSEI, MAY I HAVE YOUR AUTO-GRAPH TOO?
I'D LIKE ONE AS WELL!
GOT ANY MORE PAPER?
IS KURATA... ACKNOWL-EDGING ME?!
WHAT THE--?!
...

READ THIS WAY

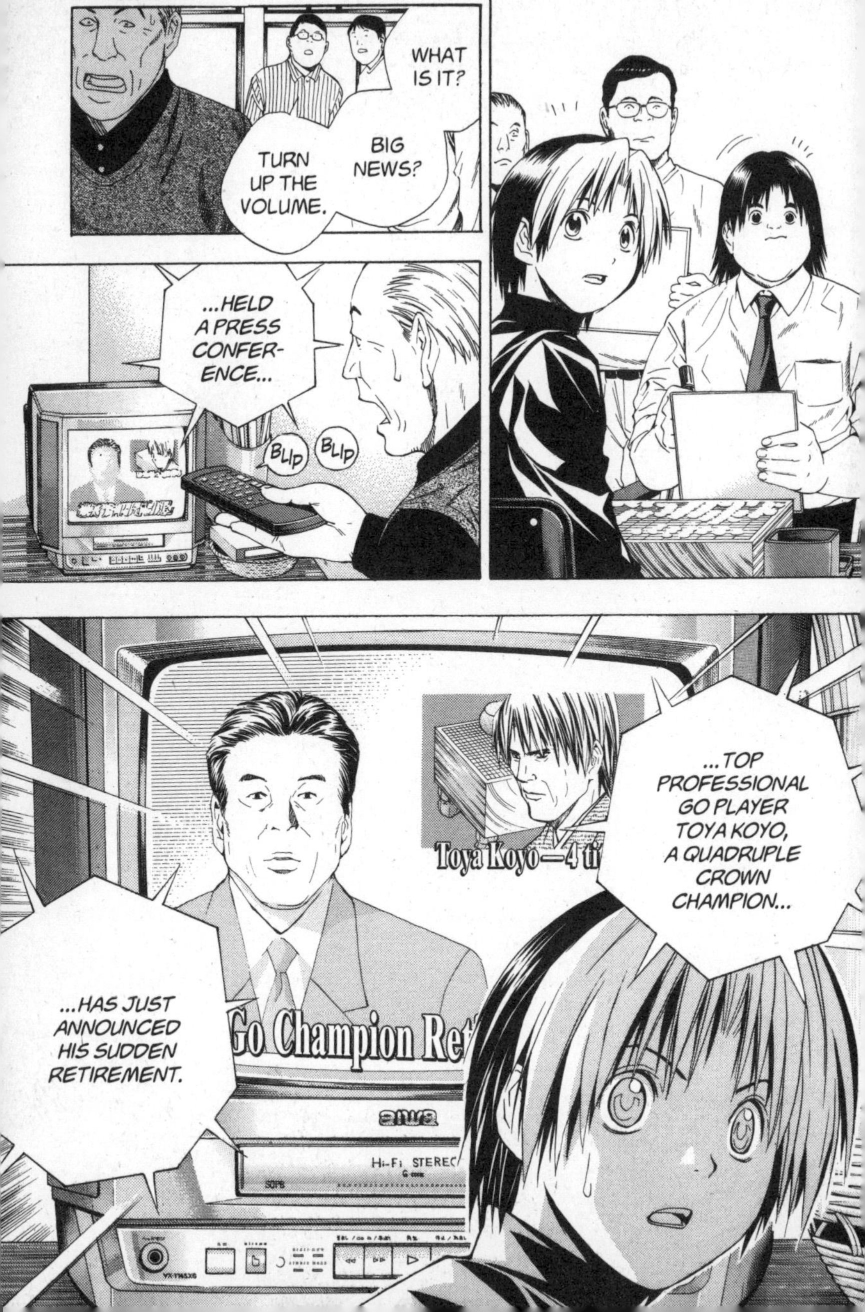
WHAT IS IT?
BIG NEWS?
TURN UP THE VOLUME.
...HELD A PRESS CONFERENCE...
BLIP
BLIP
...TOP PROFESSIONAL GO PLAYER TOYA KOYO, A QUADRUPLE CROWN CHAMPION...
Toya Koyo—4 ti
Go Champion Ret
...HAS JUST ANNOUNCED HIS SUDDEN RETIREMENT.
aiwa
Hi-Fi STEREO

HIKARU NO GO STORYBOARDS

38

YUMI HOTTA

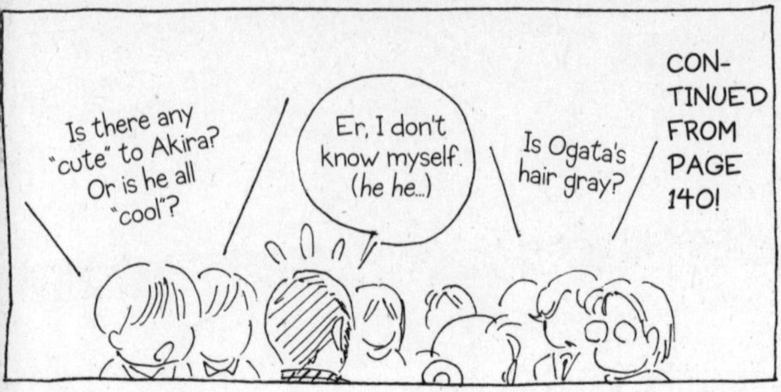
CON-TINUED FROM PAGE 140!
Is Ogata's hair gray?
Er, I don't know myself. (he he...)
Is there any "cute" to Akira? Or is he all "cool"?

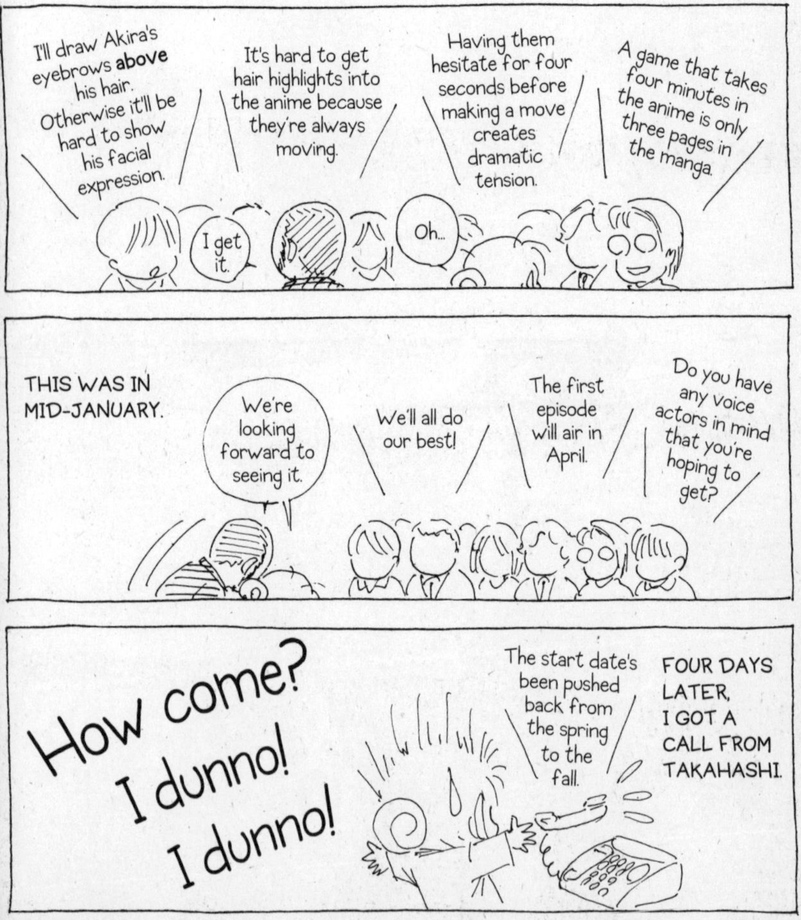
A game that takes four minutes in the anime is only three pages in the manga.
Having them hesitate for four seconds before making a move creates dramatic tension.
It's hard to get hair highlights into the anime because they're always moving.
I'll draw Akira's eyebrows **above** his hair. Otherwise it'll be hard to show his facial expression.
Oh...
I get it.
Do you have any voice actors in mind that you're hoping to get?
The first episode will air in April.
We'll all do our best!
We're looking forward to seeing it.
THIS WAS IN MID-JANUARY.
FOUR DAYS LATER, I GOT A CALL FROM TAKAHASHI.
The start date's been pushed back from the spring to the fall.
How come? I dunno! I dunno!

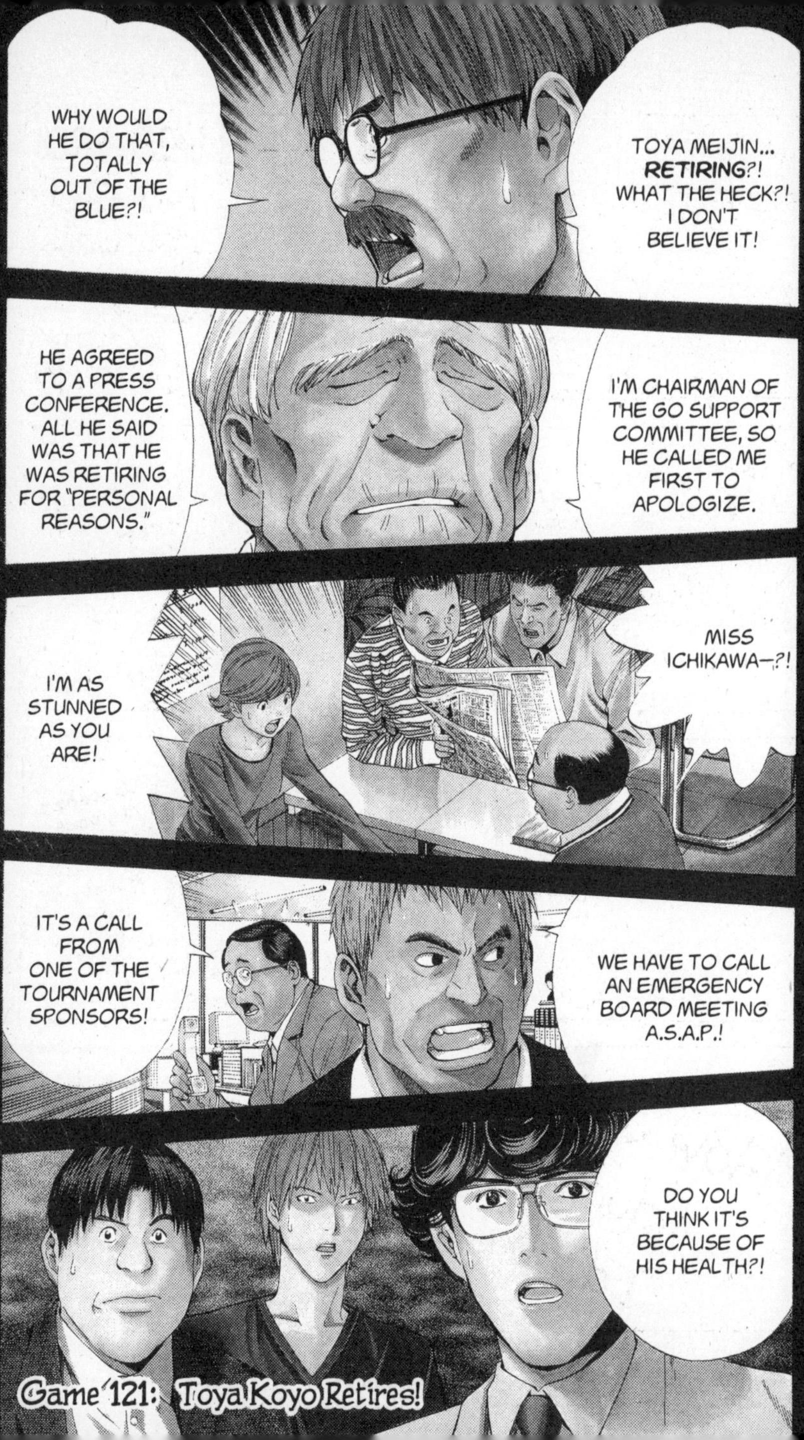
TOYA MEIJIN... **RETIRING**?! WHAT THE HECK?! I DON'T BELIEVE IT!
WHY WOULD HE DO THAT, TOTALLY OUT OF THE BLUE?!
I'M CHAIRMAN OF THE GO SUPPORT COMMITTEE, SO HE CALLED ME FIRST TO APOLOGIZE.
HE AGREED TO A PRESS CONFERENCE. ALL HE SAID WAS THAT HE WAS RETIRING FOR "PERSONAL REASONS."
MISS ICHIKAWA—?!
I'M AS STUNNED AS YOU ARE!
WE HAVE TO CALL AN EMERGENCY BOARD MEETING A.S.A.P.!
IT'S A CALL FROM ONE OF THE TOURNAMENT SPONSORS!
DO YOU THINK IT'S BECAUSE OF HIS HEALTH?!
Game 121: Toya Koyo Retires!

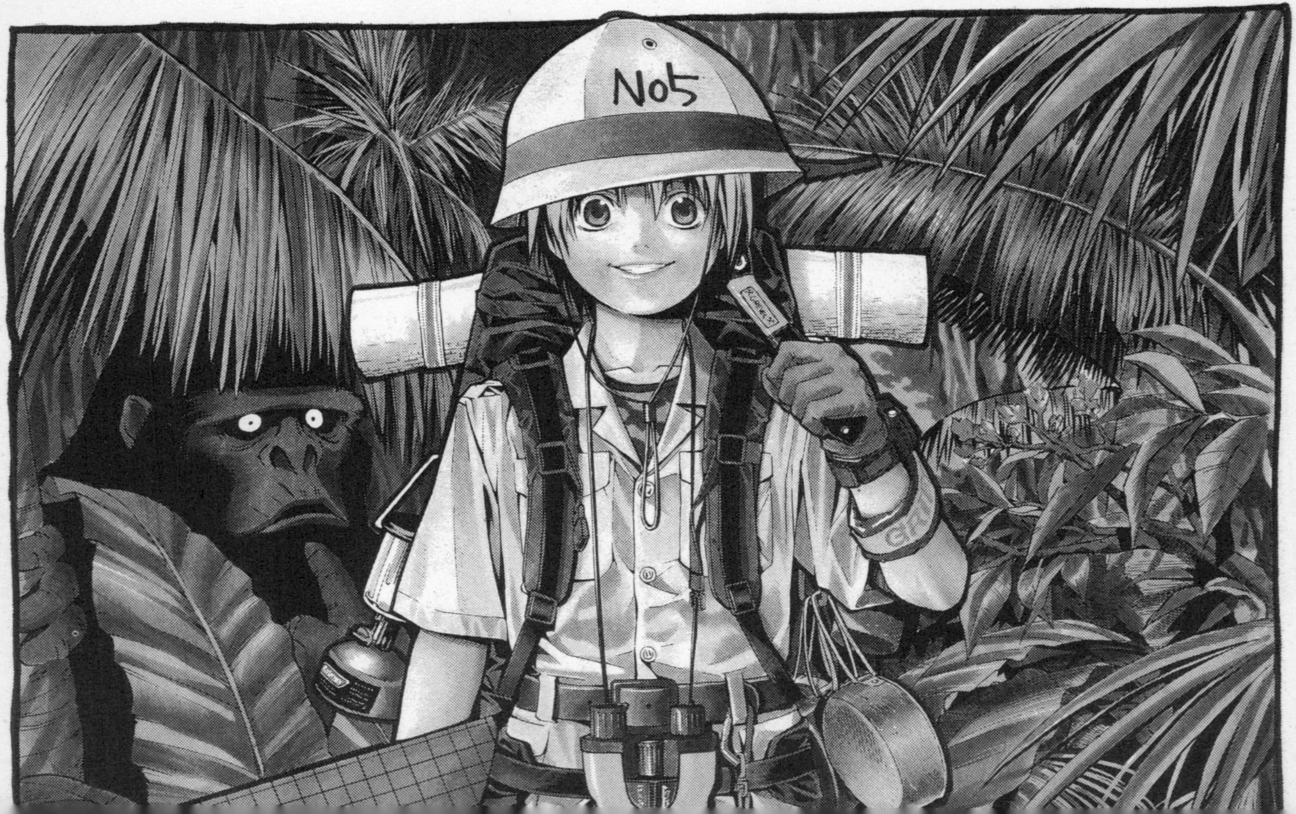
No5

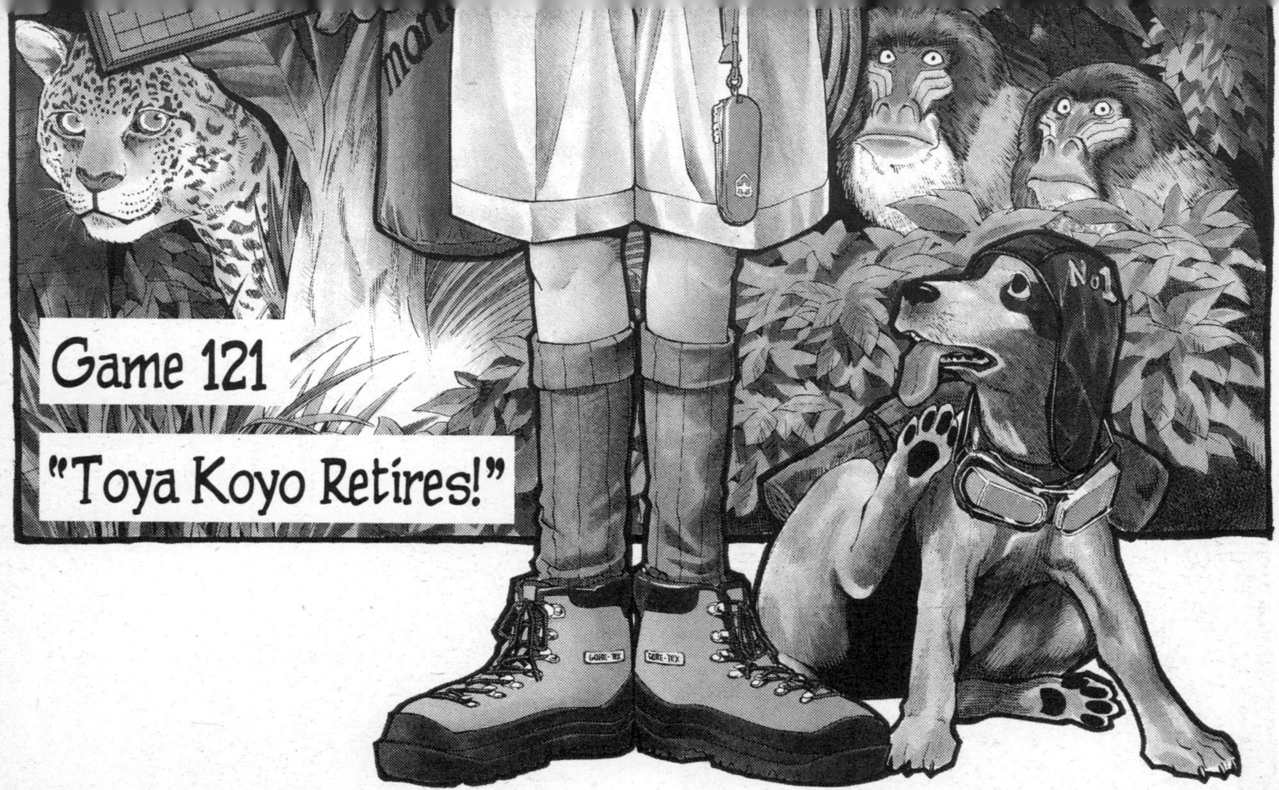
Game 121
"Toya Koyo Retires!"
GORE-TEX
GORE-TEX
No1

AKIRA

TOYA

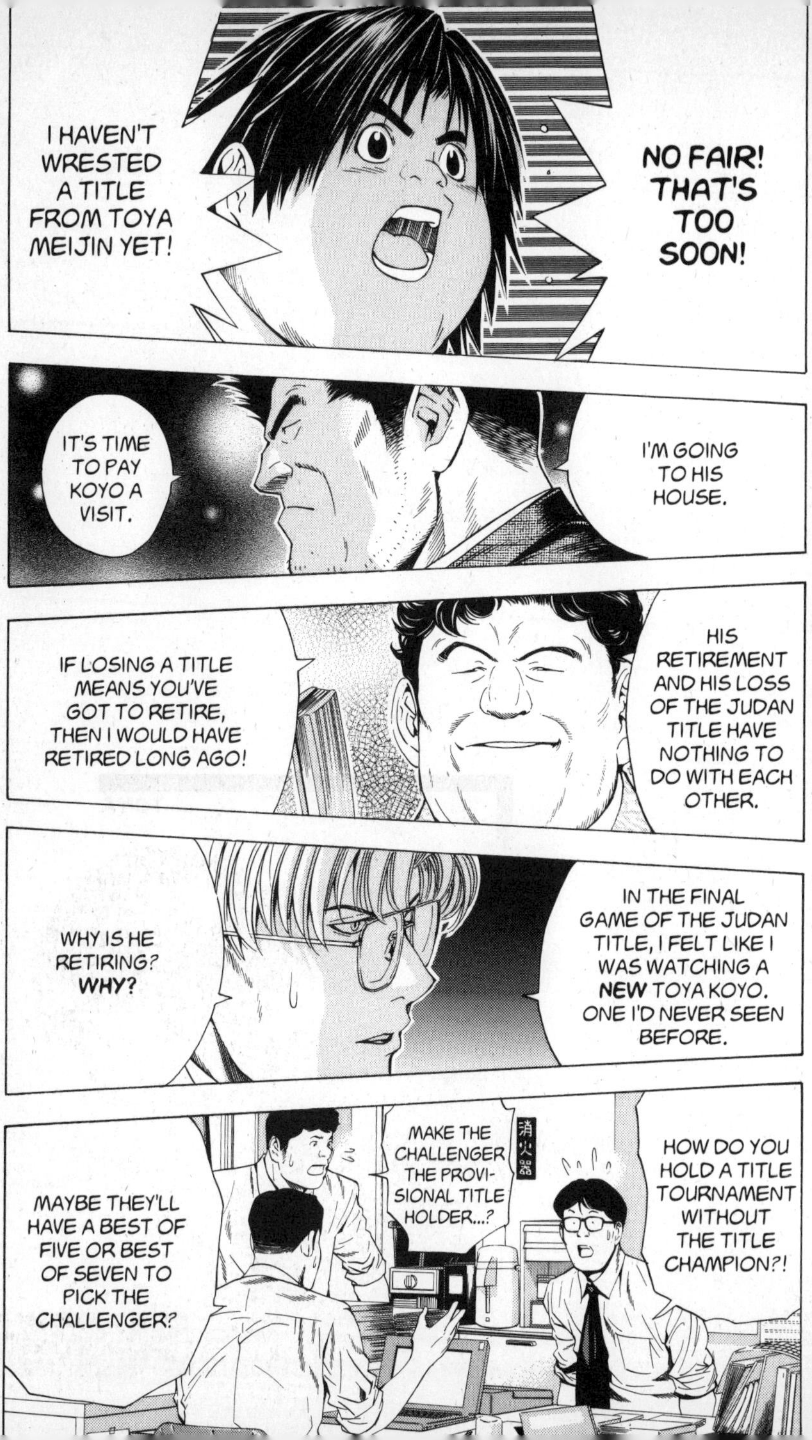
NO FAIR! THAT'S TOO SOON!
I HAVEN'T WRESTED A TITLE FROM TOYA MEIJIN YET!
I'M GOING TO HIS HOUSE.
IT'S TIME TO PAY KOYO A VISIT.
HIS RETIREMENT AND HIS LOSS OF THE JUDAN TITLE HAVE NOTHING TO DO WITH EACH OTHER.
IF LOSING A TITLE MEANS YOU'VE GOT TO RETIRE, THEN I WOULD HAVE RETIRED LONG AGO!
IN THE FINAL GAME OF THE JUDAN TITLE, I FELT LIKE I WAS WATCHING A NEW TOYA KOYO. ONE I'D NEVER SEEN BEFORE.
WHY IS HE RETIRING? WHY?
HOW DO YOU HOLD A TITLE TOURNAMENT WITHOUT THE TITLE CHAMPION?!
消火器
MAKE THE CHALLENGER THE PROVI-SIONAL TITLE HOLDER...?
MAYBE THEY'LL HAVE A BEST OF FIVE OR BEST OF SEVEN TO PICK THE CHALLENGER?

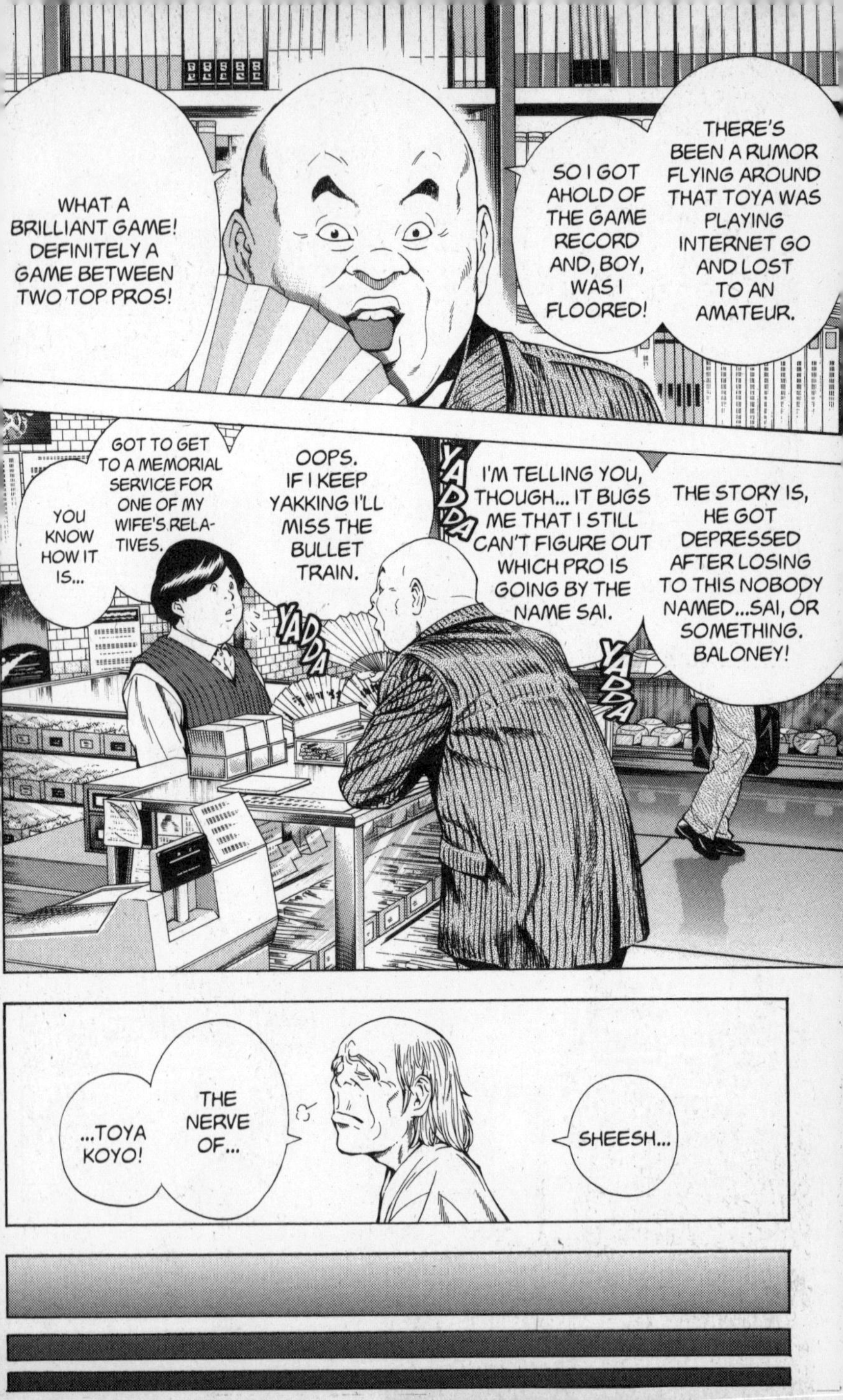
THERE'S BEEN A RUMOR FLYING AROUND THAT TOYA WAS PLAYING INTERNET GO AND LOST TO AN AMATEUR.
SO I GOT AHOLD OF THE GAME RECORD AND, BOY, WAS I FLOORED!
WHAT A BRILLIANT GAME! DEFINITELY A GAME BETWEEN TWO TOP PROS!
THE STORY IS, HE GOT DEPRESSED AFTER LOSING TO THIS NOBODY NAMED...SAI, OR SOMETHING. BALONEY!
YADDA
I'M TELLING YOU, THOUGH... IT BUGS ME THAT I STILL CAN'T FIGURE OUT WHICH PRO IS GOING BY THE NAME SAI.
YADDA
YADDA
OOPS. IF I KEEP YAKKING I'LL MISS THE BULLET TRAIN.
GOT TO GET TO A MEMORIAL SERVICE FOR ONE OF MY WIFE'S RELA- TIVES.
YOU KNOW HOW IT IS...
SHEESH...
THE NERVE OF...
...TOYA KOYO!

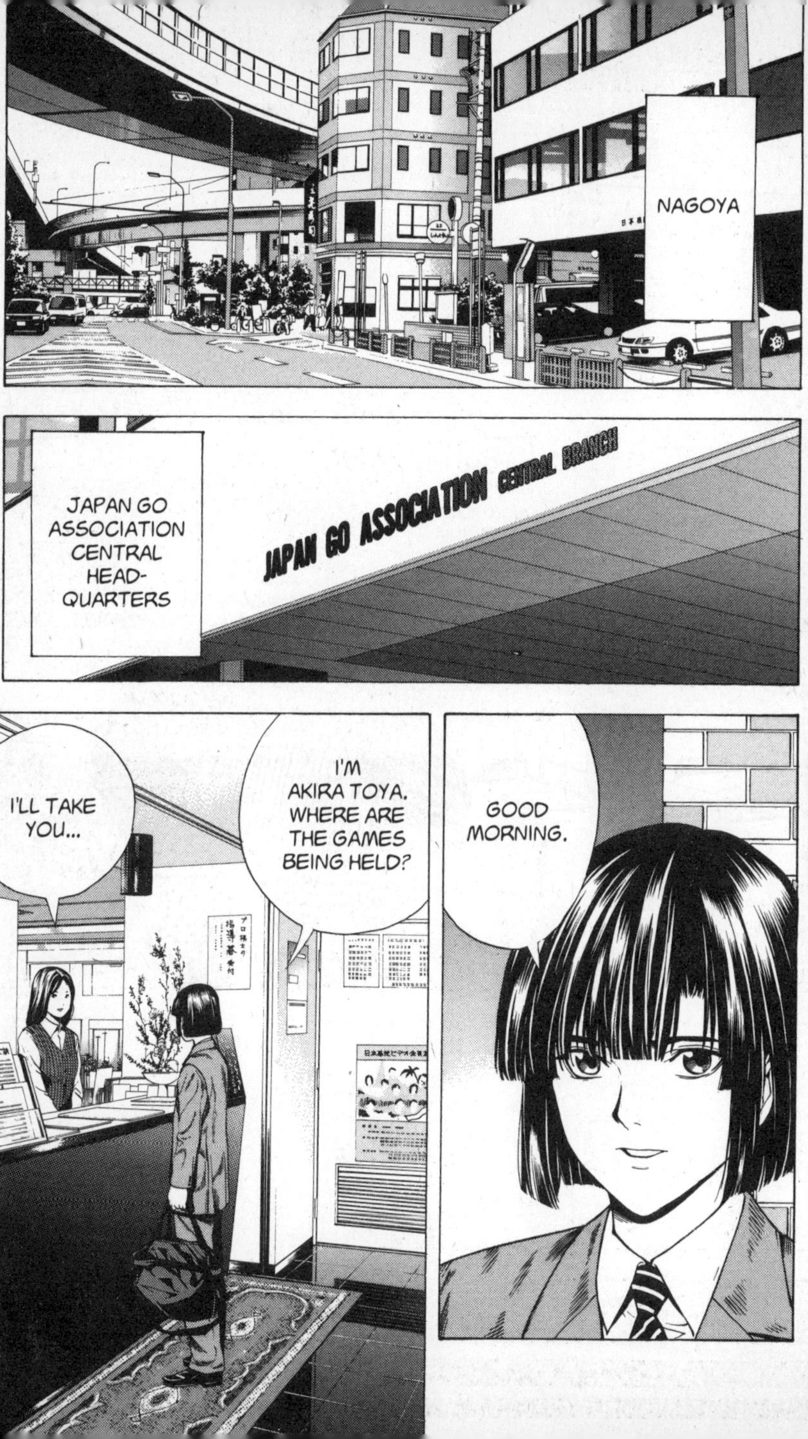
NAGOYA
JAPAN GO ASSOCIATION CENTRAL HEAD-QUARTERS
JAPAN GO ASSOCIATION CENTRAL BRANCH
GOOD MORNING.
I'M AKIRA TOYA. WHERE ARE THE GAMES BEING HELD?
I'LL TAKE YOU...

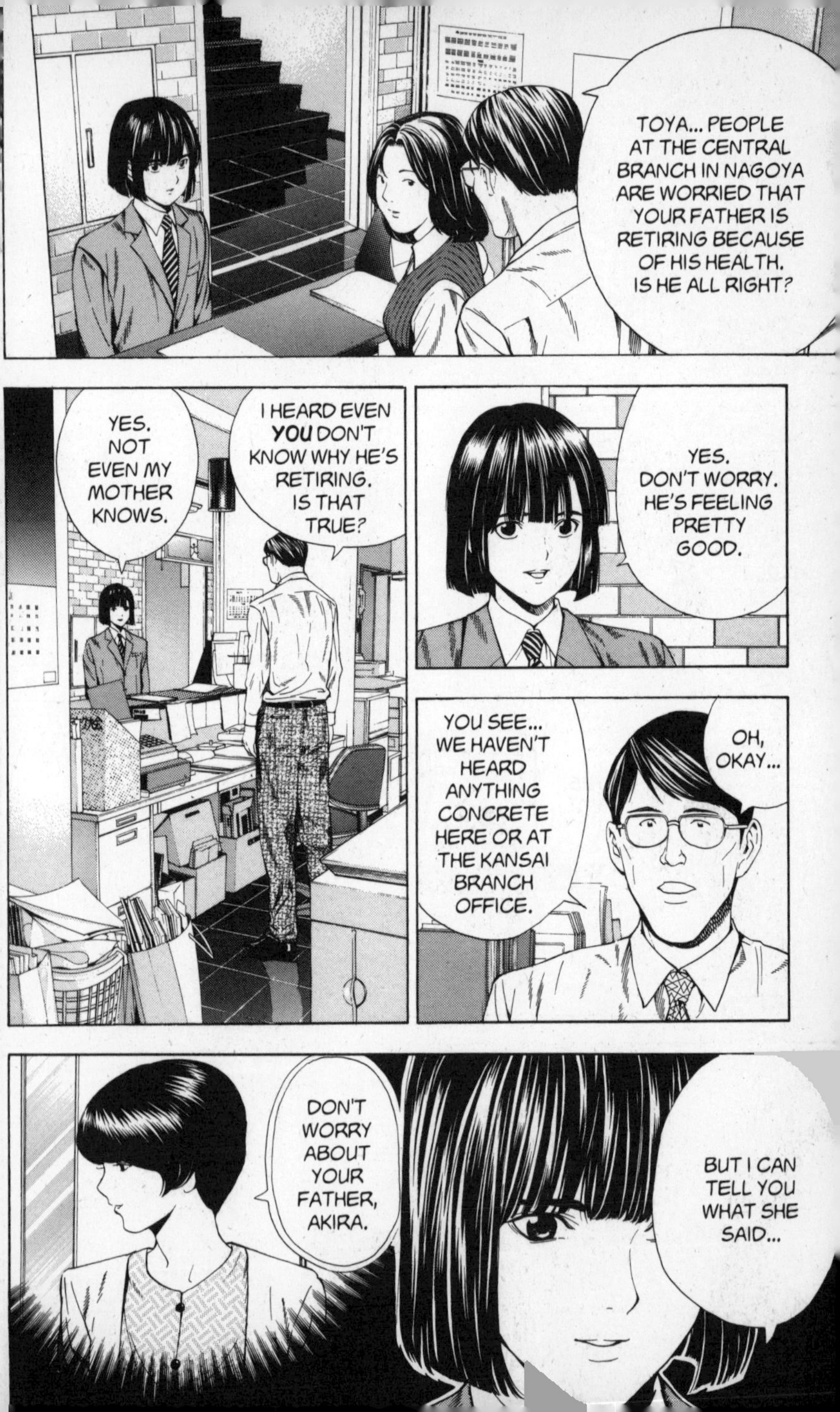
TOYA... PEOPLE AT THE CENTRAL BRANCH IN NAGOYA ARE WORRIED THAT YOUR FATHER IS RETIRING BECAUSE OF HIS HEALTH. IS HE ALL RIGHT?
YES. DON'T WORRY. HE'S FEELING PRETTY GOOD.
OH, OKAY...
YOU SEE... WE HAVEN'T HEARD ANYTHING CONCRETE HERE OR AT THE KANSAI BRANCH OFFICE.
I HEARD EVEN **YOU** DON'T KNOW WHY HE'S RETIRING. IS THAT TRUE?
YES. NOT EVEN MY MOTHER KNOWS.
BUT I CAN TELL YOU WHAT SHE SAID...
DON'T WORRY ABOUT YOUR FATHER, AKIRA.

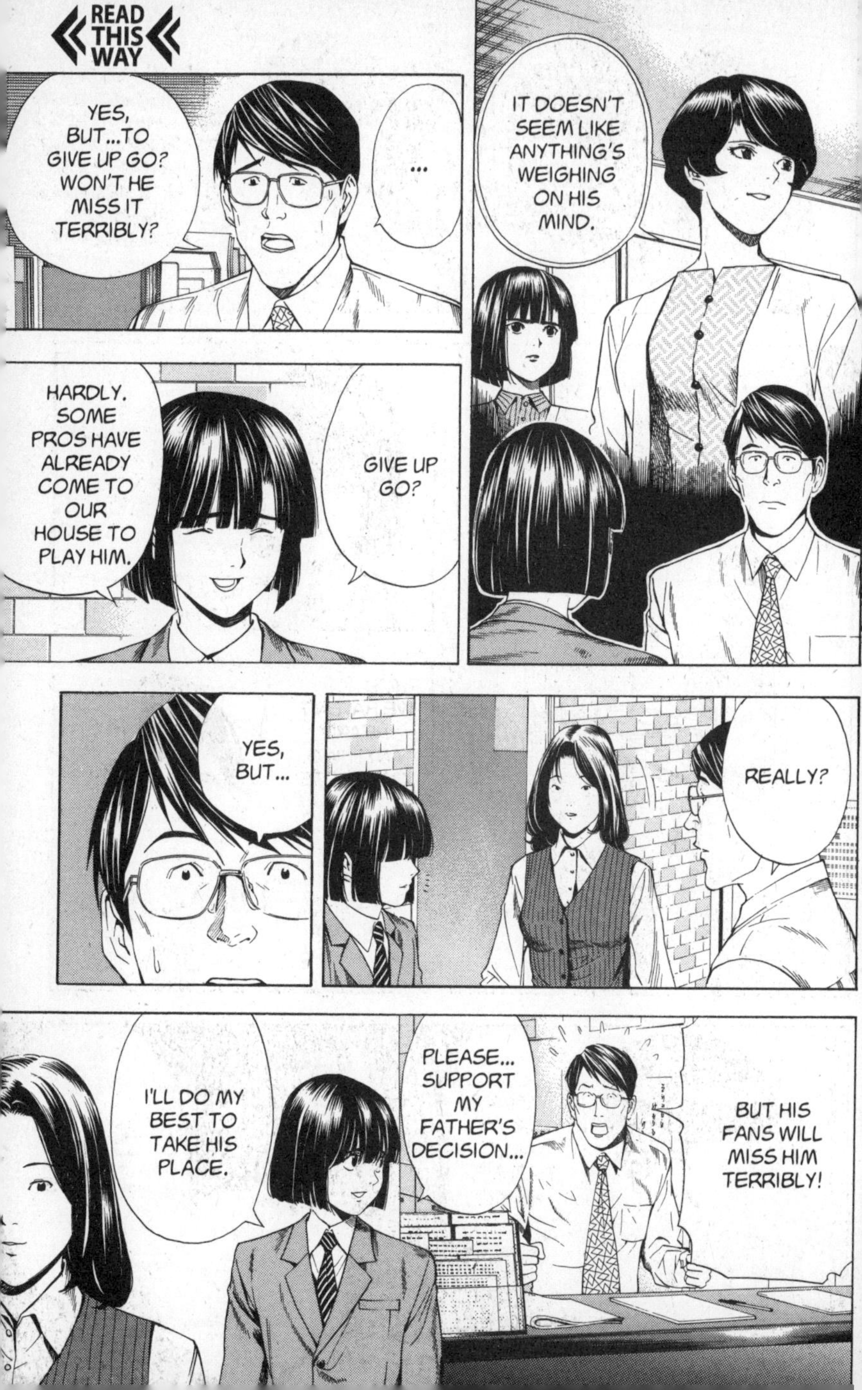
READ THIS WAY
IT DOESN'T SEEM LIKE ANYTHING'S WEIGHING ON HIS MIND.
...
YES, BUT...TO GIVE UP GO? WON'T HE MISS IT TERRIBLY?
GIVE UP GO?
HARDLY. SOME PROS HAVE ALREADY COME TO OUR HOUSE TO PLAY HIM.
REALLY?
YES, BUT...
BUT HIS FANS WILL MISS HIM TERRIBLY!
PLEASE... SUPPORT MY FATHER'S DECISION...
I'LL DO MY BEST TO TAKE HIS PLACE.

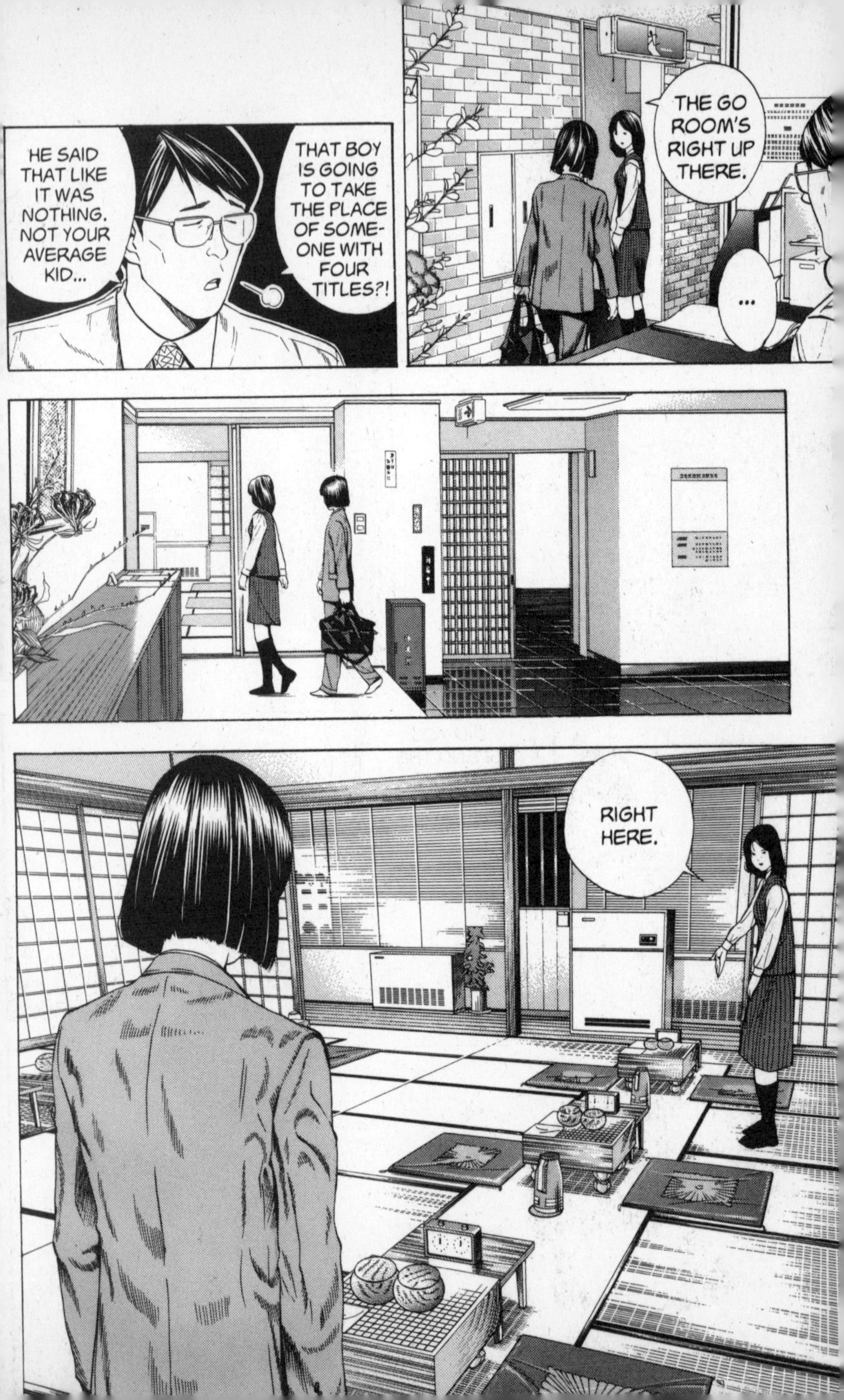
THE GO ROOM'S RIGHT UP THERE.
...
THAT BOY IS GOING TO TAKE THE PLACE OF SOME-ONE WITH FOUR TITLES?!
HE SAID THAT LIKE IT WAS NOTHING. NOT YOUR AVERAGE KID...
RIGHT HERE.

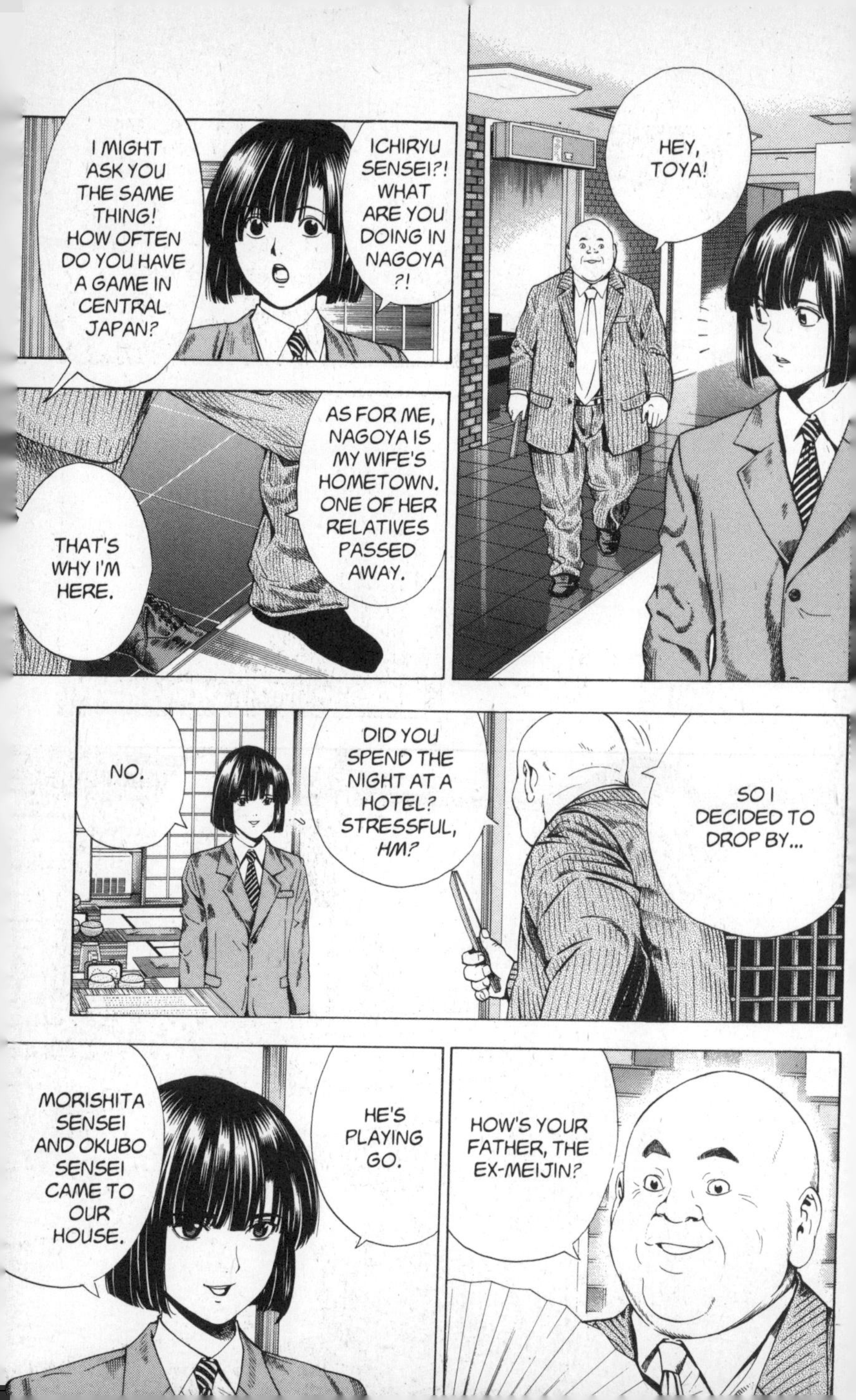
HEY, TOYA!
ICHIRYU SENSEI?! WHAT ARE YOU DOING IN NAGOYA?!
I MIGHT ASK YOU THE SAME THING! HOW OFTEN DO YOU HAVE A GAME IN CENTRAL JAPAN?
AS FOR ME, NAGOYA IS MY WIFE'S HOMETOWN. ONE OF HER RELATIVES PASSED AWAY.
THAT'S WHY I'M HERE.
SO I DECIDED TO DROP BY...
DID YOU SPEND THE NIGHT AT A HOTEL? STRESSFUL, HM?
NO.
HOW'S YOUR FATHER, THE EX-MEIJIN?
HE'S PLAYING GO.
MORISHITA SENSEI AND OKUBO SENSEI CAME TO OUR HOUSE.

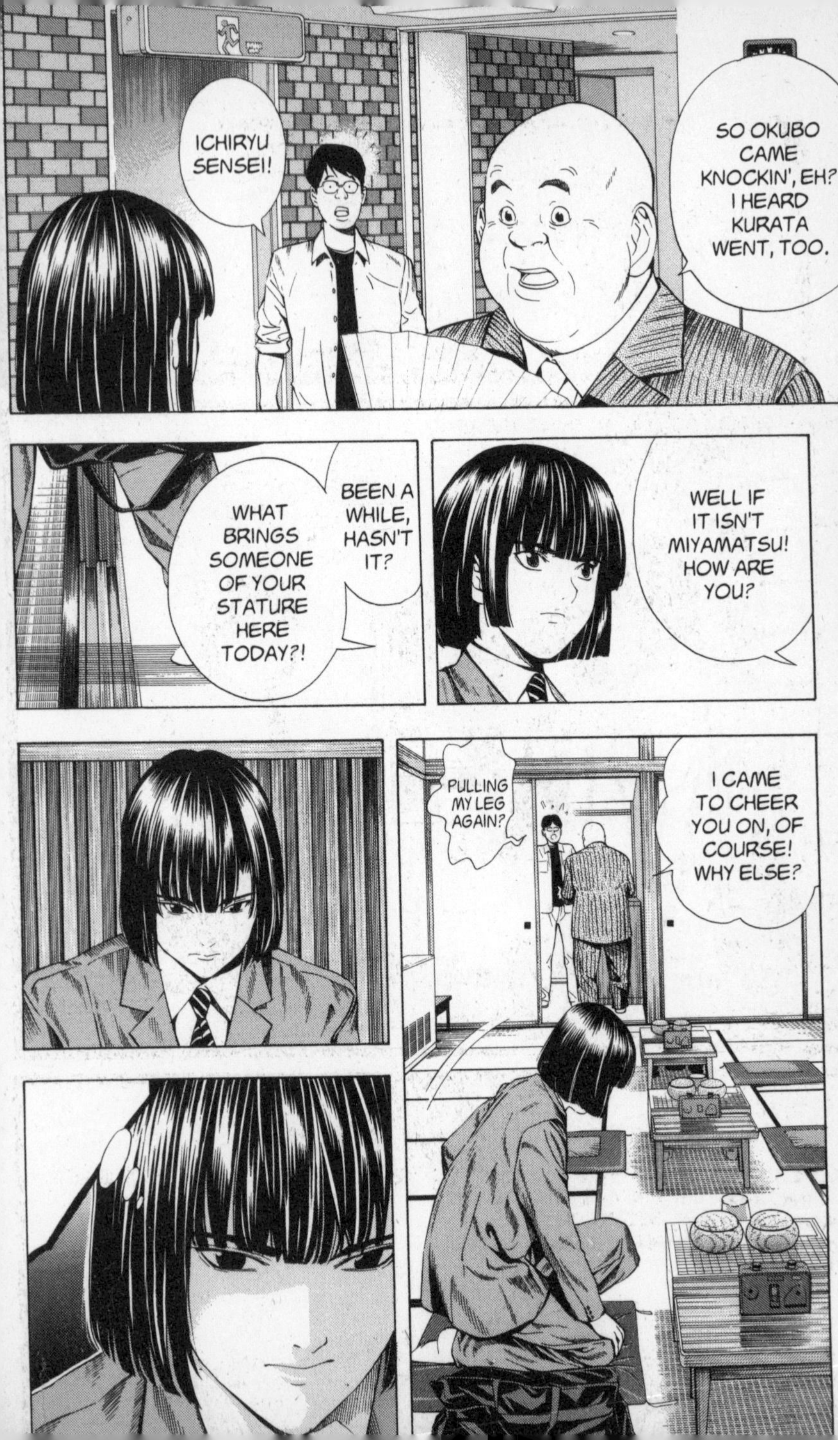
SO OKUBO CAME KNOCKIN', EH? I HEARD KURATA WENT, TOO.
ICHIRYU SENSEI!
WELL IF IT ISN'T MIYAMATSU! HOW ARE YOU?
BEEN A WHILE, HASN'T IT?
WHAT BRINGS SOMEONE OF YOUR STATURE HERE TODAY?!
I CAME TO CHEER YOU ON, OF COURSE! WHY ELSE?
PULLING MY LEG AGAIN?

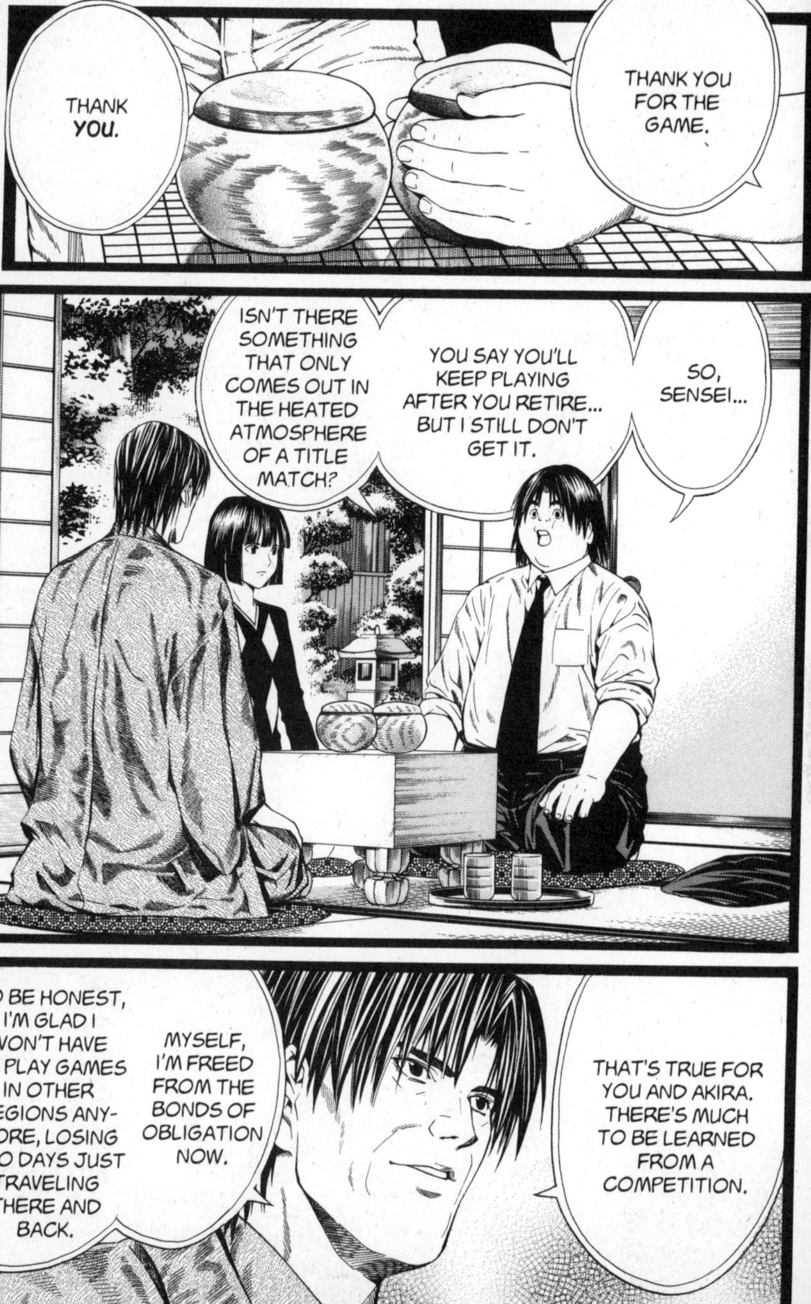
THANK YOU FOR THE GAME.
THANK YOU.
SO, SENSEI...
YOU SAY YOU'LL KEEP PLAYING AFTER YOU RETIRE... BUT I STILL DON'T GET IT.
ISN'T THERE SOMETHING THAT ONLY COMES OUT IN THE HEATED ATMOSPHERE OF A TITLE MATCH?
THAT'S TRUE FOR YOU AND AKIRA. THERE'S MUCH TO BE LEARNED FROM A COMPETITION.
MYSELF, I'M FREED FROM THE BONDS OF OBLIGATION NOW.
TO BE HONEST, I'M GLAD I WON'T HAVE TO PLAY GAMES IN OTHER REGIONS ANY-MORE, LOSING TWO DAYS JUST TRAVELING THERE AND BACK.

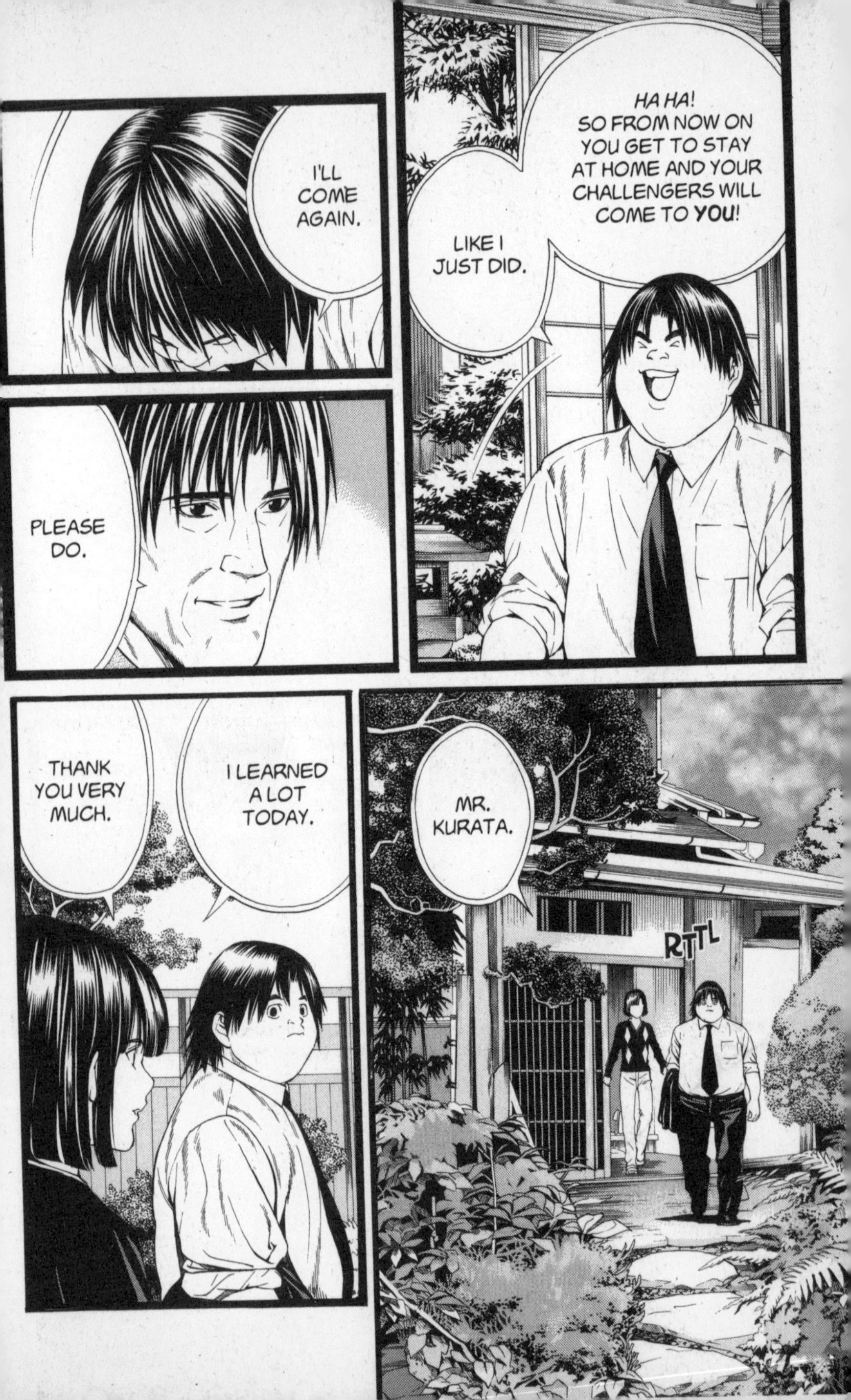
HA HA! SO FROM NOW ON YOU GET TO STAY AT HOME AND YOUR CHALLENGERS WILL COME TO **YOU**!
LIKE I JUST DID.
I'LL COME AGAIN.
PLEASE DO.
MR. KURATA.
RTTL
I LEARNED A LOT TODAY.
THANK YOU VERY MUCH.

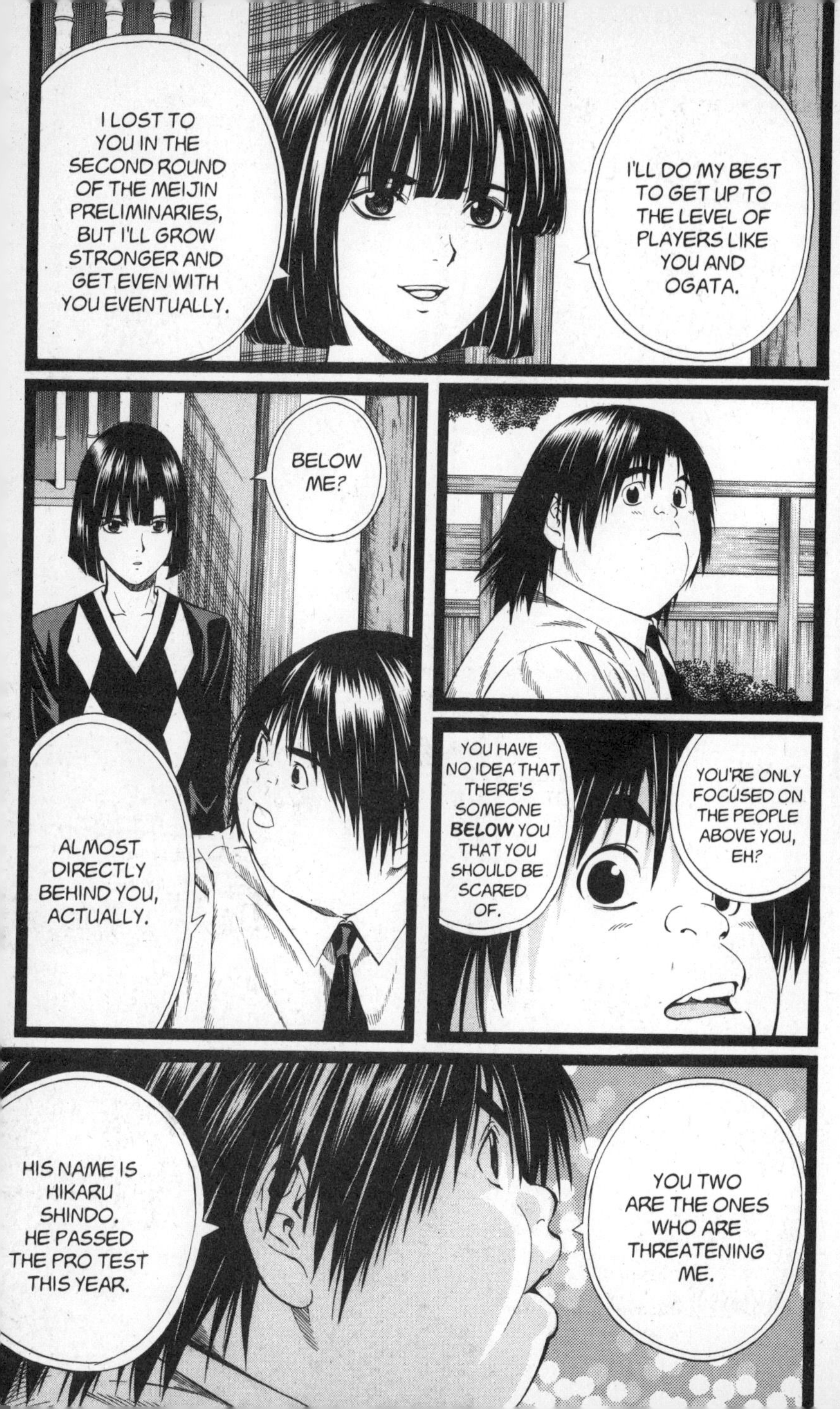
I'LL DO MY BEST TO GET UP TO THE LEVEL OF PLAYERS LIKE YOU AND OGATA.
I LOST TO YOU IN THE SECOND ROUND OF THE MEIJIN PRELIMINARIES, BUT I'LL GROW STRONGER AND GET EVEN WITH YOU EVENTUALLY.
YOU'RE ONLY FOCUSED ON THE PEOPLE ABOVE YOU, EH?
YOU HAVE NO IDEA THAT THERE'S SOMEONE **BELOW** YOU THAT YOU SHOULD BE SCARED OF.
BELOW ME?
ALMOST DIRECTLY BEHIND YOU, ACTUALLY.
YOU TWO ARE THE ONES WHO ARE THREATENING ME.
HIS NAME IS HIKARU SHINDO. HE PASSED THE PRO TEST THIS YEAR.

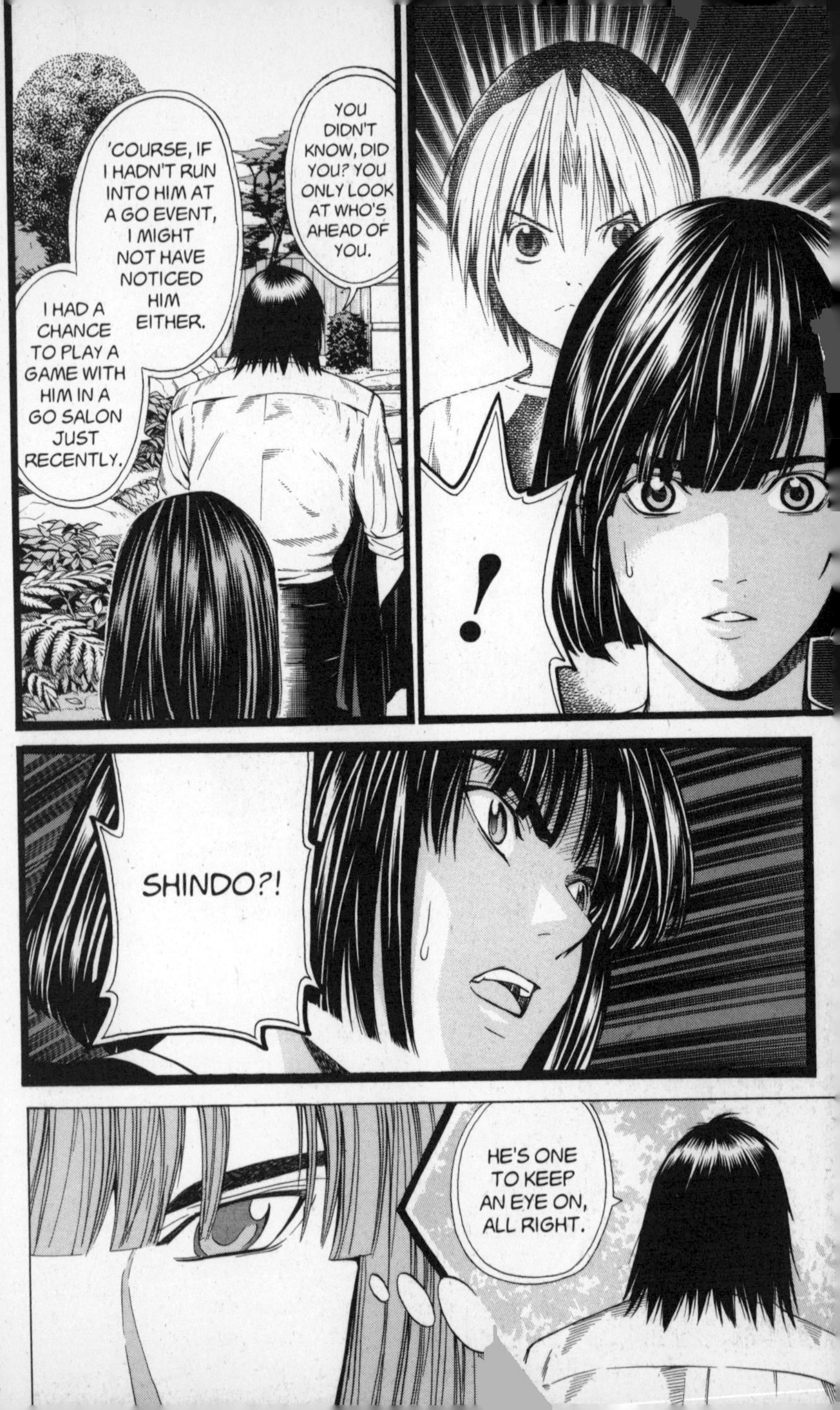
!
YOU DIDN'T KNOW, DID YOU? YOU ONLY LOOK AT WHO'S AHEAD OF YOU.
'COURSE, IF I HADN'T RUN INTO HIM AT A GO EVENT, I MIGHT NOT HAVE NOTICED HIM EITHER.
I HAD A CHANCE TO PLAY A GAME WITH HIM IN A GO SALON JUST RECENTLY.
SHINDO?!
HE'S ONE TO KEEP AN EYE ON, ALL RIGHT.

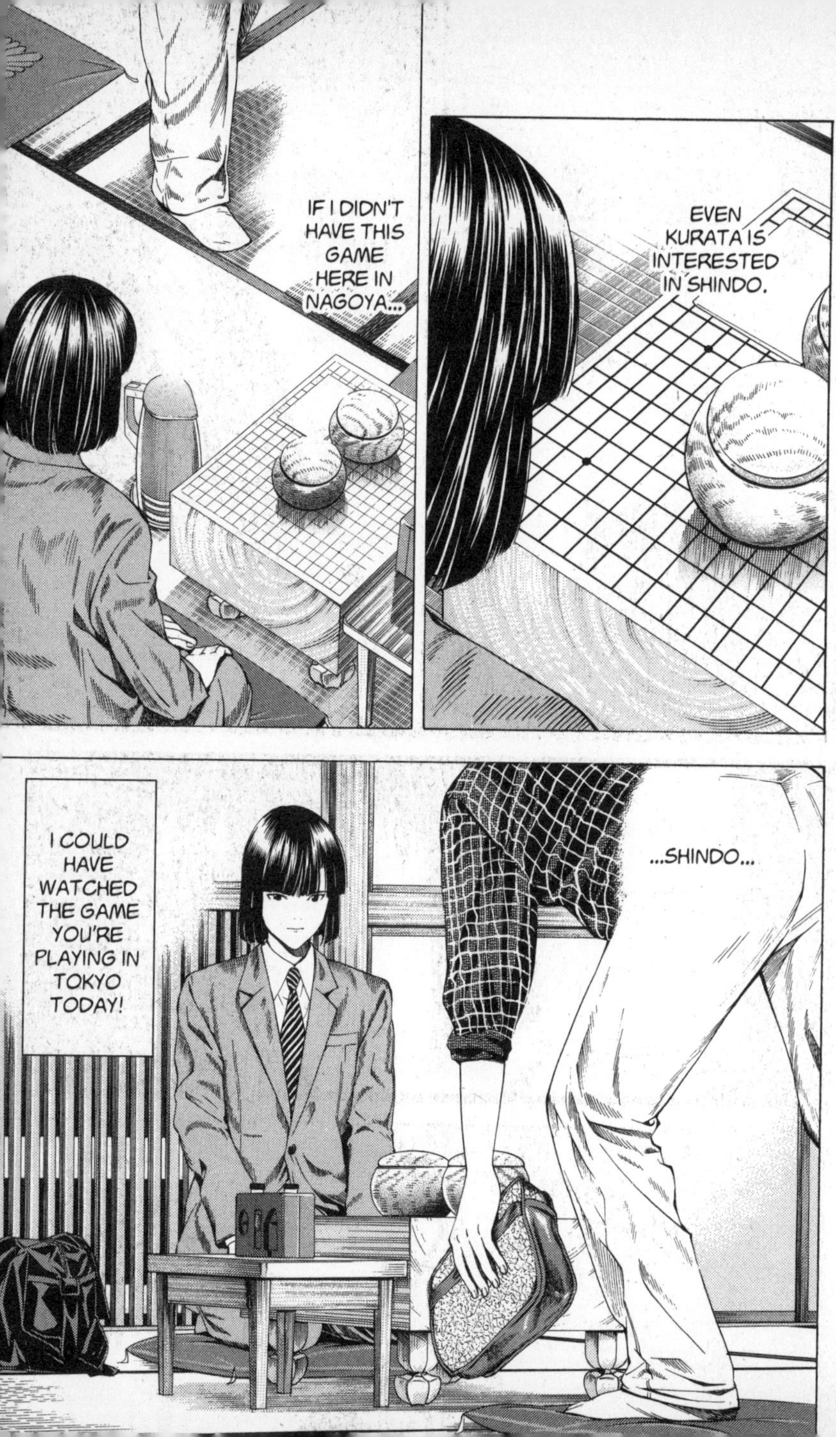
EVEN KURATA IS INTERESTED IN SHINDO.
IF I DIDN'T HAVE THIS GAME HERE IN NAGOYA...
...SHINDO...
I COULD HAVE WATCHED THE GAME YOU'RE PLAYING IN TOKYO TODAY!

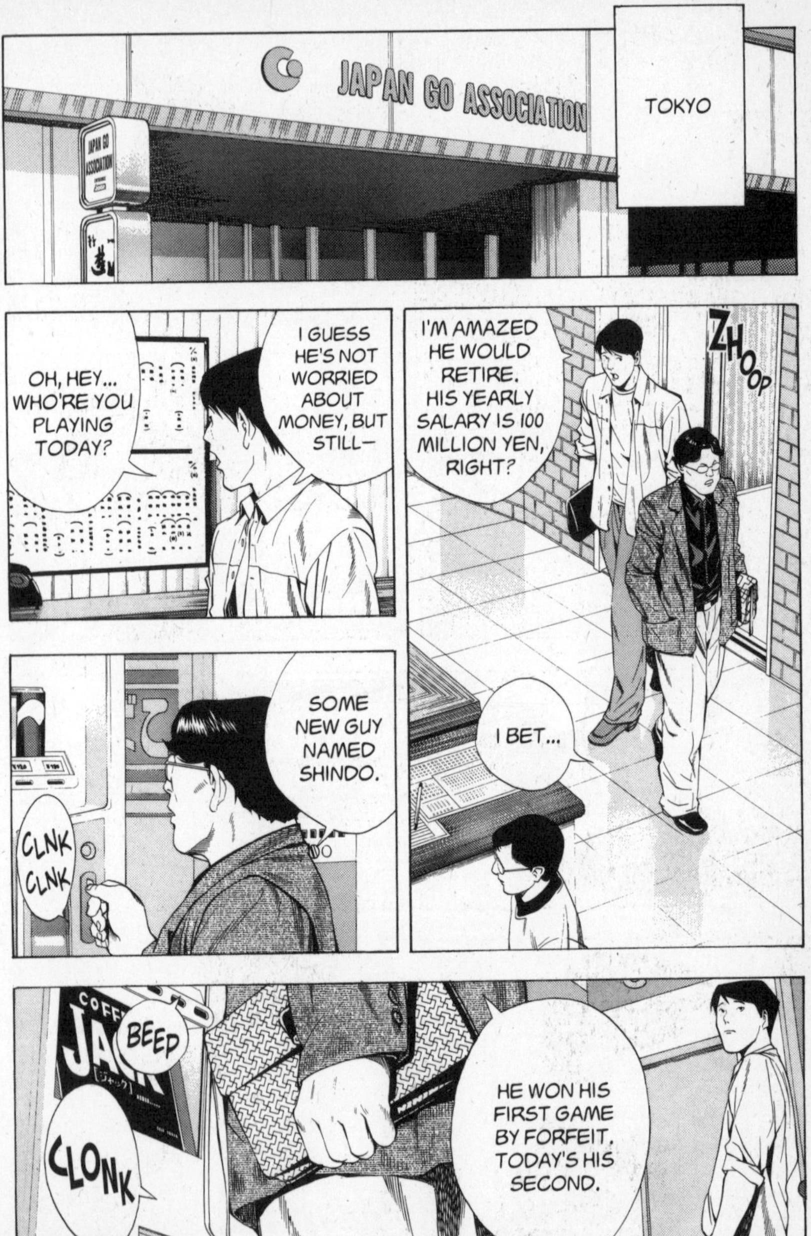
TOKYO
JAPAN GO ASSOCIATION
JAPAN GO ASSOCIATION
ZHOOP
I'M AMAZED HE WOULD RETIRE. HIS YEARLY SALARY IS 100 MILLION YEN, RIGHT?
I BET...
I GUESS HE'S NOT WORRIED ABOUT MONEY, BUT STILL—
OH, HEY... WHO'RE YOU PLAYING TODAY?
SOME NEW GUY NAMED SHINDO.
CLNK CLNK
HE WON HIS FIRST GAME BY FORFEIT. TODAY'S HIS SECOND.
BEEP
CLONK

OH...

HIS OPPONENT WAS TOYA AKIRA, BUT HE DIDN'T SHOW.

BY FORFEIT?

...IT WAS THE MORNING TOYA SENSEI COLLAPSED.

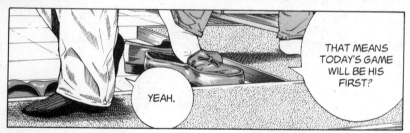

THAT MEANS TODAY'S GAME WILL BE HIS FIRST?

YEAH.

!

HE'LL PROBABLY BE INCREDIBLY NERVOUS!

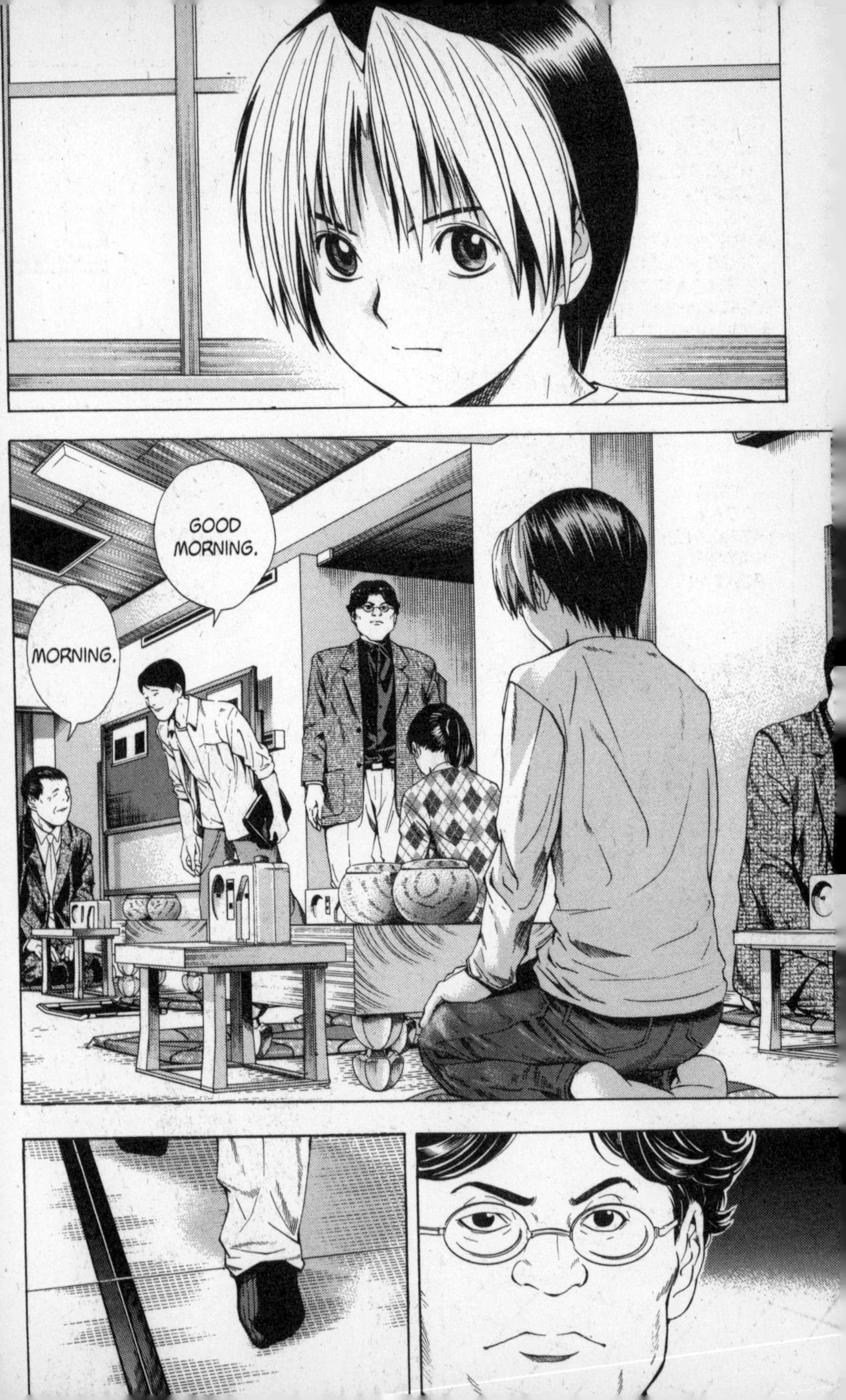
GOOD MORNING.
MORNING.

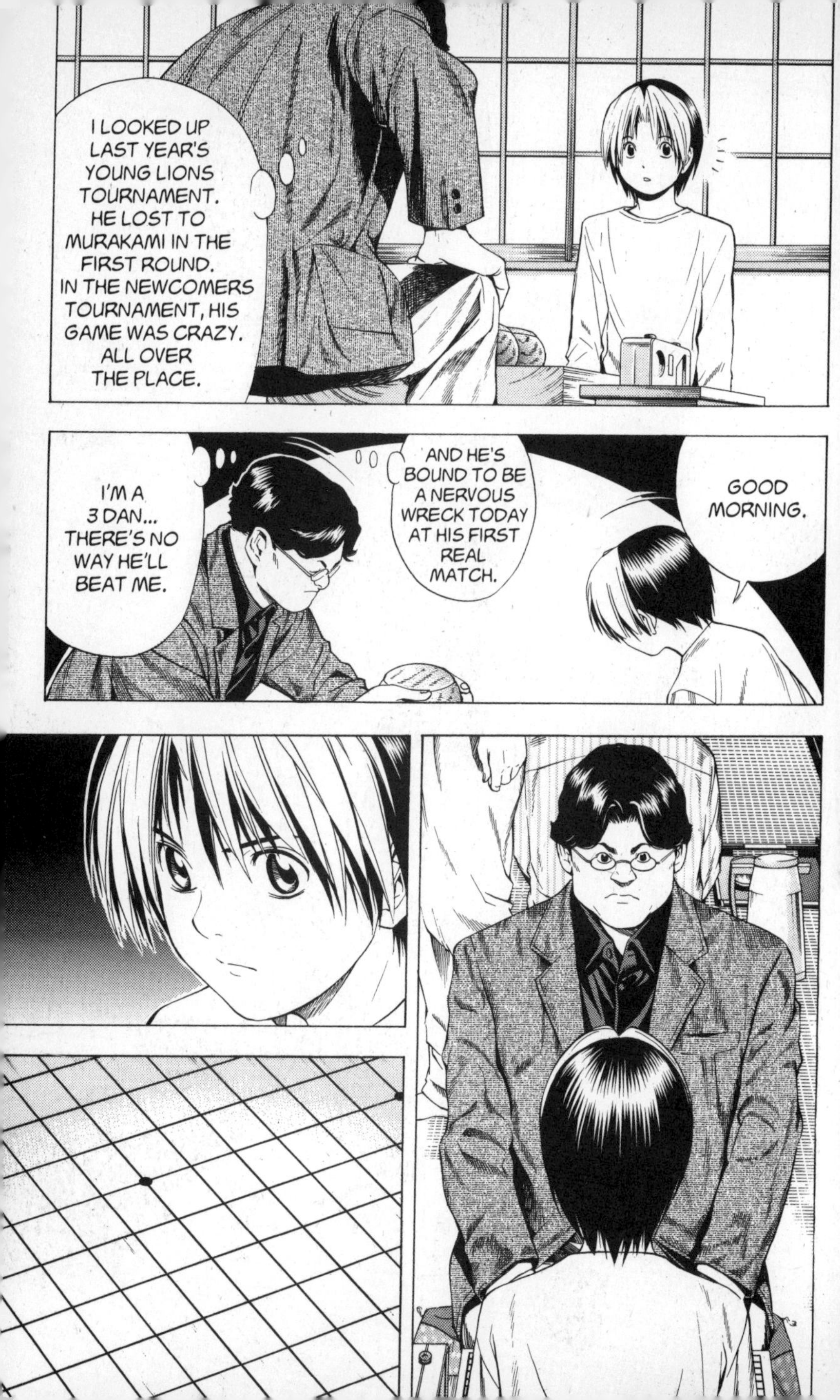
I LOOKED UP LAST YEAR'S YOUNG LIONS TOURNAMENT. HE LOST TO MURAKAMI IN THE FIRST ROUND. IN THE NEWCOMERS TOURNAMENT, HIS GAME WAS CRAZY. ALL OVER THE PLACE.
GOOD MORNING.
AND HE'S BOUND TO BE A NERVOUS WRECK TODAY AT HIS FIRST REAL MATCH.
I'M A 3 DAN... THERE'S NO WAY HE'LL BEAT ME.

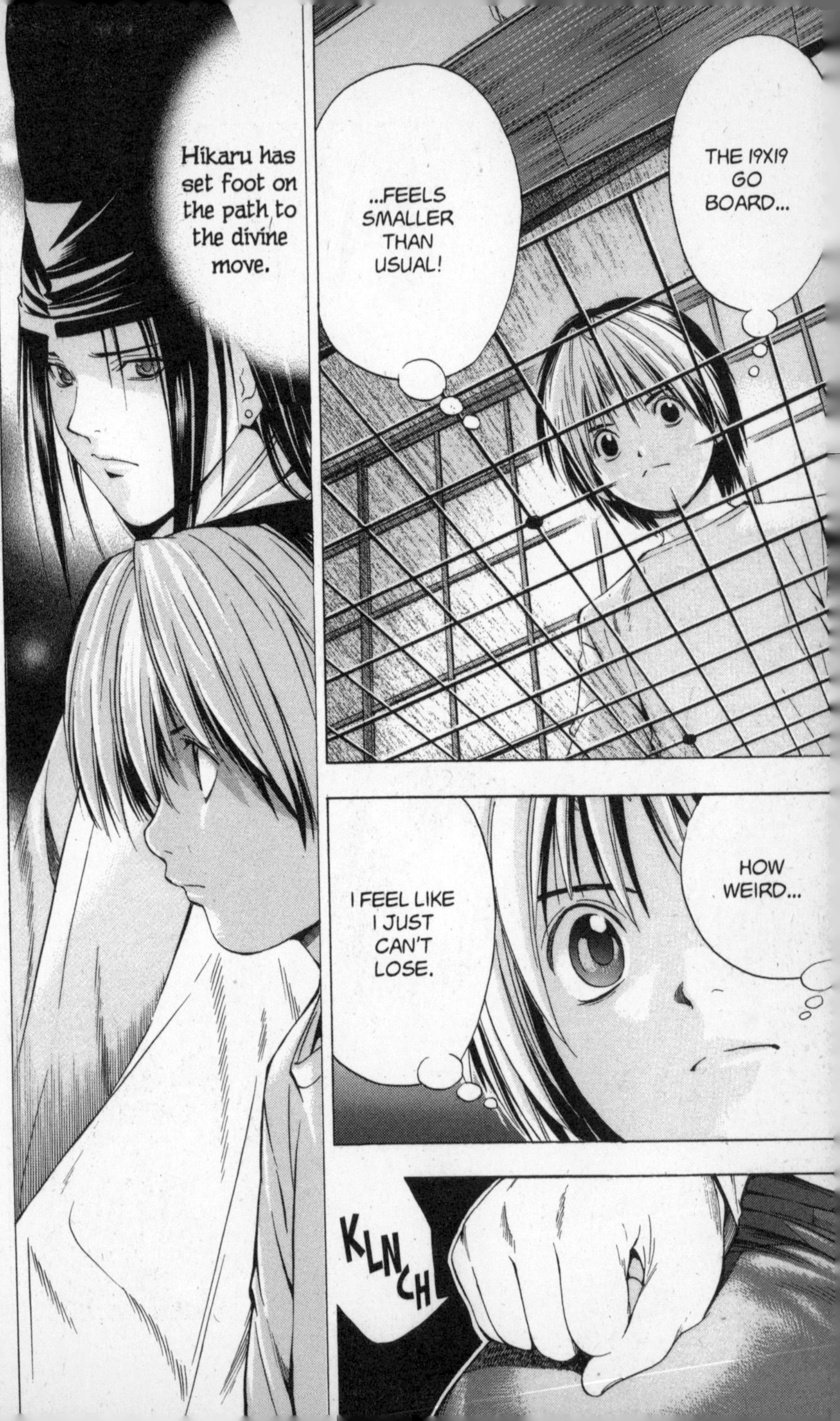
THE 19X19 GO BOARD...
...FEELS SMALLER THAN USUAL!
HOW WEIRD...
I FEEL LIKE I JUST CAN'T LOSE.
KLNCH
Hikaru has set foot on the path to the divine move.

READ THIS WAY

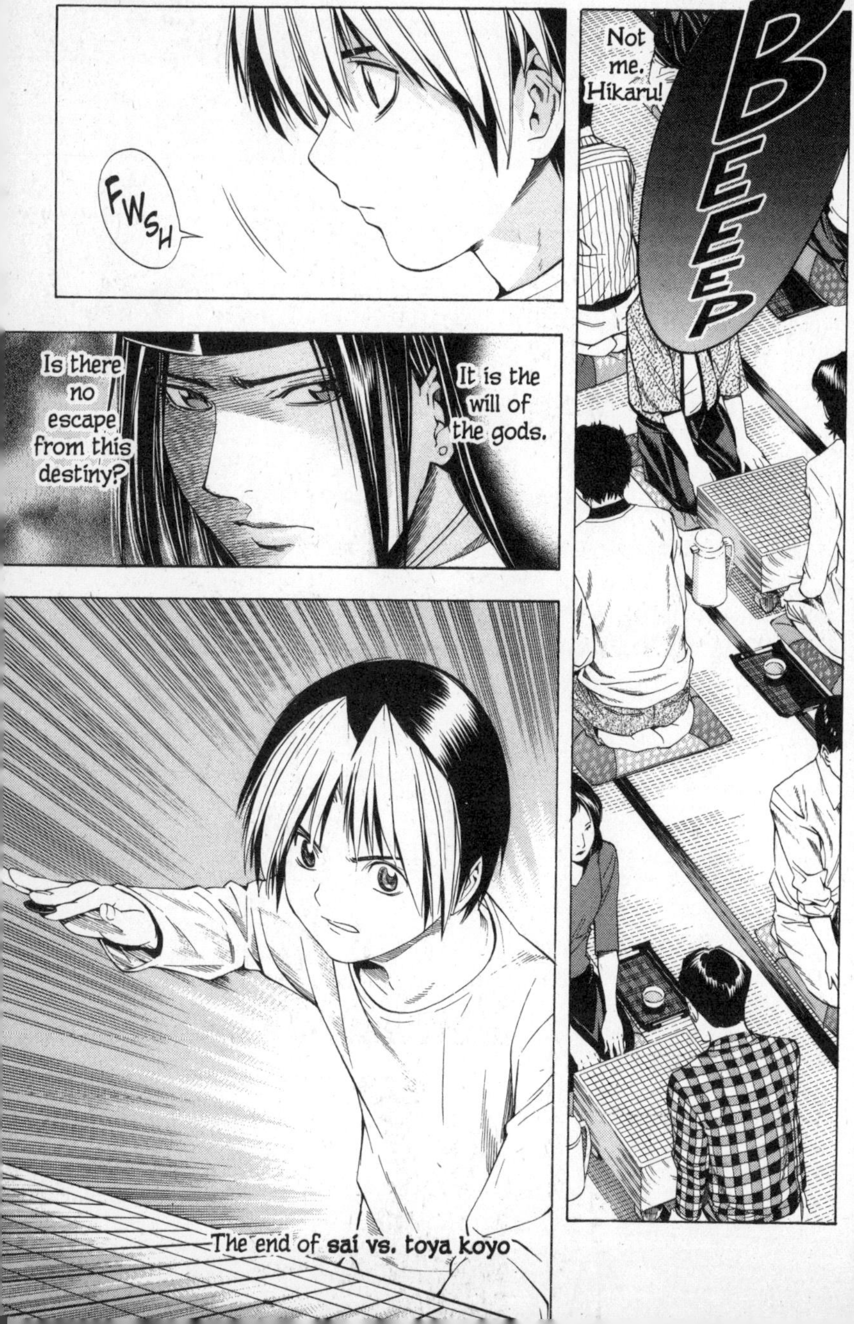
BEEEEP
Not me. Hikaru!
FWSH
It is the will of the gods.
Is there no escape from this destiny?
The end of sai vs. toya koyo

A WORD ABOUT HIKARU NO GO

CHUBU CENTER

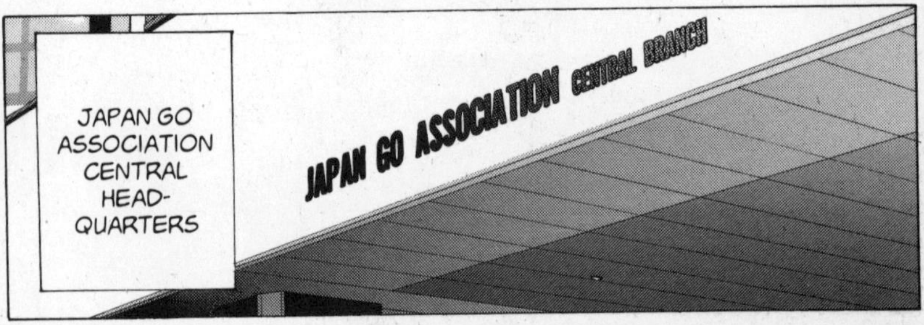
JAPAN GO ASSOCIATION CENTRAL HEAD-QUARTERS
JAPAN GO ASSOCIATION CENTRAL BRANCH

THIS CENTER IS IN NAGOYA.
THE KANSAI CENTER IS IN OSAKA.

PRO PLAYERS IN THE CHUBU, OR CENTRAL, REGION MOSTLY PLAY WITHIN CHUBU. SAME GOES FOR THOSE IN THE KANSAI REGION. BUT SOMETIMES THEY PLAY PROS FROM TOKYO. WHEN THIS OCCURS, IT'S THE LOWER RANKED PLAYER WHO TRAVELS. TRANSPORTATION AND LODGING COSTS ARE COVERED BY THE GO ASSOCIATION.

DO YOU THINK AKIRA BUYS UIRO* WHEN HE'S IN NAGOYA? OR SOME DELICIOUS TEN MUSU**?

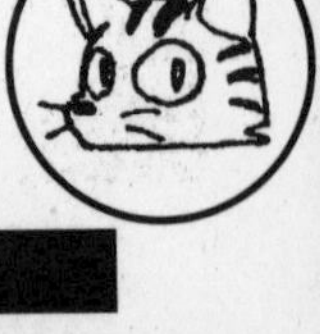

*a steamed rice-flour sweet
**a shrimp tempura rice ball

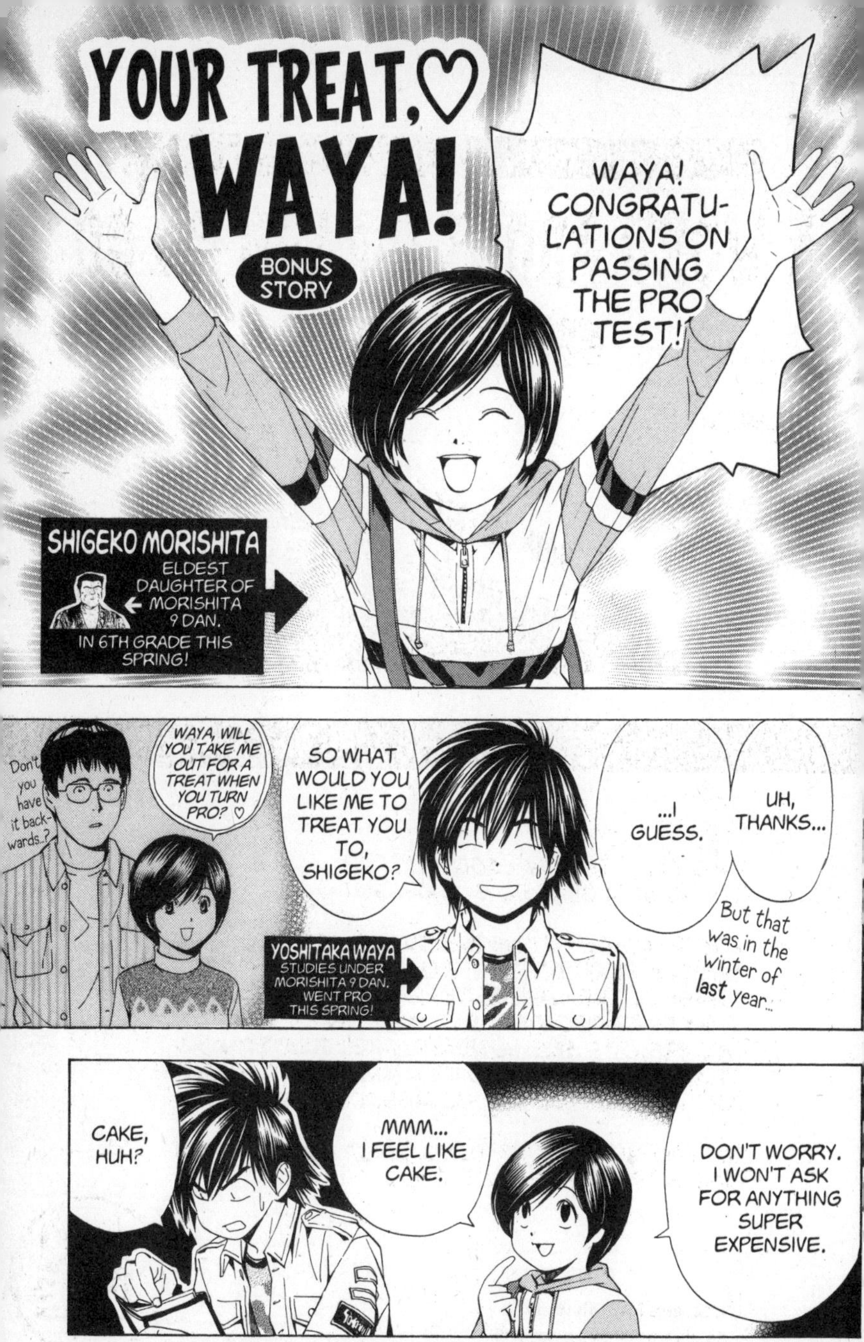
YOUR TREAT, ♡ WAYA!
BONUS STORY
WAYA! CONGRATULATIONS ON PASSING THE PRO TEST!
SHIGEKO MORISHITA
ELDEST DAUGHTER OF MORISHITA 9 DAN.
IN 6TH GRADE THIS SPRING!
UH, THANKS...
...I GUESS.
But that was in the winter of last year...
SO WHAT WOULD YOU LIKE ME TO TREAT YOU TO, SHIGEKO?
YOSHITAKA WAYA
STUDIES UNDER MORISHITA 9 DAN. WENT PRO THIS SPRING!
WAYA, WILL YOU TAKE ME OUT FOR A TREAT WHEN YOU TURN PRO? ♡
Don't you have it backwards..?
DON'T WORRY. I WON'T ASK FOR ANYTHING SUPER EXPENSIVE.
MMM... I FEEL LIKE CAKE.
CAKE, HUH?

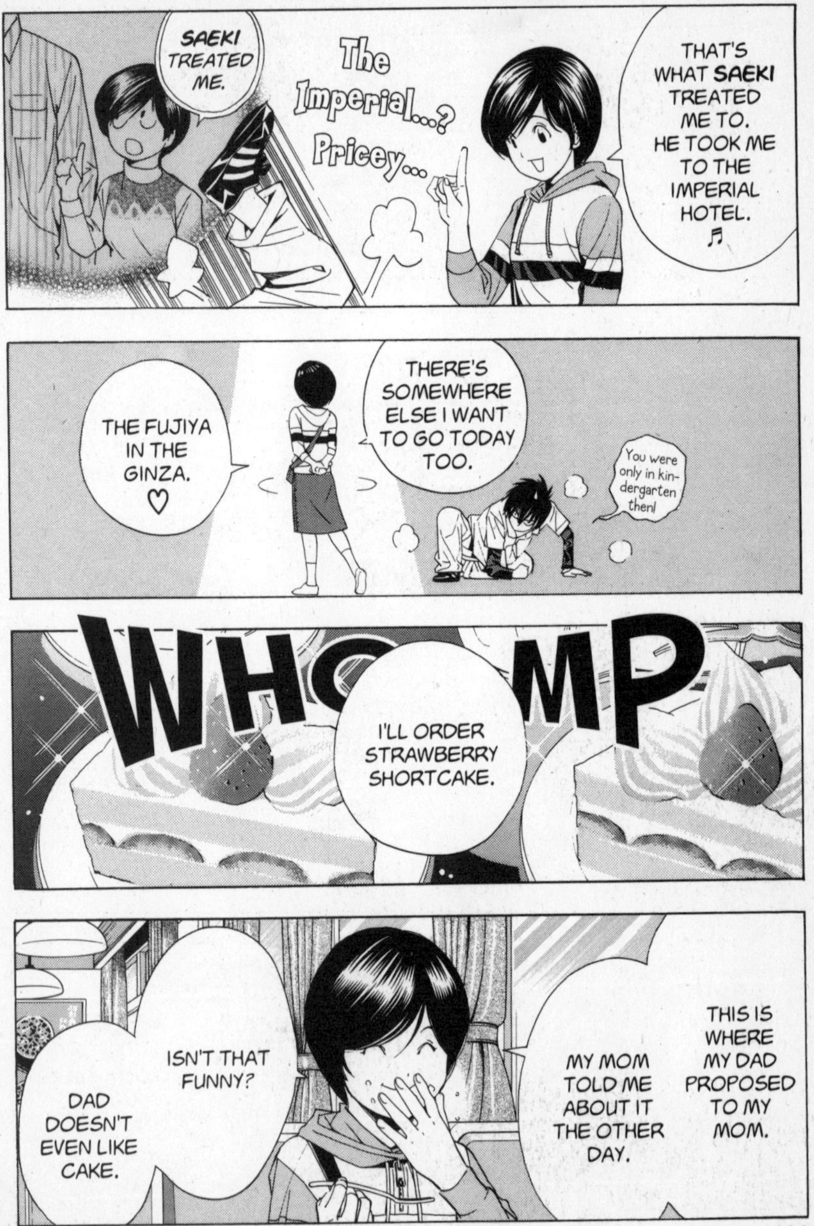
THAT'S WHAT SAEKI TREATED ME TO. HE TOOK ME TO THE IMPERIAL HOTEL. ♬
The Imperial...? Pricey...
SAEKI TREATED ME.
THERE'S SOMEWHERE ELSE I WANT TO GO TODAY TOO.
You were only in kindergarten then!
THE FUJIYA IN THE GINZA. ♡
WHOMP
I'LL ORDER STRAWBERRY SHORTCAKE.
THIS IS WHERE MY DAD PROPOSED TO MY MOM.
MY MOM TOLD ME ABOUT IT THE OTHER DAY.
ISN'T THAT FUNNY?
DAD DOESN'T EVEN LIKE CAKE.

READ THIS WAY

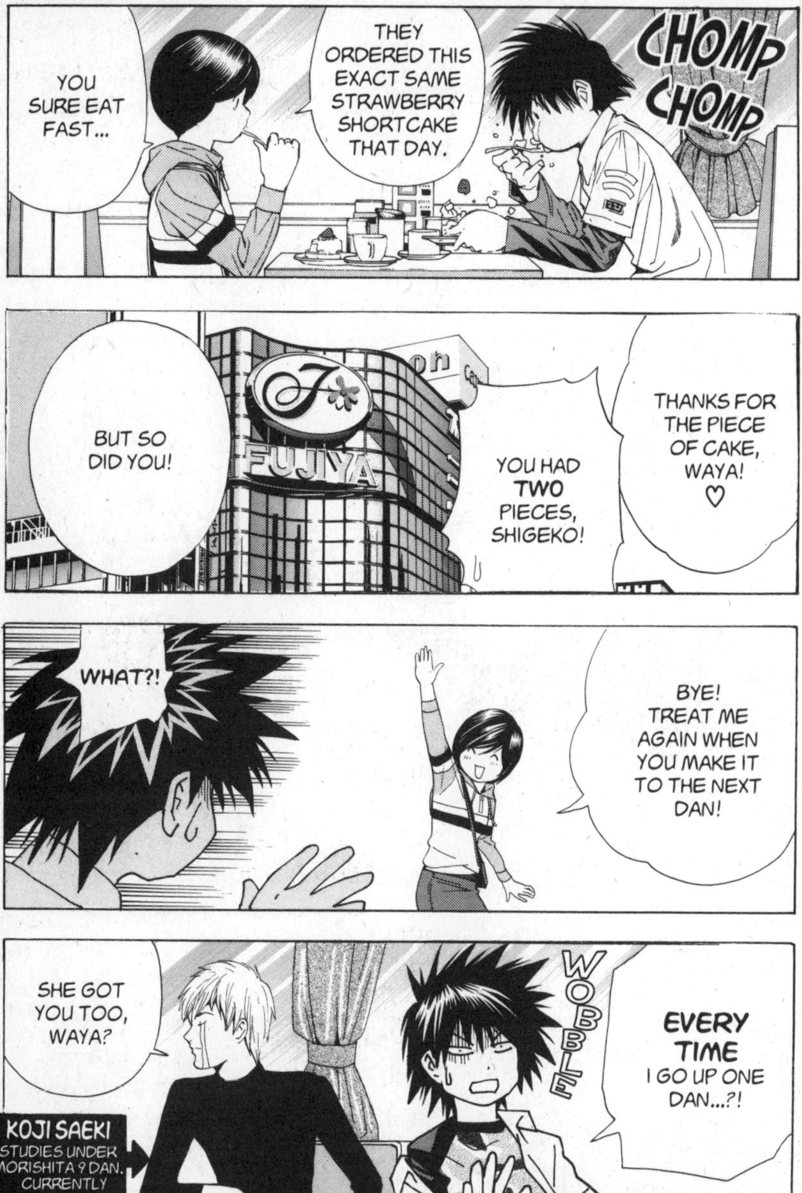
CHOMP CHOMP
THEY ORDERED THIS EXACT SAME STRAWBERRY SHORTCAKE THAT DAY.
YOU SURE EAT FAST...
THANKS FOR THE PIECE OF CAKE, WAYA! ♡
YOU HAD TWO PIECES, SHIGEKO!
FUJIYA
BUT SO DID YOU!
BYE! TREAT ME AGAIN WHEN YOU MAKE IT TO THE NEXT DAN!
WHAT?!
EVERY TIME I GO UP ONE DAN...?!
WOBBLE
SHE GOT YOU TOO, WAYA?
KOJI SAEKI
STUDIES UNDER MORISHITA 9 DAN. CURRENTLY 4 DAN.

Treat me, Waya! ♡ (END)

Next Volume Preview

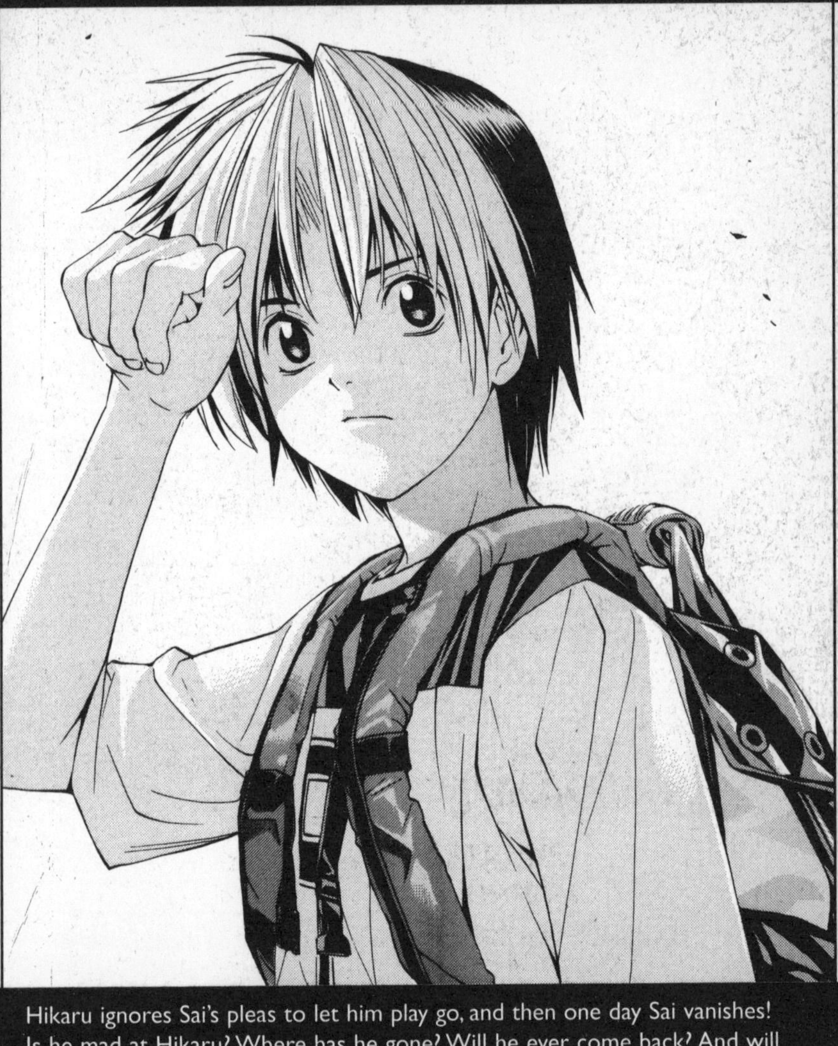

Hikaru ignores Sai's pleas to let him play go, and then one day Sai vanishes! Is he mad at Hikaru? Where has he gone? Will he ever come back? And will Hikaru be able to play without Sai's coaching...?

COMING MAY 2009

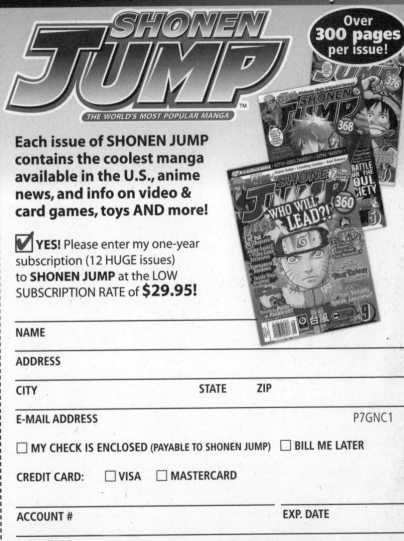